The New Complete Guide to

Nutritional Health

The New Complete Guide to Nutritional Health
Pierre Jean Cousin and Kirsten Hartvig

Distributed in the USA and Canada by
Sterling Publishing Co., Inc.
387 Park Avenue South
New York, NY 10016-8810

This revised and updated edition first published in the UK and USA in 2011
by Duncan Baird Publishers Ltd
Sixth Floor
Castle House
75–76 Wells Street
London W1T 3QH

Material from this book was first published in the UK and Ireland in 2001 and 2002 by Duncan Baird Publishers
Ltd in two separate volumes: *Food is Medicine* and *Eat for Immunity*.

Managing Editors: Judy Barratt, Grace Cheetham
Editors: Richard Emerson, Ingrid Court-Jones
Editorial Assistants: Jessica Hughes, Elinor Brett
Managing Designer: Manisha Patel
Designers: Steve Painter, Suzanne Tuhrim, Joy Wheeler, Gail Jones
Commissioned Photography: William Lingwood, Toby Scott
Stylists: David Morgan, Helen Trent, Sunil Vijayakar, Mari Mererid Williams

Library of Congress Cataloging-in-Publication Data

Cousin, Pierre Jean.
 The new complete guide to nutritional health : more than 600 foods and recipes for overcoming illness & boosting
your immunity / Pierre Jean Cousin & Kirsten Hartvig.
    p. cm.
Includes bibliographical references and index.
ISBN 978-1-84483-965-0
1. Nutrition. 2. Diet therapy. 3. Diet in disease. 4. Cooking. I. Hartvig, Kirsten. II. Title.
 RA784.C6227 2011
 613.2--dc22
                                2010033540

ISBN: 978-1-84483-965-0

10 9 8 7 6 5 4 3 2 1

Typeset in Helvetica Neue
Color reproduction by Imageright, UK
Printed and bound in China

For information about custom editions, special sales, premium and corporate purchases, please contact Sterling
Special Sales Department at 800-805-5489 or specialsales@sterlingpub.com.

The abbreviation BCE is used in this book:
BCE Before the Common Era (the equivalent of BC)

The New Complete Guide to Nutritional Health

MORE THAN 600 FOODS AND RECIPES for Overcoming Illness & Boosting Your Immunity

PIERRE JEAN COUSIN & KIRSTEN HARTVIG

DUNCAN BAIRD PUBLISHERS

LONDON

contents

foreword

trust this book

Knowledge is often the enemy of wisdom. The more information we store, the less understanding we gain. These cautionary thoughts have special force applied to nutrition and health, as you can see by browsing the "lifestyle" sections of bookstores, periodicals, or websites. Who to believe? And can all these tall tales of "a new you in 25 days" really be true? Do you want to enjoy delicious food and drink, and thereby also give yourself and your family the best chance of avoiding disease and celebrating long, active, healthy lives? Of course you do. But where to start and who should be your guide? Well, right now you are holding an answer in your hand, in the form of this beautiful and practical book, full of wise information and advice.

Modern nutritional science is mostly a branch of biochemistry and is heavily influenced by the conventional "medical model" whereby "health" means the absence of disease, and "health care" refers to drugs and other medical or surgical treatments of disease. This is a wrong turn up a blind alley. We should be aiming to inhabit a world in which it is normal to live a long, healthy, and active life, and to die of old age in good health. And we should look to the authentic origins of nutrition, which lie in the ancient discipline of dietetics as taught and practiced in both the East and West for thousands of years, and as still followed by developed nations: the practical philosophy of the good life well led, within which food and drink is, of course, integral.

If you want to change the world, begin with yourself, within your community. The most important message in *The New Complete Guide to Nutritional Health* can be expressed in a few words: food and nutrition are crucial to health. And because health is not only physical but also mental, emotional and spiritual, it might be better to say that the nature and quality of what we eat and drink are the most important determinants of our state of being.

This is an old truth to which writers such as Pierre Jean Cousin and my colleague and friend Kirsten Hartvig are bearing new witness. Everybody now knows that the incidence of tooth decay, constipation, gut diseases, obesity, high blood pressure, diabetes, osteoporosis, stroke, heart disease, and most cancers, in all populations and communities, is mostly determined by food and nutrition, together with tobacco habits and level of physical activity.

In the parallel work that we do, both Kirsten and I may be a little too respectful of the current conventions of nutritional science. As director of science at the World Cancer Research Fund, and then later, I have directed, then edited, two massive reports on food, nutrition, and the prevention of cancer, whose conclusions are based on meticulous literature reviews. They are good work—the best there is. Yet I can't help feeling that their recommendations, derived from systematic examination of thousands of studies of what people mostly in economically rich countries such as the UK and the USA actually consume, are too cautious. Most common serious chronic diseases were uncommon or rare at any stage of life, including old age, until recently in history. One finger points at industrialized products. The issue, that is to say, is not food or nutrients, so much as what is done to food before we buy and eat it—processing, which may be benign, but is often malign. You won't find this said in an expert report.

My own life's journey has led me to live and work in Brazil, and I'm writing this celebration of *The New Complete Guide to Nutritional Health* in Rio de Janeiro. Being in Brazil has turned out to be a good move for me, for "all human life is here." People are naturally aware of the social, economic, and environmental dimensions and determinants of health, although some of this knowledge has faded. One good sign, though, is that Brazilian shoppers are still not bothered by "imperfect" fresh vegetables and fruits. Anything that's good for worms is good for us. And to mention one of the superfoods in this book, it's nice to live in a country where I can harvest windfall avocados.

We are not mere bodies that eventually must suffer from this or that infirmity. We are living systems. Each and every one of us lives symbiotically with billions of microbes on and in all our outer and inner surfaces, which protect us from all forms of ailments, mental, emotional, and spiritual, as well as physical. These, together

foreword

with the tissues in which these bacteria live, are our immune system. The authors of this book propose that when we nourish our bugs, and their places of habitation on and in us, we stay strong and give ourselves the best chance of avoiding all types of disease, and of enjoying good health and happiness throughout our lives. This makes sound sense. The best time to start is at our beginning, in childhood, so buy more copies of *The New Complete Guide to Nutritional Health* and gift them to the young parents you know, or better still, to those hoping to become parents.

Geoffrey Cannon

World Public Health Nutrition Association

Access me on www.wphna.org

how to use this book

Now revised, expanded and updated, *The New Complete Guide to Nutritional Health* brings together the knowledge and experience of two experts on the links between good food and good health. Pierre Jean Cousin is a practicing herbalist and acupuncturist with a thriving complementary medicine practice based in London. Kirsten Hartvig is a registered naturopath and medical herbalist who lives in Denmark. Since 1994, she has run retreats and courses on the art of living and healing naturally, as well as seeing private clients.

In this book, the two authors give their own unique insights into the subject of nutrition. Citing the latest scientific research, they have added more superfoods and included extra ailments, as well as information on the Glycemic Index, and such topics as obesity. Pierre Jean looks at how various foods, including fruits, vegetables, dairy products, and fish, can help prevent and treat a wide range of common conditions. Kirsten takes a vegetarian approach to nutritional health, focusing on the way the right choice of foods can strengthen the immune system, thereby enabling the body's innate defensive mechanisms to combat disease.

In both Part One, Food is Medicine, and Part Two, Eat for Immunity, the authors list the "superfoods" they regard as having exceptional health-promoting qualities. Shown below are the symbols used to highlight important facts about these foods. For the most part, the products selected are not rare or exotic fruits and vegetables that are difficult to obtain, but everyday items available from most food shops or supermarkets. On the following pages you can read all about their medicinal properties, and then use the handy cross-references to discover a host of delicious and nutritious recipes that present these medicinal foods at their mouth-watering best. **The recipes are for four people**, unless otherwise stated, with the exception of the juices, syrups, and herbal drinks.

In other sections, Pierre Jean and Kirsten describe a wide range of common ailments and offer their personal suggestions for the best combination of foods to prevent or treat these disorders.

But this book is about health, not illness. By using *The New Complete Guide to Nutritional Health* to develop your understanding of the therapeutic value of fresh, natural, nutrient-packed foods, you will go a long way to ensuring life-long good health and vitality—not to mention enjoyable mealtimes—for you and your family.

KEY TO SYMBOLS USED IN FOOD IS MEDICINE

★ IMPORTANT NUTRIENTS AND OTHER ACTIVE INGREDIENTS

● BODY SYSTEM AND AILMENT

! WARNING

✔ BENEFICIAL FOODS AND OTHER RECOMMENDATIONS

✗ FOODS, DRINKS AND PRACTICES TO AVOID

KEY TO SYMBOLS USED IN EAT FOR IMMUNITY

★ IMPORTANT NUTRIENTS AND OTHER ACTIVE INGREDIENTS

✔ IMMUNE-BOOSTING ACTION AND OTHER BENEFICIAL PROPERTIES

! WARNING

♀ INTERESTING FACTS AND HANDY HINTS

USEFUL CONVERSIONS FROM METRIC TO IMPERIAL

30g = 1oz

100g = 3½oz

500g = 1lb 2oz

1kg = 2lb 4oz

30ml = 1fl oz

100ml = 3½fl oz

600ml = 21fl oz

1 litre = 35fl oz

1 tsp = 5ml

1 tbsp =15ml

part one: food is medicine

pierre jean cousin

introduction

One of the most important ways in which we can influence our health is by monitoring what we eat. Eating unhealthily—too much animal fat, salt, sugar, and artificial additives—can cause irreparable damage to our bodies, especially to the cardiovascular system and the kidneys. Eating healthily can increase vitality, immunity, and life expectancy. We can also influence the health of future generations by teaching our children healthy eating habits.

Food can be used not only to prevent illness, but also to treat it. Throughout the ages, and in all cultures, food has played an important role in healing the sick. Yet in contemporary Western societies the emphasis in healthcare has moved from traditional methods, such as diet, to modern medical techniques and a reliance on pharmaceuticals. As a result, self-help dietary remedies are rarely considered. As an experienced practitioner of a range of complementary therapies, I firmly believe in bringing the healing power of foods back to where it belongs—in our homes.

the principles of healthy eating

The mainstay of a healthy diet is plenty of unrefined complex carbohydrates and fiber. Foods such as beans, lentils, potatoes, wholewheat pasta, wholegrain bread, and cereals should make up—quite literally—the bulk of our diet. Protein-rich foods, such as meat or fish, can be added to this carbohydrate base in small amounts. Contrary to popular belief, we don't need very much protein for good health and it is not necessary to eat meat, fish, and dairy products as a daily source of protein. The other essential ingredients in a healthy diet are vitamins, minerals, and phytochemicals (biologically-active substances in plants), which are found in abundance in fruit and vegetables, and essential fatty acids from nuts, seeds, oily fish, and oils such as olive oil.

This basic template for healthy eating closely matches the traditional diet that is—or was—eaten in many cultures. Civilizations throughout history have relied upon a combination of cereals and legumes for their staple diet. In Asia, this combination is rice and soy; in America, corn and beans; in Europe, wheat, rye, barley, oats, or buckwheat, and beans, lentils, or other legumes; and in Africa, it is wheat, millet, or sorghum, and beans or garbanzos. Traditionally, a variety of fruit and vegetables (often eaten raw) has complemented this diet, together with small amounts of meat and fish when available. Fermented foods, such as cheese, yogurt, curd, fish sauce, pickled vegetables, cider, beer, and wine—all of which have a beneficial effect on the intestine—also feature in the traditional diet. This diet is ideally suited to the human body—it is rich in friendly bacteria, fiber, and nutrients and helps to maintain a healthy biological balance in the intestine.

It is very easy to adopt the healthy eating habits that are characteristic of such diets by following these simple commonsense measures:

● Buy more fresh fruit and vegetables (they are rich in antioxidants—substances that help to prevent degenerative disease such as cancer and heart disease), cereals, legumes, and fish.
● Cut down on meat, dairy products, and convenience food.
● Replace meat with oily fish.
● Tailor food intake to match your actual calorie needs (for most people this means eating less).
● Buy a cookbook that focuses on the Mediterranean diet.
● Reduce your intake of sugar, coffee, tea, sodas, and alcohol.
● Eat at regular intervals (up to five times a day if this suits your needs).

- Eat food that is in season and, ideally, locally produced according to organic principles.
- Make sure that your diet is as varied as possible.
- Use fresh ingredients as often as possible; avoid canned or dried food that contains additives.
- Be flexible in your eating—aim for balance and enjoyment. Avoid rigid dietary programs.

how the modern diet fails

These principles of healthy eating contrast starkly with the diet that is increasingly common in the West. Whereas the diet of our preindustrial ancestors was rich in fresh produce, the modern diet, which has evolved over the last 60–70 years, is characterized by food that contains preservatives, colorants, taste enhancers, sugar, caffeine, and even traces of fertilizers, pesticides, antibiotics, hormones, and metals. This leads to a proliferation of unhealthy bacteria in the gut, an accumulation of toxins in the body, poor digestion, and an increased likelihood of allergies, cardiovascular disease, and a range of cancers, including breast and colonic cancer.

In the West, food is abundant and relatively cheap owing to modern production and processing techniques. These techniques have created what has been termed "food industrialization"—the production of large amounts of food quickly and cheaply at the expense of quality and nutritional content. Paradoxically, although we now have more choice in what we can eat, less time is devoted to the selection, preparation, and consumption of food. Our diets often consist of a limited number of ingredients that we continue eating out of routine and convenience.

Much of the food that we buy is impoverished. For example, when fresh produce is out of season in one country, it is often imported from another, and much of its vitamin content is lost during transit or storage in refrigerators or on supermarket shelves.

Goodness is also depleted in the process of sterilization: In order to make fresh food "safe" and prolong shelf life by eliminating microorganisms, it is often sterilized or irradiated—yet this procedure renders it, quite literally, lifeless. Although all unhealthy, disease-causing bacteria are killed in the process, all the "good" bacteria and ferments are also destroyed. These are important for digestion and in maintaining a healthy and balanced environment in the intestine. Most milk, for example, is pasteurized, with the result that it does not contain natural ferments and is difficult for many people to break down and digest. Milk products that have not been pasteurized, such as live yogurt (which is full of lactobacilli bacteria), are well tolerated by most people. Another consequence of sterilization is that, if food is left out of the refrigerator for too long or is reheated too many times, microorganisms, such as listeria, will re-establish themselves. Without competition from good bacteria, unhealthy ones can proliferate unchecked and cause disease.

Industrialized food production is partly responsible for a range of contemporary health problems, such as male hormone imbalance (linked to the misuse of hormones in animals), the advent of antibiotic-resistant strains of bacteria (linked to the routine addition of antibiotics to animal feed), salmonella in poultry and eggs (linked to poor living conditions among animals), and Creutzfeldt-Jacob disease (linked to bovine spongiform encephalopathy or BSE, a disease affecting cows that is caused by contaminated cattle feed). Genetic modification of food is the

experiment that I believe may have harmful, long-term effects on human health and the environment. The defensive attitude of scientists who argue that "no evidence exists that genetically-modified (GM) food is unsafe" needs to be challenged—this kind of negative statement does not constitute proof that GM food is safe.

Owing to the wide-ranging effects of food industrialization it is important that, as consumers, we make informed choices about what we buy—not just favoring foods that are unprocessed and grown according to organic principles, but also excluding products that are nutritionally empty and preserved and enhanced in artificial ways.

the medicinal value of food

Our knowledge of the healing power of food is based upon thousands of years of tradition and empirical observation. Modern scientific research now confirms the curative abilities of foods that have been used therapeutically through the ages. A huge variety of foods is known to contain compounds that have medicinal properties. For example, the potent antibacterial action of allicin, a substance found in garlic, is well documented. So, too, are the protective and healing properties of antioxidants and essential oils in fruit, vegetables, herbs, and spices. Some pharmacologically active ingredients are extracted from food and sold in tablet form. Cynarin, for example, is an active ingredient that is extracted from artichoke. An extensive body of research has shown that this substance can play an important role in treating liver disease and help damaged liver tissue to regenerate. The great advantage of using food as medicine is that food is readily available to all of us and can be self-administered with relative safety. Food cures work in a purely holistic way, by enhancing the body's natural functions and encouraging it to heal itself.

using *Food is Medicine*

The aim of *Food is Medicine* is to provide inspiration and practical advice that will help you to adopt healthy eating habits and to use food in medicinal ways. *Food is Medicine* is divided into four chapters. The first chapter—Guide to Healing Foods—lists more than 140 common foods, their nutrients, and their most important medicinal properties. It also identifies seven "star" foods that are renowned for their beneficial properties. Chapter two—Foods for Common Ailments—specifies the foods that can play a part in treating over 80 common medical conditions. The third chapter—Healing Recipes—is a collection of recipes that use medicinal foods in interesting and delicious combinations. The final chapter—Diet in Practice—offers a practical guide to vitamins and minerals and the foods in which they are found. It also explains how to detoxify your body with a simple diet based on fruit, vegetables, juices, and herbal infusions.

Most of the recipes and techniques that I have selected are straightforward to make or carry out, and use easily available ingredients. The recipes can be used in three different ways:

● As everyday dishes for people who are healthy, but interested in preserving their long-term well-being by incorporating health-giving foods in their diet.

● As remedies for acute and chronic illnesses. The recipes for juices (pages 117–119) and medicinal drinks (pages 123–131) will be the most useful as they are the most medicinally potent.

Food remedies can be used in conjunction with conventional medical treatment to manage or heal a variety of severe or chronic complaints. The time that it takes to witness improvements depends on your ailment and state of health—try to be patient and persevere with food remedies. Illnesses that are stress-related are also amenable to dietary treatment.

● As first-aid treatments and for symptom relief. Some of the foods used in the recipes can alleviate problems such as indigestion and menstrual cramp. Others can be applied to the skin as remedies for bites, burns, stings, and skin problems, such as eczema, or as beauty treatments.

Some of the medicinal-drink recipes contain alcohol in the form of wine or vodka. Although in large quantities alcohol is bad for health, it is an excellent solvent that concentrates the active ingredients of plants. Macerating an herb such as basil in vodka, for example, preserves its medicinal compounds in a form that is easy and convenient to take (basil is good for indigestion, nausea, and to ease feelings of bloatedness). Most medicinal drinks that contain alcohol need be taken in only small doses or for a short period of time—just long enough to help a particular symptom or condition. The medicinal infusions and decoctions often fall into the category of traditional herbal medicine rather than dietary remedies. Since all of the medicinal drinks are potent, they should be used with caution and should not be given to children unless the recipe states that this is acceptable. If you are in doubt about whether it is appropriate to treat yourself with herbal or food remedies, or you are worried about a health problem, consult your doctor.

In a few recipes, a little cream may be added to the finished dish—this is entirely optional. If you have a health problem such as lactose intolerance, use soy milk and soy yogurt instead of milk products. If you suffer from hypertension, high cholesterol, heart disease, or diabetes, you should avoid adding sugar, salt, and fat to any of the recipes.

selecting and harvesting ingredients

Whenever possible, use organically-grown fruit and vegetables, make sure they are fresh, and avoid keeping them in a refrigerator for too long. When buying meat, buy organically-produced, free-range, or farm-raised meat; buy small quantities of quality cuts rather than larger amounts of cheaper meat. Try to buy fish on the same day that it is delivered to the store.

If possible, try to harvest wild ingredients from your yard or local countryside. When picking ingredients, such as borage leaves, nettles, and dandelion leaves, choose young plants that are growing away from main highways, rail tracks, and paths that are regularly used by animals. Make sure that you can confidently identify the plants that you need and that what you pick is in good condition and fit for consumption. You can cultivate many herbs, such as camomile, lemon balm, savory, mint, basil, thyme, and rosemary, in your yard or in pots on a patio or balcony. When harvesting wild fruit, such as berries, choose bushes and trees that are not exposed to pollution from roads. Collect only undamaged, ripe fruit and don't be tempted to eat it on the spot—it must be washed thoroughly, and preferably cooked.

Pierre Jean Cousin

chapter one

guide to healing foods

Many people consider food as fuel—they need it simply to keep them going through the day. But food can also prevent and treat illness, offering an astounding medicine-chest of natural remedies. The foods in this section are arranged by type to help you to make informed choices about which specific foods may be beneficial to you. Included are eight star foods—true wonders of nature that we should all include in our diet to boost and protect good health.

vegetables, cereals, and legumes
ROOT VEGETABLES

POTATO

★ VITAMINS B, C, FOLIC ACID, COPPER, PHOSPHORUS, POTASSIUM, SULFUR, CARBOHYDRATE

● DIGESTIVE SYSTEM Diabetes, gastritis, peptic ulcers.

Potatoes are good for mild digestive problems. Potato juice, mixed with equal amounts of carrot and cabbage juice and a little lemon juice to taste, can ease the symptoms of gastritis and peptic ulcers. The juice or pulp of raw potatoes can be applied directly to burns, insect bites, eczema, and boils. Germinated or green potatoes should not be eaten as they may cause stomach upset.
RECIPES chicken breasts with celery root mash (page 108), dandelion, bacon, and potato cakes (page 108), potato and watercress mash (page 111), potatoes with herb sauce (page 113).

PARSNIP

★ VITAMINS C, FOLIC ACID, E, K, MANGANESE, PHOSPHORUS, POTASSIUM, CARBOHYDRATE, FIBER

Parsnips belong to the same family as carrots and parsley. They contain small quantities of essential oils (mostly terpenes) that are thought to have anti-cancer properties.

TURNIP

★ VITAMINS A, B, C, FOLIC ACID, CALCIUM, MAGNESIUM, PHOSPHORUS, POTASSIUM, SULFUR, NATURAL SUGAR

Turnips, together with several other vegetables, such as broccoli, cabbage, cauliflower, and rutabaga, are cruciferous (see Broccoli, page 24). Both the root and the young leaves of the turnip can be eaten (the root can be eaten raw, grated in salads).
RECIPES young turnip salad (page 100).

ONION AND SHALLOT

★ VITAMINS B, C, MANGANESE, PHOSPHORUS, POTASSIUM, SULFUR COMPOUNDS, BIOFLAVONOIDS, ESSENTIAL OIL, NATURAL SUGAR

● BONES AND JOINTS Arthritis (rheumatoid), gout, rheumatism.
● BLOOD AND CIRCULATION Arteriosclerosis.
● DIGESTIVE SYSTEM Diabetes, diarrhea.
● IMMUNE SYSTEM Colds, influenza.
● WOMEN'S HEALTH Menstrual cramp.

Onions have antibiotic and antifungal properties, can block tumor formation, reduce levels of blood cholesterol, and prevent blood clots forming. They ease fluid retention and promote the elimination of urea. Onions are beneficial to both the digestive and circulatory systems. They can be juiced or used in a decoction to treat digestive problems, diarrhea, coughs, colds, and influenza.
Onions can be eaten raw (macerating in olive oil makes them more palatable). Onion juice can be drunk mixed with water or carrot juice; it can also be applied neat to insect stings, warts, and boils.
RECIPES onions in cider (page 111).

BEET

★ VITAMINS A, B, C, IRON, MAGNESIUM, MANGANESE, POTASSIUM, ZINC, ASPARAGINE, BETAINE, BIOFLAVONOIDS, NATURAL SUGAR

● BLOOD AND CIRCULATION Anemia.

Beet is nutritious, easy to digest, and a rich source of minerals. It contains betaine, a substance that regulates gastric pH and facilitates digestion. Beet can be eaten raw, chopped or grated in salads, or drunk as a juice (one glass per day for a month is the recommended dosage for improving digestive function). The leafy greens of the beet plant can also be cooked and eaten; they are rich in vitamins and minerals and good for the liver.
RECIPES borscht (page 94), beet and celery juice (page 121), pickled beets (page 122).

CELERY ROOT

★ VITAMINS B, C, K, IODINE, IRON, MAGNESIUM, MANGANESE, POTASSIUM, ANTIOXIDANTS

● BLOOD AND CIRCULATION Hyperlipidemia.

The root of a variety of celery plant, it helps to lower levels of blood cholesterol and reduce the risk of bowel cancer.
RECIPES chicken breasts with celery root mash (page 108).

RADISH (RED AND BLACK)

★ VITAMIN C, FOLIC ACID, SULFUR, RAPHANOL, WATER

● BONES AND JOINTS Arthritis (rheumatoid).

● DIGESTIVE SYSTEM Dyspepsia.

● RESPIRATORY SYSTEM Cough, whooping cough.

Although radishes are of poor overall nutritional value, they contain an active ingredient called raphanol that promotes bile flow and the emptying of the gallbladder. There are different types of radish. Black radishes are much larger than the common red variety and contain a greater concentration of raphanol. A combination of carrot and black radish juice is recommended for people with poor liver function and gallbladder problems such as gallstones—mix together ⅓ cup of each juice. Both black and red radishes are best eaten raw in salads. A syrup of black radish can be used as an expectorant cough mixture that is appropriate for whooping cough. The young leaves of red radishes contain valuable minerals and are an excellent addition to soups.
RECIPES radish and kumquat salad (page 98), escarole salad (page 101), black radish salad (page 101), black radish syrup (page 132).

LEEK

★ VITAMINS A, B, C, K, CALCIUM, IRON, MAGNESIUM, MANGANESE, PHOSPHORUS, POTASSIUM, SILICA, SULFUR

● BONES AND JOINTS Arthritis (rheumatoid), gout.

● KIDNEYS AND BLADDER Bladder stones.

Leeks belong to the same family as garlic and onion, and contain smaller amounts of the same active ingredients. Leeks are diuretic, laxative, and antiseptic, and are excellent for a healthy digestive tract. Leek juice can be used externally on abscesses, skin inflammation, stings, and bites. *RECIPES buckwheat with leek sauce (page 105), leek and chive mimosa with polenta (page 107), leek syrup (page 132).*

continues on page 24

carrot

CARROTS ARE RICH IN ANTIOXIDANTS AND PROTECT THE BODY FROM
CERTAIN TYPES OF CANCER. THEY BOOST THE IMMUNE SYSTEM AND
ARE USEFUL IN TREATING A RANGE OF AILMENTS, FROM POOR NIGHT
VISION TO STOMACH ULCERS.

The properties of carrot

The medicinal properties of carrots were known to the Greeks
and Romans. Carrots then were long, thin yellow roots with a
strong scent. Modern carrots, which originated in Holland in the
17th century, tend to be orange-coloured, plump, and short.

Carrots are one of the most precious vegetables in a
medicinal kitchen—they contains vitamin A (400% RDA in 100
grams), vitamin K, folic acid, potassium, manganese, sulfur,
copper, carotenes, and pectin. Their high fiber and fluid content
makes them gently laxative and good for constipation, but they
also have astringent properties that makes them good for
diarrhea—they can be used as a remedy for either problem in
children. A treatment for diarrhea in adults consists of eating
boiled carrots and boiled rice and drinking black tea. The young
leaves of carrots are rich in minerals and can be added to
soups or cooked with cereals as a tonic for children or people
recovering from illness.

Raw carrots inhibit the activity of listeria and salmonella,
and thus help to prevent or reduce the risk of food poisoning.
Carrots are recommended for chronic fatigue, anemia, poor
immune defenses, poor night vision, stomach ulcers, and
intestinal problems. They can also promote lactation in nursing
mothers. Carrot juice contains more medicinally active
ingredients than cooked carrots and the juice is recommended
for young children. Raw carrots were traditionally given to
horses suffering from bronchitis.

Carrots should be peeled to remove organophosphates
(and other artificial residues from pesticides and fertilizers) that
may accumulate in the outer part of the vegetable. If
possible, buy organically grown carrots that are free from
organophosphates and fertilizers.

Long-term health benefits

Carrots are an excellent source of antioxidants and are known
to have a protective action against lung and other types of
cancer. A diet that includes plenty of carrots also lowers
unhealthy levels of cholesterol in the blood—preventing the
buildup of fatty deposits in artery walls—and boosts the body's
immune system.

Carrots are a cheap and easily available source of
antioxidants and, ideally, they should be consumed two or
three times a week either raw in salads (or as snacks) or in
juice form.

Medicinal preparations

Carrot seeds can be made into a medicinal infusion (page 126)
that stimulates appetite and digestion, and is diuretic and
carminative (relieves flatulence). Externally, carrot juice can be
mixed with other ingredients, including cucumber, strawberries,
and chervil, to make a beauty treatment that rejuvenates the
face and neck. An external application of carrot juice can also
help to alleviate eczema and acne.

STAR FOOD PROFILE

- **BONES AND JOINTS** Arthritis (rheumatoid), rheumatism.
- **BLOOD AND CIRCULATION** Raynaud's disease.
- **DIGESTIVE SYSTEM** Colitis, diverticulitis, gastritis, peptic ulcers.
- **RESPIRATORY SYSTEM** Asthma, cough.

carrots with rosemary

2 tablespoons butter
1 red onion, sliced
2¼ pounds carrots, peeled and sliced
1 heaping tablespoon finely chopped rosemary
5 tablespoons fresh cream or yogurt
Salt and pepper
1 tablespoon chopped parsley

In a saucepan, melt the butter and add the onion, carrots, and rosemary. Cover and let the ingredients cook slowly for 30 minutes (or until the carrots are tender) in their own juices. Add a little water if the saucepan becomes dry. When the carrots are cooked, add the cream or yogurt and season to taste. Serve sprinkled with parsley.

carrot salad

1¼ pounds carrots, grated
Juice of 1 lemon
Juice of 1 orange
Pinch of salt

Mix the ingredients in a large bowl. Cover and chill before serving.

carrot, cabbage, and bell pepper juice

4 carrots, roughly chopped
½ cabbage, core removed and quartered
1 red or green bell pepper, deseeded
2 small shallots

In a juicer, process the ingredients, adding water if necessary. Chill and serve soon after making.

pumpkin

FAR MORE THAN JUST A VEGETABLE FOR CARVING JACK-O'-LANTERNS,
PUMPKIN EARNS ITS PLACE AMONG THE STAR FOODS FOR ITS
NUTRIENT-PACKED ORANGE FLESH AS WELL AS FOR ITS FLOWERS AND
SEEDS—ALL OF WHICH HAVE STRONG CURATIVE PROPERTIES.

The history of pumpkin

The name pumpkin originates from the Greek word pepon,
meaning "large melon," but the discovery of pumpkin seeds
dating back more than 7,000 years in Mexico suggests that
the vegetable's origins lie in South America. The Native North
Americans and the Aztecs used pumpkins for both food and
medicine, and archaeological evidence suggests that they were
one of the first plants to be cultivated in the Western world. The
American tradition of using a carved-out pumpkin as a light on
Halloween originates from an Irish myth. According to the story,
after his death a man named Stingy Jack was permitted neither
into Heaven nor into Hell. Instead, Jack was cursed to wander
the Earth with only a piece of coal in a hollow turnip for light.
When Irish immigrants took this story to the New World, the
turnip became a pumpkin, a vegetable native to the Americas.

Pumpkins are now grown on every continent except
Antarctica and are much prized for their versatility because
so much of the plant is edible (the flowers and seeds as well
as the flesh). They are also relatively easy to grow. Yellow
pumpkins usually weigh 9 to 18lb., but the world record for the
largest pumpkin stands at 1725lb.!

Using pumpkin

Ripe pumpkin can be boiled, baked, steamed, or mashed, and
the seeds make a delicious toasted snack. In the Middle East,
India, and Thailand, pumpkin is often used as an ingredient
in sweet dishes, and in Africa and China, the leaves are used
in soups and as cooked greens. The Japanese serve small
pumpkins in a variety of savoury dishes, and the Italians mix
pumpkin with cheese as a ravioli filling.

Pumpkin as a cure

Pumpkin is low in calories and high in water and fiber. It also
contains significant amounts of alpha- and beta-carotene and
other carotenoids—all important antioxidants—as well as good
levels of vitamin C, magnesium, and potassium.

Alpha-carotene protects against cataracts and
some cancers, and beta-carotene is a potent anti-
inflammatory that also prevents cholesterol
build up in the bloodstream, reducing the
risk of heart disease. Recent research
shows that pumpkin can aid the
regeneration of pancreatic cells, so
it may help manage some cases
of diabetes.

Pumpkin seeds contain protein,
tryptophan, essential fatty acids,
vitamins B1, B2, B3, and E,
and zinc, iron, manganese,
magnesium, selenium,
phosphorus, copper, and
potassium. Herbalists prescribe
them to counter age-related
prostate enlargement and also use
them as a diuretic and as a remedy
for intestinal worms.

Their high tryptophan content makes
pumpkin seeds potentially useful in the
treatment of anxiety, depression, and other mood
disorders, and the essential fatty acids they contain
help maintain healthy skin, nerves, and blood vessels.

STAR FOOD PROFILE

- **BONES AND JOINTS:** Arthritis (rheumatoid).
- **BLOOD AND CIRCULATION:** Atherosclerosis, heart disease, high cholesterol, thrombosis.
- **DIGESTIVE SYSTEM:** Intestinal worms.
- **IMMUNE SYSTEM:** Cancer, diabetes.
- **KIDNEYS AND BLADDER:** Diuretic.
- **MEN'S HEALTH:** Enlarged prostate.
- **NERVOUS SYSTEM, MIND, AND EMOTIONS:** Anxiety, depression, mood swings.
- **SKIN, HAIR, AND NAILS:** Slows the aging process.

pumpkin risotto *(above)*

2 tablespoons olive oil	1 chilli pepper, sliced
1 red onion, finely chopped	1⅓ cups risotto rice, rinsed
2 cloves of garlic, minced	2¼ pounds pumpkin, peeled,
2 celery ribs (with leaves), finely sliced	seeded, and cubed
	2¼ cups chopped tomatoes
1 red pepper, seeded and sliced	2 teaspoons dried oregano
2-in piece cinnamon stick	4⅓ cups vegetable stock

Heat the oil in a heavy-bottomed saucepan over a medium heat. Sauté the onion, garlic, celery, cinnamon, and chilli for 3 minutes, then add the rice and pumpkin. Continue cooking, stirring, for another 3 minutes. Add the tomatoes and oregano. Slowly add the stock, stirring continuously. Bring to boil, then reduce the heat to low and cook, stirring, until the liquid is absorbed and the rice is al dente, about 15 minutes.

pumpkin sauce

1 pound pumpkin, peeled, seeded, and cut into chunks	3 tablespoons olive oil
	1 bunch basil, chopped
1 red onion, sliced	1 cup grated Parmesan (or soy)
8 ounces ripe tomatoes, chopped	cheese

Put the pumpkin, onion, and tomatoes in a saucepan with the oil. Sprinkle with the basil and season with salt and pepper. Cover and cook over a low heat for 30 minutes, stirring occasionally, until the pumpkin is soft. Just before serving, sprinkle with the cheese and mix to combine. Serve as a sauce for pasta or as a side dish.

norfolk million tart

1 pound 2 ounces pumpkin, peeled, seeded, and sliced	1 egg
	1½ tablespoons raw cane sugar
butter, for greasing	½ teaspoon nutmeg
9 ounces piecrust dough	¼ cup raisins
2 tablespoons apricot jam	

Preheat the oven to 400°F. Boil the pumpkin for 5–10 minutes until soft. Drain and cool. Grease an 8in. tart pan with a little butter. Roll out the dough and line the pan with it. Trim the dough, reserving the trimmings. Spread the jam over the dough. Blend together the egg, sugar, nutmeg, and pumpkin, then mix in the raisins and spread it over the jam. Using the dough trimmings, make a lattice over the top. Bake for 20 minutes or until the crust is golden. Serve hot with cream or ice cream.

GREENS AND LEAFY VEGETABLES

BROCCOLI

★ VITAMINS A, C, FOLIC ACID, E, K, CALCIUM, IRON, ZINC

● BLOOD AND CIRCULATION High blood pressure.

Broccoli, together with vegetables such as turnips, cabbage, Brussels sprouts, cauliflower, and rutabaga, are cruciferous vegetables. They are rich in antioxidants and are believed to reduce the risk of certain types of cancer, including lung and colon cancer. Avoid overcooking broccoli as approximately half of its beneficial substances may be destroyed in the process.

RECIPES *broccoli and green bean juice (page 121).*

BRUSSELS SPROUT

★ VITAMINS A, B, C, FOLIC ACID, K, IRON, MANGANESE, POTASSIUM

See Broccoli, above.

RECIPES *Brussels sprouts with chestnuts (page 112).*

CAULIFLOWER

★ VITAMINS C, FOLIC ACID, E, POTASSIUM, ZINC, CAROTENES

● BONES AND JOINTS Arthritis (rheumatoid).

See Broccoli, above.

RECIPES *pickled cauliflower (page 122).*

GREEN BEAN

★ VITAMIN A, FOLIC ACID, COPPER, PHOSPHORUS, SILICA, CARBOHYDRATE, CHLOROPHYLL

● BONES AND JOINTS Arthritis (rheumatoid), gout, rheumatism.

● KIDNEYS AND BLADDER Kidney stones.

Green beans have diuretic properties and are good for kidney function and preventing water retention. They stimulate the production of white blood cells (needed to defend the body against infection) and are gently cardiotonic. For rheumatism, water retention, or as a general cardiotonic, green beans should be eaten every day for a month (the cooking water can be also be drunk or used as a stock for soup). Alternatively, half a glass of green bean juice every morning for four to five weeks has the same medicinal benefits.

RECIPES *green bean salad (page 99), green beans with dijon mustard (page 113), green bean and garlic juice (page 121), broccoli and green bean juice (page 121).*

SWISS CHARD

★ VITAMINS A, C, E, K, IRON, MAGNESIUM

Chard is a form of beet that is grown for its greens. It has diuretic and laxative properties and is useful for treating kidney and bladder inflammation. The cooked leaves can be used in a poultice for burns, abscesses, and boils.

DANDELION

★ VITAMINS A, B, C, FOLIC ACID, K, CALCIUM, IRON, MANGANESE, POTASSIUM, SILICA, BIOFLAVONOIDS, BITTER PRINCIPLE, CHLOROPHYLL, INULIN

● BLOOD AND CIRCULATION Anemia, hyperlipidemia.

● DIGESTIVE SYSTEM Colitis, constipation, gallstones.

● KIDNEYS AND BLADDER Kidney stones.

● SKIN, HAIR, AND NAILS Eczema.

Dandelion leaves improve liver function and combat gall-bladder or kidney stones. The young leaves can be used in salads or cooked in the same way as other green leafy vegetables. When choosing young dandelion plants for salads or soups, include the flowerbuds. Dandelion sap is an effective topical treatment for verrucas. The root is used in herbal medicine for its detoxifying properties.

RECIPES *dandelion, bacon, and potato cakes (page 108), dandelion infusion (page 125).*

NETTLE

★ VITAMINS A, B, C, K, CAROTENE, CALCIUM, IRON, MAGNESIUM, POTASSIUM, SILICA, SULFUR

● BONES AND JOINTS Arthritis (rheumatoid), gout, rheumatism.

● BLOOD AND CIRCULATION Anemia.

● DIGESTIVE SYSTEM Diarrhea.

Nettles are a novel addition to many recipes. They are diuretic, astringent, and depurative; they promote the elimination of uric acid, stimulate liver function, appetite, and bile flow; and they help combat infection. Nettles can be used as a fortifying ingredient in recipes for children and convalescents. They are also good for diminishing menstrual and other types of bleeding.

RECIPES nettle soup (page 96), nettle risotto (page 105), halibut steak and nettle butter (page 109).

SPINACH

★ VITAMIN A, B, C, E, K, FOLIC ACID, CALCIUM, IRON, MAGNESIUM, MANGANESE, POTASSIUM, ZINC, CAROTENE

Spinach is rich in antioxidants and stimulates pancreas function. Its juice is a powerful tonic; an infusion of the seeds is good for mild constipation (cover 1½ teaspoons of seeds in 1 cup boiling water, infuse for 10 minutes, then strain); and the leaves can be used topically for burns or eczema. Avoid over-consumption of spinach as it may reduce calcium absorption. People who suffer from gout, arthritis, or digestive-tract inflammation should avoid excess spinach.

RECIPES lamb with spinach and lentils (page 107), spicy spinach, prunes, and peas (page 109), red snapper with raw spinach salad (page 111).

WATERCRESS

★ VITAMINS A, B, C, E, K, IODINE, CALCIUM, IRON, MANGANESE, PHOSPHORUS, ZINC

● BONES AND JOINTS Arthritis (rheumatoid), rheumatism.

● BLOOD AND CIRCULATION Anemia.

● DIGESTIVE SYSTEM Intestinal parasites.

● RESPIRATORY SYSTEM Bronchitis.

Watercress stimulates the appetite and has tonic, depurative, diuretic, energizing, expectorant, and anti-cancer properties. Apply watercress leaves or juice to the skin to ease inflammation, ulcers, boils, diminish freckles, and heal scars. The juice is a hair tonic.

RECIPES cottage cheese with watercress (page 103), potato and watercress mash (page 111).

SALAD VEGETABLES

LETTUCE

★ VITAMINS A, C, FOLIC ACID, K, IRON, MANGANESE, POTASSIUM, ZINC, LACTUCARIUM

● NERVOUS SYSTEM, MIND, AND EMOTIONS Insomnia.

During the Middle Ages lettuce was served at the start of a meal in order to stimulate the appetite. Because it is rich in fiber it helps food to pass quickly through the intestines, and aids digestion. Lettuce contains lactucarium, a substance that has sedative and analgesic properties, and is thought to be useful in the treatment of mild insomnia. Lettuce seeds are the most valuable part of the plant from a medicinal perspective. A decoction of the seeds is helpful for asthma, bronchitis, spasmodic cough, and insomnia. A decoction of lettuce leaves can be used externally as an anti-inflammatory treatment for conjunctivitis and acne.

RECIPES lettuce and basil juice (page 121), lettuce-seed decoction (page 128).

MÂCHE (CORN SALAD)

★ VITAMINS A, B, C, FOLIC ACID, K, IRON, CHLOROPHYLL, FIBER

● BONES AND JOINTS Arthritis (rheumatoid).

● BLOOD AND CIRCULATION Anemia, arteriosclerosis.

● DIGESTIVE SYSTEM Constipation, gastroenteritis.

● KIDNEYS AND BLADDER Bladder stones.

Mâche is recommended for digestive problems. It has detoxifying and slight diuretic properties, it facilitates the elimination of urea (which prevents the formation of uric acid crystals), and is said to be good for respiratory disorders, probably by helping the elimination of mucus. Mâche is best eaten raw in salads but can also be cooked or taken in juice form.

ARUGULA

★ VITAMINS A, B, C, FOLIC ACID, K, IRON, CHLOROPHYLL, FIBER

● DIGESTIVE SYSTEM Dyspepsia.

Arugula was once considered to be an aphrodisiac and its cultivation in monasteries was forbidden. It is widely used in Italian cuisine and can be used in salads or lightly cooked with pasta and ravioli. It has tonic properties and stimulates appetite and digestion.

continues on page 26

cabbage

CABBAGE IS A LONG-ESTABLISHED REMEDY FOR A VARIETY OF DIGESTIVE AILMENTS. IT IS ALSO RICH IN ANTIOXIDANTS AND CAN STRENGTHEN THE IMMUNE SYSTEM AND HELP THE BODY TO OVERCOME INFECTION.

The history of cabbage

The therapeutic benefits of the common cabbage have been known and appreciated across Europe for thousands of years: The Slavs, Celts, Basques, and Germans all used cabbage for both food and medicine and the Romans considered it to be a panacea for almost any disease. It is thought that cultivation of the cabbage plant may go back as far as the Neolithic period. Cabbage belongs to the cruciferous family of vegetables, which also includes broccoli and turnip. There are many different colors, sizes, and varieties of cabbage.

The properties of cabbage

Cabbage is rich in vitamins A, B, C, and K, iron, potassium, sulfur, and copper. It also contains a variety of antioxidants that help to reduce the risk of bowel cancer and cardiovascular disease. Cabbage is anti-inflammatory, diuretic, and helps to lower blood sugar. Medicinal uses of cabbage focus on digestive ailments such as gastritis, stomach ulcers, colitis, and diverticulitis. Research shows that cabbage juice is an effective treatment for stomach ulcers. A recommended remedy for inflammation of the digestive tract is a small glass of cabbage juice every morning for a few weeks. Cabbage juice is also a natural cleansing and purifying agent.

An immune system stimulant, cabbage is also good for treating common colds and mucus, laryngitis, and other upper respiratory tract infections. The abundance of sulfur compounds in cabbage also makes it an effective remedy for rheumatism and arthritis. Cabbage contains a small amount of a substance called glucobrassinin, which reduces the activity of the thyroid gland. Excessive consumption of cabbage among people who receive insufficient iodine may lead to a mild and rare form of hypothyroidism.

Cabbage in the diet

Many of the active ingredients contained in cabbage are lost in prolonged cooking; raw cabbage and cabbage juice are of greater medicinal value. A good way of eating raw cabbage is chopped and pickled in the form of sauerkraut. This contains a high concentration of lactobacilli—bacteria that are beneficial to the intestines.

Using cabbage externally

Cabbage leaves made into a poultice can be applied externally to heal wounds, fractures, sprains, burns, and joint inflammation caused by rheumatism, arthritis, and gout. The juice can be applied to the skin in the treatment of eczema and acne. Cabbage leaves placed on the eyes can relieve local inflammation.

STAR FOOD PROFILE

- **BONES AND JOINTS** Arthritis (rheumatoid), gout.
- **BLOOD AND CIRCULATION** Raynaud's disease.
- **DIGESTIVE SYSTEM** Colitis, diverticulitis, gastritis, peptic ulcers.
- **RESPIRATORY SYSTEM** Asthma, cough.

cabbage with chestnuts

This dish goes well with roast pork.

1 white cabbage (or red cabbage or Brussels sprouts)
2 tablespoons olive oil
4 medium-size red onions, sliced
11 ounces chestnuts, peeled and cooked
To serve: cumin seeds

Chop the cabbage into thin strips, then blanch in salted, boiling water for a few minutes. In another large pan, soften the onions in the olive oil over low heat, then add the cabbage and chestnuts, and cook for a further 5 minutes. Sprinkle over some cumin seeds before serving hot.

cabbage, carrot, and blueberry juice

2 parts fresh cabbage juice
2 parts fresh carrot juice
1 part blueberry juice

Combine the juices thoroughly. Chill and serve.

CELERY

★ VITAMINS A, B, C, K, CALCIUM, MAGNESIUM, MANGANESE, POTASSIUM, ESSENTIAL OIL

● BONES AND JOINTS Gout, rheumatism.

● KIDNEYS AND BLADDER Kidney or bladder stones.

● IMMUNE SYSTEM Sore throat.

Celery is good for digestive problems and poor appetite. It is best eaten raw in salads but can also be consumed as a juice mixed with carrot or green vegetable juice. It is particularly easy to digest in soup form. Fresh celery juice is antiseptic and can ease mouth ulcers and sore throats. The juice can also be mixed with an equal amount of carrot juice and applied to the skin to promote healing. Celery is very low in calories and is a useful part of a weight-loss diet.

RECIPES *celery with wine and herbs (page 112), cabbage, carrot, and celery juice (page 121), beet and celery juice (page 121).*

CUCUMBER

★ VITAMINS B, C, K, MAGNESIUM, MANGANESE, POTASSIUM, SULFUR

● BONES AND JOINTS Gout, rheumatism.

● DIGESTIVE SYSTEM Ulcerative colitis.

Cucumbers have a very high water content; they are diuretic, anti-inflammatory, help to dissolve uric acid, and are good for intestinal health. They should be eaten with the skin on (whenever possible buy organically-produced, unwaxed cucumbers). Cucumber flesh or juice can be used externally to reduce inflammation and hydrate and protect the skin. A face mask can be made from blending 1 tablespoon of fresh cream with equal amounts of cucumber, melon, and pumpkin seeds in a food processor. The cream should be applied to the face, left for 30 minutes, and then rinsed off.

RECIPES *pineapple and cucumber salad (page 101), cucumber salad (page 101), rice with cucumber balls (page 111), cucumber and lettuce heart juice (page 121).*

BELL PEPPER

★ VITAMINS A, B, C, FOLIC ACID, ANTIOXIDANTS

● BONES AND JOINTS Rheumatism.

● DIGESTIVE SYSTEM Diarrhea, dyspepsia, gas.

The color of a bell pepper—green, yellow, or red—indicates its stage of maturity. Bell peppers can be eaten raw in salads and broiled or roasted in a variety of Mediterranean dishes. Hot peppers are used in spicy dishes such as curry; they contain up to 1 per cent capsaicin, a pungent-smelling and -tasting substance that is good for the heart and circulation.

RECIPES *stuffed bell peppers (page 106).*

TOMATO

★ VITAMINS A, B, C, FOLIC ACID, K, TRACE ELEMENTS, ANTIOXIDANTS,

● BONES AND JOINTS Rheumatism.

● DIGESTIVE SYSTEM Cholecystitis, constipation, gallstones.

● KIDNEYS AND BLADDER Bladder stones

Tomatoes help to dissolve urea (preventing the formation of uric acid crystals) and reduce inflammation of the digestive tract and bacterial activity in the bowel. Many commercially available tomatoes are grown too quickly in hothouses or are genetically modified. Organically produced varieties of tomato offer greater medicinal benefits.

RECIPES *tomato coulis (page 105), polenta with basil tomato sauce (page 107), celery and tomato juice (page 120).*

ZUCCHINI

★ VITAMINS A, B, C, MAGNESIUM, MANGANESE, PHOSPHORUS, POTASSIUM, ZINC, CAROTENES

● DIGESTIVE SYSTEM Dyspepsia, gastroenteritis.

● NERVOUS SYSTEM, MIND AND EMOTIONS Insomnia.

Zucchini are gentle on the intestines, mildly laxative, diuretic, and good for reducing bladder and kidney inflammation. They are recommended for diabetic people who manage their illness through diet. Zucchini can be eaten raw in salads or lightly cooked. The juice can be mixed with other vegetable juices and drunk daily. The juice (or the mashed flesh) can also be applied to the skin as a remedy for inflammation and abscesses; clay can be added to make an effective beauty mask.

RECIPES *zucchini cake (page 105).*

SALAD GREENS

★ VITAMINS B, C, FOLIC ACID, K, IRON, MAGNESIUM, BIOFLAVONOIDS

Salad greens, such as endive, escarole, frisée, and Belgian endive, have mild diuretic properties and contain a bitter compound that is good for the liver and gallbladder. They are an important source of nutrients. Endive root may be dried and roasted and used as a caffeine-free alternative to coffee. Belgian endive is grown without light and has little nutritional value.

RECIPES *escarole salad (page 101).*

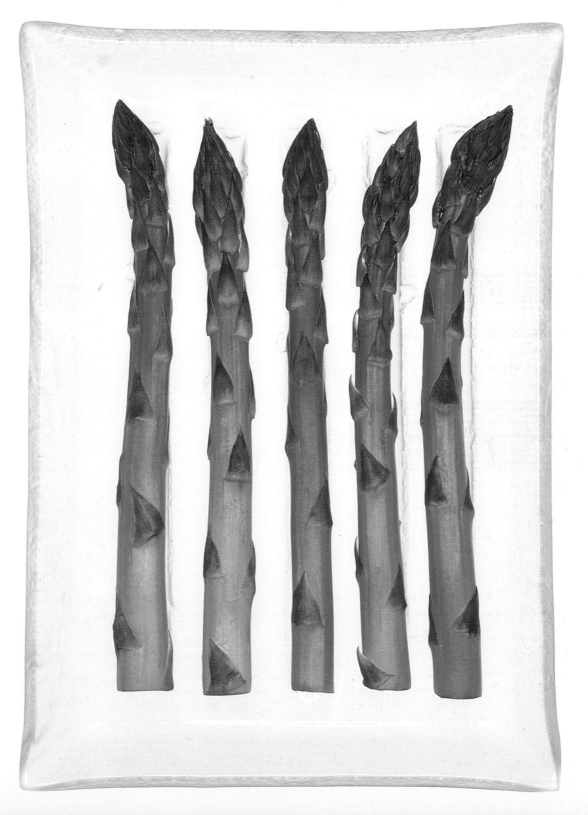

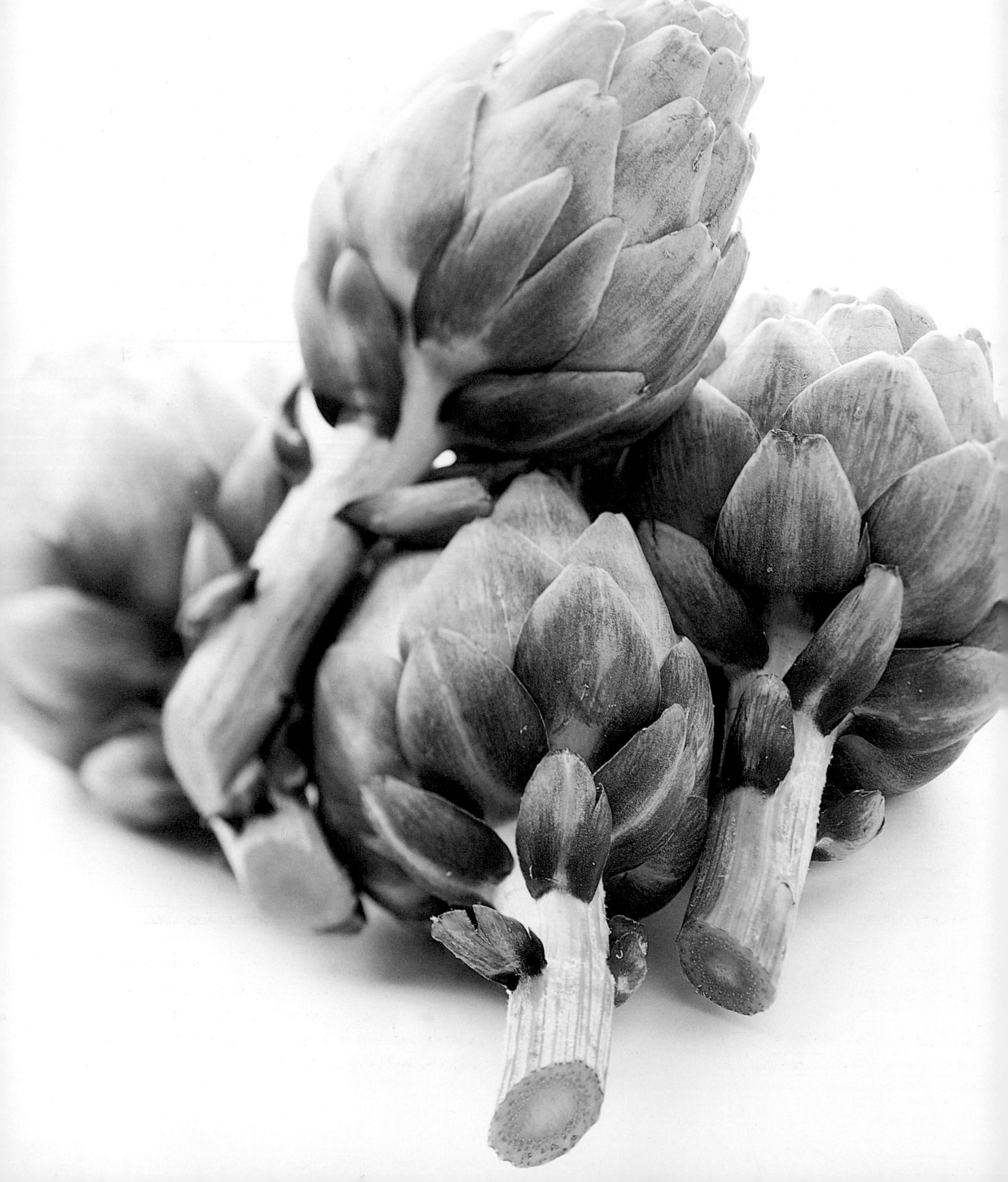

GOURMET VEGETABLES

ASPARAGUS

★ VITAMINS A, B, C, FOLIC ACID, K, COPPER, FLUORIDE, IRON, MANGANESE, POTASSIUM, ASPARAGINE

● BLOOD AND CIRCULATION Arteriosclerosis, high blood pressure, hyperlipidemia.

● DIGESTIVE SYSTEM Constipation.

Asparagus is diuretic, low in calories, and, owing to its high fiber content, good for intestinal health. It inhibits bacterial activity in the intestines, promotes lactation, and has anti-cancer properties. Asparagine is an active ingredient in asparagus that has an irritant effect—for this reason, asparagus should be avoided by people suffering from ailments that involve inflammation, such as gout, rheumatism, and cystitis. Asparagus may be grated and eaten raw in salads, although it is more commonly boiled or steamed until tender.
RECIPES warm asparagus salad (page 101), asparagus syrup (page 133).

ARTICHOKE

★ VITAMINS A, B, C, K, IRON, MANGANESE, PHOSPHORUS, CYNARIN

Artichoke contains substances that are proven to be beneficial to the kidneys (by promoting diuresis) and to the liver (by promoting detoxification). Artichoke improves the secretion of bile and emulsification and is therefore good for fat digestion. It also helps to lower levels of blood cholesterol. Some types of young artichokes can be eaten raw in salad; other varieties should be steamed or boiled (the cooking water contains most of the bitter active ingredient and should be drunk for maximum benefit). An infusion made with artichoke leaves is good for liver and kidney problems. Artichoke buds are detoxifying and can help to alleviate rheumatism, gout, and water retention. Nursing mothers should avoid artichoke—it makes breast milk taste bitter and slows down the production of milk.
RECIPES Roman-style artichoke (page 103), artichoke-leaf wine (page 130), artichoke-leaf tincture (page 132).

JERUSALEM ARTICHOKE

★ VITAMINS B, C, TRACE ELEMENTS, INULIN

● DIGESTIVE SYSTEM Constipation, gastritis.

Jerusalem artichoke is a nutritious vegetable often overlooked in cooking—it is recommended for people with diabetes. To retain its nutritional value, grate the Jerusalem artichoke in salads, steam, or boil lightly; keep the cooking water for use in soups.

AVOCADO

★ VITAMINS B, C, E, FOLIC ACID, K, ESSENTIAL FATTY ACIDS

Avocado, a fruit that is widely used as a vegetable, inhibits certain types of bacteria in the intestine, and helps to regulate cholesterol (studies suggest that it may lower blood cholesterol levels). Mashed avocado flesh can be applied to the skin as a treatment for aging or dryness, or made into a beauty mask by combining with egg white, egg yolk, or honey.
RECIPES avocado dressing (page 97), avocado tartar (page 103).

FENNEL

★ VITAMINS A, B, C, MANGANESE, PHOSPHORUS, POTASSIUM, SULFUR, ESSENTIAL OILS

● DIGESTIVE SYSTEM Abdominal cramp and colic, nausea.

● NERVOUS SYSTEM, MIND, AND EMOTIONS Headache.

● WOMEN'S HEALTH Menstrual cramp.

Fennel stimulates appetite, facilitates digestion, and promotes the secretion of bile. It is best eaten raw in salads (it goes very well with radicchio) but is also excellent cooked. If fennel is eaten in combination with legumes, it facilitates their digestion and prevents the formation of digestive gases. An infusion of fennel seeds has the same medicinal effects as eating the bulb. Fennel can be eaten by breast-feeding mothers to stimulate the baby's appetite and to prevent colic and digestive problems.
RECIPES fennel and radicchio salad (page 99), fennel with wine (page 112), fennel infusion (page 125), corn-hair and fennel-seed decoction (page 127), fennel-seed decoction (page 128).

SEAWEED

★ VITAMIN C, CALCIUM, IODINE, IRON, MAGNESIUM, PHOSPHORUS, POTASSIUM, SODIUM

● BLOOD AND CIRCULATION Atherosclerosis, high blood pressure.

Seaweed has bactericidal and anti-cancer properties, it boosts the immune system, heals ulcers, reduces levels of cholesterol in the blood, lowers blood pressure, thins the blood, and helps to prevent stroke and other cardiovascular diseases.

SALSIFY

★ FOLIC ACID, POTASSIUM, INULIN

● BONES AND JOINTS Arthritis (rheumatoid), gout.

● DIGESTIVE SYSTEM Diabetes.

● SKIN, HAIR, AND NAILS Eczema.

Salsify belongs to the daisy family and has a long root similar to that of a parsnip. Salsify is often overlooked in cooking. It has detoxifying properties and is good for liver and kidney function. When peeling salsify, plunge it in cold water with the juice of half a lemon (or 2 tablespoons of vinegar) to prevent it turning black. The juice is a natural remedy for verrucas—apply it directly to the skin.
RECIPES *salsify (page 112).*

PUMPKIN (SEE ALSO PAGES 22-3)

★ VITAMINS A, C, POTASSIUM, ANTIOXIDANTS, CAROTENE

● DIGESTIVE SYSTEM Diabetes, dysentery, dyspepsia.

● KIDNEYS AND BLADDER Cystitis.

● NERVOUS SYSTEM, MIND, AND EMOTIONS Insomnia.

Pumpkins are low in calories, high in water, calming, and cooling. The juice is a good laxative, and the flesh can be applied to the skin to calm inflammation, burns, and abscesses. Pumpkin seeds, peeled and cooked in water or milk, can ease insomnia and cystitis. The roasted seeds are a good source of essential fatty acids, magnesium, phosphorus, zinc, and potassium.
RECIPES *baked pumpkin strudel (page 109), pumpkin in syrup (page 114).*

EGGPLANT

★ VITAMINS B, C, COPPER, MAGNESIUM, MANGANESE, PHOSPHORUS, POTASSIUM, BIOFLAVONOIDS

● DIGESTIVE SYSTEM Constipation.

Eggplant is a low-calorie vegetable that is widely used in Mediterranean, Indian, and Asian cuisine. It has laxative properties, it calms the mind, and gently stimulates liver and pancreas function. The unripe eggplant is slightly toxic. Eggplant should always be cooked before eating—sprinkling salt on slices of eggplant 1 hour before cooking can reduce the water content and the amount of fat that is absorbed during cooking. Eggplant leaves are cooling and anti-inflammatory: They can be applied to burns, abscesses, and eczema.
RECIPES *bell pepper and eggplant salad (page 97), smoked salmon with eggplant sauce (page 105).*

MUSHROOM

★ VITAMIN B, COPPER, IODINE, MANGANESE, POTASSIUM, SELENIUM, ZINC, PROTEIN

Mushrooms have stimulant properties and can help to strengthen immunity. They are a vegetarian source of protein. Edible mushrooms harvested from the wild should be cooked thoroughly before eating (do not add them raw to salads as some are toxic).
RECIPES *buckwheat crêpes with field mushrooms (page 106).*

LEGUMES

BEAN (RED KIDNEY, NAVY, SMALL NAVY, BORLOTTI)

★ VITAMINS B, K, FOLIC ACID, CALCIUM, IRON, MAGNESIUM, PHOSPHORUS, POTASSIUM, CARBOHYDRATE, FIBER, PROTEIN

● DIGESTIVE SYSTEM Diabetes.

Beans are good for people with diabetes or weak liver function, but should be eaten in moderation by gout and rheumatism sufferers. Germinated beans are particularly tasty and nutritious. Beans are easier to digest if they are cooked and eaten with aromatic herbs such as garlic, thyme, and bay leaves. Red kidney beans contain a substance that can upset the stomach—soaking and boiling them vigorously for 15 minutes renders this substance harmless.
RECIPES *mediterranean bean salad (page 98), spicy spinach, prunes, and peas (page 109), beans with carrots and onions (page 112).*

FAVA BEAN

★ VITAMINS C, K, FOLIC ACID, CALCIUM, IRON, MAGNESIUM, PHOSPHORUS, POTASSIUM, CARBOHYDRATE, PROTEIN

● DIGESTIVE SYSTEM Diarrhea, dysentery.

Fava beans are good for the kidneys and bladder. An infusion of fava bean flowers (steep a handful of flowers in ⅔ cup of boiling water for 10 minutes) eases pain from kidney stones and sciatica.
RECIPES *fava bean soup (page 94).*

LENTIL

★ VITAMIN B, FOLIC ACID, CALCIUM, IRON, POTASSIUM, PROTEIN, CARBOHYDRATE

● BLOOD AND CIRCULATION Atherosclerosis, high blood pressure.

● DIGESTIVE SYSTEM Diabetes, constipation.

Lentils regulate colon function. They are recommended for pregnant women and people on a cholesterol-lowering diet. Lentils

and other legumes may help to inhibit cancerous growth.
RECIPES lentil soup (page 97), lamb with spinach and lentils (page 107).

PEA

★ VITAMINS A, B, C, K, FOLIC ACID, IRON, MAGNESIUM, PHOSPHORUS, ZINC, CARBOHYDRATE, FIBER, PROTEIN

Peas are an energy-providing food that has tonic properties and helps to regulate bowel function.
RECIPES peas with bacon pieces (page 112).

GARBANZO BEAN

★ VITAMIN B, FOLIC ACID, CALCIUM, COPPER, IRON, MAGNESIUM, MANGANESE, PHOSPHORUS, POTASSIUM, SELENIUM, SILICA, ZINC, CARBOHYDRATE, PROTEIN

Garbanzos are a staple food in many Mediterranean and North African countries. They are nutritious, easy to digest, and have antiseptic and diuretic properties. They are good for inflammation of the urinary tract and for poor digestion.
RECIPES garbanzo bean broth (page 94).

SOY

★ VITAMINS B, FOLIC ACID, CALCIUM, IRON, MAGNESIUM, POTASSIUM, SELENIUM, ZINC, CARBOHYDRATE, FIBER, LECITHIN, PROTEIN

Soy is a staple food in the East. Most non-organic soy is genetically modified. Soy bean sprouts are anti-inflammatory, can reduce stomach acidity, and relieve rheumatism.

CEREALS

BUCKWHEAT

★ VITAMIN B, IRON, MAGNESIUM, SELENIUM, ZINC, CARBOHYDRATE, PROTEIN, RUTIN

Buckwheat contains rutin—a substance that protects the heart—and is free of gluten, a protein that is insoluble in water and can be difficult to eliminate. It is a useful alternative to wheat for people who suffer from celiac disease or are gluten-intolerant. Buckwheat flour can be used instead of wheat

flour during illnesses characterized by mucus production (gluten has a glue-like quality and acts in a similar way to mucus).
RECIPES buckwheat with leek sauce (page 105), buckwheat crêpes with field mushrooms (page 106).

CORN

★ VITAMINS B, C, FOLIC ACID, MAGNESIUM, MANGANESE, PHOSPHORUS, POTASSIUM, CARBOHYDRATE, FIBER, FATTY ACIDS

Corn should be eaten from the cob or as coarse-ground polenta. Other forms of corn are depleted of nutrients by milling and processing. Corn is suitable for people with gluten intolerance. It is said to be a gentle moderator of the thyroid gland. Cold-pressed corn oil is rich in polyunsaturated fat (mostly oleic acid) and helps to reduce high cholesterol levels. It is good in salad dressings but is rapidly damaged by heat and loses its therapeutic value when used in cooking and frying. Organic corn oil is difficult to find.

RECIPES polenta with basil tomato sauce (page 107), corn-hair and fennel-seed decoction (page 127)

MILLET

★ VITAMIN B, FOLIC ACID, IRON, MAGNESIUM, PHOSPHORUS, SILICA, CARBOHYDRATE, FIBER, PROTEIN

Millet is a useful cereal for people who need to follow a gluten-free diet. It also eases fatigue, has a balancing effect upon the nervous system, and is recommended during pregnancy and recovery from illness. Millet increases in volume when cooked in water—because it is very filling, it is a useful part of a weight-reducing diet.
RECIPES chicken, millet, barley, and celery root pilaf (page 109).

BARLEY

★ VITAMINS B, E, CALCIUM, COPPER, IODINE, IRON, MAGNESIUM, POTASSIUM, CARBOHYDRATE, FIBER, L-TRYPTOPHAN

● DIGESTIVE SYSTEM Diarrhea, dyspepsia.

● NERVOUS SYSTEM, MIND, AND EMOTIONS Mild insomnia.

● WOMEN'S HEALTH Premenstrual syndrome.

Barley is good for the digestive and nervous systems, and contains L-tryptophan, an amino acid useful in the treatment of mild insomnia and premenstrual syndrome. It also lowers blood sugar and contains hordenine, a substance with cardiotonic and anti-diarrheic properties. A variety of enzymes that can relieve dyspepsia and hyperacidity can be found in germinated barley. However, because cooking destroys these enzymes, the best way to benefit from the medicinal properties of this cereal is to drink barley water made from germinated barley. The whole barley grain—germinated if possible—should be eaten for maximum nutritional and health benefits (the polished grain is of little therapeutic value).
RECIPES barley and fruit porridge (page 177), garbanzo bean broth (page 94), chicken, millet, barley, and celery root pilaf (page 109), barley infusion (page 126), barley water (page 129).

OAT

★ VITAMIN B, FOLIC ACID, CALCIUM, IRON, MAGNESIUM, PHOSPHORUS, POTASSIUM, ZINC, CARBOHYDRATE, FATTY ACIDS, FIBER, PROTEIN

● DIGESTIVE SYSTEM Diabetes.

● NERVOUS SYSTEM, MIND, AND EMOTIONS Depression, insomnia, mental fatigue.

Oats are nutritious and help to lower levels of cholesterol in the body. They have diuretic properties, stimulate thyroid function, and are good for diabetes. A tincture of oats (*Avena sativa*) is often prescribed by herbalists and homeopaths for insomnia, mild depression, and mental fatigue.
RECIPES barley and fruit porridge (page 77).

RICE

★ VITAMINS B, E, IRON, MAGNESIUM, SELENIUM, ZINC, CARBOHYDRATE, FIBER, PROTEIN

● DIGESTIVE SYSTEM Diarrhea, diabetes, diverticulitis.

Rice is an energy-providing food that helps lower blood pressure and has astringent properties. The water in which rice is cooked (rice water) is a remedy for mild diarrhea: In Vietnam, a cup of rice is soaked in a mixture of water and honey, strained and stir-fried in a wok without oil; then, when the rice has colored, 8¾ cups of water are added and the rice is simmered until overcooked. The resulting water is drunk as a diarrhea remedy. The same recipe can be used as an energy-providing drink for convalescents. Rice is suitable for people on a gluten-free diet. Because polished white rice has lost most of its important ingredients, it is preferable to eat organically-produced brown rice.
RECIPES nettle risotto (page 105), stuffed bell peppers (page 106), rice with cucumber balls (page 111).

WHEAT

★ VITAMINS B, E, FOLIC ACID, COPPER, IRON, MAGNESIUM, POTASSIUM, ZINC, CARBOHYDRATE, FIBER, PROTEIN

Wheat is the staple food of the West. Unfortunately, extensive processing and genetic modification have meant that wheat is largely stripped of its healing potential. Wheat that is allowed to germinate has increased vitamin and protein content. Wheat bran contains enzymes that ease digestion, dyspepsia and hyperacidity.
RECIPES tabouleh (page 102).

RYE

★ VITAMINS B, E, K, FOLIC ACID, COPPER, IRON, MAGNESIUM, POTASSIUM, SELENIUM, SULFUR, CARBOHYDRATE, FIBER

● BLOOD AND CIRCULATION Arteriosclerosis, high blood pressure.

Rye contains a substance that reduces blood viscosity and helps to maintain the healthy functioning of the heart. The rate of cardiovascular problems is low in populations where rye is eaten as a staple food.

olive

OLIVES FORM A MAJOR PART OF THE MEDITERRANEAN DIET AND, IN
CONJUNCTION WITH A LOW INTAKE OF ANIMAL FAT, ARE THOUGHT TO
BE IMPORTANT IN REGULATING BLOOD CHOLESTEROL LEVELS AND
REDUCING THE RISK OF CARDIOVASCULAR DISEASE.

The properties of olives

There are numerous references to olive trees in the Bible and
it is thought that olives were cultivated in Syria around 6000
years ago. Today, major olive producers include Italy, Greece,
France, Spain, Portugal, Turkey, Israel, Australia, Africa, and
many Middle Eastern countries.

Olives contain vitamins A and E, phosphorus, potassium,
magnesium, manganese, antioxidants, oleic and linoleic acid.
Black olives are easier to digest and have a higher vitamin and
antioxidant content than green olives. Only the black olive is
edible in its natural state; green olives are washed repeatedly
in brine to remove their bitter taste.

Research has demonstrated that people who follow a
Mediterranean diet—which is rich in olives and olive oil, and low
in animal fat—have a low incidence of cardiovascular disease
compared to people who eat a high proportion of animal fat.
Studies show that the high oleic acid content in olive oil helps
to regulate the balance between high-density lipoprotein (the
"good" type of cholesterol) and low-density lipoprotein (the
"bad" type of cholesterol) in the blood. This prevents fatty
deposits being laid down in the arteries and reduces the risk
of atherosclerosis and other types of cardiovascular disease.

Olives are also good for diabetes, constipation, and
gallstones. A remedy for constipation and gallstones is 2
tablespoons of cold-pressed olive oil taken every morning on
an empty stomach (an equal amount of lemon juice can be
added). The leaves of the olive tree can be used as a remedy
for high blood pressure, atherosclerosis, bladder stones,
diabetes, and angina: Bring 2 cups dried leaves (or 1⅔ cups
fresh leaves) and 4 cups of water to a boil. Cover and infuse
for 10 minutes, and then strain. Drink ⅔ cups of this decoction
three or four times a day. Olive oil has been used as a skin
treatment for centuries; it is thought to be invaluable in relieving
psoriasis, dry skin, and eczema.

Choosing olive oil

Olive oil is traditionally obtained by crushing olives in a stone
mill. However, modern extraction techniques have superseded
traditional ones and centrifugal or chemical methods are now
the most widely used.

The best olive oil to buy is first cold-pressed extra virgin oil.
Although the taste and colour may vary from one country to
another, or from year to year, this oil is the most nutritious. Try
to avoid buying semi-fine or refined olive oil. Check that olive
oil falls into one of the following categories:

● Extra virgin olive oil: This is obtained from
the first cold pressing of the olives; it is
low in acidity (below 1 per cent) and is
perfect for medicinal purposes and
use in salads.

● Fine virgin olive oil:
This is obtained from the
second pressing of the
olives. Although it has a
higher acidity, the taste and
medicinal qualities are good.

STAR FOOD PROFILE

- **BLOOD AND CIRCULATION** Angina, atherosclerosis, high blood pressure.
- **DIGESTIVE SYSTEM** Constipation, diabetes, gallstones.
- **KIDNEYS AND BLADDER** Bladder stones.
- **SKIN, HAIR, AND NAILS** Dermatitis and eczema.

black olive tapenade

1¾ cups pitted black olives
2–3 cloves of garlic, peeled
1 cup capers
3¾ ounces anchovy fillet, soaked in milk for 10 minutes
1 teaspoon Dijon mustard
2 tablespoons olive oil

Blend the ingredients to a thick paste. Serve on toast, or with salads, or pasta.

aromatic olive oil

Use in vinaigrette and marinades or to brush food prior to cooking.

6 sprigs thyme
1–2 sprigs rosemary
1 sprig sweet marjoram
1 teaspoon black peppercorns
3 cloves of garlic, peeled and left whole
2 shallots, left whole
6 bay leaves
4 cups olive oil

Seal all ingredients in a pickling jar. Leave for 1 month (page 122).

green olives and lemon

3½ cups green olives in brine
Lemons preserved in salt (page 45)
Several small thyme sprigs
Cold-pressed olive oil (see method for amount)
¼ cup dry white wine

Drain the olives, setting aside half the brine. In a pickling jar, arrange the olives and lemons in alternate layers. Add the thyme sprigs. Mix the brine with an equal amount of olive oil and the wine. Pour this over the olives and lemons so that they are covered. Tightly seal the jar and leave for 2 or 3 weeks before using as a starter or with salad.

fruits and nuts

EXOTIC FRUIT

COCONUT

★ NATURAL SUGAR, PALMITIC AND OLEIC ACIDS

Coconut is an excellent between-meal snack. It has slight diuretic and laxative properties. The milk can be used to treat stomach ulcers and gastritis.

DATE

★ VITAMINS A, B, CALCIUM, MAGNESIUM, POTASSIUM, NATURAL SUGAR

● BLOOD AND CIRCULATION Anemia.

● RESPIRATORY SYSTEM Bronchitis.

● NERVOUS SYSTEM, MIND, AND EMOTIONS Mental fatigue.

Dates may help to prevent cancer. They are a traditional remedy for tuberculosis. In North Africa, respiratory problems are treated with powdered or boiled date stones.

RECIPE banana and date salad (page 114).

FIG

★ VITAMINS A, B, C, FOLIC ACID, CALCIUM, COPPER, IRON, MANGANESE, POTASSIUM, ZINC, NATURAL SUGAR

● DIGESTIVE SYSTEM Constipation, dyspepsia, gastritis, gingivitis.

● RESPIRATORY SYSTEM Bronchitis.

● IMMUNE SYSTEM Sore throat.'

Figs are laxative and slightly diuretic. For constipation, cook 4 or 5 fresh figs in milk with 2 dates and a few raisins—eat for breakfast. For respiratory problems, boil 4 ounces fresh figs in 4 cups water for 15 minutes, strain, and drink. This mixture can also be used as a gargle for sore throats or gingivitis. Figs are good for pregnant women, people recovering from illness, and elderly people.

RECIPES fresh figs with raspberry cheese (page 117)

BANANA

★ VITAMINS B, C, FOLIC ACID, IODINE, IRON, MAGNESIUM, POTASSIUM, CARBOHYDRATE, TRYPTOPHAN

Bananas have antacid and mild antibacterial properties. Consult your doctor about eating bananas if you suffer from diabetes.

RECIPE banana and date salad (page 114).

GUAVA

★ VITAMINS A, C, POTASSIUM, SULFUR, CAROTENE, NATURAL SUGAR

● DIGESTIVE SYSTEM Dyspepsia.

Guava has astringent properties and is good for digestion. However, the unripe fruit is difficult to digest and the seeds should not be eaten by people with intestinal problems.

KUMQUAT

★ VITAMIN C, CITRUS FLAVONOIDS, NATURAL SUGAR

Kumquats have the same properties as oranges (page 41).

RECIPES radish and kumquat salad (page 98).

LYCHEE

★ VITAMIN C, MAGNESIUM, PHOSPHORUS, POTASSIUM, BIOFLAVONOIDS, NATURAL SUGAR

Lychees stimulate digestion and are slightly astringent. For abdominal pain, drink a decoction of lychee seeds.

RECIPES lychee fruit salad (page 114), lychee-seed decoction (page 128).

MANGO

★ VITAMINS A, B, C, E, SULFUR, CAROTENES, NATURAL SUGAR

● DIGESTIVE SYSTEM Colitis, diarrhea, ulcerative colitis.

Mango has an astringent effect on the gut, which means that it promotes contractions and enhances digestive processes.

PINEAPPLE

★ VITAMINS B, C, CITRIC, FOLIC AND MALIC ACIDS, MAGNESIUM, POTASSIUM, BROMELAIN, NATURAL SUGAR

● BONES AND JOINTS Arthritis (rheumatism), gout.

● BLOOD AND CIRCULATION Arteriosclerosis.

● DIGESTIVE SYSTEM Dyspepsia.

Pineapple contains bromelain enzymes which reduce inflammation, aid digestion, and help to break down proteins. Bromelain is used

to make various medicines, including anti-inflammatory drugs; it is most concentrated in the core of the pineapple.

RECIPES pineapple and cucumber salad (page 101).

PAPAYA

★ VITAMINS A, B, C, FOLIC ACID, POTASSIUM, NATURAL SUGAR, PAPAIN

Papaya contains papain, an enzyme that aids the digestive process by facilitating the breakdown of protein. Papaya is useful for reducing fever.

RECIPES baked papaya with ginger (page 117).

SOFT FRUIT AND BERRIES

APRICOT

★ VITAMINS A, B, C, IRON, MAGNESIUM, MANGANESE, PHOSPHORUS, POTASSIUM, NATURAL SUGAR

● BLOOD AND CIRCULATION Anemia.

● NERVOUS SYSTEM, MIND, AND EMOTIONS Mental fatigue, mild anxiety, insomnia.

Apricots have a balancing effect on the nervous system. Both fresh and dried apricots are beneficial for pregnant women, people recovering from illness, and elderly people.

RECIPES poached apricots with cardamom (page 117), apricot, lime, and mint juice (page 119).

GRAPE AND RAISIN

★ VITAMINS B, C, K, CALCIUM, IODINE, MANGANESE, POTASSIUM, SODIUM, BIOFLAVONOIDS, NATURAL SUGAR

● BONES AND JOINTS Arthritis (rheumatoid), gout.

● SKIN, HAIR, AND NAILS Dermatitis and eczema.

Grapes are diuretic, detoxifying, and laxative. They promote the elimination of uric acid and enhance liver function and bile flow. Black grapes are rich in bioflavonoids, particularly quercetin, which is good for the heart and circulation. Raisins are recommended as a snack for children, pregnant women, convalescents, and elderly people. A cold-pressing of grape pips (grape seed oil) is rich in polyunsaturated fatty acids and good for cardiovascular health.

RECIPES autumn fruit compote (page 116).

GOOSEBERRY

★ VITAMINS A, B, C, IRON, PHOSPHORUS, POTASSIUM, MALIC AND CITRIC ACIDS, NATURAL SUGAR

● BONES AND JOINTS Arthritis (rheumatoid), gout.

Gooseberries are laxative and diuretic. They stimulate liver function and ease inflammation of the digestive and urinary tracts.

PEACH

★ VITAMINS A, B, C, COPPER, MAGNESIUM, PHOSPHORUS, POTASSIUM, ZINC, NATURAL SUGAR

● DIGESTIVE SYSTEM Dyspepsia.

● KIDNEYS AND BLADDER Bladder stones.

Peaches are diuretic and laxative. Peach blossom is traditionally used to make an infusion or syrup that has calming and laxative properties (suitable for children). An infusion of peach leaves has an even stronger purgative effect. Fresh peach juice may be applied to the skin as a beauty treatment.

RECIPES peach syrup (page 132).

PLUM AND PRUNE

★ CALCIUM, IRON, MAGNESIUM, PHOSPHORUS, POTASSIUM, FIBER, NATURAL SUGAR

● BONES AND JOINTS Gout, rheumatism.

● BLOOD AND CIRCULATION Atherosclerosis.

● DIGESTIVE SYSTEM Constipation.

Both plums and prunes are a good source of fiber—prunes are well known for their laxative effects. Prunes also aid liver function, help to lower levels of cholesterol in the blood, and have anti-cancer properties.

RECIPES spicy spinach, prunes, and peas (page 109).

MELON (ALL TYPES)

★ VITAMINS A, B, C, NATURAL SUGAR

● BONES AND JOINTS Gout, rheumatism.

● DIGESTIVE SYSTEM Constipation, dyspepsia, irritable bowel syndrome.

Melon is cooling, laxative, and diuretic. Applied topically, crushed melon flesh eases the pain of mild burns, including sunburn. A beauty lotion for dry skin can be made with equal amounts of distilled water, milk, and melon juice.

RECIPES minted melon (page 114), watermelon and summer fruits (page 114).

BLACK CURRANT

★ VITAMIN C, CALCIUM, MAGNESIUM, PHOSPHORUS, POTASSIUM, NATURAL SUGAR

● BONES AND JOINTS Gout, rheumatism.

● IMMUNE SYSTEM Sore throat.

Black currants promote vitality and speed recovery after illness. They may aid bone remineralization after fractures. The leaves have the same properties as the berries and are also diuretic.

RECIPES black currant wine (page 129).

RED CURRANT

★ VITAMINS C, K, CALCIUM, IRON, PHOSPHORUS, POTASSIUM, CITRIC ACID, PECTIN, NATURAL SUGAR

● BONES AND JOINTS Arthritis (rheumatoid), gout.

● DIGESTIVE SYSTEM Constipation.

● KIDNEYS AND BLADDER Cystitis.

Red currants are laxative, diuretic, and depurative. They ease inflammation of the digestive tract, mild fever, and liver problems. Red currants are very acidic and should not be eaten in excess.

RECIPES red and white currants with raspberry coulis (page 115), red currant, blackberry, and blueberry juice (page 120).

BLACKBERRY

★ VITAMINS B, C, E, K, COPPER, MANGANESE, POTASSIUM, NATURAL SUGAR, PECTIN, TANNIN, ESSENTIAL OIL

● DIGESTIVE SYSTEM Diarrhea.

● IMMUNE SYSTEM Sore throat.

Blackberries are astringent, laxative, tonic, and depurative. The syrup is a good remedy for diarrhea in babies, respiratory infections, and sore throats. An infusion of the leaves is a traditional gargle for acute sore throat.

RECIPES watermelon and summer fruits (page 114), fruit salad with lemon balm (page 115), red currant, blackberry, and blueberry juice (page 120), blackberry syrup (page 134).

CHERRY

★ VITAMINS C, MAGNESIUM, POTASSIUM, ELLAGIC ACID, NATURAL SUGAR

● BONES AND JOINTS Arthritis (rheumatoid), gout, rheumatism.

● BLOOD AND CIRCULATION Atherosclerosis, arteriosclerosis.

● KIDNEYS AND BLADDER Bladder stones, cystitis.

Cherries are diuretic, laxative, depurative; they stimulate the immune system and help to prevent infection. Cherry-stem decoction can be used to treat cystitis, rheumatism, and edema.

RECIPES cherry-stem decoction (page 127), cherry-stem and apple decoction (page 128), cherry-leaf wine (page 130).

STRAWBERRY

★ VITAMINS B, C, IRON, MAGNESIUM, PHOSPHORUS, SILICA, SULFUR, NATURAL SUGAR, SALICYLIC ACID

● BONES AND JOINTS Gout.

● BLOOD AND CIRCULATION High blood pressure.

● DIGESTIVE SYSTEM Colitis, constipation, diarrhea.

● KIDNEYS AND BLADDER Cystitis.

Strawberries are tonic, laxative, and antibacterial. They enhance liver and gallbladder function. Strawberries may cause an allergic response (in the form of a rash) or exacerbate allergic dermatitis. The leaves and roots can be made into a medicinal decoction.

RECIPES carrot and strawberry salad (page 97), fruit salad with lemon balm (page 115), strawberry and raspberry juice (page 120), strawberry-leaf decoction (page 128).

RASPBERRY

★ VITAMINS B, C, K, IRON, MAGNESIUM, POTASSIUM, CITRIC, MALIC AND SALICYLIC ACIDS, NATURAL SUGAR

● BONES AND JOINTS Gout.

● DIGESTIVE SYSTEM Indigestion, vomiting.

● SKIN, HAIR, AND NAILS Eczema.

Raspberries are slightly diuretic and laxative. They are good for frequent urination. Raspberry-leaf infusion can facilitate labor.

RECIPES red and white currants with raspberry coulis (page 115), apple and raspberry juice (page 119), cherry and raspberry juice (page 120), strawberry and raspberry juice (page 120), raspberry vinegar (page 122).

CITRUS FRUIT

ORANGE

★ VITAMINS B, C, CALCIUM, COPPER, MANGANESE, PHOSPHORUS, POTASSIUM, ZINC, BIOFLAVONOIDS, NATURAL SUGAR, PECTIN

● DIGESTIVE SYSTEM Dyspepsia.

Oranges have tonic, diuretic, and laxative properties. They stimulate the immune system, liver function and appetite.

continues on page 45

blueberry

BLUEBERRIES HAVE ANTI-CANCER AND ANTIBACTERIAL PROPERTIES. THEY ARE GOOD FOR THE HEALTH OF THE EYES, INTESTINES, CIRCULATORY SYSTEM, AND URINARY TRACT.

The properties of blueberry

Blueberries are part of the *Vaccinium* species, which also includes cranberries and bilberries. They are small, purple berries that are commonly found in western and central Europe, and North America. Thought to have been used in European folk medicine since the 16th century, blueberries have excellent antioxidant properties, which make them useful for preventing cancer and other degenerative diseases. In fact, when compared to other fruits, blueberries are among the top sources of antioxidants.

Blueberries have a powerful antibacterial action in the intestine—especially upon coli bacteria—they promote the healing of gastric ulcers, and the leaves of the blueberry plant contain tannin, which has strong antidiarrheal properties.

Blood circulation is enhanced by substances found in blueberries, such as vitamins A and C, bioflavonoids, anthocyanosides, glycosides, and delphininol. Blueberries may help to lower blood sugar, decrease the chances of blood clots forming, and enhance the health of blood capillaries.

Blueberries can improve eye health and sight. This is thought to be due to compounds in the berries that enhance the health of capillaries in the eye.

Cranberries (*Vaccinium oxycoccos*) are a close relative of blueberries and are native to North America. They are a well-known and popular treatment for urinary-tract infections, such as cystitis (an inflammation of the bladder resulting in frequent, urgent, and often painful urination). Drinking the fresh juice of either blueberries or cranberries can help to prevent urinary-tract infections.

Blueberries in the diet

Since blueberries are an excellent source of antioxidants, they are important in the diet to promote long-term health and to prevent age-related physical changes, and chronic diseases. In particular, people with cardiovascular problems, mild diabetes, eye problems, urinary-tract or intestinal infections should eat blueberries regularly. Blueberries make wonderful pies, syrups, and jelly and are much enjoyed by children. They can be made into liqueurs or preserves for adults, or the berries can be added to fruit salad, or simply eaten as a snack on their own.

Medicinal preparations

Blueberries and their leaves can be made into medicinal preparations. Blueberry decoction is useful for diarrhea, colitis, and poor night vision. It can be used as a mouthwash for sore throats and ulcers, and as a face wash for eczema. To make, boil ¾ cup blueberries in 4 cups of water until the volume of water has halved. Strain and use as appropriate.

Blueberry- and strawberry-leaf decoction is good for mild diabetes, intestinal problems, arteriosclerosis, rheumatism and arthritis, and it can be drunk throughout the day. Boil ¾ cup each of blueberry and strawberry leaves in 4 cups of water for 3 minutes. Then leave to infuse for 10 minutes, strain, and drink. To make a tincture of blueberries, add scant 1 cup fresh blueberries, a handful of blueberry leaves, and the zest of one lemon to generous 3 cups vodka. Leave in a cool, dark place for 3 weeks and then press and strain the mixture and store in a tightly sealed bottle. Take 20–30 drops of this tincture in a glass of water every day for diarrhea, intestinal problems, circulatory problems, and mild diabetes.

STAR FOOD PROFILE

- **BONES AND JOINTS** Arthritis (rheumatoid), rheumatism.

- **BLOOD AND CIRCULATION** Atherosclerosis, arteriosclerosis, Raynaud's disease.

- **DIGESTIVE SYSTEM** Abdominal cramp and colic, colitis, diarrhea, gastroenteritis, intestinal infections, ulcerative colitis.

- **KIDNEYS AND BLADDER** Cystitis and urethritis.

- **IMMUNE SYSTEM** Sore throat.

blueberry vinegar

Use in dressings or take a teaspoon, diluted in water, every morning.

2¾ cups blueberries
Generous 3 cups white wine vinegar or cider vinegar

Put the blueberries in a hermetically sealable pickling jar. Pour over the white-wine or cider vinegar and seal the jar tightly. Leave to macerate in a cool, dark place for 2 weeks. Strain and bottle the vinegar.

blueberries and cottage cheese

Scant 1 cup cottage cheese
3 tablespoons superfine sugar
3 tablespoons live yogurt
1¾ cups fresh blueberries
1 apple, peeled and grated
Lemon juice to taste
To garnish: a few raspberries

Beat the cottage cheese with the sugar and yogurt. Stir in the blueberries, apple, and lemon juice. Garnish with raspberries. Chill and serve.

blueberry syrup

This can be added to water for children or to white wine for adults.

9 cups blueberries
1¼ cups water
Sugar

In a stainless steel saucepan bring the blueberries and water to a boil. Strain them through cheesecloth. Allow the juice to ferment at room temperature for 24 hours. Weigh the juice and add an equal amount of sugar. Dissolve the sugar in the juice, bring to a boil, simmer for 1 minute, and allow to cool. Store the syrup in sterilized bottles in the refrigerator.

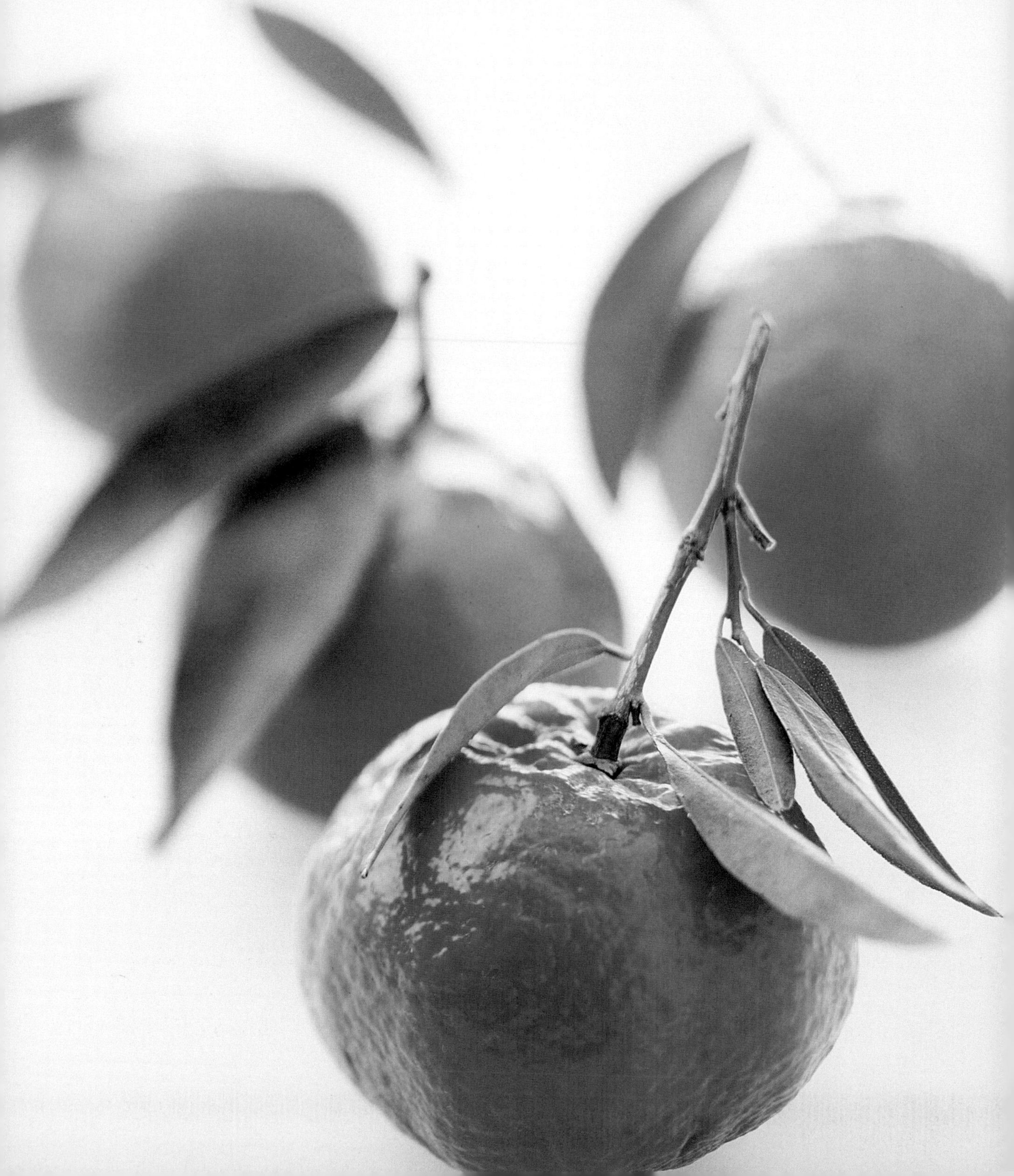

Oranges also help to lower levels of cholesterol in the blood and they are rich in antioxidants. Eating whole oranges is preferable to drinking concentrated juice.

RECIPES radish and kumquat salad (page 98), orange-zest infusion (page 125).

MANDARIN AND TANGERINE

★ VITAMINS B, C, CALCIUM, COPPER, MANGANESE, PHOSPHORUS, POTASSIUM, ZINC, BIOFLAVONOIDS, NATURAL SUGAR, PECTIN

Mandarin and tangerine have similar properties to orange. Mandarin rind contains an essential oil that acts as a sedative and, in Chinese medicine, an infusion of dried tangerine peel is used for poor digestion, abdominal distension, and irritability.

GRAPEFRUIT

★ VITAMINS B, C, COPPER, MAGNESIUM, POTASSIUM, ANTIOXIDANTS, BIOFLAVONOIDS, ESSENTIAL OIL, NATURAL SUGAR, PECTIN

● BONES AND JOINTS Arthritis (rheumatoid).

● DIGESTIVE SYSTEM Dyspepsia, obesity.

Grapefruit has strong antioxidant and cholesterol-lowering properties. It contains an astringent essential oil, stimulates appetite and liver function, aids detoxification, and is slightly diuretic. Grapefruit is recommended for circulatory problems and obesity. It may interact with a variety of prescribed drugs—consult your doctor if in doubt.

OTHER FRUIT

APPLE

★ VITAMINS B, IRON, MAGNESIUM, MANGANESE, POTASSIUM, SULFUR, NATURAL SUGAR, PECTIN, MALIC ACID

● BONES AND JOINTS Arthritis (rheumatoid), gout, rheumatism.

● DIGESTIVE SYSTEM Constipation, diarrhea, dyspepsia, peptic ulcers.

Apples are diuretic, they aid the elimination of uric acid, and lower cholesterol levels in the blood. Traditionally, raw apples are eaten to ease constipation and cooked apples are eaten as a remedy for diarrhea. Apple blossom infusion eases coughs and soothes sore throats.

RECIPES autumn fruit compote (page 116), apple and raspberry juice (page 119), cherry and apple juice (page 120), pear and apple infusion (page 126), cherry-stem and apple decoction (page 128).

PEAR

★ VITAMINS A, B, C, K, FOLIC ACID, COPPER, IODINE, MAGNESIUM, SULFUR, NATURAL SUGAR, PECTIN

● BONES AND JOINTS Arthritis (rheumatoid), gout, rheumatism.

● DIGESTIVE SYSTEM Diarrhea.

Pears are laxative, diuretic, astringent, and calming. They aid uric acid elimination and prevent bacteria proliferating in the intestines. They are good for pregnant women, the elderly and convalescents. An infusion of pear tree leaves can ease urinary problems.

RECIPES autumn fruit compote (page 116), pears with herbs (page 116), pear and apple infusion (page 126).

PHYSALIS (GROUND CHERRY)

★ VITAMIN C, PHYSALIN

● BONES AND JOINTS Arthritis (rheumatoid), gout.

● KIDNEYS AND BLADDER Bladder stones.

Physalis contains physalin, which is diuretic and facilitates the elimination of urea. The jelly helps kidney or bladder inflammation.

RECIPES physalis jelly (page 124), physalis-berry decoction (page 128).

PERSIMMON

★ VITAMINS A, B, C, COPPER, IODINE, IRON, MAGNESIUM, PHOSPHORUS, SULFUR, ZINC, NATURAL SUGAR, PECTIN

● DIGESTIVE SYSTEM Crohn's disease.

Persimmon is a nutritious fruit that prevents the proliferation of bacteria in the intestines. It has laxative and astringent properties.

POMEGRANATE

★ VITAMINS B, C, K, COPPER, MANGANESE, PHOSPHORUS, POTASSIUM, NATURAL SUGAR

● BLOOD AND CIRCULATION High blood pressure.

● DIGESTIVE SYSTEM Constipation.

Pomegranate is considered to be a tonic for the heart, kidneys, and bladder. The juice is recommended for people with bladder disorders and tapeworm.

QUINCE

★ VITAMINS C, COPPER, IRON, POTASSIUM, NATURAL SUGAR, PECTIN, TANNIN

● DIGESTIVE SYSTEM Diarrhea.

Quince is astringent and enhances digestion and liver function.

RECIPES quince liqueur (page 131).

continues on page 47

lemon

LEMON IS A NATURAL DISINFECTANT. IT IS RICH IN VITAMIN C AND CITRUS FLAVONOIDS THAT HAVE A POWERFUL ANTIOXIDANT FUNCTION. LEMON IS GOOD FOR STRENGTHENING THE IMMUNE SYSTEM AND PREVENTING INFECTION AND DISEASE.

The properties of lemon

The lemon tree (*Citrus limon*) is a small evergreen indigenous to the forests of northern India. It bears bright yellow segmented fruit that, together with lime, orange, and grapefruit, belong to the citrus family (page 41).

Although there is some doubt about their origin and distribution, it is thought that lemon trees were introduced to Europe by Arabs, probably around the 11th century. In the past, lemons were the mainstay of prevention and treatment for scurvy, a disease that results from a deficiency of vitamin C. Lemons were traditionally taken on long sea voyages and the juice given to sailors in order to prevent scurvy. Today, lemons are widely produced in the US, Spain, Portugal, Italy, and, to a lesser extent, southern France.

Lemons are rich in citrus flavonoids that, alongside vitamin C, have an important antioxidant function. Citrus flavonoids are phytochemicals (biologically active plant compounds) that can assist the healing of wounds, strengthen the walls of blood capillaries, and prevent diseases such as arteriosclerosis. Vitamin C also helps to fight infection, strengthen the immune system, make collagen (the main protein found in connective tissue), keep the skin and joints healthy, and prevent cancer. Other substances found in lemon are citric and malic acid, vitamin B, folic acid, glucose, fructose, potassium, and silica.

Pectin is another important component of lemon. It is concentrated in the skin around the segments and can help to lower levels of unhealthy cholesterol in the blood.

Lemon as a cure

Lemons can be used to treat a range of ailments. They are a natural booster of the immune system; they can help to reduce mild fever, lower blood pressure, reduce gastric acidity, promote liver function, and increase the fluidity of blood. They also have diuretic properties.

Specific illnesses that can be treated with lemon are rheumatism, arthritis, high blood cholesterol, dyspepsia, colds, and influenza. As well as using lemons in recipes, try to use the juice freely as a flavouring in cooking, as a dressing for salads and fish, and in cold drinks and teas.

Lemon juice is a natural disinfectant and antiseptic—prior to the development of modern antiseptics, it was used in hospitals for this purpose. The juice can be applied directly to the skin (it is an astringent and a bactericide) and is a useful ingredient in homemade beauty masks. Lemon juice can be used as a skin toner, an anti-aging treatment, and to reduce or eliminate freckles.

A fragrant essential oil is found in the outer skin of the lemon and this can be extracted under pressure. This essential oil has excellent antibacterial properties and is available from healthfood stores, aromatherapy suppliers, and some pharmacies. It can be used to treat colds, sore throats, gingivitis, or mouth ulcers. Take four drops in a teaspoon of honey for colds and sore throats. For gingivitis or mouth ulcers, use one drop of essential oil on a toothbrush with a small amount of toothpaste. This will disinfect the teeth and mouth. Lemon essential oil is also antiparasitic.

STAR FOOD PROFILE

- **BONES AND JOINTS** Arthritis (rheumatoid), rheumatism.
- **BLOOD AND CIRCULATION** Atherosclerosis, palpitations.
- **DIGESTIVE SYSTEM** Dyspepsia.
- **IMMUNE SYSTEM** Colds, influenza, sore throat.

lemonade

2 lemons, wiped and sliced
¼ cup brown sugar
4 cups water

Mix the lemons with the water and sugar. Macerate for 12 hours in the refrigerator, stirring intermittently to dissolve the sugar, and then drink cold.

lemon preserved in salt

Use in salads or stews. The lemon juice can also be used, sparingly, as a seasoning.

3 lemons, wiped and quartered
Salt

In a small, hermetically-sealable pickling jar, put a ½-inch-deep layer of salt. Place one layer of lemon quarters on top and cover with salt. Continue until the last layer of lemon is covered in salt and then tightly seal the jar and store in a cool, dark place for 1 month. After a month, wash the lemon quarters under cold, running water and use.

lemon in oil

Lemons will keep for months if they are covered in oil—use them in salads or with meat or fish dishes. The oil can be used in dressings.

6 lemons, wiped and sliced or quartered
3 tablespoons salt
Olive oil
1 bay leaf

Place the lemons in a bowl and sprinkle them with the salt. Toss and then refrigerate for 24 hours. Drain the juice from the lemons, then leave in a colander for 2 hours, or press the lemon gently to remove as much juice as possible. Wipe the salt off the lemons and place in a hermetically-sealable pickling jar. Cover the lemons with the olive oil—press them down to make sure they are covered—and add the bay leaf.

RHUBARB

★ **VITAMINS C, K, IRON, CALCIUM, MAGNESIUM, MANGANESE, POTASSIUM**

● **DIGESTIVE SYSTEM** Constipation.

Rhubarb has tonic, laxative, and antiparasitic properties. It facilitates bile flow and prevents the proliferation of bacteria in the gut. The root may be used in powder or tincture form as a laxative. Rhubarb should be avoided by people suffering from hyperacidity, gout, kidney stones, or gallstones. The leaves are poisonous.
RECIPES rhubarb and ginger tart (page 115).

NUTS

HAZELNUT

★ **VITAMINS B, E, K, FOLIC ACID, CALCIUM, COPPER, IRON, MAGNESIUM, MANGANESE, PHOSPHORUS, POTASSIUM, ZINC, SULFUR, FATTY ACIDS**

Hazelnuts are excellent energy-providing snacks that are also rich in fiber. They are recommended for people who are prone to kidney or gall bladder stones. They may also help get rid of intestinal worms—treatment consists of 1 tablespoon of cold-pressed hazelnut oil every morning on an empty stomach for 15 days. Cold-pressed hazelnut oil can also be used externally. It is particularly recommended for oily skin owing to its regulatory effect on sebum secretion. It can help treat acne, dermatitis, and seborrheic eczema. An infusion of hazelnut leaves makes an excellent astringent fluid that can be applied to the skin for the treatment of varicose veins. Cover 2 cups of dried leaves with 4 cups of boiling water and infuse for 12 hours—strain and use as a skin wash two or three times a day. A fluid extract from the leaves (available commercially) can be taken internally for the same condition.
RECIPES green beans with dijon mustard (page 113).

ALMOND

★ **VITAMINS B, E, FOLIC ACID, CALCIUM, COPPER, IRON, MAGNESIUM, MANGANESE, PHOSPHORUS, POTASSIUM, ZINC, OLEIC ACID, FATTY ACIDS**

● **DIGESTIVE SYSTEM** Irritable bowel syndrome.

Almonds provide energy. They balance the nervous system and are useful for digestive problems. Almond milk relieves intestinal spasm and inflammation in cases of irritable bowel syndrome; sweet almond oil is a mild laxative suitable for children. Externally, almond paste and oil can be used for eczema, rashes, and as an ingredient in beauty masks. Bitter almonds are toxic and should be avoided.
RECIPES almond milk (page 79)

CHESTNUT

★ **VITAMINS B, C, IRON, MAGNESIUM, POTASSIUM, ZINC**

● **BLOOD AND CIRCULATION** Anemia.

● **DIGESTIVE SYSTEM** Dyspepsia.

Chestnuts are good for convalescents, elderly people, and those prone to varicose veins and hemorrhoids. A handful of the leaves infused for 10 minutes in 4 cups of water is a good expectorant.
RECIPES Brussels sprouts with chestnuts (page 112).

PINE NUT

★ **VITAMINS B, E, FOLIC ACID, COPPER, IRON, MAGNESIUM, MANGANESE, PHOSPHORUS, POTASSIUM, ZINC, OLEIC ACID, FATTY ACIDS**

Pine nuts are energy-providing and nutritious; they have laxative properties and are good for digestive problems.

PEANUT

★ **VITAMINS B, E, FOLIC ACID, CALCIUM, IRON, MAGNESIUM, SELENIUM, ZINC, AMYLASE, FATTY ACIDS**

● **DIGESTIVE SYSTEM** Dyspepsia.

Peanuts contain amylase, an enzyme that eases dyspepsia and hyperacidity. Some people are allergic to peanuts: The symptoms include vomiting and diarrhea. In severe cases the allergy is fatal.

WALNUT

★ **VITAMINS B, E, K, FOLIC ACID, CALCIUM, COPPER, IRON, MAGNESIUM, POTASSIUM, SELENIUM, ZINC, LINOLEIC ACID, FATTY ACIDS**

● **DIGESTIVE SYSTEM** Diarrhea.

Walnuts have cholesterol-lowering properties and are good for intestinal parasites and heart and circulatory problems. Apply walnut oil to skin affected by dermatitis or eczema.
RECIPES garlic and walnut sauce (page 57).

herbs, spices, and condiments

HERBS

PARSLEY

★ VITAMINS A, B, C, K, FOLIC ACID, IRON, ZINC, ESSENTIAL OIL

● BLOOD AND CIRCULATION Anemia.

● DIGESTIVE SYSTEM Dyspepsia, flatulence.

Parsley has diuretic, depurative, tonic, and laxative properties. It stimulates appetite and liver function, regulates bile flow, and is a good antiseptic for the lungs. Parsley is best eaten raw in salads or chopped and sprinkled generously over casseroles, meat, fish, and other main-course dishes. It can also be used in broths or in raw juice cocktails. Freshly chopped parsley can be rubbed into the skin as an anti-aging treatment or as a remedy for insect bites and stings. An infusion of parsley seeds can be used to treat urine retention and digestive problems such as dyspepsia.

RECIPES parsley, onion, and lemon salad (page 101), tabouleh (page 102), potatoes with herb sauce (page 113).

MINT

★ ESSENTIAL OIL

● BLOOD AND CIRCULATION Palpitations.

● DIGESTIVE SYSTEM Colic, colitis, intestinal parasites, irritable bowel syndrome, nausea and vomiting (including morning sickness).

● RESPIRATORY SYSTEM Asthma, bronchitis.

● NERVOUS SYSTEM, MIND, AND EMOTIONS Mental fatigue, migraine, neuralgia.

Mint is a nervous-system stimulant (an infusion of mint taken in the evening may prevent sleep). Mint essential oil is a powerful antispasmodic, analgesic, anti-inflammatory, and antiseptic agent for the intestines; it may also help to expel intestinal worms.

RECIPES tabouleh (page 102), minted melon (page 114), fresh mint sorbet (page 115), mint syrup (page 133).

BASIL

★ ESSENTIAL OIL

● BONES AND JOINTS Gout.

● DIGESTIVE SYSTEM Abdominal cramp, colic, intestinal infections.

● NERVOUS SYSTEM, MIND, AND EMOTIONS Anxiety, insomnia, mental fatigue, migraine.

Basil is a popular herb in Mediterranean countries. It contains a powerful essential oil that has antispasmodic and antiseptic properties; it acts as a tonic for the nervous system and helps to ease digestive complaints, including intestinal infections. Basil can be used in soups, sauces, medicinal drinks, such as basil liqueur, and raw in salads. Fresh basil leaves can be preserved by freezing or storing in oil. To preserve basil in oil, choose leaves from the top part of the plant, rinse gently in cold water and allow to dry on paper towels. Sprinkle the leaves with salt, wait 30 minutes, gently wipe the salt off, place the leaves in a sterilized jar or bottle, and fill with cold-pressed olive oil. Keep the jar tightly closed and store in the refrigerator.

RECIPES polenta with basil tomato sauce (page 107), pasta twists with pesto (page 106), basil liqueur (page 131).

MARJORAM AND OREGANO

★ ESSENTIAL OIL

● DIGESTIVE SYSTEM Abdominal pain, distention, and gas.

● RESPIRATORY SYSTEM Bronchitis, colds, influenza.

Marjoram and oregano are two distinct plants, but for culinary and medicinal purposes they are interchangeable. Both are potent bactericides, expectorants, and digestive-system stimulants. They are good natural remedies for ear, nose, throat, and lung infections. The essential oils of these herbs can be applied to the skin as a treatment for rheumatism and skin infections. They should be diluted with a base oil, such as almond, before they are applied to the skin.

RECIPES marjoram infusion (page 125).

ROSEMARY

★ ESSENTIAL OIL

● BONES AND JOINTS Gout.

● DIGESTIVE SYSTEM Colitis, diarrhea, flatulence, intestinal infections, irritable bowel syndrome.

● RESPIRATORY SYSTEM Asthma.

● NERVOUS SYSTEM, MIND, AND EMOTIONS Headache, neuralgia.

● IMMUNE SYSTEM Colds, influenza.

Rosemary contains a potent essential oil that is diuretic, promotes perspiration, stimulates the production and flow of bile, improves digestion, and acts as an antiseptic for the lungs and the digestive system. It can be diluted with a base oil, such as almond, and massaged into the skin for muscular cramps and rheumatism.

RECIPES *carrots with rosemary (page 21).*

THYME

★ ESSENTIAL OIL

● BONES AND JOINTS Rheumatism.

● DIGESTIVE SYSTEM Intestinal infections and parasites.

● RESPIRATORY SYSTEM Bronchitis, cough.

● KIDNEYS AND BLADDER Cystitis.

● IMMUNE SYSTEM Colds, influenza.

Thyme has powerful antibacterial properties. It is a general stimulant and acts as an antiseptic for the throat, lungs, and digestive system. Thyme may improve poor circulation.

RECIPES *amazingly aromatic vinegar (page 124).*

TARRAGON

★ ESSENTIAL OIL

● DIGESTIVE SYSTEM Colic, intestinal parasites.

● WOMEN'S HEALTH Menstrual cramp.

Tarragon is a general stimulant, it is antispasmodic and improves digestive function. The infused oil can be applied to the skin to treat rheumatism, muscular spasms, and cramps. Fill a jar with tarragon leaves, cover with olive oil, and leave for two weeks.

RECIPES *tarragon vinegar (page 124), amazingly aromatic vinegar (page 124).*

SAGE

★ ESSENTIAL OIL

● WOMEN'S HEALTH Irregular or painful menstrual cycle, menopausal symptoms.

There are more than 200 species of sage but the species most commonly used in cooking is *Salvia officinalis*. Sage is a general stimulant and a digestive-system tonic. It is good for hypotension, excessive perspiration, and fatigue.

RECIPES *garlic and sage soup (page 57).*

BAY

★ ESSENTIAL OIL

● DIGESTIVE SYSTEM Dyspepsia, flatulence.

● WOMEN'S HEALTH Menstrual cramp.

Bay leaves have antiseptic, stimulant and antispasmodic properties. They can be used in casseroles and soups or made into an infusion for indigestion and bloated stomach, or as a gargle for mouth and throat infections (add 3–4 leaves to a cup of boiling water, cover, infuse for 10 minutes, and then strain).

RECIPES *orange-zest infusion (page 125).*

CHIVE AND SCALLION

★ VITAMINS A, B, C, CALCIUM, MAGNESIUM, PHOSPHORUS, POTASSIUM, SULFUR COMPOUNDS, BIOFLAVONOIDS, ESSENTIAL OIL

● BONES AND JOINTS Arthritis (rheumatoid), gout, rheumatism.

● BLOOD AND CIRCULATION Arteriosclerosis.

● DIGESTIVE SYSTEM Diabetes, diarrhea, intestinal infections and parasites.

● WOMEN'S HEALTH Menstrual cramp.

Chives and scallions are antibacterial, antiviral, antifungal, and diuretic; they prevent tumor and blood-clot formation and help to lower levels of cholesterol in the body. Chives and scallions also prevent water retention, promote the elimination of urea and the expectoration of mucus, and are good for the digestive system and the circulatory system. Both chives and scallions may be eaten raw, chopped and sprinkled over main courses and salads, or made into raw juice cocktails. A broth containing chives or scallions (especially combined with garlic, clove, and ginger) is good for colds and influenza as well as digestive problems, such as diarrhea. The fresh juice can be applied to insect stings, warts, and boils.

RECIPES *chive and ginger broth (page 96), leek and chive mimosa with polenta (page 107).*

CILANTRO (CORIANDER LEAVES)

★ VITAMIN B, FOLIC ACID, ESSENTIAL OIL

- **DIGESTIVE SYSTEM** Abdominal pain, dyspepsia, flatulence, indigestion, irritable bowel syndrome.

Cilantro is an aromatic herb that has antibiotic properties and helps to treat a range of digestive problems. It is widely used in Asian and North African cooking. The leaves can be chopped and sprinkled on salads, main dishes, and soups. The seeds contain a greater concentration of active ingredients than the leaves and can be made into medicinal drinks.

RECIPES cilantro dressing (page 97), coriander-seed infusion (page 127), coriander-seed tincture (page 132).

CHERVIL

- ★ **VITAMINS A, B, C, IRON, ESSENTIAL OIL**
- **BONES AND JOINTS** Gout.
- **BLOOD AND CIRCULATION** Anemia.
- **RESPIRATORY SYSTEM** Bronchitis.

Chervil has diuretic, tonic, and laxative properties. It stimulates appetite and liver function and regulates the flow of bile. It is also a good antiseptic for the lungs and helps to get rid of phlegm in the chest. Chervil can be eaten raw in salad or sprinkled generously over casseroles, fish, meat, and main course dishes. It can also be used in broths or raw juice cocktails. Freshly chopped chervil can also be rubbed on the skin to treat insect bites or stings.

RECIPES herbal broth (page 94), parsley, onion, and lemon salad (page 101), potatoes with herb sauce (page 113).

BORAGE

- ★ **GAMMA-LINOLEIC ACID (GLA)**
- **RESPIRATORY SYSTEM** Bronchitis.

Borage has depurative, diuretic, and laxative properties and promotes the elimination of toxins. Borage seeds contain gamma-linoleic acid (GLA), an essential fatty acid that helps the body to make prostaglandins. Prostaglandins are hormone-like substances that have numerous health benefits, such as keeping the blood thin, lowering blood pressure, maintaining water balance, and regulating blood sugar. Another good, but less abundant, source of GLA is evening primrose oil. Borage oil can be applied to the skin as a treatment for mature skin and for dry, scaly eczema. Young borage leaves are excellent raw in salads, especially with dandelion and watercress. They can also be added to soups or included in a variety of raw juice cocktails.

RECIPES borage leaves in vinegar (page 124).

SORREL

- ★ **VITAMIN C, IRON, CHLOROPHYLL, OXALATE**

Sorrel has laxative and depurative properties and is a traditional remedy for digestive and lung infections. It contains a substance known as oxalate that gives the herb its sour taste. In sufficient quantities oxalate is poisonous—for this reason sorrel should be eaten in moderation.

RECIPES herbal broth (page 94).

SAVORY

- ★ **ESSENTIAL OIL**
- **DIGESTIVE SYSTEM** Diarrhea, flatulence.
- **RESPIRATORY SYSTEM** Asthma, bronchitis.

Two species of savory are commonly used in cooking: summer savory (usually grown in the yard), and winter savory (usually found in the wild). Savory is a nervous-system stimulant and a tonic. It is particularly effective for poor digestion.

CAMOMILE

- ★ **COMPLEX CHEMICALS SUCH AS NOBILINE AND CHAMAZULENE, ESSENTIAL OIL**
- **DIGESTIVE SYSTEM** Diarrhea, indigestion, irritable bowel syndrome.
- **NERVOUS SYSTEM, MIND, AND EMOTIONS** Insomnia, migraine, neuralgia.
- **WOMEN'S HEALTH** Menstrual cramp.

Camomile contains nobiline, which is a bitter tonic, and chamazulene, which is a potent anti-inflammatory agent. An infusion of camomile is widely recommended for its calming properties and its ability to improve digestion and ease digestive problems. Camomile infusion stimulates liver function, regulates the flow of bile, and can be used externally as a douche for thrush, a wash for inflamed skin, mild burns, sunburn, dermatitis and eczema, and as an eyewash for conjunctivitis. Camomile flowers and white wine can be made into an excellent bitter aperitif.
RECIPES lemon-balm and camomile infusion (page 126), elder and camomile infusion (page 126), camomile and citrus wine (page 131), camomile aperitif (page 131).

ELDER

★ ESSENTIAL OIL

The flowers, berries, and bark of the elder tree can all be used medicinally. The flowers promote perspiration (useful for colds and influenza) and skin eruptions in chicken pox, German measles, and scarlet fever. They are also diuretic and promote detoxification and bile flow. The berries are good for constipation, headache, and mild neuralgia. The bark is diuretic, and is useful for rheumatism, arthritis, nephritis (inflammation of the kidneys), and bladder stones. All parts of the plant have anti-inflammatory properties.
RECIPES elder and camomile infusion (page 126), elderberry syrup (page 133).

LINDEN (LIME TREE)

★ ESSENTIAL OIL

Linden- or lime-tree blossom has antispasmodic, sedative, and slight hypnotic properties. It also induces sweating. Research suggests that lime flowers may reduce the viscosity and rate of coagulation of the blood. This may help to prevent cardiovascular problems. An infusion of lime blossom has a delicate fragrance and is a good remedy for insomnia in children as well as adults (steep a small handful of the blossom in 1¼ cups water for 5 minutes).
RECIPES pears with herbs (page 116).

LEMON BALM (MELISSA)

★ ESSENTIAL OIL

● DIGESTIVE SYSTEM Indigestion.

● NERVOUS SYSTEM, MIND, AND EMOTIONS Anxiety, insomnia, migraine, neuralgia.

Lemon balm contains a potent essential oil that has tonic and antispasmodic properties. Although rarely used in cooking, lemon balm is often included in herbal liqueurs such as Chartreuse, Benedictine and Eau de Melissa des Carmes. Lemon balm can help to relieve spasms (muscular, digestive, or asthmatic).
RECIPES lemon-balm and camomile infusion (page 126), sparkling lemon-balm infusion (page 127).

DILL WEED

★ ESSENTIAL OIL

● DIGESTIVE SYSTEM Abdominal cramp, colic.

● WOMEN'S HEALTH Irregular menstrual cycle or menstrual cramp.

Dill weed is a type of wild fennel that is often used in fish recipes or in pickling vinegar. Both the leaves and the seeds can be used. Dill weed is recommended for lactating mothers as its aromatic compounds pass into breast milk and enhance the flavor.
RECIPES lentil soup (page 97), dill-seed decoction (page 128), amazingly aromatic vinegar (page 124).

SPICES AND SEEDS

CHILI

★ VITAMINS A, B, C, K, TRACE ELEMENTS, ESSENTIAL OIL CONTAINING UP TO 1 PER CENT CAPSAICIN

● DIGESTIVE SYSTEM Diarrhea, dyspepsia, flatulence.

● IMMUNE SYSTEM Colds.

There may be over 50 species of chili of varying shapes and sizes. The colour of a chili—green, yellow, red or purple—indicates its stage of maturity. An essential oil in chilies contains capsaicin, which is thought to be good for the heart and circulation. Chilies are recommended for digestive problems and circulatory problems such as chilblains. Excessive consumption of chilies should be avoided as it may cause chronic inflammation of the stomach and intestines.
RECIPES cardamom hot sauce (page 113).

CARDAMOM

★ ESSENTIAL OIL

● DIGESTIVE SYSTEM Diarrhea.

Cardamom seeds are strongly aromatic and are widely used in Indian cooking in curries and to flavor candies and desserts. They

continues on page 56

garlic

GARLIC IS AN ANTICOAGULANT AND HELPS TO REDUCE CHOLESTEROL LEVELS IN THE BLOOD. IT ALSO HAS ANTIBACTERIAL AND ANTIFUNGAL PROPERTIES.

The history of garlic

Garlic is part of the Liliacaea family, which also includes onions, shallots, leeks, chives, and scallions. It is native to central Asia, and its cultivation began in China, Mesopotamia (modern Turkey, Iran, and Iraq), and Egypt thousands of years ago. Garlic has a long reputation as a health-giving food, used both to prevent and to cure illness. In Egypt, as early as 2600BCE, workers building the pyramids were given garlic to keep them strong. Ancient Greek soldiers ate the herb to improve their strength and increase their resistance to infection. In Europe, garlic has long been used to protect against disease—16th-century monks took it to ward off the plague, and its use was widespread during the cholera epidemics of the 19th century.

The properties of garlic

The principal active ingredients in garlic are a volatile oil called allicin, released when the cloves are crushed, and several sulfur compounds, released when garlic is steamed or boiled.

Recent scientific research has shown that allicin is a powerful anticoagulant. It inhibits blood-clotting and helps to break down existing clots, allowing the blood to flow more freely and reducing blood pressure. Garlic suppresses the production of cholesterol in the liver and increases the rate at which dietary cholesterol is expelled from the body. As a result, it is extremely useful for those who suffer from high cholesterol levels, thrombosis (obstructive blood clots), heart disease, and other circulatory problems.

Allicin has potent antibacterial and antifungal properties, and raw garlic is effective in relieving the symptoms of colds and respiratory infections, such as nasal congestion. It is also useful in combating digestive system infections and controlling the balance of bacteria in the gut, as well as helping to repel parasites, such as intestinal worms. Boiling a head of garlic in milk and drinking the resulting decoction every morning is a remedy for intestinal parasites.

Recent research has suggested that diallyl sulfide, a component of garlic, may help to prevent the growth of certain malignant tumors.

Garlic as a cure

A traditional European folk custom involved placing a head of garlic in a small bag and tying it around a child's neck as a protection against colds or influenza. Fixing the bag around the abdomen was thought to protect against worms. Scientists have now discovered that some of the sulfur compounds found in garlic can indeed be absorbed through the skin.

For maximum therapeutic value, at least two raw garlic cloves should be eaten every day. For many people, however, this is unpalatable: Odorless garlic supplements can provide a useful additional source of this important food. If you are worried about bad breath, try chewing cardamom seeds, parsley leaves, or a few roasted coffee beans to help disguise the smell.

Garlic can also be used to great effect in tinctures, drinks, soups, and sauces. To make a garlic tincture, soak 2 ounces of garlic in 1 cup of strong vodka; leave it to macerate in a sealed opaque bottle for two weeks. Strain the mixture, pressing the garlic with the back of a spoon to extract all the remaining liquid. Add up to 15 drops to a small amount of water and take twice a day to reduce high blood pressure and high cholesterol, to combat colds and chronic bronchitis, or as an antiseptic for the digestive system. Keep the tincture in an airtight bottle, away from light, and it will last for up to two years.

STAR FOOD PROFILE

- **BLOOD AND CIRCULATION** Atherosclerosis, high blood pressure, thrombosis.
- **DIGESTIVE SYSTEM** Gastroenteritis, intestinal parasites, ulcerative colitis.
- **IMMUNE SYSTEM** Colds, influenza.

garlic and sage soup

4–5 garlic bulbs, peeled
8¾ cups water
Approximately 10 sage leaves
Salt and pepper
3 or 4 thick slices of rye bread
⅔ cup cold-pressed olive oil
To serve: fresh parsley or chervil, finely chopped

Peel the cloves from the bulbs of garlic and boil in the water for 20 minutes. Add the sage and season with salt and pepper. Infuse for a few minutes. Place the rye bread in a large dish, and pour the olive oil over the bread. Pour the garlic and sage soup over the bread. Sprinkle with the parsley or chervil and serve immediately.

garlic, carrot, and spinach cocktail

4 carrots, peeled and chopped
4 ounces fresh spinach leaves
2 cloves of garlic, peeled
Crushed ice
Salt and pepper

Process all the ingredients in a juicer and mix with some crushed ice. Add salt and pepper to taste. Serve immediately.

garlic and walnut sauce

2 ounces garlic cloves, peeled
¾ cup shelled walnuts
1 cup walnut oil
Salt and pepper
1 tablespoon finely chopped parsley

Process all the ingredients in a blender, adding ice water if necessary.

stimulate the appetite and aid digestion. They contain an essential oil that is an effective breath freshener: After eating an excessive amount of garlic, cardamom seeds will both freshen the breath and prevent heartburn.

RECIPES *cardamom hot sauce (page 113), poached apricots with cardamom (page 117).*

CINNAMON

★ ESSENTIAL OIL

● IMMUNE SYSTEM Colds, influenza.

Cinnamon is a bactericide that promotes the functioning of the respiratory and cardiovascular systems. It is also antispasmodic and stimulates digestion. Chinese herbalists use cinnamon to promote vitality, warm the body, and treat colds and influenza.

RECIPES *cinnamon wine (page 129).*

CLOVES

★ ESSENTIAL OIL

● DIGESTIVE SYSTEM Diarrhea.

● IMMUNE SYSTEM Colds, influenza.

Clove essential oil acts as a powerful antiseptic. Cloves are good for intestinal infections and travelers used to chew them in order to prevent both intestinal infections and hepatitis. They also have a slight anesthetic action. Clove oil can be used externally to treat infected wounds, dental pain, and mouth ulcers.

GINGER

★ VITAMIN B, C, MAGNESIUM, POTASSIUM, ESSENTIAL OIL

● DIGESTIVE SYSTEM Nausea and vomiting.

● IMMUNE SYSTEM Colds, influenza.

● WOMEN'S HEALTH Morning sickness.

Ginger is one of the most widely used spices in Asia. It stimulates the appetite, has antiseptic and tonic properties, and is good for nausea, particularly morning sickness. Combined in a broth with scallions, garlic, and cloves, it promotes sweating and alleviates cold symptoms. Ginger can also be used as a massage oil for rheumatism and to improve blood circulation in muscles. Combine ½ teaspoon ginger essential oil, ¼ teaspoon rosemary essential oil, ¼ teaspoon juniper-berry essential oil, and ½ cup vegetable oil.

RECIPES *honey and ginger broiled salmon (page 65), chive and ginger broth (page 96), rhubarb and ginger tart (page 115), baked papaya with ginger (page 117), ginger infusion (page 127).*

CUMIN

★ ESSENTIAL OIL

● DIGESTIVE SYSTEM Flatulence.

Cumin seeds are rich in an essential oil that has sedative and carminative properties. They can help to treat poor digestion and are recommended for lactating mothers.

RECIPES *cumin-seed decoction (page 128).*

SAFFRON

★ BITTER COMPOUNDS, ESSENTIAL OIL

● DIGESTIVE SYSTEM Dyspepsia.

● WOMEN'S HEALTH Menstrual cramp.

Saffron has calming and antispasmodic properties. It can be used to treat bronchial spasms. It can also be applied to sore and inflamed gums as a painkiller.

HORSERADISH

★ VITAMIN C, FOLIC ACID, CALCIUM, IRON, MAGNESIUM, MANGANESE, PHOSPHORUS, POTASSIUM, SELENIUM, SULFUR, ZINC, ESSENTIAL OIL

● BONES AND JOINTS Arthritis (rheumatoid), gout, rheumatism.

● RESPIRATORY SYSTEM Bronchitis, colds, coughs.

Horseradish has antispasmodic properties, promotes the flow of bile, and is good for sinus problems.

RECIPES *horseradish sauce (page 113).*

ANISE

★ ESSENTIAL OIL

● DIGESTIVE SYSTEM Colic, distention and gas, dyspepsia, flatulence, nausea and vomiting.

● NERVOUS SYSTEM, MIND, AND EMOTIONS Migraine.

● WOMEN'S HEALTH Irregular menstrual cycle and menstrual cramp.

Aniseed (the seeds of the anise plant) and star anise (the fruit) have the same properties. They both contain a potent essential oil that is strongly antispasmodic and acts as a stimulant to the heart, respiratory and digestive systems. Anise is slightly diuretic and helps to promote bile flow and digestion. It is recommended for lactating mothers.

RECIPES *pears with herbs (page 116), anisette (page 131), aniseed tincture (page 132).*

JUNIPER BERRIES

★ ESSENTIAL OIL

● BONES AND JOINTS Gout, rheumatism.

TIVE SYSTEM Intestinal infections.

S AND BLADDER Cystitis.

erries have tonic, antiseptic, depurative, and diuretic
s. They help to eliminate uric acid and toxins from the
 contain a powerful antibacterial essential oil. In France
 nboring countries, houses and stables are traditionally
 d by burning juniper twigs and leaves—their disinfectant
 lps to eliminate parasites and insects. Juniper berries
 for poor digestion and chest infections; they are also
ended for diabetes because they stimulate the pancreas
 n that produces insulin). To treat acne, eczema, and slow
ounds: Boil 2 ounces juniper berries and twigs in 4 cups
for 10 minutes; strain, and use the cooled water as a
 .

ckled turnips (page 122), juniper-berry wine (page 130).

G

TIAL OIL

TIVE SYSTEM Diarrhea.

contains a potent essential oil that is poisonous in large
 ut beneficial in small amounts. It is a good general
 for the digestive system, has analgesic properties, and
 s the brain and nervous system. Nutmeg is recommended
 reath, poor digestion, and other digestive ailments. The
 ssential oil can be applied to the skin for rheumatism and
 (dilute with a base oil such as almond).

VANILLA

★ ESSENTIAL OIL

Vanilla is a mild excitant and a tonic. It also stimulates the digestive
system. Vanilla essential oil has antiseptic properties.

COCOA

★ VITAMIN B, CALCIUM, IRON, MAGNESIUM, POTASSIUM, SELENIUM, ZINC,
   THEOBROMINE, VEGETABLE FAT

Cocoa contains theobromine, a substance that has a similar
effect to caffeine, but is less toxic, does not raise blood pressure,
accumulate in the body, or result in addiction. Good-quality cocoa
is slightly diuretic and helps to eliminate toxins from the body. In
some cases, cocoa may trigger migraines. Good brands of
chocolate contain at least 60 per cent cocoa.

SUNFLOWER SEED

★ LINOLEIC, STEARIC AND PALMITIC ACIDS, POLYUNSATURATED OILS

● DIGESTIVE SYSTEM Constipation.

Sunflower seeds are a useful part of a low-cholesterol diet. They
are delicious toasted and provide essential fatty acids.

FENNEL SEED

★ ESSENTIAL OILS

● BONES AND JOINTS Gout.

● DIGESTIVE SYSTEM Abdominal pain, colic, nausea, and vomiting
   (including morning sickness).

Fennel seeds are gently tonic and diuretic. They have an
estrogen-like effect and can help to regulate menstruation. The
main medicinal use of fennel seeds is for digestive problems, such
as poor appetite and digestion, bloating, nausea, and flatulence.
The seeds also promote urination and the elimination of uric acid.
RECIPES fennel-seed decoction (page 128).

CONDIMENTS, HONEY, AND WINE

PEPPERCORNS

★ TRACE ELEMENTS (INCLUDING CHROMIUM), COMPLEX ESSENTIAL OIL (PIPERIN)

● DIGESTIVE SYSTEM Diarrhea, dyspepsia.

● IMMUNE SYSTEM Colds, sore throat.

Peppercorns are good for digestive problems and circulatory problems, such as chilblains. They stimulate the heart and peripheral circulation, although excessive consumption of pepper may aggravate any inflammation of the stomach and intestines.

VINEGAR

★ POTASSIUM, PHOSPHORUS, TRACE ELEMENTS SUCH AS COPPER AND ZINC

● BONES AND JOINTS Arthritis (rheumatoid), gout, rheumatism.

● IMMUNE SYSTEM Sore throat.

Vinegar is good for a variety of conditions. A gargle made of honey, vinegar, and water may help to ease sore throats. Vinegar is also a traditional toner and disinfectant for the skin. Because it acts as a solvent it is able to take up the active ingredients of the medicinal plants that are preserved in it. Homemade aromatic vinegar can be added to salads or used in cooking, thereby increasing the medicinal value of other foods. Excessive consumption of vinegar should be avoided as it may upset the stomach and cause digestive problems, such as gastritis.

RECIPES pickled turnips (page 122), pickled beet (page 122), pickled cauliflower (page 122), blackberry vinegar (page 122), raspberry vinegar (page 122), borage leaves in vinegar (page 124), tarragon vinegar (page 124), shallot vinegar (page 124), herb vinegar (page 124), amazingly aromatic vinegar (page 124).

MUSTARD

★ ESSENTIAL OIL, FERMENTING AGENTS

● DIGESTIVE SYSTEM Constipation.

The white mustard seed is used as a condiment and the black seed is commonly used by herbalists. Mustard causes a sensation of heat in the stomach and stimulates the digestion.

RECIPES table mustard (page 124).

HONEY

★ AROMATIC SUBSTANCES, FRUCTOSE, GLUCOSE, POLLEN

● DIGESTIVE SYSTEM Diarrhea.

● RESPIRATORY SYSTEM Asthma, bronchitis.

● IMMUNE SYSTEM Sore throat.

Honey is a natural antibiotic that works both internally and externally. It eases respiratory infections, calms the nerves, induces sleep, and disinfects wounds and sores. As well as being an effective treatment for diarrhea, it also has laxative properties. A few drops of lemon juice mixed with a teaspoon of honey is an excellent sore throat remedy.

RECIPES honey and ginger broiled salmon (page 65), peach syrup (page 132).

POLLEN

★ VITAMINS B, C, E, MAGNESIUM, POTASSIUM, TRACE ELEMENTS, ESSENTIAL AMINO ACIDS, ANTIOXIDANTS

Pollen is an easily assimilated natural food supplement that is recommended for anyone suffering from low energy levels. One tablespoon a day is the standard recommended dose, although some specialists recommend more.

ROYAL JELLY

★ VITAMINS B, C, AMINO ACIDS

● BLOOD AND CIRCULATION Anemia.

● NERVOUS SYSTEM, MIND, AND EMOTIONS Depression, mental fatigue.

Royal jelly is a white substance produced by bees to feed to the larvae of potential queen bees. It is a powerful tonic that is particularly recommended for children and elderly people.

WINE

★ BIOFLAVONOIDS, TANNINS

● BLOOD AND CIRCULATION High blood pressure.

Small amounts of wine (no more than 2 glasses a day) are recommended for enhancing the health of the cardiovascular system. Red wine, in particular, has been found to reduce the incidence of heart disease, particularly among those suffering from high cholesterol and high blood pressure.

RECIPES black currant wine (page 129), cinnamon wine (page 129), artichoke-leaf wine (page 130), cherry-leaf wine (page 130), juniper-berry wine (page 130), camomile and citrus wine (page 131), camomile aperitif (page 131).

meat, fish, and dairy produce

POULTRY AND GAME

★ VITAMIN B, IRON, TRACE ELEMENTS, ZINC, PROTEIN

The main advantage of poultry and game is that they are usually leaner than other types of meat. Red meat, for example, contains a large amount of hidden fat—this can have an adverse effect on cholesterol levels and increase the risk of fatty deposits building up in the arteries. Reducing your intake of red meat and eating game and poultry instead can reduce the risk of cardiovascular disease.
RECIPES chicken breasts with celery root mash (page 108), chicken, millet, barley, and celery root pilaf (page 109).

RED MEAT

★ VITAMIN B, SELENIUM, ZINC, PROTEIN

Red meat should be eaten in moderation because of its high fat content. Lean cuts of lamb, pork, and beef should be selected and visible fat trimmed off. Modern food production methods mean that there may be traces of antibiotics and hormones in meat. As with all food, use organic produce where possible.
RECIPES lamb with spinach and lentils (page 107).

SHELLFISH

★ IODINE, IRON, SELENIUM, ZINC AND OTHER TRACE ELEMENTS, PROTEIN

Shellfish provide energy and are a good source of the antioxidant minerals zinc and selenium. They help to boost the immune system and are a low-fat source of protein. It is a good idea to eat shellfish on a regular basis as an alternative to meat.

MILK, CHEESE, BUTTER, YOGURT

★ VITAMINS A, B, D, CALCIUM, PROTEIN

Although milk and milk products are good sources of protein and calcium, they are also difficult to digest. This is because during the sterilization process milk is subjected to intense heat that destroys its natural ferments. These ferments help the digestion of lactose—the sugar found in milk. Without the aid of these bacteria, lactose intolerance becomes more likely. Symptoms of lactose intolerance include diarrhea, bloating, abdominal pain, and gas. Milk can also exacerbate eczema and respiratory problems involving mucus. If you suspect that you suffer from lactose intolerance, eliminate milk and milk products from your diet for two weeks and see if your symptoms diminish in frequency and intensity. Cheese, butter, and cream should be consumed only in small quantities because they are rich in saturated fat and can contribute to the buildup of fatty deposits in the arteries. Avoid these foods altogether if you are overweight or have high cholesterol levels (or switch to low-fat products). Live yogurt is good for the health of the digestive tract and retains the natural bacteria that help to digest lactose. Dairy products can be made more digestible by mixing them with live yogurt. For example, mix cottage cheese with 2–3 tablespoons of live yogurt.
RECIPES cottage cheese with watercress (page 103), halibut steak and nettle butter (page 100), fresh figs with raspberry cheese (page 117).

EGG

★ VITAMINS B, D, CALCIUM, CHROMIUM, IODINE, IRON, SELENIUM, ZINC, CHOLESTEROL, PROTEIN

Eggs are a good source of protein but they should be avoided by people with high cholesterol levels. Choose organically produced free-range eggs.
RECIPES buckwheat with leek sauce (page 105), leek and chive mimosa with polenta (page 107).

 oily fish

OILY FISH, SUCH AS MACKEREL, SALMON, HERRING, AND TUNA, ARE
RICH IN POLYUNSATURATED FATS KNOWN AS OMEGA-3 FATTY ACIDS. A
SUBSTANTIAL BODY OF RESEARCH HAS LINKED DIETS RICH IN OMEGA-3
FATTY ACIDS WITH A LOW INCIDENCE OF CARDIOVASCULAR DISEASE.

The properties of oily fish

Both freshwater and saltwater oily fish are an important part of
a nutritious, medicinal diet. Most nutrition experts suggest that
they should be eaten frequently, particularly as a replacement
for red meat. Oily fish are rich in vitamin D and omega-3
fatty acids, which makes them good for the health of the
cardiovascular system. Research shows that the incidence of
cardiovascular disease is lowest in populations that eat a diet
high in omega-3 fatty acids—the Eskimo population, whose
diet is dominated by oily fish, is an excellent example of this.

Preventing illness

Oily fish can help to reduce some major health problems, such
as high blood pressure, atherosclerosis and arteriosclerosis. It
is estimated that regular consumption of fish and fish oil can
reduce the risk of heart attack by approximately one third. Oily
fish have an anti-inflammatory action that makes them good
for health problems, such as ulcerative colitis and rheumatoid
arthritis, that are characterized by inflammation. Oily fish are also
recommended for eczema, psoriasis, and multiple sclerosis,
and they may help to protect the body from cancer. Research
suggests that omega-3 fatty acids may counteract certain types
of allergies and assist brain development in children.

An important role of omega-3 fatty acids is the creation of
prostaglandins. Prostaglandins are hormone-like substances
that have numerous health benefits, such as keeping the blood
thin, lowering blood pressure, maintaining water balance, and
regulating blood sugar.

Including fish in the diet

Omega-3 fatty acids are found in a range of fish and shellfish
but the most abundant sources are mackerel, herring,
anchovies, trout, salmon, sardine, whitebait, pilchards, and red
tuna. People who have had a heart attack or who suffer from
chronic cardiovascular illness are advised to eat 1 ounce of
these types of oily fish every day. Those who are in reasonable
health and do not have cardiovascular disease are advised to
eat oily fish twice weekly in order to maintain long-term health.

Oily fish and cod liver oil both contain omega-3 fatty acids.
Many people take cod liver oil in supplement form during the
winter months (care should be taken as overdosing on this may
damage your health). Cod liver oil is an excellent source of the
fat-soluble vitamins A and D, as well as a source of omega-3
fatty acids, but the best source of omega-3 fatty acids is fresh
oily fish; if this is not available, canned sardine or mackerel
is a good alternative.

STAR FOOD PROFILE

● **BONES AND JOINTS** Arthritis (rheumatoid).

● **BLOOD AND CIRCULATION** Atherosclerosis, arteriosclerosis, high
blood pressure.

● **DIGESTIVE SYSTEM** Ulcerative colitis.

● **SKIN, HAIR, AND NAILS** Eczema, psoriasis.

cotriade of mackerel

3 potatoes, sliced
2 medium tomatoes, sliced
5 ounces small onions, halved
2 cloves
2 cloves of garlic
1 bouquet garni
Pinch of saffron
Salt and pepper
⅝ cup dry white wine
1¼ cups water
2¼ pounds mackerel, cleaned and gutted
2 tablespoons chopped parsley or chives

Spread the potatoes on the bottom of a large, well-oiled ovenproof dish. Add the other ingredients, except the parsley or chives. Put the dish in a preheated oven at 400°F for 20 minutes or until the fish is cooked. Serve hot or warm sprinkled with parsley or chives.

honey and ginger broiled salmon

1¾ pounds salmon fillet
2-inch piece ginger root, peeled and grated
2 cloves of garlic
3 tablespoons soy sauce
½ teaspoon Chinese five spice powder
2 tablespoons clear honey
2 scallions, chopped

In a large bowl, combine all of the ingredients. Mix well, cover with plastic wrap and refrigerate for 30 minutes. Remove the salmon from the marinade (keep the marinade) and pat dry. Broil or pan fry for 5 minutes on either side, brushing with the marinade during cooking.

foods for common ailments

When the body is fighting disease it needs all the help it can get—informed dietary choices can provide this help. To guide you through these choices, the following pages list over 80 ailments, organized by the body system that they affect. Symptom profiles, lists of beneficial foods and foods to avoid, menu suggestions to ensure the healthy function of each body system, and page references to useful recipes are all designed to help you to help your body combat illness and glow with health.

bones and joints

STAR FOODS FOR BONES AND JOINTS: ARTICHOKE, CABBAGE, CHEESE, CUCUMBER, DANDELION, FISH OIL, GINGER, GREEN BEAN, LEEK, MILK, NETTLE, OILY FISH, ONION, RADISH.

Our muscles, bones, and joints suffer constantly from small traumas and everyday wear and tear. The musculo-skeletal system also changes gradually over the years, which may result in pain, stiffness, inflammation, and restriction of movement.

Good circulation and the elimination of uric acid are important factors in retaining maximum mobility and staying free of aches and pains. To protect your bones and joints, a constitutional approach is best: Avoid alcohol, acid-forming foods, and too much red meat; increase your intake of foods that are rich in minerals (such as green beans), foods that promote detoxification (artichokes, dandelion, and radishes), and foods that are diuretic (cucumber, leeks, and onions). Calcium and vitamin D help to strengthen the bones—calcium-rich foods include cheese, milk and fresh vegetables, and oily fish is a good source of vitamin D. Juices and infusions are useful for both bone mineralization and the elimination of waste. If you suffer from chronic arthritis or rheumatism, you should follow a strict detox program (such as the one outlined on pages 136–139) at regular intervals.

Regular gentle exercise helps you to stay mobile. Excess weight can have an adverse effect on weight-bearing joints, such as the hips, knees and the lower part of the spine. If you experience pain or discomfort in these joints, you may need to consider losing weight by following a low-calorie diet. (N.B. To make a medicinal infusion, steep 1 tablespoon of the dried ingredient in a cup of boiling water for 10 minutes.)

ARTHRITIS (RHEUMATOID)

PAIN, INFLAMMATION AND SWELLING IN ANY OF THE JOINTS WITH OVERALL ACHING OR STIFFNESS. ARTHRITIS IS A CHRONIC, HEREDITARY ILLNESS INVOLVING AN AUTO-IMMUNE REACTION.

! ALLERGIES TO DAIRY, WHEAT, FAT, OR OTHER FOOD CAN SOMETIMES EXACERBATE OR EVEN TRIGGER AN ATTACK. IF YOU SUSPECT THAT THIS IS THE CASE, ELIMINATE A FOOD FROM YOUR DIET FOR 2–3 WEEKS, REINTRODUCE IT GRADUALLY, AND MONITOR SYMPTOMS.

✔ Apple, artichoke, asparagus, banana, bell pepper, black currant, blueberry, cabbage, cauliflower, celery, cherry, chive and scallion, corn, cucumber, dandelion, endive, fennel, garlic, gooseberry, grapefruit, grape and raisin, green bean, horseradish, juniper berry, leek, lemon, lettuce, mâche, melon, millet, nettle, oily fish, onion, parsnip, pear, pineapple, potato, prune, radish, red currant, salsify, tarragon, thyme, tomato, vinegar, watercress. Ginger has analgesic properties and promotes circulation— massage painful joints with a combination of ginger, rosemary and juniper-berry essential oils mixed with vegetable oil (page 58).

✘ Alcohol, coffee, cooked fat and oil, dairy products, dried beans and lentils, game and poultry, peanuts, processed food, red meat, refined oils, sorrel, sugar, tea, white flour.

RECIPES carrot, cabbage, and bell pepper juice (page 21), garbanzo bean broth (page 94), broccoli and green bean juice (page 121), pear and apple infusion (page 126), cherry-stem decoction (page 127), cherry-stem and apple decoction (page 128), strawberry-leaf decoction (page 128), cherry-leaf wine (page 130).

ANKYLOSING SPONDYLITIS

PROGRESSIVE, CHRONIC INFLAMMATION OF THE SPINE CAUSING
FLARE-UPS OF PAIN AND STIFFNESS. MOST COMMON AMONG
YOUNG MEN.

✔ To relieve pain, rub some olive oil infused with bay leaves,
juniper berries, camomile, and rosemary flowers on the affected
area of the back. Take infusions of black currant leaves or
strawberry root and leaves. SEE ALSO Arthritis (rheumatoid).

✘ SEE Arthritis (rheumatoid).

RECIPES strawberry-leaf decoction (page 128), artichoke-leaf wine
(page 130).

BURSITIS

INFLAMMATION OF A FLUID-FILLED SAC (BURSA) THAT PROTECTS A
JOINT FROM FRICTION. SYMPTOMS INCLUDE PAIN, SWELLING, AND
RESTRICTION OF MOVEMENT IN AFFECTED JOINTS, TYPICALLY THE
SHOULDER, WRIST, ELBOW, KNEE, AND FINGERS.

✔ Drink pear- or black currant-leaf infusion. Apply a poultice of
fresh cabbage leaves to the affected joints two or three times a
day to reduce inflammation. SEE ALSO general advice on the care
of muscles and joints.

RECIPES pear and apple infusion (page 126).

CARPAL TUNNEL SYNDROME

COMPRESSION OF A NERVE THAT TRAVELS THROUGH THE WRIST.
SYMPTOMS INCLUDE PAIN THAT SHOOTS UP THE ARM, AND NUMB,
TINGLING, OR BURNING SENSATIONS IN THE HAND AND FINGERS. MAY
BE HORMONAL (IT CAN OCCUR SPONTANEOUSLY DURING PREGNANCY),
OR CAUSED BY A REPETITIVE STRAIN INJURY.

✔ Frequent application of a poultice of cabbage leaves or a
mixture of green clay, cabbage leaves (processed in a blender),
and mashed cucumber may help to reduce pain and inflammation
in the wrist. SEE ALSO general advice on the care of bones and
joints and Bursitis.

SUGGESTED MENUS FOR INFLAMED JOINTS AND OTHER PAINFUL JOINT CONDITIONS

The following menus are designed for people
suffering from arthritis, rheumatism, joint pain
and inflammation, fibrositis or polymyalgia
rheumatica, and include foods that have
anti-inflammatory properties. Arthritis sufferers
whose condition is exacerbated by an allergy
to alcohol, dairy products, or wheat should
avoid the foods marked with an asterisk.

MENU 1

BREAKFAST

A bowl of sugar-free porridge with skim
milk*, yogurt*, and a small glass of juice
made from green beans, cabbage, or other
vegetables; or a fruit juice combination
such as pineapple, apple, and strawberry.

SNACKS

Dried fruit, especially raisins or apricots,
and dandelion coffee.

LUNCH

Garbanzo bean or leek and potato soup
with brown bread*; a mixed salad of
mâche, green beans, and radishes with
olive oil and lemon juice; poached salmon
with potatoes; a pear or an apple.

DINNER

Steamed vegetables with ginger and garlic
and a small amount of rice or noodles; an
infusion of dandelion or black currant leaves
or a small glass of artichoke-leaf wine*.

MENU 2

BREAKFAST

A bowl of cottage cheese* mixed with two
or three tablespoons of yogurt*, a glass of
fruit juice (grape, apple, or cherry), and a
slice of melon or a banana.

SNACKS

Dried fruit, especially black currants or
raisins, and dandelion coffee.

LUNCH

Pasta with vegetables, smoked salmon and
brown bread*; a piece of fruit.

DINNER

A mixed salad with brown bread*; an
infusion of camomile or black currant
leaves, or a small glass of artichoke-
leaf wine*.

CHRONIC BACK PAIN

! MAY REQUIRE OSTEOPATHIC OR CHIROPRACTIC TREATMENT.

✔ *SEE* Arthritis (rheumatoid) and Osteoarthritis.

CRAMPS (MUSCULAR)

A SUDDEN MUSCULAR SPASM CAUSING TEMPORARY PAIN AND
DISCOMFORT—MAY BE DUE TO A CIRCULATORY PROBLEM.

✔ Tarragon is well known for its antispasmodic action. Eat plenty
of magnesium-rich foods, such as wholegrain cereals, nuts, seeds,
seafood, and green vegetables. *SEE ALSO* general advice in Heart
and Circulation.

FIBROMYALGIA

PAIN AND MUSCULAR STIFFNESS IN AREAS SUCH AS THE BACK, NECK,
AND SHOULDERS OF UNCERTAIN CAUSES.

✔ Massage some olive oil infused with rosemary and juniper or
bay berries into the affected area. *SEE ALSO* Arthritis (rheumatoid),
Gout, and Ankylosing spondylitis.

GOUT

SUDDEN ATTACK OF SEVERE PAIN, SWELLING, AND INFLAMMATION,
OFTEN IN THE BIG TOES, ANKLES, KNEES, OR ELBOWS, OWING TO
A BUILDUP OF URIC ACID CRYSTALS IN THE JOINTS. RECURRENT
ATTACKS MAY BE FREQUENT.

✔ Basil, celery, chervil, nettle, raisin, raspberry, rosemary,
strawberry. Apply a poultice of fresh cabbage leaves to affected
joints to reduce pain and inflammation. *SEE ALSO* Arthritis
(rheumatoid).

✗ Tea, coffee, rhubarb.

*RECIPES apple and raspberry juice (page 119), dandelion infusion
(page 125), strawberry-leaf decoction (page 128), artichoke-leaf
tincture (page132).*

OSTEOARTHRITIS

A CHRONIC, DEGENERATIVE CONDITION AFFECTING MOSTLY
THE WEIGHT-BEARING JOINTS, COMMON IN PEOPLE AGED 40
AND OVER.

✔ Apple, asparagus, bean, black currant, cabbage, celery, chervil,
dandelion, ginger, leek, olive, radish, salsify, yogurt. Drink fresh
vegetable or fruit juice every day and increase the amount of oily
fish, fish oil, and shellfish in your diet. *SEE ALSO* general advice on
Bones and Joints.

OSTEOPOROSIS

LITERALLY "POROUS BONE"—A GRADUAL LOSS OF CALCIUM CAUSES
BONES TO BECOME WEAK, BRITTLE, AND PRONE TO FRACTURE.
OSTEOPOROSIS IS COMMON IN POSTMENOPAUSAL WOMEN WHO HAVE
LOW ESTROGEN LEVELS (THIS HORMONE REGULATES THE UPTAKE
OF CALCIUM).

! A CALCIUM- AND MAGNESIUM-RICH DIET MUST BE SUPPORTED BY
REGULAR LOW-INTENSITY EXERCISE AND EXPOSURE TO SUNLIGHT.

✔ Bean curd, cottage cheese, fish oil, fresh fruit, goat cheese, all
leafy greens, hard cheese such as Parmesan, oily fish, soy, yogurt.

POLYMYALGIA RHEUMATICA

INFLAMMATION OF MUSCLES CAUSING CAUSING PAIN AND STIFFNESS
OF THE SHOUDERS AND HIPS. ITS EXACT CAUSE IS UNKNOWN BUT
AUTOIMMUNITY, GENETICS, AND INFECTION HAVE ALL BEEN IMPLICATED.

✔ *SEE* Anemia, Arthritis (rheumatoid), and Fibrositis.

RESTLESS LEGS SYNDROME

BURNING, ACHING SENSATION IN THE LEGS CAUSING RESTLESSNESS
AND TWITCHING. THE SUFFERER BECOMES IRRITABLE AND FIDGETY.

! MAY BE ASSOCIATED WITH IRON AND VITAMIN-B DEFICIENCY.

✔ Take infusions of camomile, elderberry, ginger, lemon balm,
limeflower, rosemary. Use ginger, chilies, and rosemary regularly in
cooking. *SEE ALSO* general advice in Heart and Circulation.

✗ Tea, coffee.

*RECIPES lemon-balm and camomile infusion (page 126), elder and
camomile infusion (page 126), ginger infusion (page 127).*

RHEUMATISM

ANY DISEASE THAT IS CHARACTERIZED BY INFLAMMATION IN THE
MUSCLES AND JOINTS, PARTICULARLY RHEUMATOID ARTHRITIS.

✔ *SEE* Arthritis (rheumatoid) and Fibrositis.

TENDINITIS

INFLAMMATION OF A TENDON (THE FIBROUS TISSUE THAT CONNECTS
MUSCLES AND BONES).

✔ *SEE* Bursitis.

TENOSYNOVITIS

INFLAMMATION OF A TENDON AND THE PROTECTIVE SHEATH THAT
SURROUNDS IT.

✔ *SEE* Bursitis.

heart and circulation

STAR FOODS FOR HEART AND CIRCULATION: BARLEY, BUCKWHEAT, CLOVE, ENDIVE, GARLIC, GINGER, GREEN BEAN, LEEK, LEGUMES, LEMON, LETTUCE, LIME, OAT, OILY FISH, OLIVE OIL, OLIVE, ONION, ORANGE, PARSLEY, PARSNIP, POTATO, ROSEMARY, SHALLOT, AND SPINACH.

Diet plays a fundamental role in the health of the heart and blood vessels. A good diet can help to keep the cardiovascular system working efficiently throughout life whereas a bad diet is a major risk factor for hypertension, atherosclerosis, heart attack, and stroke. The Western diet, which tends to be high in saturated fat, sugar, and salt, encourages the development of fatty deposits, known as atheroma, in the arteries. The arteries narrow and problems such as blood clots and heart attacks become more likely.

If you have suffered a heart attack, the most effective way to avoid a second attack is to follow a diet that protects your cardiovascular system. Increase your intake of oily fish and fiber-rich foods; eat more potassium-rich vegetables, garlic, ginger, greens, and fruit, as these may help to lower your blood pressure. Bioflavonoids, found in yellow, orange, red, and green vegetables and fruit, are antioxidants that help to reduce the formation of fatty deposits and clots in the arteries. Reduce your consumption of red or fatty meat (especially pork), full-fat dairy products, eggs, sugar, salt, and alcohol. Eliminate fried and fast foods from your diet. Take regular, low-intensity exercise, such as swimming, cycling, walking, or jogging, three times a week for at least one hour at a time. If you are overweight, start following a low-calorie diet. If you smoke, it is vital that you make every effort to give up. (N.B. To make a medicinal infusion, steep 1 tablespoon of the dried ingredient in a cup of boiling water for 10 minutes.)

ANEMIA

A DEFICIENCY OF IRON IN THE BLOOD, COMMONLY CAUSED BY A LACK OF IRON-RICH FOODS IN THE DIET OR BY A LOSS OF BLOOD, OFTEN THROUGH HEAVY MENSTRUATION. PERNICIOUS ANEMIA IS CAUSED BY AN INABILITY TO ABSORB VITAMIN B12.

✔ Iron-rich foods: apricot (dried), beet, blackberry, black currant, broccoli, carrot, chervil, chestnut, dandelion, fresh fruit and vegetable juices, green bean, mâche, nettle, parsley, prune, royal jelly, spinach, watercress. Vitamin B-rich foods: lean red meat, molasses, yeast extract. Drink plenty of fresh fruit and vegetable juices including blackberry, black cherry, grape, lettuce, spinach, fennel. If you are a vegan, it may be helpful to take a daily vitamin B12 supplement (this should be available from most healthfood stores).

RECIPES nettle soup (page 96), cabbage, carrot, and celery juice (page 121), green bean and garlic juice (page 121), broccoli and green bean juice (page 121), celery and red onion juice (page 121), fennel infusion (page 125), fennel-seed decoction (page 128), black currant wine (page 129).

ANGINA

EPISODES OF CRUSHING PAIN RESULTING FROM POOR BLOOD SUPPLY TO THE HEART. USUALLY CAUSED BY BLOCKED AND NARROWED ARTERIES. ATTACKS ARE TRIGGERED BY STRESS AND EXERTION.

! DO NOT STOP TAKING MEDICATION PRESCRIBED BY YOUR DOCTOR.

SEVERE CHEST PAIN THAT IS NOT ALLEVIATED BY REST SHOULD BE TREATED AS A MEDICAL EMERGENCY.

✔ Eat a small portion of oily fish every day. Increase your intake of magnesium-rich food, such as wholegrain cereal products, nuts, and seeds. Drink infusions of olive leaves and limeflower. *SEE ALSO* Atherosclerosis, Arteriosclerosis, High blood pressure, and Stress (page 85).

✘ Fatty red meat, full-fat dairy products (such as butter, high-fat cheese, and cream), egg, sugary foods, salt, and alcohol. Avoid fried and fast foods.

RECIPES garlic tincture (page 56), green bean and garlic juice (page 121), broccoli and green bean juice (page 121), celery and red onion juice (page 121), lemon-balm and camomile infusion (page 126), ginger infusion (page 127).

ARTERIOSCLEROSIS

THE HARDENING OF ARTERIES IN OLD AGE, A CONDITION OFTEN ACCELERATED OR AGGRAVATED BY A DIET THAT CONTAINS AN EXCESS OF ALCOHOL, FAT, SALT, AND SUGAR.

! DO NOT STOP TAKING MEDICATION PRESCRIBED BY YOUR DOCTOR.

✔ Apricot, artichoke leaf, asparagus, black radish, blueberry, camomile, celery, dandelion, endive, fish, garlic, grape, lettuce, limeflower, mâche, onion, orange, parsley, pineapple, potato, pumpkin, raspberry, rosemary, rye, saffron, scallion and chive, strawberry. *SEE ALSO* Atherosclerosis.

✘ Alcohol, fast and processed foods, fatty red meat, fried or oily foods, full-fat dairy products, salt, sugar.

RECIPES garlic tincture (page 56), strawberry-leaf decoction (page 128), artichoke-leaf wine (page 130).

ATHEROSCLEROSIS

THE CLOGGING UP OF ARTERIES BY FATTY DEPOSITS KNOWN AS ATHEROMA. THIS CONDITION IS DIRECTLY LINKED TO AN EXCESS OF FAT AND SUGAR IN THE DIET.

! DO NOT STOP TAKING MEDICATION PRESCRIBED BY YOUR DOCTOR.

✔ Apricot, black currant, blueberry, celery, cherry, fig, garlic, germinated barley, ginger, grape, lemon, oat, olive, pineapple, prune, sage, seaweed. Eat oily fish as often as possible and plenty of yellow, orange, red, and leafy greens. Take artichoke, black currant (leaves and fruit), and strawberry-leaf infusions or decoctions. Drink blueberry juice.

✘ Fatty red meat, full-fat dairy products, fried or oily foods, fast and processed foods, foods that are high in sugar.

RECIPES cabbage, carrot, and blueberry juice (page 27), cabbage, carrot, and celery juice (page 121), ginger infusion (page 127), strawberry-leaf decoction (page 128), barley water (page 129).

SUGGESTED MENUS FOR HIGH BLOOD PRESSURE

The following menus are designed to promote weight loss and should ease symptoms associated with stress and high blood pressure, such as digestive problems and water retention. The menus are also recommended for anyone with a heart or circulatory condition. If you are not trying to lose weight, simply increase the amount of

MENU 1

BREAKFAST

A bowl of sugar-free cereal with skim milk; yogurt; a small glass of lettuce, cucumber, and garlic juice or pineapple, apple, and strawberry juice.

SNACKS

Any dried fruit; dandelion coffee substitute.

LUNCH

Lentil soup with brown bread; a salad of fennel, radicchio, and olives with olive oil and lemon juice dressing; fish with potatoes; a piece of fruit.

DINNER

Steamed vegetables with ginger and garlic

on a small bed of noodles (left); a small glass of artichoke-leaf wine (page 130).

MENU 2

BREAKFAST

A bowl of porridge; grape or apple juice.

SNACKS

Any dried fruit; dandelion coffee substitute.

LUNCH

Leek and potato soup; cottage cheese, smoked salmon, and brown bread; a piece of fruit.

DINNER

A mixed salad with brown bread; an infusion of camomile or black currant

CHILBLAINS

PAINFUL, ITCHY SWELLINGS OF THE SKIN CAUSED BY EXPOSURE TO COLD AND POOR CIRCULATION. MOST COMMON ON THE TOES, FINGERS, NOSE AND EARLOBES.

✔ To improve circulation: black currant, blackberry, blueberry, cabbage, carrot, chervil, garlic, ginger, red currant. Consume warm food and drinks. Drink blackberry-leaf infusion. SEE ALSO Anemia.
RECIPES ginger infusion (page 127).

HIGH BLOOD PRESSURE

HIGH BLOOD PRESSURE (HYPERTENSION) OCCURS WHEN THERE IS RESISTANCE IN THE BLOOD VESSELS TO THE FLOW OF BLOOD. IT IS OFTEN SYMPTOMLESS AND ASSOCIATED WITH HIGH CHOLESTEROL AND ARTERIOSCLEROSIS. RISK FACTORS INCLUDE CHRONIC STRESS, AGE, POOR DIET, AND ALCOHOL CONSUMPTION. HIGH BLOOD PRESSURE GREATLY INCREASES THE PATIENT'S RISK OF SUFFERING A STROKE OR HEART ATTACK.

! DO NOT STOP TAKING MEDICATION PRESCRIBED BY YOUR DOCTOR.

✔ Artichoke, asparagus, broccoli, celery, dandelion, garlic, grape, leek, lettuce, oat, oily fish, olive and olive oil, olive-leaf infusion, onion, pomegranate, potassium-rich vegetables, red wine, rice, rye, sunflower seeds and oil, tomato. Increase your intake of magnesium-rich food, such as wholegrain cereal products, nuts, and seeds. In many cases, overcoming obesity is the most effective way of lowering high blood pressure—follow a low-calorie, dairy-free, wheat-free diet for as long as necessary. Combine this diet with regular low-intensity, prolonged exercise. Drink grape juice and infusions of artichoke and olive leaf. SEE ALSO Atherosclerosis.

✘ High-fat foods, including dairy products, and wheat.
RECIPES cabbage, carrot, and blueberry juice (page 27), garlic tincture (page 56), celery and tomato juice (page 120), green bean and garlic juice (page 121), celery and red onion juice (page 121), cucumber and lettuce heart juice (page 121), lettuce and basil juice (page 121), dandelion infusion (page 125).

HYPERLIPIDEMIA

AN EXCESSIVE AMOUNT OF FAT IN THE BLOOD. OFTEN LINKED TO HEAVY ALCOHOL CONSUMPTION, SMOKING, LACK OF EXERCISE, AND A DIET THAT IS HIGH IN FAT.

! DO NOT STOP TAKING MEDICATION PRESCRIBED BY YOUR DOCTOR.

✔ Celery root, dandelion, fig, garlic, germinated barley, nuts, oat, oily fish, onion, papaya. Drink infusions of artichoke and olive leaf.

Include plenty of olive oil in your diet. SEE ALSO Atherosclerosis and Arteriosclerosis.

✘ Avoid fatty foods, except oily fish.
RECIPES garlic tincture (page 56), artichoke-leaf wine (page 130).

PALPITATIONS/ARRHYTHMIA

AN IRREGULAR HEARTBEAT, WHICH MAY BE CAUSED BY CONGENITAL FACTORS, OR MAY BE THE RESULT OF EXERTION, STRESS, OR HEART DISEASE. SUDDEN ONSET REQUIRES MEDICAL ATTENTION.

! DO NOT STOP TAKING MEDICATION PRESCRIBED BY YOUR DOCTOR.

✔ Buckwheat, clove, endive, garlic, germinated barley, green bean, leek, lemon, lemon balm, lettuce, limeflower, mint, parsley, parsnip, passion fruit, oat, olive leaf (in infusion) and oil, onion, rosemary, shallot, tarragon, valerian.

✘ Alcohol, coffee, tea, tobacco.
RECIPES green bean and garlic juice (page 121), celery and red onion juice (page 121), lettuce and basil juice (page 121), lemon-balm and camomile infusion (page 126), barley water (page 129).

THROMBOSIS

FORMATION OF A BLOOD CLOT WITHIN A BLOOD VESSEL OR INSIDE THE HEART, IMPEDING THE FLOW OF BLOOD.

! DO NOT STOP TAKING MEDICATION PRESCRIBED BY YOUR DOCTOR.

✔ Borage oil, buckwheat, camomile, fenugreek, garlic, lemon, limeflower, oily fish, olive oil, orange, pineapple, pumpkin, raspberry, strawberry, tarragon. Eat oily fish on a regular basis.

✘ Alcohol, tobacco.
RECIPES garlic tincture (page 56), strawberry and raspberry juice (page 120), green bean and garlic juice (page 121), celery and red onion juice (page 121), strawberry-leaf decoction (page 128).

RAYNAUD'S DISEASE

INADEQUATE CIRCULATION IN THE HANDS OR FEET DUE TO ARTERIAL SPASM CAUSES FINGERS OR TOES TO TURN WHITE AND STING ON EXPOSURE TO COLD. THE CHEEKS, EARS, AND NOSE MAY ALSO BE AFFECTED.

✔ Blackberry, black currant, black pepper, blueberry, cabbage, carrot, cayenne pepper, chervil, cinnamon, garlic, ginger, red currant. Consume a lot of warm food and drinks. Increase your intake of magnesium-rich food, such as wholegrain cereal products, nuts, and seeds. Drink blackberry leaf infusion. SEE ALSO Anemia.
RECIPES ginger infusion (page 127).

digestive system

STAR FOODS FOR THE DIGESTIVE SYSTEM: ALL BITTER GREENS, ARTICHOKE, BASIL, BLACK CURRANT, BLACK RADISH, BLUEBERRY, CARROT, CHERVIL, DANDELION, ENDIVE, FENNEL, FIG, GARLIC, GERMINATED BARLEY, GINGER, GRAPEFRUIT, JUNIPER BERRY, LEMON, LETTUCE, NUTMEG, OLIVE OIL, PAPAYA, PARSLEY, PINEAPPLE, QUINCE, RADISH, ROSEMARY, THYME, WATERCRESS, ZUCCHINI.

The digestive system includes the mouth, esophagus, stomach, liver, pancreas, gallbladder, and small and large intestine. A diet that consists largely of convenience foods and is high in sugar and fat—as well as alcohol, sodas, spicy snacks, and tobacco—puts the digestive tract under constant strain. The digestive system is also notoriously sensitive to stress and emotional conditions. If you often experience minor digestive problems, or suffer from a chronic condition, you should try to reduce your stress levels as much as possible.

Many digestive problems can be alleviated by eliminating alcohol, coffee, spicy or salty snacks, fatty food (such as cream, cheese, and butter), and junk food from your diet. Eating less, but at regular intervals, can also help. Increase your food intake in the morning, eat moderately at lunchtime and eat lightly in the evening. Some people feel better if they eat five small meals a day.

Two or three times a year, go on a wheat- and dairy-free diet for two to three weeks at a time, or follow the detox program outlined on pages 136–139. In general, try to increase the amount of fiber in your diet by eating plenty of fresh vegetables (don't just rely on cereals as a source of fiber). Fiber encourages food to pass quickly though the gut. When cooking, use plenty of herbs, such as basil, garlic, ginger, juniper, rosemary, and thyme—these are naturally antibacterial and promote digestion. Cabbage, carrots, zucchini, lettuce,

fennel, blueberries, figs, papaya, and pineapple are beneficial to the stomach and intestines; germinated barley is good for dyspepsia. Efficient liver function is important for healthy digestion—bitter greens, artichokes, black currant berries and leaves, black radishes, chervil, dandelion, endive, grapefruit, lemon, olive oil, parsley, quince, and watercress all help the liver to function efficiently and also promote the flow and emulsification of bile.

(N.B. To make a medicinal infusion, steep 1 tablespoon of the dried ingredient in a cup of boiling water for 10 minutes.)

ABDOMINAL PAIN

SUDDEN ONSET OF SEVERE ABDOMINAL PAIN, WHICH MAY BE ACCOMPANIED BY ABDOMINAL SWELLING, DIARRHEA OR VOMITING.
! MAY RAPIDLY TURN INTO A MEDICAL EMERGENCY—SEE A DOCTOR AS SOON AS POSSIBLE. USE SELF-HELP MEASURES ONLY WHEN POTENTIALLY SERIOUS CONDITIONS HAVE BEEN RULED OUT.

ABDOMINAL CRAMP

DISCOMFORT IN THE ABDOMEN WITH VARIOUS CAUSES INCLUDING TRAPPED GAS, CONSTIPATION, OR IRRITABLE BOWEL SYNDROME.
✔ Infusions of aniseed, basil, bay leaf, camomile, cilantro, cumin seed, dill weed, fennel seed, ginger, lemon balm, lychee seed, marjoram, mint, oregano, tarragon. Blueberry, cucumber, carrot, and garlic may alleviate intestinal fermentation and inflammation.

SEE ALSO general advice on the care of the digestive system, and Distention and Gas.

RECIPES cabbage, carrot, and blueberry juice (page 27), blueberry decoction (page 42), cucumber and lettuce heart juice (page 121), fennel infusion (page 125), lemon-balm and camomile infusion (page 126), lychee-seed decoction (page 128), dill-seed decoction (page 128), fennel-seed decoction (page 128), cumin-seed decoction (page 128), camomile and citrus wine (page 131), anisette (page 131), basil liqueur (page 131).

BLOATING

SEE ABDOMINAL PAIN, DISTENTION AND GAS.

CHOLECYSTITIS

AN ACUTE OR CHRONIC INFLAMMATION OF THE GALLBLADDER, OWING TO BLOCKAGE (USUALLY BY GALLSTONES) OR INFECTION, CAUSING PAIN IN THE UPPER RIGHT ABDOMEN AND/OR BETWEEN THE SHOULDERS. THE CONDITION IS OFTEN ACCOMPANIED BY INDIGESTION AND NAUSEA AFTER EATING FATTY FOOD.

! ACUTE PAIN MAY RAPIDLY TURN INTO A MEDICAL EMERGENCY — SEE A DOCTOR AS SOON AS POSSIBLE. USE SELF-HELP MEASURES ONLY WHEN POTENTIALLY SERIOUS CONDITIONS HAVE BEEN RULED OUT.

✔ Bitter greens, dandelion, fresh fruit and vegetables, hazelnut. Try to use plenty of rosemary in your cooking. Every morning drink some olive oil mixed with lemon juice (see page 36) followed by a glass of black radish and carrot juice (see below). Artichoke-leaf, lemon, lemon-peel, or rosemary infusions or fresh cherry juice may also provide some relief.

✘ Cookies and other refined carbohydrates, fatty foods, rhubarb.
RECIPES cherry and raspberry juice (page 120), cherry and apple juice (page 120), black radish and carrot juice (page 121), dandelion infusion (page 125), artichoke-leaf wine (page 130), lemon liqueur (page 131), artichoke-leaf tincture (page 132).

COLIC

SEE ABDOMINAL CRAMP, CONSTIPATION, INDIGESTION.

SUGGESTED MENUS TO AID DIGESTION

The following menus are helpful for anyone suffering from minor problems, such as constipation, distention, and gas, caused by a weak or sluggish digestive system.

MENU 1

BREAKFAST

A bowl of porridge; yogurt; a small glass of juice made of carrot, cabbage, and green or red bell pepper; or fruit juice combinations such as black currant, blueberry, and blackberry or pineapple, apple, and strawberry.

SNACKS

Dried fruit, especially blueberries, pineapple or papaya; dandelion coffee substitute; fennel, ginger, and basil infusion or lemon-balm infusion.

LUNCH

Fish or chicken with potatoes and herb sauce (page 113), or buckwheat with leek sauce (page 105), or tabouleh (page 102) with a broiled lamb chop and a carrot and orange salad; rhubarb and ginger tart (page 115).

DINNER

Fava bean soup or herbal broth (page 94) cooked with barley; fresh fruit salad; a camomile infusion; a small glass of basil liqueur (page 131) or a teaspoon of anisette (page 131) in a glass of water.

MENU 2

BREAKFAST

A bowl of rice or corn flakes with soy milk or an autumn fruit compote; fruit juice (grape, apple, or blueberry); half a grapefruit, a banana, or a kiwi fruit.

SNACKS

Dried fruit, especially raisins, papaya, pineapple, or blueberries; dandelion coffee substitute; fennel, ginger, or cumin-seed infusion.

LUNCH

Honey and ginger broiled salmon (page 63) with steamed vegetables; pumpkin in syrup (page 112).

DINNER

Roman-style artichoke (page 101) or lentil soup (page 95); pears with herbs (page 114); a small glass of camomile and citrus wine (page 129).

COLITIS

SEE ABDOMINAL PAIN, IRRITABLE BOWEL SYNDROME, ULCERATIVE COLITIS.

CONSTIPATION

SLOW INTESTINAL TRANSIT CAUSING IRREGULAR BOWEL MOVEMENTS AND HARD STOOLS.

! STRONG LAXATIVES SHOULD BE AVOIDED. A HIGH-FIBER DIET AND AN INCREASED INTAKE OF RAW FRUIT AND VEGETABLES OFTEN HELPS TO RELIEVE THIS CONDITION.

✔ All leafy greens, apple, asparagus, Brussels sprout, chervil, coconut, cooked rhubarb, cucumber, elderberry, fig, grapefruit, hazelnut, Jerusalem artichoke, kumquat, leek, live yogurt, melon, mustard, olive, orange, peach, pea, persimmon, pomegranate, prune, raspberry, raw apple, red currant, sorrel, strawberry, turnip, tomato, watermelon. Drink plenty of water and apple, melon, prune, or tomato juice—mixed with yogurt if desired. Each morning have olive oil with lemon juice (page 36) and figs boiled in milk (page 38).

✘ Guava seeds. If the condition worsens when you eat foods that contain wheat, you should suspect a wheat allergy and eliminate it from your diet.

RECIPES almond milk (page 79), rhubarb and ginger tart (page 115), apple and raspberry juice (page 119), prune juice (page 120), celery and tomato juice (page 120), cucumber and lettuce heart juice (page 121), elderberry syrup (page 133).

CROHN'S DISEASE

A RECURRENT INFLAMMATION OF THE INTESTINE THAT MAY NECESSITATE SURGERY. SYMPTOMS—WHICH ARE NOT ALWAYS PRESENT, EVEN IN SERIOUS CASES—INCLUDE CRAMPING PAIN, DIARRHEA, WEIGHT LOSS, ANEMIA, AND SOMETIMES JOINT PAIN.

! DO NOT STOP TAKING MEDICATION PRESCRIBED BY YOUR DOCTOR.

✔ Almond, blueberry, cabbage, carrot, fig, ginger, grapefruit, mint, peach, pollen, pumpkin, quince, tarragon, zucchini. Aniseed or mint infusion or fennel tea may also provide some relief. SEE ALSO general advice on the care of the digestive system.

✘ Guava seeds and all dairy products except live yogurt.

RECIPES cabbage, carrot, and blueberry juice (page 27), almond milk (page 79), cabbage, carrot, and celery juice (page 121), fennel infusion (page 125), coriander-seed infusion (page 127), anisette (page 131), quince liqueur (page 131).

DIABETES MELLITUS

A CHRONIC CONDITION IN WHICH AN ABSENCE OR INSUFFICIENCY OF INSULIN LEADS TO PROBLEMS IN THE METABOLISM OF SUGAR. AS A RESULT, SUGAR LEVELS RISE IN THE BLOOD AND URINE.

! DO NOT STOP TAKING MEDICATION PRESCRIBED BY YOUR DOCTOR. YOUR DOCTOR MAY REFER YOU TO A REGISTERED DIETICIAN.

✔ Artichoke, bean, blueberry, brown bread and pasta, brown flour, cabbage, chive and scallion, fruit, garlic, Jerusalem artichoke, legumes, nut, oat, olive, onion, potato, pumpkin, salsify, shallot, rice, unrefined cereals. Drink fresh blueberry, cabbage, celery, or citrus-fruit juice and blueberry, blueberry-leaf, or juniper infusion.

✘ Excessive amounts of animal fat. Consult your doctor before eating bananas.

RECIPES blueberry tincture (page 42), cabbage, carrot, and celery juice (page 121), beet and celery juice (page 121), juniper-berry wine (page 130).

DIARRHEA

THE PASSING OF FREQUENT LIQUID STOOLS CAUSED BY BOWEL INFLAMMATION, FOOD INTOLERANCE, STRESS, OR DRUG TREATMENT.

! DIARRHEA CAN CAUSE RAPID DEHYDRATION. SEE YOUR DOCTOR IF THE ATTACK IS PROLONGED.

✔ Barley, bell pepper, blackberry, blueberry, boiled carrot, boiled rice, cabbage, camomile, cardamom, chili, chive, clove, cooked apple, fava bean, honey, lychee, nettle, nutmeg, onion, pear, peppercorns, quince, rice water, rosemary, savory, strawberry, walnut. Drink fresh blackberry, blueberry, or carrot juice and fennel-seed or rice-water infusion.

RECIPES blueberry decoction (page 42), blueberry tincture (page 42), fennel infusion (page 125), fennel-seed decoction (page 128), quince liqueur (page 131), blackberry syrup (page 133).

DISTENTION AND GAS

ABDOMINAL BLOATING, DISCOMFORT OR PAIN CAUSED BY FERMENTATION OF FOOD, FAT MALABSORPTION, INFECTION, OR STRESS.

✔ Anise, bell pepper, blackberry, blueberry, carrot, chili, garlic, lettuce, marjoram, oregano, savory. Use plenty of bay leaves, clove, coriander, cumin seed, fennel, juniper and rosemary in your cooking. Drink fresh blackberry, blueberry, or lettuce and garlic juice and aniseed, camomile, cumin-seed, dill-seed, or fennel-seed infusion.

✘ Alcohol, fermented foods and foods that may ferment, such as bread, flour-based foods, legumes, and sugary foods.
RECIPES bay-leaf infusion (page 52), lettuce and basil juice (page 121), dill-seed decoction (page 128), fennel-seed decoction (page 128), cumin-seed decoction (page 128).

DIVERTICULITIS

SMALL POUCHES IN THE LARGE INTESTINE WHICH BECOME INFLAMED, CAUSING PAIN, GAS, DIARRHEA, OR CONSTIPATION.

✔ High-fiber foods: apple, bean, blackberry, blueberry, brown bread, brown rice, Brussels sprout, cabbage, chestnut, dried fruit, garbanzo bean, grapefruit, green vegetables, Jerusalem artichoke, lentil, melon, orange, parsnip, pea, porridge, potato, turnip, watermelon. As some of these foods may increase the production of gas, use plenty of fresh herbs and garlic in your cooking.
✘ Guava seeds.
RECIPES cabbage, carrot, and blueberry juice (page 27), garlic and sage soup (page 57), cucumber and lettuce heart juice (page 121), fennel infusion (page 125), lemon-balm and camomile infusion (page 126), dill-seed decoction (page 128), fennel-seed decoction (page 128), cumin-seed decoction (page 128), anisette (page 131).

DYSPEPSIA AND HEARTBURN

INDIGESTION AND A BURNING SENSATION IN THE UPPER ABDOMEN/ CHEST, OFTEN TRIGGERED BY RICH OR SWEET FOOD, OVEREATING, ALCOHOL, OR STRESS.

✔ Anise, apple, arugula, banana, barley, bay leaf, bell pepper, carrot, chestnut, chili, cilantro, fennel, fig, grapefruit, guava (seeded), Jerusalem artichoke, lemon, lettuce, melon, orange, peach, peanut, peppercorns, persimmon, pineapple, potato, pumpkin, quince, radish, saffron, zucchini.
✘ Alcohol, coffee, fatty food, tea. Do not eat late at night.
RECIPES lemon-balm and camomile infusion (page 126), coriander-seed infusion (page 127), fennel-seed decoction (page 128), anisette (page 131), aniseed tincture (page 132).

FLATULENCE

SEE DISTENTION AND GAS.

FOOD POISONING

SEE GASTROENTERITIS, INDIGESTION, NAUSEA AND VOMITING.

GALLSTONES

SEE CHOLECYSTITIS.

GASTRITIS

A GENERAL INFLAMMATION OF THE LINING OF THE STOMACH, CAUSING SYMPTOMS SIMILAR TO THOSE OF INDIGESTION.

✔ A 20-hour fast, drinking only barley water or rice water (see Rice; page 35), may reduce the symptoms considerably. Follow this with a diet of bland foods such as: banana, barley, cabbage, carrot, fennel, fig, Jerusalem artichoke, potato, pumpkin, quince, rice, watermelon, zucchini. Drink fresh carrot, cabbage or zucchini juice, and aniseed, dill-seed, fennel-seed or mint infusions.
SEE ALSO general advice on the care of the digestive system, Dyspepsia, and Indigestion.
RECIPES cabbage, carrot, and celery juice (page 121), lettuce and basil juice (page 121), coriander-seed infusion (page 127), dill-seed decoction (page 128), fennel-seed decoction (page 128).

BARLEY AND FRUIT PORRIDGE

This recipe by Hanne Glasse, which was first published in 1747, can help to boost a sluggish digestive system.

---

2 ounces germinated barley
4 cups water (or equal parts of water and milk)
3 tablespoons raisins
2 tablespoons dried black currants or blueberries
Pinch of ground nutmeg
2 tablespoons brown sugar
¼ cup white wine or a little brandy
2 egg yolks (optional)

In a large saucepan, boil the barley in the water with the raisins, black currants or blueberries, and nutmeg until the barley is tender. Remove from the heat and stir in the brown sugar and white wine. Return to the heat, bring to a boil, and cook over low heat for a further 2 minutes. Add the egg yolks at this stage if desired, but remove from the heat before stirring them in. The end result should resemble rice pudding.

GASTROENTERITIS

AN INFLAMMATION OF THE DIGESTIVE TRACT CAUSED BY MICRO-ORGANISMS AND RESULTING IN NAUSEA, VOMITING, DIARRHEA, ABDOMINAL PAIN AND FEVER.

! DO NOT EAT ANYTHING FOR 24 HOURS. DRINK SMALL AMOUNTS OF FLUIDS FREQUENTLY. GINGER, FENNEL, OR MINT TEA OR AN INFUSION OF THYME, JUNIPER, OR BASIL MAY HELP.

✔ When you feel you can start eating again, eat very lightly, preferably food cooked with garlic, basil, juniper, marjoram, mint, rosemary, or thyme to reduce the infection. Also eat: blueberry, boiled carrot, chive and scallion, garbanzo bean, mâche, persimmon, pumpkin, quince, watercress, zucchini.

RECIPES garlic and sage soup (page 57), almond milk (see opposite page), herbal broth (page 94), ginger infusion (page 127), fennel-seed decoction (page 128), barley water (page 129), basil liqueur (page 131).

GINGIVITIS

INFECTED OR BLEEDING GUMS, OFTEN CAUSED BY BACTERIAL ACTIVITY AND OCCASIONALLY BY VITAMIN DEFICIENCY.

! ALWAYS BRUSH TEETH AND GUMS THOROUGHLY.

✔ Chew lemon peel, cloves, fresh or dried blueberries, or figs. Add a tablespoon of salt and a drop or two of lemon essential oil to a strong thyme infusion to make a mouthwash. A strong sage infusion with a teaspoon of lemon juice added also makes a good mouthwash, as does fig water (see Fig; page 38).

✘ Sugary food.

HALITOSIS (BAD BREATH)

BAD BREATH IS OFTEN CAUSED BY YEAST OR BACTERIAL ACTIVITY IN THE MOUTH AND VARIOUS DIGESTIVE PROBLEMS.

✔ Nutmeg and an infusion of cardamom seeds. SEE ALSO Gingivitis.

HANGOVER

DELAYED EFFECTS OF DRINKING AN EXCESSIVE AMOUNT OF ALCOHOL, INCLUDING FATIGUE, HEADACHE, NAUSEA, INDIGESTION.

✔ Drink plenty of water and infusions throughout the day. SEE ALSO Indigestion.

RECIPES garlic and sage soup (page 57), dandelion infusion (page 125), fennel infusion (page 125), ginger infusion (page 127).

HEPATITIS (A, B, OR C)

ACUTE AND CHRONIC INFECTIONS OF THE LIVER CAUSED BY VIRUSES. SYMPTOMS INCLUDE FATIGUE, INDIGESTION, JAUNDICE, AND LOSS OF APPETITE.

! IT IS IMPERATIVE TO FOLLOW MEDICAL ADVICE.

✔ Bitter greens, apple, artichoke, asparagus, black radish, blueberry, cabbage, celery, chervil, dandelion, endive, grapefruit, green bean, horseradish, lemon, olive and olive oil, parsley, swiss chard. Drink fresh lettuce juice, mint tea, or some olive oil mixed with lemon juice (page 36) .

✘ Alcohol, fatty food, meat, tobacco.

RECIPES dandelion infusion (page 125).

INDIGESTION

A VARIETY OF SYMPTOMS, WHICH MAY INCLUDE NAUSEA, VOMITING, HEARTBURN, AND BELCHING. INDIGESTION IS OFTEN CAUSED BY EXCESSIVE CONSUMPTION OF FATTY FOOD OR ALCOHOL.

✔ Drink water or take a decoction, infusion, or tincture (see below). Eat as little as possible until symptoms have cleared.

RECIPES garlic and sage soup (page 57), herbal broth (page 94), fennel infusion (page 125), lemon-balm and camomile infusion (page 126), coriander-seed infusion (page 127), ginger infusion (page 127), fennel-seed decoction (page 128), aniseed tincture (page 132).

INTESTINAL INFECTIONS AND PARASITES

SEE GASTROENTERITIS

IRRITABLE BOWEL SYNDROME

ABDOMINAL CRAMPS AND SPASMS, AND ALTERNATING OR IRREGULAR BOUTS OF CONSTIPATION AND DIARRHEA. OFTEN ASSOCIATED WITH STRESS, PSYCHOLOGICAL PROBLEMS, AND CHANGE OF ROUTINE.

! AVOID ALL DAIRY PRODUCTS AND WHEAT FOR 2 WEEKS. A WEEK OR TWO LATER REINTRODUCE WHEAT, THEN DAIRY INTO YOUR DIET—IF EITHER CAUSES A SUDDEN RETURN OR AGGRAVATION OF THE CONDITION, ELIMINATE IT FROM YOUR DIET FOR GOOD.

✔ Almond milk, barley, blueberry, camomile, carrot, cilantro, germinated legumes, ginger, melon, mint, persimmon, potato, pumpkin, quince, rice, rosemary, tarragon, zucchini. Drink parsley-seed or mint infusion.

✘ Dairy products and wheat (if they exacerbate symptoms).

RECIPES almond milk (see below), fennel infusion (page 125), dill-seed decoction (page 127), fennel-seed decoction (page 128), anisette (page 131), basil liqueur (page 131).

NAUSEA AND VOMITING

MAY BE A SYMPTOM OF INDIGESTION OR GASTROENTERITIS, BUT OCCASIONALLY INDICATES A SERIOUS DISORDER.

! SEE A DOCTOR IF SYMPTOMS ARE PROLONGED. SEE A DOCTOR IMMEDIATELY IF YOU ARE IN PAIN, WORRIED ABOUT THE CAUSE OF VOMITING, OR IF THERE IS BLOOD IN THE VOMIT.

✔ Infusions of anise, fennel, ginger, mint. SEE ALSO Cholecystitis, Gastritis, Hangover, Indigestion, and Migraine (page 84–5). RECIPES ginger infusion (page 127), fennel-seed decoction (page 128), basil liqueur (page 131).

OBESITY

EXCESSIVE BODY WEIGHT THAT IMPAIRS MOVEMENT AND MAY LEAD TO SERIOUS HEALTH DISORDERS. OBESITY IS OFTEN DUE TO OVER-EATING COMBINED WITH A LACK OF EXERCISE. OTHER CAUSES OFTEN INCLUDE SLOW METABOLISM OR A MALFUNCTIONING THYROID GLAND.

! IT IS NOT POSSIBLE TO REDUCE WEIGHT WITHOUT DECREASING CALORIE INTAKE (EATING LESS) AND INCREASING THE RATE AT WHICH CALORIES ARE USED (EXERCISING MORE).

✔ Eat plenty of foods that are both low-calorie and high-volume, such as greens, legumes, and potato.

✗ Dairy products, wheat (if they cause an allergy). SEE ALSO the detox program (pages 136–139).

PEPTIC ULCERS

INCLUDES GASTRIC AND DUODENAL ULCERS; A SMALL AREA OF THE LINING OF THE STOMACH OR DUODENUM BECOMES INFLAMED, THEN ERODED. SYMPTOMS OF PEPTIC ULCERS INCLUDE A BURNING, GNAWING PAIN IN THE UPPER ABDOMEN OR CHEST, INDIGESTION, NAUSEA, AND VOMITING.

! DO NOT STOP TAKING MEDICATION PRESCRIBED BY YOUR DOCTOR. SEVERE PAIN AND VOMITING BRIGHT RED BLOOD MAY INDICATE THAT THE ULCER HAS BECOME PERFORATED—SEE A DOCTOR IMMEDIATELY. GIVE UP SMOKING.

✔ Apple, banana, cabbage, carrot, fennel, fig, lettuce, potato, quince, rice barley. Eat small meals. Drink a potato-juice remedy (page 18) mixed with fresh carrot juice.

✗ Acidic, fatty or spicy foods, alcohol, coffee, tea. RECIPES cabbage, carrot, and blueberry juice (page 27), fennel infusion (page 125), coriander-seed infusion (page 127), fennel-seed decoction (page 128), aniseed tincture (page 132).

ULCERATIVE COLITIS

CHRONIC INFLAMMATION AND ULCERATION OF THE LOWER PART OF THE COLON CAUSING ABDOMINAL PAIN, AND DIARRHEA WITH BLOOD AND MUCUS.

! DO NOT STOP TAKING MEDICATION PRESCRIBED BY YOUR DOCTOR.

✔ Barley, beet, blackberry, blueberry, cabbage, carrot, cauliflower, cereals, cooked apple, cucumber, dandelion, fava bean, fresh fruit and vegetables, garlic, gooseberry, lettuce, lychee, mâche, mango, nettle, oily fish, pear, persimmon, potato, quince, rosemary, strawberry, zucchini. Eat high-fiber foods and reduce your meat intake. SEE ALSO Anemia (page 71).

✗ Alcohol, dairy products, guava seeds, tobacco. RECIPES almond milk (left), cabbage, carrot, and blueberry juice (page 27), mango juice (page 120), fennel infusion (page 125), lemon-balm and camomile infusion (page 126), elder and camomile infusion (page 126), fennel-seed decoction (page 128).

ALMOND MILK

Almond milk is helpful for people suffering from constipation, Crohn's disease, gastroenteritis, irritable bowel syndrome, and ulcerative colitis. It also acts as a mild laxative for children and is good for coughs and bronchial inflammation (page 80).

Scant 1 cup almonds
1 tablespoon water
¼ cup clear honey
4 cups water
2 tablespoons orange-blossom water

Blend the almonds and the tablespoon of water in a food processor until you have a paste. Add the honey and then dilute the paste with the 4 cups of water. Filter and add the orange-blossom water. Take 3 tablespoons 3 times a day.

respiratory system

STAR FOODS FOR THE RESPIRATORY SYSTEM: BASIL, CHERVIL, CHIVE AND SCALLION, GARLIC, GINGER, LETTUCE, MÂCHE, MARJORAM, MINT, PARSLEY, RED AND BLACK RADISH, ROSEMARY, SAVORY, THYME, WATERCRESS.

Common problems that affect the lungs include irritation and inflammation accompanied by excess mucus. Some mucus is normal and healthy as it helps to keep the lungs lubricated. However, when the lungs are exposed to allergens, bacteria, viruses, or pollutants, mucus production increases.

One of the most harmful pollutants to which the lungs are exposed is tobacco smoke. If you have respiratory problems and you smoke, it is imperative that you stop. Exercise is also very important—long walks in the open air are ideal. Avoid mucus-forming foods, such as wheat and dairy products, and use herbs, such as basil, chives, garlic, ginger, marjoram, mint, rosemary, savory, and thyme, in cooking. Drink plenty of fresh juices—they are rich in zinc and vitamin C, which boosts the immune system, making the lungs less prone to infection. (N.B. To make a medicinal infusion, steep 1 tablespoon of the dried ingredient in a cup of boiling water for 10 minutes.)

ASTHMA

AN INFLAMMATION AND CONSTRICTION OF THE BRONCHI AND BRONCHIOLES, CAUSING BREATHLESSNESS, WHEEZING, TIGHT CHEST, AND COUGHING. ASTHMA MAY BE HEREDITARY. TRIGGERS INCLUDE ALLERGIES, STRESS, EXERCISE, AND EXPOSURE TO COLD AIR.

! DO NOT STOP TAKING MEDICATION PRESCRIBED BY YOUR DOCTOR.

✔ Black currant, cabbage, carrot, chervil, grapefruit, honey, horseradish, lettuce, mint, radish, rosemary, savory, sorrel, watercress. Drink chervil, carrot, cabbage, lemon, watercress,

and apple juices and infusions of mint, thyme (with lemon juice), and rosemary. During an attack, eat a lump of sugar infused with three drops of fennel essential oil.

✘ Dairy products.

RECIPES *carrot, apple, and ginger juice (page 120), cabbage, carrot, and celery juice (page 121), lemon-balm and camomile infusion (page 126), ginger infusion (page 127), lettuce-seed decoction (page 128), strawberry-leaf decoction (page 128).*

BRONCHITIS

AN INFLAMMATION OF THE LINING OF THE BRONCHI, RESULTING IN COUGHING, SPUTUM PRODUCTION, AND BREATHLESSNESS. MAY BE ACUTE (CAUSED BY VIRUSES AND BACTERIA) OR CHRONIC (DUE TO RECURRENT INFECTIONS, SMOKING, OR POLLUTION).

✔ Black currants, borage, carrot, chervil, fig, garlic, grape, honey, horseradish, lettuce, mint, quince, radish, sage, savory, thyme, watercress. Drink infusions of rosemary and borage. SEE ALSO general advice on the care of the respiratory system.

✘ Dairy products, wheat.

RECIPES *almond milk (page 79), carrot, apple, and ginger juice (page 120), marjoram infusion (page 125), lemon-balm and camomile infusion (page 126), ginger infusion (page 127), lettuce-seed decoction (page 128), leek syrup (page 132).*

COUGH

A SYMPTOM OF AN INFECTION, INFLAMMATION, OR IRRITATION OF THE

THROAT, USUALLY ASSOCIATED WITH A COLD, INFLUENZA, BRONCHITIS, OR SORE THROAT. SEE ALSO IMMUNE SYSTEM.

! IF THE COUGH IS PERSISTENT, OR IF MUCUS IS SPECKLED WITH BLOOD, SEE A DOCTOR IMMEDIATELY.

✔ SEE Asthma, Bronchitis, and Sore throat (page 87).

HAY FEVER (ALLERGIC RHINITIS)

AN ALLERGIC REACTION TO TREE, FLOWER, OR GRASS POLLEN, HOUSE DUST, ANIMAL FUR OR OTHER AIRBORNE PARTICLES CAUSING SNEEZING, RUNNY NOSE, AND ITCHY EYES, NOSE, AND THROAT.

✔ SEE general advice on the respiratory system and Asthma.
RECIPES *marjoram infusion (page 125), lemon-balm and camomile infusion (page 126), elder and camomile infusion (page 126).*

PLEURISY

SEVERE LOCALIZED CHEST PAIN, OFTEN ONE-SIDED AND MADE WORSE BY COUGHING, CAUSED BY INFLAMED MEMBRANES SURROUNDING THE LUNGS RESULTING FROM AN UNDERLYING ILLNESS.

✔ Cabbage, carrot, cherry, chervil, fig, garlic, leek, onion, radish, saffron, watercress. SEE ALSO Asthma, Bronchitis.
RECIPES *cabbage, carrot, and celery juice (page 121), marjoram infusion (page 125), lemon-balm and camomile infusion (page 126), elder and camomile infusion (page 126), cherry-stem decoction (page 127), lettuce-seed decoction (page 128).*

PNEUMONIA

SEVERE INFLAMMATION OF THE LUNGS, CAUSED BY VIRAL OR

BACTERIAL INFECTION OR CHEMICAL IRRITATION. SYMPTOMS INCLUDE BREATHLESSNESS, A COUGH THAT MAY PRODUCE BLOODY SPUTUM, FEVER, AND CHEST PAIN. SEVERE CASES MAY BE LIFE THREATENING.

! DO NOT STOP TAKING MEDICATION PRESCRIBED BY YOUR DOCTOR.

✔ Foods rich in vitamin C and zinc plus blackberry, borage, carrot, chervil, clove, fig, garlic, juniper berry, leek, mâche, nettle, onion, rosemary, savory, thyme. SEE ALSO Asthma, Bronchitis.
RECIPES *cherry and apple juice (page 120), cabbage, carrot, and celery juice (page 121), green bean and garlic juice (page 121), lettuce and basil juice (page 121), celery and red onion juice (page 121), marjoram infusion (page 125), lemon-balm and camomile infusion (page 126), elder and camomile infusion (page 126), cherry-stem decoction (page 127).*

SORE THROAT AND TONSILLITIS

SEE SORE THROAT AND TONSILLITIS (PAGE 85).

WHOOPING COUGH

A HIGHLY CONTAGIOUS BACTERIAL INFECTION, CAUSING SEVERE SPASMODIC COUGH. OCCURS PRIMARILY IN INFANTS.

! ANTIBIOTICS CAN REDUCE LENGTH OF ILLNESS IF PRESCRIBED EARLY.

✔ Take a mixture of lemon juice and honey. SEE ALSO Asthma, Bronchitis and Immune system.
RECIPES *almond milk (page 79), marjoram infusion (page 125), lemon-balm and camomile infusion (page 126), elder and camomile infusion (page 126), leek syrup (page 132), black radish syrup (page 132).*

SUGGESTED MENU FOR CHRONIC LUNG DISORDERS

The following menu is designed for someone suffering from a chronic lung disorder such as asthma or bronchitis.

BREAKFAST
A bowl of rice cereal with soy milk; a small glass of carrot juice; a cup of coffee; grapefruit or kiwi fruit.

SNACKS
Dried fruit, especially raisins and figs; fresh fruit, such as orange, kiwi, papaya, and pineapple; ginger infusion.

LUNCH
Black radish salad and broiled fish with mustard or horseradish sauce; melon with fresh mint.

DINNER
Lentil soup (page 97) with rye bread; avocado tartar (page 103); lettuce-seed, marjoram, or lemon-balm infusion.

kidneys and bladder

STAR FOODS FOR THE KIDNEYS AND BLADDER: BARLEY, BLACK CURRANT, BLUEBERRY, CABBAGE, CELERY, CRANBERRY, CUCUMBER, DANDELION, FIG, FRESH FRUIT, GRAPE, LEEK, ONION, UNPROCESSED CEREALS, WATERCRESS, WHEATGERM.

The kidneys' role in the body is to filter waste products from the blood. The waste is then eliminated from the body via the bladder and urethra in the form of urine. The body produces approximately 6 to 8 cups of urine per 24 hours on average and the bladder is evacuated, on average, four to six times a day. The appearance of your urine provides a rough indication of whether you are drinking enough: Dark orange or amber is a sign that you need to increase your fluid intake. Changes in urinary habits or function that warrant medical attention include: cloudy or discolored urine, unexplained changes in urinary output, and pain or discomfort on urination. A problem that becomes common in men over the age of 50 is enlarged prostate gland (page 91). This typically causes a hesitant, weak, or trickling flow of urine.

You can enhance your kidney function by drinking more water, fruit juices, and herbal infusions, and regularly eating foods from the above list. Reduce your intake of coffee, tea, and alcohol: Alcohol suppresses the production of antidiuretic hormone in the body, with the result that urine output by the kidneys increases dramatically. Foods that are rich in fiber and magnesium, such as fresh fruit, unprocessed cereals, and wheatgerm, are beneficial to the kidneys and bladder. It is also important to prevent kidney, bladder, and urethral infections by keeping your immune system healthy (pages 86–87). (N.B. To make a medicinal infusion, steep 1 tablespoon of the dried ingredient in a cup of boiling water for 10 minutes.)

BLADDER AND KIDNEY STONES

SMALL HARD MASSES OF CALCIUM AND OTHER SALTS OCCURRING ANYWHERE IN THE URINARY TRACT. STONES MAY LODGE IN THE BLADDER CAUSING FREQUENT, PAINFUL URINATION AND BLOOD IN THE URINE; THEY MAY OCCUR IN THE URINE-COLLECTING DUCT OF THE KIDNEYS CAUSING SEVERE PAIN; OR THEY MAY REMAIN IN THE KIDNEYS. KIDNEY OR BLADDER STONES MAY NECESSITATE SURGERY OR ANOTHER MEDICAL PROCEDURE.

! DRINK AT LEAST 6–8 GLASSES OF WATER PER DAY AND 1 DURING THE NIGHT.

✔ Almond, artichoke, bean, blackberry, black currant, cabbage, celery, cherry, dandelion, endive, fava bean, garbanzo bean, grape, green bean, leek, lettuce, mâche, melon, nettle, olive, onion, peach, physalis, radish, red currant, strawberry, tomato, watercress. Drink olive-leaf infusion and black currant, grape, cranberry, cherry, and watercress juices.

✘ Animal protein, chocolate, coffee, gooseberry, peanut, rhubarb, sorrel, spinach, tea.

RECIPES *fava bean-flower infusion (page 32), garbanzo bean broth (page 94), cabbage, carrot, and celery juice (page 121), celery and red onion juice (page 121), cucumber and lettuce heart juice (page 121), physalis jelly (page 124), dandelion infusion (page 125), pear and apple infusion (page 126), corn-hair and fennel-seed decoction (page 127), physalis-berry decoction (page 128), strawberry-leaf decoction (page 128), barley water (page 129), juniper-berry wine (page 130).*

CYSTITIS AND URETHRITIS

INFLAMMATION OF THE BLADDER AND URETHRA CAUSED BY CHEMICAL IRRITATION OR INFECTION. SYMPTOMS INCLUDE PAIN IN THE LOWER ABDOMEN, FREQUENT, URGENT, AND PAINFUL URINATION, AND BLOOD IN THE URINE. CYSTITIS IS MOST COMMON IN WOMEN.

✔ Artichoke, blueberry, cherry, cranberry, cucumber, dandelion, juniper berry, melon, pumpkin, red currant, strawberry, thyme, watermelon. Drink plenty of water and watercress, black currant, blueberry, cranberry, and grape juices.

✘ Asparagus.

RECIPES cabbage, carrot, and blueberry juice (page 27), garbanzo bean broth (page 94), cherry and raspberry juice (page 120), cherry and apple juice (page 120), cabbage, carrot, and celery juice (page 121), celery and red onion juice (page 121), cucumber and lettuce heart juice (page 121), physalis jelly (page 124), corn-hair and fennel-seed decoction (page 127), physalis-berry decoction (page 128), strawberry-leaf decoction (page 128), barley water (page 129).

ENLARGED PROSTATE GLAND

THE ENLARGING GLAND CAUSES NARROWING OF THE URETHRA AND IMPEDES THE FLOW OF URINE. SEE MEN'S HEALTH.

IRRITABLE BLADDER

A FREQUENT URGE TO PASS URINE. SEE CYSTITIS AND URETHRITIS.

PYELONEPHRITIS

AN INFECTION OF THE KIDNEYS (ACUTE OR CHRONIC) CAUSING PAIN IN THE BACK AND LOWER ABDOMEN, FEVER, AND PAINFUL URINATION.

! ANTIBIOTICS MAY BE URGENTLY REQUIRED.

✔ Almond, artichoke, bean, blackberry, black currant, borage, cabbage, celery, cherry, cucumber, dandelion, endive, fava bean, garbanzo bean, garlic, grape, leek, lettuce, melon, onion, peach, physalis, radish, red currant, strawberry, watercress, watermelon. Drink plenty of water and onion, cabbage, celery, cucumber, watercress, grape, cranberry, cherry, and blueberry juices.

RECIPES cabbage, carrot, and blueberry juice (page 27), garbanzo bean broth (page 94), cherry and apple juice (page 120), celery and red onion juice (page 121), cucumber and lettuce heart juice (page 121), physalis jelly (page 124), corn-hair and fennel-seed decoction (page 127), physalis-berry decoction (page 128), strawberry-leaf decoction (page 128), barley water (page 129).

SUGGESTED MENUS FOR KIDNEY AND BLADDER PROBLEMS

The following menus are designed to enhance the health of the urinary tract for people who are suffering from problems such as kidney or bladder stones. The emphasis is on drinking plenty of fluids and eating foods that have diuretic and anti-inflammatory properties such as garbanzo bean, leek, and onion.

MENU 1

BREAKFAST

A bowl of cereal or porridge; a small glass of celery and carrot juice; a cup of herbal tea; grapefruit or kiwi fruit.

SNACKS

Dried fruit, such as fig, or fresh fruit rich in vitamin C, such as orange; dandelion or ginger infusion; cranberry juice.

LUNCH

Zucchini cake (page 105) and broiled fish with rice and cucumber; barley water (page 129); melon with fresh mint.

DINNER

Buckwheat with leek sauce (page 105); blueberries and cottage cheese (page 43); lettuce-seed or thyme infusion.

MENU 2

BREAKFAST

A boiled egg with rye bread; a juice (celery and onion, or green bean, lettuce, and garlic); live yogurt; a cup of herbal tea.

SNACKS

Dried fruit, especially raisin and fig; fresh fruit, such as black currant, blueberry and pear; barley water (page 129).

LUNCH

Onions in cider (page 111) with a slice of roast meat, bread, and a little table mustard; a cucumber salad; a piece of fruit.

DINNER

Garbanzo bean broth (page 94) with bread; barley water (page 129); thyme or camomile infusion.

nervous system, mind, and emotions

STAR FOODS FOR THE NERVOUS SYSTEM: APPLE, APRICOT, ASPARAGUS, AVOCADO, BANANA, BEET, CABBAGE, CAMOMILE, CELERY, DILL SEED, FISH, GREENS, LEGUMES, LETTUCE, NUTS, OAT, PEACH, POTATO, PUMPKIN, QUINCE, SHELLFISH, UNREFINED CEREALS.

Good stress management, relaxation, meditation, and open-air exercise combined with small dietary changes can alleviate many symptoms of common nervous system disorders. Foods that have a calming effect on the nervous system are those that are rich in vitamin B, folic acid, magnesium, potassium, zinc, selenium, and manganese. Try to eat plenty of fish, greens, legumes, nuts, potatoes, and unrefined cereals. Increase your intake of proteins and cut down on alcohol, coffee, and tea. Drink infusions of camomile, lemon verbena, lemon balm, limeflower, olive-tree leaf, orange blossom, or valerian. Bear in mind that problems such as irritability and poor concentration—as well as headaches and dizziness—may be caused by mild hypoglycemia, in which case you should eat regular carbohydrate-based meals or snacks. (N.B. To make a medicinal infusion, steep 1 tablespoon of the dried ingredient in a cup of boiling water for 10 minutes.)

ANXIETY

FEELINGS OF FEAR ARE ASSOCIATED WITH TENSION, SWEATING, PALPITATIONS, INSOMNIA, AND LOSS OF APPETITE.

✔ Almond, apple, apricot, basil, bean, beet, celery, eggplant, legumes, lemon balm, lettuce, peach, quince. Drink fresh apple, apricot, cucumber, lettuce, or peach juices and aniseed, basil, camomile, lemon-balm, lettuce-seed, limeflower, rosemary, or thyme infusions. Eat more carbohydrates. Eating sugary snacks may reduce anxiety—this should be an occasional measure only.

✘ Coffee, cola drinks, tea.

RECIPES lemon-balm and camomile infusion (page 126), sparkling lemon-balm infusion (page 127), lettuce-seed decoction (page 128), camomile and citrus wine (page 131), asparagus syrup (page 133).

DEPRESSION

A NEGATIVE MENTAL STATE ASSOCIATED WITH A BROAD SPECTRUM OF PHYSICAL SYMPTOMS.

✔ Oats, walnuts, fresh fruit and vegetables that are rich in vitamin B complex. *SEE ALSO* Anxiety.

✘ Alcohol.

HEADACHES AND MIGRAINE

OFTEN CAUSED BY LOCAL MUSCLE TENSION OR STRESS; MIGRAINES ARE SEVERE, PROLONGED HEADACHES THAT MAY BE TRIGGERED BY CERTAIN FOODS, HORMONAL FLUCTUATIONS, OR HYPOGLYCEMIA.

✔ Almond, anise, basil, cabbage, camomile, cherry, chive, fava bean, fennel, ginger, lemon balm, mint, oily fish, onion, peach, rosemary, white meat. Eat plenty of fresh fruit and vegetables. Drink fresh apple, apricot, and lettuce juices or aniseed, basil, camomile, fennel-seed, lemon-balm, or mint infusions. *SEE ALSO* Anxiety.

✘ Alcohol, coffee, cheese, chocolate, food with additives, ice-cream, monosodium glutamate, sweeteners, tea.

RECIPES ginger infusion (page 127), basil liqueur (page 131), anisette (page 131), aniseed tincture (page 132).

INSOMNIA

A PATTERN OF PERSISTENT SLEEPING DIFFICULTY, EITHER WITH PROBLEMS FALLING ASLEEP OR FREQUENTLY INTERRUPTED SLEEP.

✔ Basil, barley, camomile, corn, eggplant, fennel, lettuce, lime blossom, marjoram, onion, pumpkin, zucchini. Eat a carbohydrate snack 20 minutes before you go to bed. *SEE ALSO* Anxiety.

✘ Coffee, cola drinks, tea.

RECIPES lime-blossom infusion (page 54), mango juice (page 120), marjoram infusion (page 125), lemon-balm and camomile infusion (page 126), sparkling lemon-balm infusion (page 127), camomile and citrus wine (page 131), camomile aperitif (page 131), asparagus syrup (page 133).

IRRITABILITY AND STRESS

SYMPTOMS SUCH AS ANXIETY, POOR CONCENTRATION, AND INSOMNIA ARE OFTEN COMBINED WITH PHYSICAL SYMPTOMS SUCH AS DIGESTIVE DISTURBANCES AND SOMETIMES HIGH BLOOD PRESSURE.

✔ *SEE* Anxiety, Insomnia, Heart and Circulation, Digestive System.

MENTAL FATIGUE

LACK OF MENTAL FOCUS AND POOR CONCENTRATION AND MEMORY.

✔ Fruit and vegetables (especially apricots and carrots), mint, royal jelly, shellfish, foods rich in vitamin B (greens and unrefined cereals), zinc and selenium. Drink apricot, cherry, and grape juices and basil and mint infusions. *SEE ALSO* Anxiety, Insomnia.

✘ Excessive amounts of coffee and alcohol.

MULTIPLE SCLEROSIS

CHRONIC DEGENERATIVE DISORDER OF THE NERVOUS SYSTEM.

! DO NOT STOP TAKING MEDICATION PRESCRIBED BY YOUR DOCTOR.

✔ Buckwheat, corn, fresh fruit and vegetables, legumes, millet. Eat more oily fish and cold-pressed vegetable oils, such as sunflower seed and olive oil. Drink fresh apple, apricot, cabbage, grape, or lettuce juices or aniseed, basil, camomile, fennel-seed, lemon-balm, or mint infusions. Take evening primrose oil daily.

✘ Dairy products, gluten, meat.

RECIPES ginger infusion (page 127).

NEURALGIA

SEE HEADACHES AND MIGRAINE.

VERTIGO

DIZZINESS AND LOSS OF BALANCE, SOMETIMES WITH NAUSEA.

! MAY INDICATE A SERIOUS PROBLEM—CONSULT YOUR DOCTOR.

✔ Basil, fennel, lemon balm, orange, mint, sage, thyme. *SEE ALSO* general advice on the care of the nervous system.

SUGGESTED MENU FOR STRESS-RELATED SYMPTOMS

The following menu is designed for someone suffering from mild anxiety, depression, poor concentration, headaches, or mild insomnia.

MENU 1

BREAKFAST

A bowl of porridge; a small glass of carrot juice; herbal infusions such as lemon balm or camomile; a banana.

SNACKS

Dried fruit, such as raisins or figs; fresh fruit rich in vitamin C, such as orange; nuts; herbal infusions.

LUNCH

Broiled meat, beans with carrots and onions (page 112), rice with cucumber balls (page 111), or grated celery root and carrot salad (page 100); fruit salad with lemon balm (page 115).

DINNER

Broiled salmon with eggplant sauce (page 105); banana and date salad (page 114); lettuce-seed, camomile, or lemon-balm infusion.

immune system

STAR FOODS FOR THE IMMUNE SYSTEM: APPLE, ARTICHOKE, BASIL, BLACKBERRY, BLACK CURRANT, BLUEBERRY, CABBAGE, CAMOMILE, CARROT, CHERRY, CHIVE, CINNAMON, CLOVE, CUCUMBER, CUMIN, DANDELION, ELDER, GARLIC, GREEN BEAN, LEGUMES, LEMON, LEMON BALM, LEEK, LIVE YOGURT, MINT, OILY FISH, PEAR, RASPBERRY, RED ONION, RED CURRANT, SHELLFISH, THYME, UNREFINED CEREALS, WATERCRESS, WATERMELON.

The immune system protects the body from invasion and infection by bacteria, viruses, and other microbes. Allergies occur when the immune system over-reacts to a substance. Regular exercise and a healthy diet strengthen the immune system—poor nutrition, alcohol, drugs, and stress weaken it.

To boost your immune system, try to cut down on your intake of alcohol and animal fat and eliminate from your diet any foods that you suspect may be causing an allergy—the most common culprits are citrus fruit, corn, eggs, milk and cheese, nuts, pork, processed tomatoes, shellfish, wheat, and food containing monosodium glutamate or any additives.

Three categories of foods strengthen the immune system:
1) anti-infective: basil, blackberries, blueberries, cinnamon, cloves, cumin, garlic, juniper, lemon, thyme, and live yogurt, which is rich in lactobacilli.
2) anti-inflammatory: apple, artichoke, black currants, cabbage, camomile, cherries, cucumber, elder, lemon balm, mint, oily fish, pears, raspberries, red currants, watercress, watermelon.
3) diuretic and depurative: artichoke, chives, dandelion, green beans, leeks, onions.

Greens are rich in vitamins, beta-carotene, minerals, and trace elements, which help to maintain a healthy immune system. Red, green, and yellow vegetables and fruit contain antioxidants that help prevent the deterioration of immunity. Oily fish contains an oil that has important anti-inflammatory

properties. Fresh raw fruit and vegetables are the best source of vitamin C; and legumes, shellfish, and unrefined cereal provide zinc, an important immuno-stimulant.
(N.B. To make a medicinal infusion, steep 1 tablespoon of the dried ingredient in a cup of boiling water for 10 minutes.)

CANDIDA

A LOW-LEVEL INFECTION CAUSED BY THE PROLIFERATION OF *CANDIDA ALBICANS*. THIS CAN OCCUR WHEN THE BALANCE OF THE INTESTINAL FLORA IS DISTURBED AFTER TAKING ANTIBIOTICS OR IMMUNO-SUPPRESSANTS, OR FOLLOWING COMPROMISED IMMUNITY.

✔ Blueberry, garlic, live yogurt, pickled turnip; infusions of cumin seed, thyme, fennel, and aniseed. Follow the detox on pages 136–139. *SEE ALSO* general advice on the care of the immune and digestive systems.
RECIPES fennel infusion (page 125), marjoram infusion (page 125).

COMMON COLD

A VIRAL INFECTION CAUSING WATERY DISCHARGE FROM THE NOSE, SLIGHT FEVER, SORE THROAT, AND COUGH. RECURRENT COLDS ARE USUALLY A SIGN OF A WEAK IMMUNE SYSTEM.

✔ Basil, blackberry, blueberry, chili, chive, cinnamon, clove, cumin, garlic, ginger, juniper, lemon, live yogurt, onion, orange, peppercorns, rosemary, scallion, shellfish, thyme, unrefined cereal. Eat plenty of fresh, raw fruit and vegetables, especially those that are red, green, or yellow in color. Drink fresh blackberry, carrot, lemon, or orange juice.

RECIPES garlic and sage soup (page 57), chive and ginger broth (page 96), elder and camomile infusion (page 126).

INFLUENZA

MANAGEMENT, SEE COMMON COLD.

LARYNGITIS

SEE SORE THROAT.

POST-VIRAL FATIGUE

CHRONIC ILLNESS CHARACTERIZED BY LOW ENERGY LEVELS AND POOR CONCENTRATION. USUALLY FOLLOWS A VIRAL ILLNESS.

✔ Fresh apricot, beet, blueberry, cabbage, carrot, cherry, or grape juices and basil, mint, or thyme infusions. *SEE ALSO* Anemia (page 71), Mental fatigue (page 85), general advice on the care of the immune system and detoxification (pages 136–139).

RECIPES garlic tincture (page 56).

SINUSITIS

AN INFLAMMATION OF THE SINUSES, CAUSED BY RECURRENT COLDS OR FOLLOWING AN UPPER RESPIRATORY TRACT INFECTION. CHRONIC SINUSITIS MAY ALSO BE CAUSED BY AN ALLERGY. SEE COMMON COLD.

SORE THROAT

A COMMON SYMPTOM RESULTING FROM COLDS, LARYNGITIS, PHARYNGITIS, OR TONSILLITIS.

✔ Bay leaf, blackberry, black currant, blueberry, borage, carrot, celery, chervil, clove, fig, garlic, honey, juniper berry, leek, lemon, mâche, onion, peppercorns, nettle, rosemary, savory, thyme, vinegar. *SEE ALSO* general advice on the care of the immune system and the respiratory system.

RECIPES almond milk (page 79), marjoram infusion (page 125), leek syrup (page 132), black radish syrup (page 132).

TONSILLITIS

AN ACUTE INFLAMMATION OF THE TONSILS, MOST FREQUENT IN CHILDREN.

✔ A thyme infusion with honey and lemon juice may help to soothe the pain. *SEE ALSO* Common cold, Influenza, Sore throat.

RECIPES red currant, blackberry, and blueberry juice (page 120), leek syrup (page 132), black radish syrup (page 132).

SUGGESTED MENUS FOR THE IMMUNE SYSTEM

The following menus are designed to enhance the health of the immune system and prevent illness.

MENU 1

BREAKFAST

Live yogurt with kiwi fruit; a small glass of carrot juice; a cup of dandelion root coffee or a herbal infusion such as lemon balm or camomile.

SNACKS

Fresh fruit rich in vitamin C; nuts; herbal infusions.

LUNCH

Grated celery root and carrot salad (page 100); dandelion, bacon and potato cakes (page 108); lychee fruit salad (page 114).

DINNER

Spinach with green beans; camomile or lemon-balm infusion.

MENU 2

BREAKFAST

A boiled egg with wholemeal bread; a glass of carrot juice.

SNACKS

Dried fruit or nuts; dandelion infusion.

LUNCH

Mediterranean bean salad (page 98); boiled fish; fruit salad.

DINNER

Nettle or watercress soup (page 96); cottage cheese with blueberries (page 43); elderflower and camomile infusion.

skin, hair, and nails

STAR FOODS FOR SKIN, HAIR, AND NAILS: ALL RED, YELLOW, OR GREEN FRUIT AND CABBAGE, CAMOMILE, CARROT, CHERVIL, DANDELION, GREENS, OILY FISH, OLIVE, SHELLFISH, WATERCRESS.

To improve or control a skin condition, try following a detox program such as the one outlined on pages 136–39. It is important to identify any foods to which you may be allergic and to eliminate them from your diet. If you smoke, make an effort to give up. You should also treat the skin externally by applying skin washes and poultices to eliminate inflammation and bacterial activity (see specific skin problems).

The following foods promote healthy skin, hair, and nails:
1) dandelion is a general detoxifier;
2) carrots and all red, yellow, or green fruit and vegetables are rich in beta-carotene and antioxidants;
3) leafy greens contain vitamins and minerals that are beneficial for the skin;
4) camomile infusion can help to relieve stress (which may exacerbate skin problems). It can also be used as a skin wash;
5) shellfish and oily fish contain essential fatty acids and minerals. (N.B. To make a medicinal infusion, steep 1 tablespoon of the dried ingredient in a cup of boiling water for 10 minutes.)

ACNE

A SKIN CONDITION CHARACTERIZED BY INFLAMED SPOTS ON THE FACE, NECK, OR BACK, USUALLY RELATED TO HORMONAL FLUCTUATIONS.

✔ Foods that are rich in zinc and vitamin A. Apply cabbage leaves or juice, carrot juice, or a lettuce-seed decoction to very inflamed spots and use a camomile infusion as a face wash.

✘ Cheese, chocolate, food that is rich in iodine (such as shellfish and kelp), refined carbohydrate.

RECIPES cabbage, carrot, and blueberry juice (page 27), juniper-berry water (apply externally, see page 59), black radish and carrot juice (page 121).

BOILS AND CARBUNCLES

SEE ACNE.

DANDRUFF

A FLAKY SCALP, SOMETIMES CAUSED BY A FUNGAL INFECTION.

✔ Rinse your hair with a thyme or rosemary infusion. *SEE ALSO* general advice on the care of the skin, hair, and nails.

DERMATITIS AND ECZEMA

INFLAMMATION OF THE SKIN THAT IS OFTEN CHRONIC. SORES MAY BE DRY AND ITCHY OR WEEPING.

✔ Artichoke, carrot, chervil, cucumber, dandelion, all greens, grape, melon, oily fish, raspberry, salsify. An application of olive or walnut oil is effective in relieving dry skin. A camomile or thyme infusion can be used as a skin wash to reduce inflammation and prevent bacterial activity.

✘ Alcohol and spicy food. Reduce your intake of dairy products, meat, processed food and any other suspected allergens.

RECIPES cabbage, carrot, and blueberry juice (page 27), juniper-berry water (apply externally, see page 59), black radish and carrot juice (page 121), dandelion infusion (page 125).

FUNGAL INFECTIONS

AN IRRITATION OF THE SKIN BETWEEN THE TOES OR FINGERS, AROUND THE GROIN, OR ON THE SCALP.

✔ Use a thyme infusion to bathe or wash the affected area.

SEE ALSO general care of the immune system.

PSORIASIS

A CONDITION CAUSING AN EXCESSIVE PRODUCTION OF NEW SKIN CELLS. THIS RESULTS IN SORE, SCALY PATCHES ON THE SKIN. TENDS TO RUN IN FAMILIES.

! STRESS IS KNOWN TO AGGRAVATE AND EVEN TRIGGER PSORIASIS.

✔ Eat plenty of oily fish and increase your exposure to sunlight.

SEE ALSO Irritability and Stress (page 85).

✘ Animal fat and dairy products.

ROSACEA

A CHRONIC INFLAMMATION OF THE FACE CAUSING RED AREAS TO APPEAR ON THE CHEEKS, NOSE, FOREHEAD, AND CHIN.

! THE CONDITION IS EXACERBATED BY ALCOHOL AND STRESS.

✔ Try following a dairy-free diet. Use a camomile infusion as an anti-inflammatory face wash. A thyme infusion or cabbage or lettuce leaves applied to the affected area can also help to reduce the inflammation.

✘ Alcohol and spicy food.

RECIPES cabbage, carrot, and blueberry juice (page 27), black radish and carrot juice (page 121).

URTICARIA (HIVES)

RAISED RED, ITCHY PATCHES CAUSE BY AN ALLERGIC REACTION AND AGGRAVATED BY STRESS.

! THIS CONDITION MAY BE A REACTION TO A PRESCRIPTION DRUG — CONSULT YOUR DOCTOR. HIVES CAN BE DANGEROUS IF THE MOUTH, LIPS, OR TONGUE ARE AFFECTED.

✔ Artichoke, carrot, cucumber, dandelion, greens (especially nettle and watercress), radish, watermelon. Drink camomile or lemon-balm infusions. Use a mixture of equal amounts of camomile and peppermint infusion as a skin wash.

✘ Try to identify and eliminate the cause of the allergy (for example strawberries or shellfish). Avoid alcohol, animal fat, dairy products, eggs, stimulants, and wheat for a few days.

RECIPES lemon-balm and camomile infusion (page 126), sparkling lemon-balm infusion (page 127).

women's health

For specific conditions affecting women's health, see below. For lactating mothers, fennel is recommended, as it is thought to stimulate the baby's appetite and prevent colic and digestive problems; dill weed enhances the flavour of breast milk. (N.B. To make a medicinal infusion, steep 1 tablespoon of the dried ingredient in a cup of boiling water for 10 minutes.)

AMENORRHEA

IRREGULAR OR ABSENT MENSES. MAY BE CAUSED BY HORMONAL IMBALANCE, STRESS, OVER-EXERCISE, RAPID WEIGHT LOSS, OR ANOREXIA.

✔ Anise, dill, dried fruit, fennel, greens, liver, parsley, red meat, sage, yeast extract. Drink fresh apricot, broccoli, or spinach juice and aniseed, fennel-seed, or sage infusion.

RECIPES apricot, lime, and mint juice (page 119), broccoli and green bean juice (page 121), fennel infusion (page 125), carrot seed infusion (page 126), coriander-seed infusion (page 127), corn-hair and fennel-seed decoction (page 127), dill-seed decoction (page 128), fennel-seed decoction (page 128), anisette (page 131), aniseed tincture (page 132), coriander-seed tincture (page 132).

CYSTITIS

SEE KIDNEYS AND BLADDER.

DIGESTIVE PROBLEMS DURING PREGNANCY

PROBLEMS SUCH AS HEARTBURN, SLUGGISH DIGESTION, HYPER-ACIDITY, AND INDIGESTION ARE COMMON DURING PREGNANCY.

✔ Apple, banana, carrot, fig, germinated barley, ginger, papaya, peach, pineapple, potato, zucchini. Eat small, frequent meals. Drink apple, carrot, peach, or pineapple juice; and basil, camomile, fennel-seed, or lemon-balm infusion. SEE ALSO Constipation.

✘ Avoid fatty and processed foods.

RECIPES fennel infusion (page 125), lemon-balm and camomile infusion (page 126), corn-hair and fennel-seed decoction (page 127), sparkling lemon-balm infusion (page 127), ginger infusion (page 127), fennel-seed decoction (page 128), barley water (page 129).

ENDOMETRIOSIS

INFLAMMATION RESULTING FROM FRAGMENTS OF THE ENDOMETRIUM MIGRATING IN THE PELVIS AND AROUND THE INTESTINES CAUSING A WIDE VARIETY OF SYMPTOMS INCLUDING PAINFUL MENSES AND SHARP PAIN IN THE PELVIS DURING INTERCOURSE. SEE PREMENSTRUAL SYNDROME AND PAINFUL MENSES.

FLUID RETENTION

SOME WOMEN SUFFER FROM FLUID RETENTION PRIOR TO MENSTRUATION OR DURING PREGNANCY.

✔ Drink barley infusion. Leek and onion are good diuretics.
RECIPES barley infusion (page 126)

IRREGULAR MENSES

SEE AMENORRHEA.

MENOPAUSAL SYMPTOMS

THE HORMONAL CHANGES ASSOCIATED WITH THE MENOPAUSE (CESSATION OF MENSES AROUND THE AGE OF 50) GIVE RISE TO A RANGE OF SYMPTOMS INCLUDING HOT FLASHES AND MOOD SWINGS.

✔ Foods rich in calcium and manganese: avocado, bean curd, cottage cheese, chestnut, date, fig, greens, live yogurt, nut, soy, tea, unrefined cereals. Foods rich in boron: almond, raisin, prune, soy. Food rich in B vitamins (pages 140–141). Drink fresh cabbage, cherry, grape, grapefruit, and watercress juice and aniseed, camomile, cumin-seed, lemon-balm, and sage infusion, and live yogurt drinks.
RECIPES cabbage, carrot, and blueberry juice (page 27), cherry and apple juice (page 120), cherry and raspberry juice (page 120), lemon-balm and camomile infusion (page 126), sparkling lemon-balm infusion (page 127), cumin-seed decoction (page 128), anisette (page 131), aniseed tincture (page 132).

MORNING SICKNESS

NAUSEA, AND SOMETIMES VOMITING, IS A COMMON SYMPTOM IN THE FIRST TRIMESTER OF PREGNANCY.

✔ Eat small, frequent meals and increase your intake of carbohydrate (bean, bread, chestnut, pasta, and rice). Drinking

fennel, ginger, or peppermint infusions or eating a small amount of candied ginger can help alleviate nausea.
RECIPES fennel infusion (page 125), ginger infusion (page 127).

PAINFUL MENSES

PAIN IN THE LOWER ABDOMEN DURING MENSES.

✔ Aniseed, dill weed and sage have hormone-like properties— drink as infusions. The following are powerful antispasmodics and analgesics and are excellent as infusions for abdominal cramps and pain: bay leaf, camomile, chive and scallion, coriander seed, fennel, mint, onion and shallot, rosemary, saffron, tarragon.
RECIPES tarragon-infused oil (apply externally, see page 52), raspberry-leaf infusion (page 125), lemon-balm and camomile infusion (page 126), coriander-seed infusion (page 127), dill-seed decoction (page 128).

PREGNANCY (GENERAL WELL-BEING)

GOOD NUTRITION IS IMPORTANT FOR THE HEALTH OF BOTH MOTHER AND BABY DURING PREGNANCY.

✔ Eat foods rich in iron and folic acid, such as dried fruit and dark, leafy greens, including watercress, spinach, and broccoli) on a daily basis, plus beet, blackberry, celery, fennel root, germinated legumes, live yogurt, red meat, and unrefined cereals. Drink 6 cups of mineral water daily, plus fresh apple, apricot, beet, cabbage, grape, green-bean, lettuce, or watercress juice and camomile, fennel, lime-blossom flower, or mint infusion.

✘ Alcohol and fast or processed food. Do not smoke.
RECIPES cabbage, carrot, and blueberry juice (page 27), apple and raspberry juice (page 119), apricot, lime, and mint juice (page 119), cherry and apple juice (page 120), green-bean and garlic juice (page 121), beet and celery juice (page 121), lettuce and basil juice (page 121), fennel infusion (page 125), raspberry-leaf infusion (page 125), lemon-balm and camomile infusion (page 126), ginger infusion (page 127), fennel-seed decoction (page 128).

PREMENSTRUAL SYNDROME (PMS)

A VARIETY OF PHYSICAL AND EMOTIONAL SYMPTOMS OCCURRING A FEW DAYS BEFORE MENSES IS DUE, INCLUDING CONSTIPATION, FATIGUE, FLUID RETENTION, IRRITABILITY, LOWER ABDOMINAL PAIN AND DISTENSION, AND MOOD SWINGS.

✔ Increase your intake of fruit and vegetables rich in vitamin B6, calcium, magnesium, manganese, and zinc (pages 142–143). Eat small, frequent meals rich in carbohydrates (bean, bread, chestnut, pasta, and rice), and root vegetables. Aniseed, dill weed, and sage have hormone-like properties—drink as infusions; tarragon and mint are powerful antispasmodics and analgesics and are excellent as infusions for abdominal cramps. Barley contains an amino acid that may help to relieve PMS. *SEE ALSO* general advice on the care of the nervous system, and Irritability and Stress (page 85).

✘ Fatty or salty foods, stimulants such as coffee, cola drinks, and tea. Reduce your consumption of dairy products.

RECIPES celery and red onion juice (page 121), cucumber and lettuce heart juice (page 121), lettuce and basil juice (page 121), lemon-balm and camomile infusion (page 126), sparkling lemon-balm infusion (page 127).

THRUSH

A VAGINAL INFECTION RESULTING IN SORENESS AND DISCHARGE. SEE CANDIDA (PAGE 86). DOUCHE WITH CAMOMILE AND THYME INFUSION.

men's health

ENLARGED PROSTATE

A COMMON CONDITION IN MEN OVER 45. DIFFICULTY URINATING IN THE MORNING IS AN EARLY SYMPTOM OF AN ENLARGED PROSTATE.

! CANCER IS A RELATIVELY COMMON, TREATABLE CAUSE. SEEK MEDICAL ADVICE IF YOU HAVE SYMPTOMS OF AN ENLARGED PROSTATE.

✔ Bean curd, bread, chicken, corn, dried fig, egg, fish, greens, live yogurt, nettle, nut, pumpkin seed, pumpkin-seed oil, soy, and foods rich in zinc (page 143). The following remedy may help: Mix equal amounts of almond, Brazil nut, cucumber seed, flaxseed, peanut, pumpkin seed, sesame seed, soy bean, and walnut. Make into a paste. Take 2 tablespoons daily.

PROSTATITIS

SEE ENLARGED PROSTATE AND ADVICE ON THE IMMUNE SYSTEM.

✔ Infusions of juniper berries or blueberries.

children's health

Most of the advice given in this chapter also applies to children, with the exception of alcohol-based preparations.

ANXIETY, FEAR, NIGHTMARES

✔ Infusions of camomile, lemon balm, or linden in the evening.

RECIPES lemon-balm and camomile infusion (page 126), sparkling lemon-balm infusion (page 127).

CHICKENPOX

SEE MEASLES.

CONSTIPATION

SEE DIGESTIVE SYSTEM.

✔ For infants, use puréed boiled carrot or cooked apple.

RECIPES peach syrup (page 132).

DIARRHEA

SEE DIGESTIVE SYSTEM.

✔ Blueberry, boiled carrot, and rice water (see Rice; page 35) are the safest dietary remedies for children.

MEASLES AND RUBELLA

HIGHLY CONTAGIOUS VIRAL INFECTIONS CHARACTERIZED BY FEVER AND A SKIN RASH.

✔ Blackberry, celery, cherry, cucumber, onion, and thyme help reduce fever and fight infection. Camomile tea can be used as a skin wash to calm down itching and irritation. Olive oil mixed with 3 per cent of lavender essential oil is also helpful for skin rashes.

RECIPES cabbage, carrot, and blueberry juice (page 27), black radish and carrot juice (page 121), cherry-stem decoction (page 127), cherry-stem and apple decoction (page 128).

WHOOPING COUGH

SEE RESPIRATORY SYSTEM.

chapter three

healing recipes

Incorporating medicinal foods into our diet is a perfect opportunity for creative and delicious cooking. The recipes on the following pages range from quick and unusual dishes that boost good health to recipes for medicinal drinks, tinctures, and syrups that target specific ailments (bear in mind that some of the wines and liqueurs need to be prepared in advance). To find ways of using a particular medicinal food, start with the food—by looking in Chapter One of the book where you will find references to the recipes in this section. To find a dish or a remedy that will alleviate a particular ailment, start with the ailment—by looking under the appropriate body system in Chapter Two where beneficial recipes are recommended. Or simply browse through the recipes to devise your own health-giving menu.

soups and salads

The following recipes serve 4 people unless otherwise stated. Where possible, harvest your own ingredients or use fresh, organic produce. Take care to wash ingredients thoroughly.

SOUPS

croutons

1 clove of garlic
4 thick slices of bread, 1 day old at least
Olive oil

Rub the garlic on the bread, then dice the bread and fry lightly in olive oil. Leave to drain on paper towels for a few minutes.

fava bean soup *(right)*

3¼ pounds fresh or dried fava beans
2 tablespoons olive oil
1 red onion, finely chopped
2 cups fresh chervil, parsley or arugula, chopped
8¾ cups cold water
Salt and pepper
To serve: croutons (recipe above)

Soak the dried fava beans according to the instructions on the packet. In a saucepan, heat the olive oil and add the onion. Cover and sweat slowly for 10 minutes over gentle heat. Add the fava beans, chervil, and water. Bring to a boil and simmer until the beans are cooked. Blend the soup, add salt and pepper, and serve hot with croutons.

herbal broth

2 cups sorrel leaves, finely chopped
1 cup lettuce leaves, finely chopped
1 cup Swiss chard leaves, finely chopped
1 cup fresh chervil, finely chopped
½ cup leeks, chopped
Salt to taste
6¼ cups water
1 tablespoon olive oil

Blend all the ingredients. Transfer the mixture to a saucepan. Bring to a boil, and then simmer for 20 minutes or until cooked.

borscht

½ green or white cabbage
½ red cabbage
2 red beets, peeled
6¼ cups stock (meat or vegetable)
1 parsnip, peeled and halved
1 large carrot, peeled and halved
A few cumin seeds
3 tablespoons tomato paste
2 tablespoons red wine vinegar
Salt and pepper
To serve: sour cream or yogurt

Chop the cabbage and one of the beets into thin strips. In a large saucepan, bring the stock to a boil and add the cabbage, beet strips, parsnip, carrot, cumin, and tomato paste. Cover and simmer for approximately 1 hour, adding more stock if necessary. Remove the parsnip and carrot from the broth (if they have not already disintegrated), mash with a fork, and return to the saucepan. Using a juicer, extract the juice from the remaining beet. Add the juice, vinegar, salt and pepper to the broth. Serve with a little sour cream or yogurt.

garbanzo bean broth

Boiling garbanzo beans and barley together produces a medicinal decoction that has diuretic properties and can be drunk as a treatment for cystitis and edema. Simply drain off the cooking water after 30 minutes and store in the refrigerator. Fill up the pan with water and continue cooking. The finished broth is bland in taste and excellent for babies or people recovering from illness.

Generous 1 cup garbanzo beans, soaked and allowed to germinate (this
   may take up to 48 hours)
Scant 1 cup pot barley
4 cups water
Salt and pepper
2 cups fresh parsley, chopped

Boil the garbanzo beans and the barley in the water for 60 minutes or until thoroughly cooked. Season with salt and pepper. Add the parsley and leave to infuse for 10 minutes. Blend and serve.

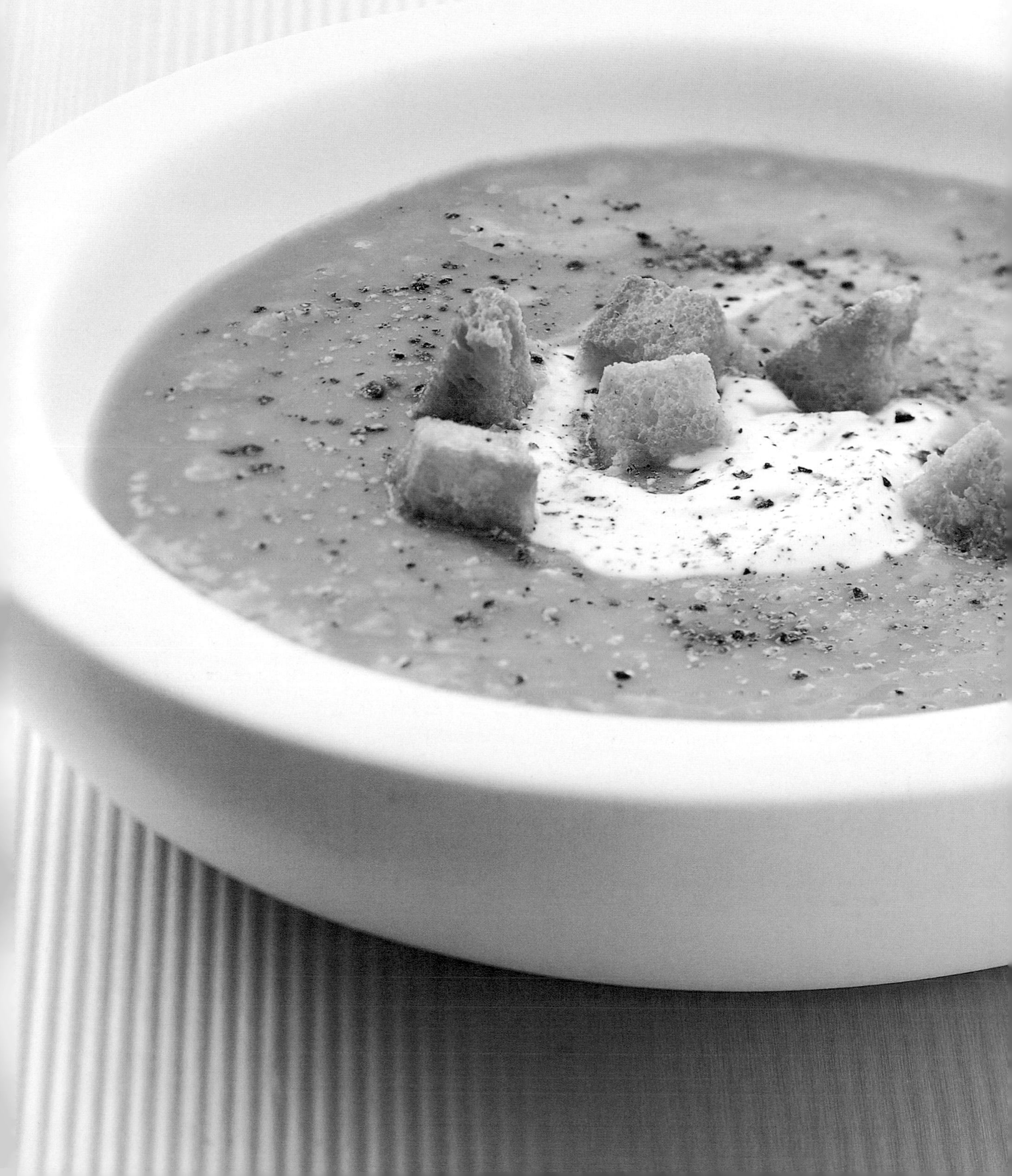

chive and ginger broth *(below)*

1 bunch of chives or 8 scallions, trimmed
1 clove
2-inch piece ginger root, peeled and sliced
2 cloves of garlic
5 black peppercorns
Small root of Chinese angelica, chopped
4 cups water

Boil all the ingredients in the water for 15 minutes and serve hot. Chicken pieces can be added to this broth—put the raw pieces in the broth and simmer for 30 minutes.

nettle soup

Harvest fresh, young nettle tops from nettles growing away from busy paths and polluted areas.

1¼ pounds potatoes, peeled and chopped
11 ounces nettle tops (leaves and stems)
Salt and pepper
5 tablespoons olive oil
2 tablespoons finely chopped fresh chervil or parsley
To serve: croutons (see page 94)

In a large pan, cover the potatoes with cold water. Bring to a boil and then simmer for about 20 minutes or until cooked. Add the nettles and simmer for 5-8 minutes. Season with salt and pepper. In a food processor, blend the soup, then stir in the olive oil and chervil or parsley. Serve hot with croutons.

lentil soup

You can use germinated lentils for this recipe. Buy whole lentils that are green on the outside and red inside rather than split red lentils. Soak them in cold water for 24 hours, then strain, rinse with cold water, and place in a flat dish. Cover the lentils with a wet cloth and leave them in a well-ventilated place for a further 24 hours to allow the shoots to grow. Leave the lentils for 48 hours for even longer shoots.

1¾ cups germinated lentils or non-germinated split red lentils
Chicken or vegetable stock (enough to cover the lentils)
3 red onions, chopped
2 tomatoes, chopped
4 cloves of garlic, crushed
2 tablespoons dill weed
Pepper
A little sour cream, cottage cheese, or yogurt

Steam the lentils for 20 minutes and then cover with chicken or vegetable stock, and simmer for a further 20 minutes. Meanwhile, steam the onions, tomatoes, and garlic, for 5 minutes and then blend in a food processor. Add the onion mixture to the simmering lentils, together with the dill weed and pepper. Simmer for a further 5 minutes and then serve immediately with a little sour cream, cottage cheese, or yogurt.

SALADS

vinaigrette dressing

1 or 2 cloves of garlic (or to taste)
2 tablespoons lemon juice
4 tablespoons olive oil
Salt and pepper

Crush the garlic, mix with the lemon juice, and then stir in the olive oil. Season with salt and pepper and then pour the dressing over the salad. Vinaigrette can be made very quickly by blending the ingredients.

avocado dressing

2 avocados, peeled and pitted
1 clove of garlic
Lemon juice to taste
1 tablespoon Dijon mustard
1 tablespoon finely chopped fresh parsley
Salt and pepper

Blend the ingredients and use as an alternative to mayonnaise or vinaigrette.

pepper and eggplant salad

1 green bell pepper, halved
1 red bell pepper, halved
1 yellow bell pepper, halved
1¼ pounds eggplants, chopped in small pieces
Salt
Juice of half a lemon
2 shallots, finely chopped
9 ounces tomatoes, quartered
Vinaigrette dressing
2 tablespoons finely chopped fresh basil or mint

Under a preheated broiler, char the bell peppers. When the skin has turned black put the bell peppers in a plastic bag and seal it. When cool enough to handle, rub off the skin and slice the bell peppers thinly. Lightly cook the eggplants in salted, boiling water with the lemon juice until tender. Drain the eggplants and mix with the bell peppers, shallots, and tomatoes. Toss in the vinaigrette and sprinkle with the basil or mint. Chill in the refrigerator for 2 hours before serving.

carrot and strawberry salad

This salad goes well with cilantro dressing.

3 tablespoons olive oil
Juice of 1 small lemon
4 cups grated carrot
2¾ cups strawberries, chopped
Thin strips of lemon zest
To garnish: 3 strawberries

Mix the olive oil and lemon juice in a bowl. Add the carrots and strawberries. Garnish with the 3 strawberries and the lemon zest. This salad will improve if it is refrigerated for 3 hours.

cilantro dressing

1 tablespoon finely chopped cilantro
1¼ cups live natural yogurt
Salt and pepper

Mix the cilantro with the yogurt, season with salt and pepper.

mediterranean bean salad *(below)*

1 cup dried navy beans, borlotti beans, or black-eyed peas
Pinch of ground cinnamon
1 onion, finely chopped
2 tomatoes, chopped
½ cup black olives
1 clove
Salt and pepper
4 tablespoons olive oil
1 tablespoon chopped fresh mint leaves
To serve: garlic bread

Soak the beans according to the instructions on the packet, then put them in cold water, bring to a boil, and simmer for about 2 hours with the cinnamon. Drain the beans and mix them with all the other ingredients, except the mint leaves. Sprinkle the mint leaves on top of the salad and refrigerate for as long as possible (up to 12 hours). Serve with garlic bread.

radish and kumquat salad *(below right)*

Large bunch of radishes, tops removed
2 oranges
12 kumquats
Lemon juice to taste
Pinch of salt
Sugar or clear honey to taste (optional)

Slice the radishes and oranges and mix in a salad bowl. Slice the kumquats in half lengthwise and add to bowl. Sprinkle on a little lemon juice and salt. Refrigerate and toss before serving. Sugar or honey can be added to taste.

fennel and radicchio salad

2 fennel bulbs, finely chopped
Radicchio leaves--one-third vinegar or lemon juice and two-thirds olive oil)

Mix the fennel and radicchio leaves in a large salad bowl. Sprinkle with vinaigrette immediately prior to serving.

green bean salad

1¼ pounds green beans
¼ cup hazelnuts, chopped
3 tablespoons vinaigrette (page 97)
½ lettuce
2 tablespoons chopped fresh parsley or chervil

In boiling, salted water cook the green beans until al dente. When they are ready, plunge them into cold water, then drain. Roast the hazelnuts in a skillet without oil. Toss the beans in the vinaigrette and place them on a bed of lettuce. Sprinkle the hazelnuts, together with the parsley, over the beans.

grated celery root and carrot salad

11 ounces celery root, peeled and grated or cut into matchsticks
11 ounces carrots, peeled and grated or cut into matchsticks
A few tablespoons avocado dressing (page 97)
2 tablespoons finely chopped fresh chervil or parsley

In boiling, salted water blanch the celery root for 5 seconds and drain. Mix together the celery root and raw carrot and toss in the mayonnaise (use just enough to coat the vegetables). Refrigerate for 2 hours, garnish with the chervil or parsley, and serve.

young turnip salad *(below)*

This salad goes well with thin slices of smoked fish.

2¼ pounds young turnips, peeled
2¼ cups chicken or vegetable stock
3 tablespoons finely chopped fresh chives
3 tablespoons finely chopped fresh tarragon
3 tablespoons finely chopped fresh chervil
2 tablespoons olive oil
1 tablespoon lemon juice

In boiling, salted water blanch the turnips for 2 minutes. Drain and then cook further in the stock for 10–15 minutes. Drain and cool. Place the turnips in a serving dish and sprinkle over the chives, tarragon, and chervil. Mix the olive oil and lemon juice together and pour over the turnips. Gently toss the salad and serve warm.

escarole salad

1 escarole (or any type of salad greens)
A few radishes, tops removed
¾ cup pitted black olives
A few anchovies (optional)
3 tomatoes, quartered
1 shallot, finely chopped
2 tablespoons finely chopped fresh chives
2 tablespoons finely chopped fresh tarragon
4 tablespoons vinaigrette dressing (page 97)
5 ounces hard goat cheese, feta cheese, or mozzarella

In a bowl, put the escarole, radishes, olives, anchovies, tomatoes, shallot, chives, and tarragon. Add the vinaigrette, toss gently, and sprinkle over the cheese. Refrigerate for 30 minutes before serving.

pineapple and cucumber salad

11 ounces cucumber, peeled and thinly sliced
Salt
11 ounces fresh pineapple, diced
2 tablespoons light mayonnaise or light cream mixed with lemon juice (optional)
A few borage leaves in vinegar (page 124), fresh borage flowers, or mint leaves

Put the cucumber into a colander, sprinkle with salt to extract the juice, and leave for 45 minutes. Rinse away the salt and squeeze the water from the cucumber. In a bowl, mix the cucumber slices and diced pineapple and refrigerate for 2 hours. Before serving, drain away excess water, toss in the mayonnaise or cream if using and decorate with the borage or mint.

warm asparagus salad

2¼ pounds fresh thick asparagus, trimmed (remove woody ends)
Salt and pepper
6 tablespoons olive oil
2 tablespoons finely chopped fresh chervil (optional)
A few capers
Parmesan cheese shavings
Balsamic vinegar

In a roasting pan, place the asparagus in a single layer (avoid overcrowding) and season well. Pour over the olive oil and roast in a preheated oven at 400°F for about 20 minutes or until tender. Carefully place the cooked asparagus on a warm serving dish and sprinkle with the chervil (if using) capers, Parmesan cheese, and a little balsamic vinegar. Serve warm.

parsley, onion, and lemon salad

Serve as a side dish with broiled fish.

2 tablespoons olive oil
1 bunch of parsley or chervil, finely chopped
1 large red onion, thinly sliced
2 lemons, peeled and diced
Salt and pepper
To serve: lettuce leaves

Mix all the ingredients in a bowl. Chill before serving. Serve on a bed of lettuce leaves.

black radish salad

1 or 2 black radishes (depending on size), peeled and sliced
Salt (to sprinkle on radish)
5 ounces Swiss cheese or a cheese of your choice, finely diced
3 tablespoons vinaigrette dressing (page 97)
2 tablespoons finely chopped fresh parsley
1 shallot, finely chopped
1 lettuce

Put the radish in a colander, sprinkle with salt to extract the juice, and leave for 45 minutes. Rinse the salt off and press down gently on the radish to squeeze out excess water. Mix the radish with some chunks of cheese in a salad bowl and add the vinaigrette. Sprinkle over the parsley and shallot, and lightly toss all the ingredients. Serve on a bed of lettuce.

cucumber salad

1 large cucumber, peeled and thinly sliced
Salt (to sprinkle on cucumber)
2 tablespoons finely chopped fresh chervil or flat-leaf parsley
1 shallot, finely chopped
¾ cup diced cooked ham or turkey
4 tablespoons vinaigrette dressing (page 97)
Salt and pepper

Put the cucumber into a colander, sprinkle with salt to extract the juice, and leave for 45 minutes. Rinse the salt off and, in a bowl, mix with the chervil or flat-leaf parsley, shallot, and cooked ham or turkey. Toss in vinaigrette, add salt and pepper to taste, and refrigerate before serving.
-

appetizers, main courses, and accompaniments

The following recipes serve 4 people unless otherwise stated. Where possible, harvest your own ingredients or use fresh, organic produce. Take care to wash ingredients thoroughly.

APPETIZERS

tabouleh *(below)*

This dish can be served as an appetizer or a main course. To serve as a main course, double the amount of bulgur wheat in the recipe and add olives, preserved lemon slices (page 47), diced cucumber, and a few chopped hard-cooked eggs.
¾ cup bulgur wheat (or couscous)

Salt and pepper
⅔ cup olive oil
Juice of 1 lemon
11 cups parsley, finely chopped
3¾ cups mint, finely chopped
3 medium shallots or scallions, chopped
To serve: ½ lettuce and 2 tomatoes, diced

Soak the bulgur wheat or couscous in warm water for about 15 minutes (or as indicated on the packet). In a sieve, drain well, pressing the grains to remove any excess water. Put the bulgur wheat or couscous in a bowl and add the salt, pepper, olive oil, and lemon juice. Allow the wheat to absorb the dressing, then add the parsley, mint, and shallots or scallions. Refrigerate for 24 hours and then serve on a bed of lettuce garnished with the tomatoes.

roman-style artichoke

This dish is also excellent served cold a day after making.

2 cups parsley, finely chopped
1 tablespoon finely chopped mint leaves
1 clove of garlic, crushed
Salt and pepper
2 tablespoons olive oil
4 medium or 8 small globe artichokes
1 cup olive oil
Juice of half a lemon

Mix the parsley and mint with the garlic, salt, pepper, and 2 tablespoons of olive oil. Rinse the artichokes in cold water. Remove the outer, damaged leaves and the middle leaves. Trim the stalks off each artichoke and remove the central "chokes" using a curved, serrated grapefruit knife. Spoon the herb mixture into the middle of each artichoke and press the remaining leaves around the mixture. In a large casserole dish, cover the artichokes with salted water and 1 cup of olive oil. Bring slowly to a boil, then transfer the casserole dish to an oven preheated to 350°F, for about 35 minutes or until cooked. Add the lemon juice and serve hot.

avocado tartar *(right)*

This can be served as a dip with carrot sticks or on toast.

2 avocados, peeled and pitted
2 shallots, finely chopped
1 tablespoon finely chopped tarragon
1 tablespoon finely chopped chervil
Juice of half a lemon
Salt and pepper

Put the ingredients in a blender and blend. Refrigerate before serving.

cottage cheese with watercress

Serve as an appetizer, or as a snack on toast.

1 bunch of watercress
1 tablespoon vinegar
Generous 1 cup low-fat cottage cheese
Salt and pepper
1 tablespoon finely chopped parsley and shallots (optional)

Wash the watercress in a bowl of cold water with the vinegar. Dry the watercress, chop finely, and combine with the cottage cheese. Season with salt and pepper and a mixture of the parsley and shallots, if desired.

green olive tapenade

Serve on toast, with eggs, or as a sauce for pasta.

1 clove of garlic, peeled
1 tablespoon finely chopped tarragon
1 tablespoon finely chopped parsley
1 or 2 anchovies, soaked in milk for 10 minutes
3 tablespoons olive oil
Juice of half a small lemon
Scant 1 cup pitted small green olives, finely chopped
Salt and pepper

Blend the garlic, tarragon, parsley, anchovies, olive oil, and lemon juice. Add the olives to the herb and oil mixture and season with salt and pepper.

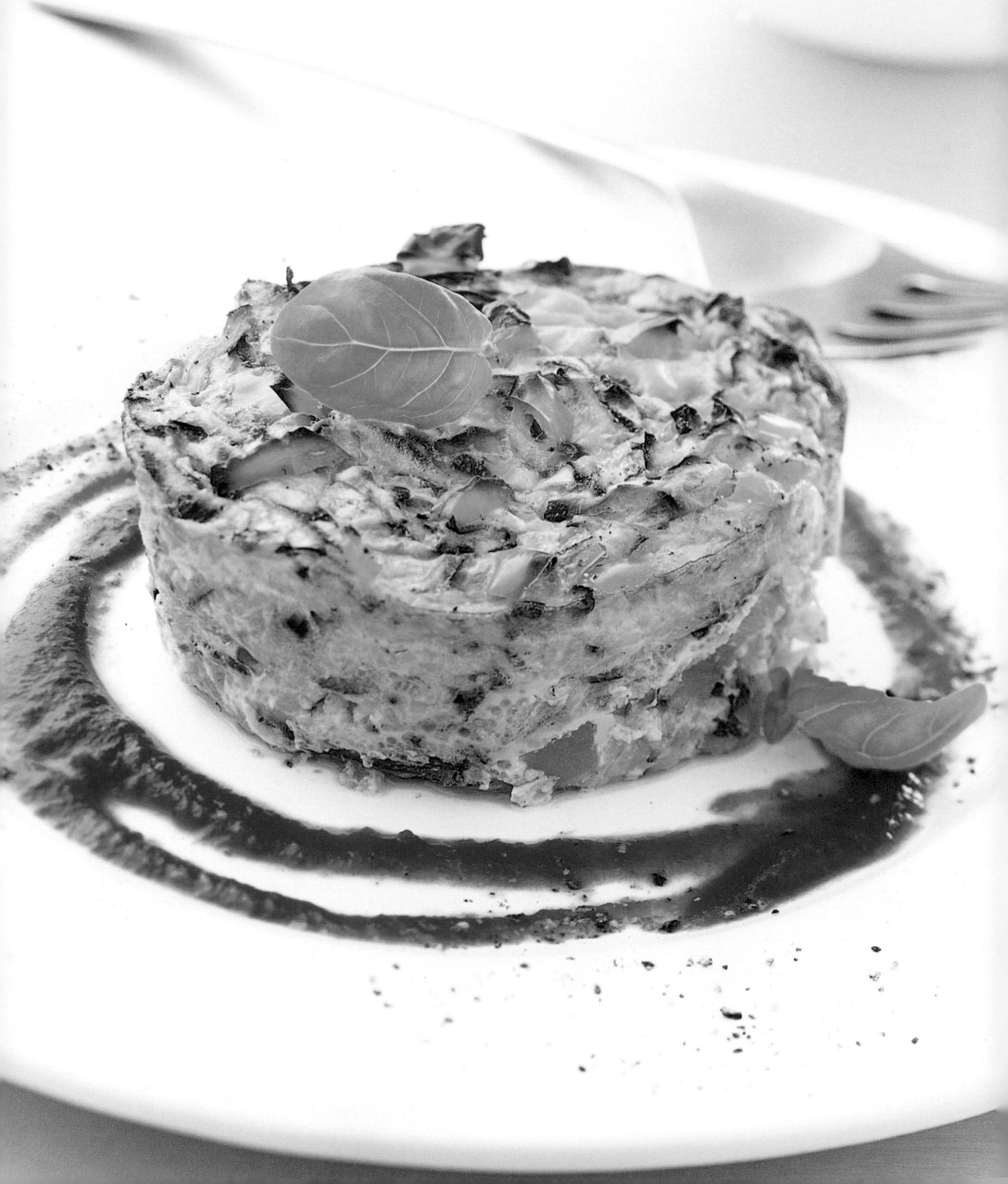

zucchini cake _(left)_

1¾ pounds zucchini, roughly chopped
1 egg
3 tablespoons cottage cheese or ricotta cheese
Salt and pepper
1 yellow bell pepper, finely diced
To serve: tomato coulis (see below)

Boil the zucchini for approximately 4 minutes. Blend them with the egg, cottage cheese or ricotta, and salt and pepper. Stir in the diced bell pepper. Divide the mixture among 4 individual dishes and place in a roasting tin, half-filled with hot water. Bake in a preheated oven at 325°F for 25 minutes. Serve hot with tomato coulis.

tomato coulis

Serve with zucchini cake (see previous recipe).

4 ripe beefsteak tomatoes, quartered
Pinch of sugar
1 teaspoon tomato paste
4 tablespoons olive oil
Salt and pepper

Blend the ingredients to an emulsion. Strain to remove skin and seeds and use as required. Serve as an appetizer or as an accompaniment to broiled meat.

MAIN COURSES
nettle risotto

See page 96 for instructions on harvesting nettles. If nettles are out of season, use young spinach leaves instead.

2 medium onions, sliced
2 tablespoons olive oil
2 cups risotto rice
⅔ cup dry white wine
4 cups vegetable or chicken stock, kept hot
3½ cups nettle tops
Salt and pepper
1¼ cups freshly grated Parmesan cheese
2 tablespoons finely chopped chervil or parsley

In a heavy-based saucepan, gently sweat the onions in the olive oil for about 10 minutes. Stir in the rice to coat with oil and cook for about 2 minutes. Pour in the wine and cook until the rice has absorbed all the liquid. Add the vegetable or chicken stock, a ladleful at a time, allowing the rice to absorb it all before adding more. Continue until the rice is cooked, but still retaining bite—the risotto should be loose and creamy. Meanwhile, steam the nettles until thoroughly wilted. Squeeze lightly and chop roughly. Stir into the risotto and heat through for 2 minutes. Season well and serve immediately, sprinkled with Parmesan and chervil or parsley.

buckwheat with leek sauce

Buckwheat comes either green or roasted. Green buckwheat has a much improved flavor if it is dry-roasted first. Cook it on its own in a pan, stirring all the time until there is a nutty, toasted aroma.

1¼ pounds dry-roasted green buckwheat
4 cups water
4 large leeks, chopped
3 eggs, beaten
Salt and pepper

For the sauce:
Half the cooked leeks (see recipe)
⅔ cup light cream, soy milk, cottage cheese, or yogurt
3 tablespoons chopped chervil or parsley
Lemon juice to taste

In a wide, heavy-based saucepan, bring the dry-roasted buckwheat and water to a boil. Simmer, covered, for 15–20 minutes or until the buckwheat is cooked. The buckwheat will absorb all the liquid and be light and fluffy in texture. Steam the leeks for 10 minutes or until cooked and divide in half. Combine one half of the leeks with the buckwheat and eggs. Season well and pour into a greased, ovenproof dish. Bake in a preheated oven at 350°F for 20 minutes or until browned. Meanwhile, blend the remaining half of the leeks with the cream, soy milk, cottage cheese, or yogurt, and the chervil or parsley. Add lemon juice to taste. Re-heat (carefully if using light cream or yogurt) and serve with the baked buckwheat and leek.

smoked salmon with eggplant sauce

3 large eggplants
6 tablespoons olive oil
Salt and pepper
2 tablespoons finely chopped basil
4 smoked salmon fillets

Using a fork, prick the eggplants all over and cook under a preheated broiler, set to maximum, turning them until the skins are completely charred. When cool enough to handle, scoop out the flesh with a spoon. Put into a strainer and, using a saucer or a small plate, press out as much juice as possible. Pound the flesh in a mortar and slowly beat in the olive oil as if making mayonnaise. Alternatively, use a food processor and drizzle oil through the feeder. Season with salt and pepper. Add the basil. Under a preheated broiler set to maximum, broil the salmon for 5 minutes on either side. Serve with a spoon of the eggplant sauce.

stuffed bell peppers
(below)

Scant 1 cup salted water
Generous ½ cup basmati rice, rinsed
2 green bell peppers
2 red bell peppers
1 large tomato, chopped
1 tablespoon chopped tarragon
¾ cup pitted green and/or black olives, chopped
1 clove of garlic, crushed
1 teaspoon oil or butter
Salt and pepper

In a medium saucepan, bring the salted water to a boil. Add the rice and cook, covered, over a low heat for about 20 minutes or until the water is fully absorbed. Slice the tops off the bell peppers, remove the core and seeds, and set aside. Stir the remaining ingredients into the cooked rice. Fill the bell peppers with the rice mixture and replace the tops. Put into an oiled, ovenproof dish and cover. Bake in a preheated oven at 350°F for about 35–40 minutes or until cooked.

buckwheat crêpes with field mushrooms

For the stuffing:
2 tablespoons vegetable oil
1 large onion, finely chopped
2 large cloves of garlic, crushed
1 teaspoon paprika
1½ pounds field mushrooms, cut into ½-inch chunks
1 red bell pepper, seeded and cut into ½-inch chunks
⅔ cup red wine
4 large sage leaves, roughly chopped
3 tablespoons finely chopped parsley
Salt and pepper

For the crêpes:
2 cups buckwheat flour
1 teaspoon salt
1 large egg
2¼ cups water
Oil to fry

To prepare the stuffing, heat the oil and cook the onion and garlic In a large skillet over low heat for about 10 minutes or until soft. Add the paprika and mushroom chunks and stir. Add the bell pepper chunks and wine and cook for a further 10 minutes until all the moisture has evaporated. Stir through the herbs and season. Keep warm while you make the crêpes. To make the batter, put the flour and salt into a large bowl and make a well in the middle. Put the egg into the well and beat together. Gradually add the water. Refrigerate for at least 30 minutes (or overnight). Pour a small ladleful of batter into a hot, lightly oiled skillet and cook on each side over a moderate heat for about 3–4 minutes or until lightly browned. Stack on a plate and keep warm. Place a little mushroom stuffing in the middle of each crêpe, roll up, and serve.

pasta twists with pesto

For the pesto:
5 cloves of garlic
15 large basil leaves (more for a stronger flavor)
½ cup pine nuts
Salt and pepper
Generous 1 cup grated Parmesan cheese
7 tablespoons olive oil

1¼ pounds fusilli pasta twists

Using a pestle and mortar, crush the garlic, basil, and pine nuts (or use a blender). Add the salt, pepper, Parmesan, and olive oil to make an emulsion. Bring a large pan of salted water to a boil. Add the pasta and return to a boil. Cook uncovered for about 12 minutes or until al dente. Do not drain the pasta completely as a little cooking water will help the pesto to coat the pasta. Toss generously in pesto and serve immediately.

leek and chive mimosa with polenta

4 leeks, coarse outer leaves removed
4 eggs, hard-cooked
2 tablespoons olive oil
2 tablespoons chopped chives, chervil, parsley, or tarragon
4 lemon wedges

For the polenta:
Scant 2 cups instant polenta
Scant 1 cup soy cream
1–2 tablespoons hot chili sauce, or to taste
7 ounces Parmesan cheese or a strong cheddar, grated
Salt and pepper

Cut the leeks lengthwise, rinse well under cold, running water, and then boil in salted water (or steam) until tender. While the leeks are cooking, separate the yolks and the whites of the eggs, and mash separately with a fork. Boil the polenta according to the instructions on the packet and then stir through the cream, chili sauce and cheese. Season well. To assemble: Spoon the polenta onto a warmed serving dish and arrange the leeks on top. Sprinkle over the mashed egg whites and yolks. Keep warm. In a small skillet, heat the olive oil, add the chives or other herbs, fry for about 30 seconds, and pour over the leeks. Serve immediately with the lemon wedges.

lamb with spinach and lentils

As a vegetarian alternative, the spinach and lentil mixture can be served with boiled rice instead of lamb.

1 cup brown lentils, soaked overnight
1 large clove of garlic
1¼ pounds fresh spinach, cut into thin strips
1 tablespoon vegetable oil
½ teaspoon ground coriander
½ teaspoon ground cumin
Salt and pepper
4 tablespoons olive oil
2 tablespoons finely chopped cilantro leaves
2 tablespoons natural yogurt (optional)
2 lamb fillets, trimmed
Oil to fry

In a large saucepan of boiling water, cook the lentils with the garlic for about 15 minutes or until soft but not mushy. Pan-fry the spinach quickly in the vegetable oil until all excess moisture has evaporated. Add the spinach, coriander, cumin, seasoning, and olive oil to the lentils. Just before serving, stir through the cilantro and natural yogurt, if using. In a very hot skillet, fry the lamb fillets quickly on all sides, turning them over with a wooden spoon, for about 12 minutes or until they are well browned and crisp on the outside. (For well-done fillets, cook on the top shelf of a preheated oven at 450°F for a further 10 minutes.) Slice the fillets thickly and serve on a bed of the spinach and lentil mixture.

polenta with basil tomato sauce *(above)*

For the sauce:
1 medium onion, chopped
2 tablespoons olive oil
1¼ pounds tomatoes
Handful of basil leaves, chopped
Salt and pepper

For the polenta:
6¼ cups water
1 teaspoon salt
2⅔ cups pre-cooked polenta
7 tablespoons butter
7 ounces Parmesan cheese, grated

Using a heavy-based saucepan, gently sweat the onion in the olive oil over low heat. Peel the tomatoes (plunging them in boiling water helps the skin to come away) and add to the onions. Season and simmer for 30–40 minutes. When the sauce is thick and pulpy, add the basil, and remove from the heat. Using a heavy-based saucepan, bring the water and salt to a boil, stir in the polenta, and cook over low heat for about 10 minutes, stirring all the time. Stir in the butter and Parmesan cheese and transfer to a rectangular, shallow dish. Spread level with a spatula and allow to set solid. Cut into slices, re-heat in the oven or microwave, or by broiling, and serve with a generous portion of basil tomato sauce.

chicken breasts with celery root mash *(below)*

4 skinless chicken breasts
Pepper
4 lettuce, large spinach, or sorrel leaves
8 slices smoked bacon
Oil to fry

For the mash:
1 celery root, peeled and cut into chunks
Same weight of potatoes, peeled and cut into chunks
A little hot milk
Olive oil or butter to taste
Salt and pepper

Make a slit the length of the chicken breasts and open like a book. Grind pepper into the opening and cover with a lettuce, spinach, or sorrel leaf. Close up the breasts and wrap each one in two pieces of bacon. Secure with a toothpick and refrigerate until ready to use. In two large saucepans, boil the celery root and potatoes separately until cooked. Drain and transfer into one large pan. Cover with a clean folded cloth so that steam is absorbed. Mash the vegetables together, beat in a little hot milk, olive oil or butter, and season to taste. Keep warm. In a skillet, heat the oil and cook the chicken breasts for about 12 minutes or until they are brown on all sides and the juices run clear. Serve with the celery root mash.

dandelion, bacon, and potato cakes

Pancetta or smoked ham can be used instead of bacon. If using smoked ham, add just before serving. Dandelion, bacon, and potato cakes are delicious served with green bean salad (page 99).

¾ cup chopped smoked bacon
1 tablespoon vegetable oil
1¼ pounds young dandelion leaves (or destalked watercress, or lettuce)
2 cloves of garlic
2 tablespoons white wine vinegar
1¼ pounds potatoes, boiled and mashed
2 tablespoons flour
1 large egg
Oil to fry

In a large, heavy-based skillet, fry the bacon in the oil. When cooked, remove, and set aside. Add the dandelion leaves, watercress, or lettuce and the garlic to the pan. Soften over low heat for about 12 minutes or until cooked. Remove the garlic, add the vinegar, and continue cooking until the liquid has evaporated and the mixture is quite dry. Mix the greens mixture into the mashed potato together with the bacon. Beat in the flour and egg thoroughly. With floured hands, make into 4 large or 8 small equal patties and fry in hot oil until they are golden brown on both sides. Serve piping hot.

baked pumpkin strudel

3 tablespoons olive oil
2 red onions, finely chopped
6 cups diced pumpkin or squash
2 cloves of garlic, crushed
1 bay leaf
Sprig of fresh thyme
Salt and pepper
1 x 14-ounce packet fresh phyllo pastry
Plenty of olive oil to brush
1 egg, beaten
1½ cups freshly grated Parmesan cheese
Generous 1 cup wholewheat bread crumbs

In a 10-inch wide pan, heat the oil, add the onion, and cook for
10 minutes or until soft. Add the pumpkin or squash, garlic, bay leaf,
thyme, and seasoning. Cover and cook over low heat, allowing the
ingredients to cook gently in their own juices. If the pumpkin starts to burn,
stir in a little water. Allow to cool slightly. Lay out 4 overlapping sheets of
phyllo pastry and brush quickly with oil. Cover with another 4 sheets and
brush with oil. Repeat once more to make three layers. Spoon over the
pumpkin mixture to within 2 inches of the edges and roll up into a
sausage. Tuck the ends under. Slip a cookie sheet underneath, brush with
beaten egg, and sprinkle over a mixture of Parmesan and bread crumbs.
Bake in a preheated oven at 400°F for about 20 minutes or until the pastry
and bread crumb mixture is golden brown. Serve immediately.

chicken, millet, barley, and celery root pilaf

To make a seafood pilaf use a mixture of shrimp, squid, and mussels
instead of chicken

4 skinless chicken breasts
8 tablespoons olive oil
1 large clove of garlic, crushed
Salt and pepper
1 cup millet
1¼ pounds celery root, peeled and finely diced
1 cup barley, soaked overnight
⅔ cup pesto (page 106)
Pepper
To serve: 8 large basil leaves

Marinate the chicken in the oil, garlic, and seasoning for at least 2 hours.
Cook the millet in twice its own volume of boiling water for about
10 minutes or until al dente. Meanwhile, steam the celery root with the
barley for 15 minutes or until both are cooked. Combine the celery root,
millet, and barley, with plenty of pesto and pepper. Keep warm. In a skillet,
cook the chicken with the marinade juices for about 6 minutes on each
side. When cool enough to handle, tear into strips and fork through the
millet mixture. Tear the basil leaves and sprinkle over the top.

spicy spinach, prunes, and peas

Cinnamon, chopped almonds, raisins, and chopped parsley can be added
to the couscous if desired. Alternatively, basmati rice can be used instead
of couscous.

1 tablespoon oil
1 red onion, chopped
⅔ cup black-eyed peas soaked overnight
½ teaspoon ground turmeric
1 teaspoon ground cinnamon
Pepper
1½ cups water
Generous ½ cup no-soak prunes
2¼ pounds young spinach leaves, picked over
1⅓ cups couscous

In a large saucepan, heat the oil and sweat the onion over low heat for
10 minutes or until soft. Drain the peas and add to the pan along with the
turmeric, cinnamon, and pepper. Cover with the water and simmer with the
lid on. When the peas are three-quarters cooked (probably after about
30 minutes), add the prunes. Add the spinach, in batches, to the stew and
cook for a further 10 minutes. Cook the couscous according to the
instructions on the packet and serve with the stew.

halibut steak and nettle butter

If nettles are out of season, use fresh sorrel leaves.

5 ounces young nettle leaves
10 tablespoons sweet butter, softened
Salt and pepper
4 tablespoons white wine
4 tablespoons salted water or fish stock
1 bay leaf
Juice of half lemon
4 halibut steaks

Steam the nettles for about 8 minutes or until wilted. Squeeze dry. Blend
the nettles and butter and season to taste. Scrape out on to waxed paper
and roll into a log. Refrigerate. Cut into discs when hard. In a large shallow
pan bring the wine and salted water or fish stock to a boil, add the bay leaf
and lemon juice. Add the halibut and simmer for 5 minutes on each side.
Serve with black pepper and a disc of butter.

red snapper with raw spinach salad *(left)*

1¼ pounds young spinach leaves, picked over
6 medium mushrooms, sliced
A few arugula leaves (optional)
Salt and pepper
3 tablespoons vinaigrette (page 97)
3 tablespoons oil
8 red snapper fillets
To serve: chervil and chives, chopped

Remove the stems from the spinach, place the leaves in a serving dish, and add the mushrooms, arugula, salt, and pepper. Toss in the vinaigrette. In a skillet, heat the oil and rapidly sauté the snapper for 5 minutes on each side or until cooked. Place the snapper on the salad. Garnish with the chervil and chives.

ACCOMPANIMENTS

onions in cider *(below right)*

4 tablespoons oil
10 medium onions
5 teaspoons hard cider
1 sprig rosemary
2 bay leaves
Salt and pepper
To serve: cooked zucchini

In a large skillet, heat the oil and slowly fry the whole onions until they are golden brown all over. Add the cider, rosemary, bay leaves, salt, and pepper, then cover, and simmer gently until the onions are well cooked (they should retain their shape). Remove the onions and reduce the sauce by boiling rapidly to a syrupy consistency. Cover the onions with the sauce and serve with the zucchini.

steamed shallots

Serve as a main dish accompaniment or use to thicken sauces.

11 ounces shallots, peeled
½ teaspoon ground cinnamon

Steam the shallots, then blend with the cinnamon.

rice with cucumber balls

2¼ cups salted water
1⅓ cups brown rice, rinsed
1 cucumber
1 shallot, finely chopped
2 tablespoons butter
1 tablespoon finely chopped cilantro or parsley

In a large saucepan, bring the salted water to a boil. Add the rice and cook, covered, over low heat for 20 minutes or until ready. Cut the cucumber in half lengthwise and, using a melon baller, make as many balls as possible. Blanch the balls in boiling water for 2 minutes, then drain, and rinse in cold water. In a skillet, cook the shallot and cucumber in the butter over low heat. As soon as they start to color, add the rice and serve sprinkled with the cilantro or parsley.

potato and watercress mash

1¼ pounds potatoes, peeled and chopped
11 ounces watercress, damaged stalks removed
1 tablespoon butter or light cream
Large pinch of nutmeg
Salt and pepper

Cook the potatoes in boiling, salted water. Drain and return to low heat to drive off excess moisture. Blend the watercress with the butter or cream. Add to the potato, and use a masher to make a smooth paste. Stir in the nutmeg and salt and pepper.

celery with wine and herbs

1 large head of celery (or 2 small ones)
5 tablespoons white wine
5 tablespoons water
4 tablespoons olive oil
2 tablespoons finely chopped parsley
2 tablespoons finely chopped tarragon
Salt and pepper
Lemon juice

Carefully wash the celery and remove the root, leaves, and stringy parts of the stalks. Cut into small pieces and cook in boiling, salted water for 4–6 minutes. Drain (the cooking water can be kept and used in a soup) and place in an ovenproof dish. Boil the wine and water for 1 minute, then pour over the celery in the ovenproof dish. Add the olive oil and cook for 20 minutes at 325°F. Add the parsley, tarragon, and seasoning. Serve hot with a few drops of lemon juice.

peas with bacon pieces

¾ cup lardons or chopped lean bacon
1¼ pounds fresh or frozen peas or 1¼ pounds can pease pudding
⅔ cup vegetable stock
Arugula, finely chopped
Black pepper

In a skillet, sauté the lardons or bacon until golden. Drain away the fat and set aside. Blend the peas, if using, with the vegetable stock. Transfer the pea mixture or pease pudding to the skillet and heat. Mix the lardons or bacon with the pea mixture or pease pudding. Transfer to a serving dish. Sprinkle over the arugula and pepper.

salsify

Salsify will keep well in the refrigerator for a few days and is an interesting accompaniment to main courses. Canned salsify can be used instead of fresh; just sauté before serving.

6¼ cups cold water
1 tablespoon all-purpose flour
3 tablespoons vinegar
Generous pinch of salt
2¼ pounds fresh salsify
Olive oil
1 tablespoon finely chopped parsley

In a large pan, mix the water, flour, vinegar, and salt. Bring to a boil, stirring well. Plunge the salsify into the boiling water, then cover, and simmer for 20 minutes or until cooked. (Cool and store the salsify in its cooking water in the refrigerator.) Before serving, lightly sauté in olive oil and garnish with the parsley.

brussels sprouts with chestnuts

1 pound 5 ounces chestnuts
4 cups meat or vegetable stock
1 pound 10 ounces Brussels sprouts, damaged outer leaves removed
¾ cup chopped bacon, lardons, or pancetta
1 tablespoon vegetable oil

Using a sharp knife, make an incision in each chestnut. Place the chestnuts in a pan and cover with cold water. Bring to a boil for 2 minutes, drain, and peel the outer and inner skin. Cook the peeled chestnuts in the meat or vegetable stock for 30 minutes. Cook the Brussels sprouts for about 15 minutes in salted, boiling water (the sprouts should remain firm). Using a skillet, sauté the bacon, lardons, or pancetta in the oil. When cooked, drain the fat and add the sprouts and chestnuts to the pan. Mix by shaking the pan, heat through for 4 minutes. Season to taste and serve immediately.

beans with carrots and onions

This is an excellent accompaniment to sausages or red meat.

7 ounces onions, sliced
7 ounces carrots, diced
3 cloves of garlic
2 tablespoons olive oil or butter
2¼ pounds dried beans (small navy, canellini or borlotti beans), soaked overnight
Bouquet garni (made with a bay leaf, 2 or 3 sprigs of thyme, 2 or 3 sprigs of parsley and 1 clove)
Salt and pepper

In a large saucepan, cook the onions, carrots, and garlic in the olive oil or butter over low heat for approximately 10 minutes or until the onions are soft. Stir frequently. Add the drained beans and cook for 3 minutes, then cover with water and bring to a boil. Add the bouquet garni, cover, and simmer for 1½ hours or until the beans are cooked. Add salt and pepper after 45 minutes. Serve hot.

fennel with wine

This dish goes very well with smoked fish or cold meat.

1¾ pounds fennel, bruised outer layer and tops removed
1¼ cups white wine
2 bay leaves
1 cinnamon stick or ½ teaspoon ground cinnamon
A few crushed black peppercorns
¼ cup pistachio nuts, shelled
2 anchovy fillets (optional)
1 teaspoon sugar
Pinch of nutmeg
3 tablespoons olive oil

1 tablespoon vinegar
Juice and grated zest of half a lemon

Cut the fennel into quarters and slice thinly. Put the white wine, bay leaves, cinnamon, peppercorns, and fennel in a saucepan, and cover with water. Bring to a boil, then cover, and simmer until the fennel is cooked but still firm. Strain the fennel and put into a deep dish. Blend the pistachio, anchovy (if using), sugar, nutmeg, olive oil, vinegar, and lemon in a food processor and spoon the sauce over the fennel. Cover with plastic wrap and refrigerate for 24 hours. Serve at room temperature.

potatoes with herb sauce

For the sauce:
Small bunch (5 or 6 sprigs) of parsley, finely chopped
Small bunch (5 or 6 sprigs) of chervil, finely chopped
2 tablespoons tarragon leaves, finely chopped
4 anchovy fillets (optional), finely chopped
1 egg, hard-cooked and finely chopped
2 small shallots, finely chopped
Pinch of black pepper
3 tablespoons olive oil
1 tablespoon white wine vinegar
1 tablespoon white wine

16 small new or salad potatoes, boiled
2 teaspoons fresh capers (replace with preserved capers if necessary)

Make the sauce by mixing the ingredients together (boil the white wine briefly before mixing, in order to allow the alcohol to evaporate). Slice the boiled potatoes while hot and place them in a serving dish. Warm the sauce over a gentle heat and then pour on the potatoes. Sprinkle over the capers and toss very gently. Serve warm.

green beans with dijon mustard *(right)*

2¼ pounds green beans
⅔ cup light cream or yogurt
Juice of 1 small lemon
1 tablespoon Dijon mustard
Scant 1 cup toasted, chopped hazelnuts
Salt and pepper

Using a steamer, cook the green beans until al dente. Rinse in cold water and then drain. Mix the cream or yogurt, lemon juice, and mustard in a bowl, then add the beans, and toss lightly. Sprinkle over the toasted hazelnuts, season, and refrigerate before serving.

cardamom hot sauce

Use this sauce to add flavor to soups or stews.

1 teaspoon black peppercorns
1 teaspoon caraway seeds
4 cardamom pods
4 dried chilies
1 bulb of garlic, peeled
Bunch of cilantro leaves, washed with stems removed

Blend all of the ingredients and use as desired.

horseradish sauce

Adjust the ingredients according to taste. Use as a condiment.

2 small shallots, finely chopped
Pinch of ground black pepper
¼ cup salt
Scant 1 cup mustard powder
1 dried red chili, ground
2 ounces fresh horseradish root, grated
1 teaspoon grated nutmeg
½ cup vinegar
¼ cup dry white wine
A little vegetable stock

Blend all the ingredients into a smooth paste. If the mixture is too dry, add some vegetable stock. To reduce the strength and sharpness, boil the blended ingredients for 5 minutes. Refrigerate.

desserts

The following recipes serve 4 people unless otherwise stated. Where possible, harvest your own ingredients or use fresh, organic produce. Take care to wash thoroughly, peel, or de-seed fruit where necessary.

watermelon and summer fruits *(right)*

1 small watermelon
Blackberries (frozen if out of season)*
Raspberries*
Strawberries*
Crushed ice
Superfine sugar to taste
2 tablespoons orange-blossom water (available in healthfood stores and supermarkets)

* Use one quarter of the weight of the watermelon of each fruit.

Cut off the top of the watermelon and spoon out all the flesh. Remove the seeds and cut the flesh into rough cubes. Mix with the other fruit and a small amount of crushed ice. Use this fruit mixture to fill up the shell of the watermelon. Sprinkle on superfine sugar and orange-blossom water. Alternatively, serve the fruit salad in individual bowls.

banana and date salad

5 ripe bananas, peeled and sliced
Scant 2 cups fresh dates, pitted and finely chopped
1¼ cups live yogurt
To decorate: toasted chopped nuts

In glass bowls, arrange the bananas and dates in alternate layers and pour on the yogurt. Refrigerate overnight. Serve sprinkled with toasted chopped nuts if desired.

lychee fruit salad

7 ounces lychees, peeled and pitted
7 ounces tangerines, peeled and separated into segments
6–8 kumquats, chopped
2 tablespoons orange-blossom water
2 glasses crushed ice made with jasmine tea

Put the fruit in a bowl and pour over the orange-blossom water and crushed ice. Serve immediately.

minted melon

2 tablespoons granulated sugar
2 tablespoons water
3 tablespoons fresh mint leaves
Juice of half a lemon
1 ripe honeydew melon, refrigerated
A few chunks candied ginger or ginger preserved in syrup (optional)

In a small saucepan, over low heat, completely dissolve the sugar in the water. Bring to a boil and add the mint and lemon juice. Cool. Slice the melon and place in glass bowls. Glaze the melon with the cold syrup. Serve with ginger if desired.

pumpkin in syrup

1 pumpkin
3¾ cups sugar
2¼ cups water
To decorate: walnuts and toasted almonds, chopped

Cut the pumpkin into eight wedges, cut the flesh from the peel, and remove the seeds and fibers. Dissolve the sugar completely in the water. Bring to a boil and add the pumpkin wedges. Simmer for 20 minutes or until tender: The bubbles should become bigger and slower. Allow to cool and serve the pumpkin and syrup sprinkled with the walnuts and toasted almonds.

rhubarb and ginger tart

For the pie dough:
2 cups all-purpose flour
Pinch of salt
½ cup butter
3 tablespoons ice water

For the filling:
1¼ pounds fresh rhubarb stalks, washed
Scant ½ cup soft brown sugar
2-inch piece ginger root, peeled and grated, or 1 teaspoon orange or
   lemon zest
1 tablespoon lemon juice
To serve: fresh cream or live yogurt (optional)

To make the pie dough: Blend the flour, salt, and butter until well combined; mix in enough water to bind. Chill for 30 minutes and then use the pastry to line a 10-inch tart pan. Cut the rhubarb into small chunks (about ½ inch long). Stack the chunks tightly in the pastry case and sprinkle with the brown sugar, ginger, and lemon juice. Bake immediately in an oven preheated to 350°F for 35 minutes or until cooked. Serve with a little fresh cream or live yogurt if desired.

fruit salad with lemon balm

1 cup wild strawberries
1 cup blackberries
1 cup blueberries
1 cup red currants
3 eating apples peeled, cored, sliced, and sprinkled with lemon juice
½ cup sugar
5 tablespoons water
⅔ cup sparkling wine (optional)
2 tablespoons lemon juice
10 lemon-balm leaves, finely chopped

In a large bowl mix the fruit together. Over low heat, dissolve the sugar in the water, wine (if using), and lemon juice. Bring to a boil and reduce to a syrup. When the syrup has cooled, pour it over the fruit, and sprinkle the lemon-balm leaves on top. Refrigerate for at least 2 hours before serving.

red and white currants with raspberry coulis

Generous 2 cups red currants
Generous 2 cups white currants
1½ cups raspberries
½ cup sugar
To decorate: fresh mint leaves
To serve: fresh cream or live yogurt (optional)

Combine the red and white currants and arrange in individual glass bowls. Crush the raspberries with a fork or blend them. Transfer to a stainless steel, enamel, or glass pan and cook over medium heat for 2 minutes. Strain through a fine strainer into a clean pan and, over low heat, dissolve the sugar in the juice. Pour, warm, over the red and white currants. Decorate with the mint. Serve with fresh cream or live yogurt if desired.

fresh mint sorbet *(left)*

1 cup sugar
1¼ cups water
3 tablespoons fresh mint leaves, washed and dried
Juice of 2 lemons
1 egg white
To decorate: whole mint leaves or lime slices (optional)

In a large saucepan, over low heat, dissolve the sugar completely in the water. Bring to a boil and reduce until syrupy. Meanwhile, chop the mint finely (setting some aside for the decoration if desired), add to the cooling syrup, and allow to infuse for 1 hour. Strain, stir in the lemon juice, and freeze until set. Break the frozen syrup into pieces and blend. Whisk the egg white until stiff and fold in. Decorate with whole mint leaves or lime slices if desired and serve.

pears with herbs

4 cups boiling water
1 handful lime flowers (linden)
2 tablespoons dried mint
2 star anise
Zest of 1 orange
4 large pears
Sugar to taste
Dried fruit such as apricots, golden raisins, or prunes (optional)
To decorate: toasted nuts (optional)

Pour the boiling water over the lime flowers, mint, star anise, and orange zest, cover, and infuse for 30 minutes. Strain the infusion and then pour it into a large steamer or pressure cooker. Steam the pears with the infusion until they are tender (in a pressure cooker this should take about 4–5 minutes). Remove the pears, reduce the infusion by half, and add sugar to taste. Pour the infusion over the pears in a serving dish and allow to cool before serving. If desired, you can add some dried fruit such as apricots, golden raisins, or prunes to the infusion before you pour it over the pears. They will swell in the liquid and take up the fragrance of the herbs. You can also serve the pears decorated with a sprinkling of toasted nuts.

autumn fruit compote

2¼ pounds eating apples, peeled, cored and roughly chopped
2¼ pounds pears, peeled, cored and roughly chopped
1¼ pounds black grapes, de-seeded
Juice and grated zest of 1 lemon or 1 tablespoon grated fresh ginger root
1 clove
½ teaspoon ground cinnamon
Pinch of nutmeg
⅔ cup water
To serve: fresh cream or live yogurt (optional)

In a heavy-based saucepan, place the apples, pears, and grapes with the lemon juice and add the remaining ingredients. Simmer for 25 minutes, or until all the fruit is cooked. Empty the fruit into a glass bowl and allow to cool. Serve with fresh cream or live yogurt if desired.

baked papaya with ginger

3 papayas, halved and de-seeded
¼ cup sweet butter
5 chunks of preserved ginger, chopped
Juice and zest of 1 lime
1 tablespoon of preserved ginger syrup
To serve: brown sugar or honey to taste (optional)

Place the papayas in a buttered ovenproof dish. Mash together or blend the butter and ginger with half the lime juice and zest. Pour the mixture into the halved papayas. Sprinkle with the remaining lime juice, followed by the ginger syrup and brown sugar, if desired. Bake in the oven preheated to 350ºF until tender, basting occasionally with the juices. Serve with a little honey spooned over the top if desired.

fresh figs with raspberry cheese *(left)*

12 figs
Scant 1 cup raspberries
Scant ½ cup cottage cheese
1 tablespoon superfine sugar
3 tablespoons live yogurt

Quarter the figs to within ½ inch of the base. Blend the raspberries, then mix with the cottage cheese, sugar, and yogurt. Pour this mixture over the figs. Refrigerate for a few hours before serving.

poached apricots with cardamom *(right)*

4 cardamom pods
2½ cups water
½ cup brown or white sugar
Zest of 1 lemon, cut into thin strips
12 apricots, pitted
Orange juice to taste
To serve: toasted chopped nuts (optional)

Using a rolling pin, crush the cardamom pods and tie into a cheesecloth bag. In a large saucepan, bring the water, sugar, and lemon zest to a boil. Add the cardamom and simmer for a few minutes until the cardamom flavor is sufficiently strong (taste the syrup). Remove the cheesecloth bag, add 12 apricots, and poach for about 10 minutes over low heat (the syrup should be barely simmering). Once the apricots are cooked, remove them, and reduce the syrup by half by boiling rapidly. Add a little orange juice to taste and pour the syrup over the apricots. Serve chilled with toasted chopped nuts if desired.

juices

To maximize the nutritional value of juice, use the freshest possible ingredients and drink the juice as soon as you have made it (make a small quantity and drink it all at once rather than storing it). Where possible, harvest your own ingredients or use fresh, organic produce. Avoid using fruit and vegetables that are damaged or overripe and take care to wash ingredients thoroughly. If fruit is difficult to obtain, buy ready-made juice from a healthfood store—always choose brands that are organic and unsweetened.

The following juices are made using either a juicer or a blender. A juicer extracts the juice from fruit and vegetables, leaving behind the solid parts, such as the rind, peel, pith, and pits—ideal for citrus fruit and apples. A blender simply liquidizes the whole fruit or vegetable—good for soft fruit such as strawberries and raspberries. If you do not have a juicer, you can add a little water to a recipe, blend the ingredients, and then strain them through a strainer or a piece of cheesecloth. Juices are best served cold, poured over crushed ice. Vegetable juices can be seasoned with salt and pepper.

Because it is hard to predict how much juice individual fruits will yield, the amounts of fruit given in these recipes may need adjusting depending on juiciness (older, riper fruit yields more juice).

FRUIT JUICES

apple and raspberry juice

11 ounces eating apples, peeled, cored and roughly chopped
¾ cup raspberries
2 tablespoons rosewater or orange-blossom water
Ice cubes made from jasmine tea
Sugar to taste

In a blender, process the apples and raspberries. Add the rosewater or orange-blossom water, then pour the liquid over jasmine tea ice cubes. Alternatively, crush the jasmine tea ice cubes in the blender with the fruit. Add sugar to taste.

apricot, lime, and mint juice

3 ripe apricots, pitted
3 tablespoons fresh lime juice
Honey to taste
1 teaspoon chopped fresh mint
Crushed ice

In a blender, process the apricots and the lime juice. Sweeten to taste with honey and pour into a glass half-filled with mint and crushed ice.

cherry and raspberry juice

¼ cup ready-made cherry juice
¼ cup ready-made raspberry juice
Juice of half a lemon
Crushed ice

Mix the juices together and add the lemon juice and crushed ice.

cherry and apple juice

3 eating apples
¼ cup ready-made cherry juice

Process the apples in a juicer and mix the apple juice with the cherry juice.

mango juice

2 mangoes, peeled and pitted
2 tablespoons orange-blossom water
A few ice cubes made from camomile tea

Using a blender, process the mango flesh with the orange-blossom water and the camomile ice cubes. Blend until the ice is well crushed.

carrot, apple, and ginger juice

6 carrots, cut in chunks
4 apples, peeled, cored and cut in chunks
1 tablespoon grated ginger root
Crushed ice

Process the carrots, apples, and ginger in a juicer. Pour over crushed ice.

prune juice

1 teaspoon lemon juice
Maple syrup to taste
⅔ cup ready-made prune juice

Mix the lemon juice and maple syrup with the prune juice.

red currant, blackberry, and blueberry juice

1 cup red currants
¾ cup blackberries
1 cup blueberries

Use frozen fruits if red currants, blackberries, or blueberries are out of season. Process the ingredients in a blender.

strawberry and raspberry juice

Scant 2 cups strawberries
Generous 1 cup raspberries
Lemon juice to taste
Crushed ice
A little water

In a blender, process the strawberries and raspberries. Add lemon juice and pour over crushed ice. Add water if necessary.

pineapple shake

½ cup soy milk
¼ cup pineapple juice
1 teaspoon grated coconut
Sugar to taste

Using a blender, process the ingredients. Add sugar to taste. Serve chilled.

VEGETABLE JUICES

celery and tomato juice

Half a celery plant
2 tomatoes
1 cucumber

Trim the celery stalks and base. Process the ingredients in a juicer.

cabbage, carrot, and celery juice

This juice can be served hot or cold.

½ red or white cabbage
4 carrots, roughly chopped
5 stalks celery, roughly chopped
½ red onion (or 2 shallots)
Water
Salt and pepper
1 teaspoon lemon juice

In a blender, process the vegetables. Add a little water to thin the consistency and add salt, pepper, and lemon juice.

green bean and garlic juice

1½ cups green beans
2 small lettuce hearts
2 tablespoons water
2 cloves of garlic
Pinch of cayenne pepper
Crushed ice

In a juicer, process the vegetables, water, and garlic, mix with the cayenne pepper, and pour over the crushed ice.

black radish and carrot juice

3½ ounces black radishes
2 ounces carrots

Process the ingredients in a juicer.

broccoli and green bean juice

A few stems and flowerets of broccoli
¾ cup green beans
2 tablespoons lemon juice
2 tablespoons water
Crushed ice

In a juicer, process the vegetables, mix with the water, and pour over the crushed ice.

celery and red onion juice

1 celery plant, leaves and outside stalks removed
2 red onions
Crushed ice
Juice of half a lemon

Trim the celery stalks and base. In a juicer, process the celery and onions and pour over the crushed ice and lemon juice.

beet and celery juice

1 head of celery, leaves and outside stalks removed
2 beets, cooked
Juice of half a lemon or lime
1 tablespoon olive oil

Trim the celery stalks and base. In a juicer, process the beets and celery and pour in a glass with the lemon juice and olive oil.

cucumber and lettuce heart juice

2 cucumbers
1 lettuce heart

Process the ingredients in a juicer.

lettuce and basil juice

1 lettuce
1 radicchio
5 basil leaves
Juice of half a lemon

Process the lettuce, radicchio, and basil in a juicer and then add the lemon juice.

pickles and preserves

When making preserves buy the best quality ingredients possible. Sterilize jars and bottles use glass or ceramic, avoid metal) by pouring boiling water over them or leaving them in a hot oven for at least 20 minutes. The main ingredient used in pickling is vinegar — this acts as a solvent, taking the aroma as well as the medicinally active ingredients from the plants. Preserves should generally be consumed within three months.

PICKLED VEGETABLES

pickled turnips

Serve with main dishes, such as pork and potatoes.

3¼ pounds turnips, peeled and grated
2 tablespoons salt
40 juniper berries
30 black peppercorns

Place the ingredients in layers in a large glass or ceramic jar, then put a sterile cloth and a plate on the top layer. Place a weight on top of the plate and keep refrigerated. The turnips will start to ferment and will take 2–3 weeks to pickle. When pickled, rinse well in cold water and dry thoroughly. Serve raw in salad or cook and serve in the same way as sauerkraut (boiled and as an accompaniment for sausages or pork).

pickled beets

2¼ pounds baby beets, unpeeled
4 cups water
2¼ cups red wine vinegar
2 bay leaves
2 sprigs of thyme
12 black peppercorns
2 cloves of garlic
¼ cup salt
Generous ½ cup granulated sugar
1 white onion, sliced

Wrap the beets in foil and bake in a preheated oven at 400°F until tender. Meanwhile, bring the water, vinegar, herbs, peppercorns, garlic, salt, and sugar to a boil and cook for 3 minutes. Leave to cool. Peel the beets and combine with the onion in hermetically sealable pickling jars. Pour over the pickling vinegar and seal the jars tightly. Store for at least 2 weeks in a cool, dark place.

pickled cauliflower *(right)*

Use in starters or salads.

1 medium cauliflower
4½ teaspoons salt
White wine vinegar or cider vinegar (enough to cover the cauliflower)
1 teaspoon green peppercorns
1 teaspoon black peppercorns
1 teaspoon pink peppercorns
1–6 fresh green, red, and yellow chilies according to taste (yellow chilies are optional, as they are not always available)

In a large saucepan, blanch the cauliflower in boiling, salted water for 5 minutes. Rinse under cold water, drain, and pat dry with paper towels. Carefully cut away small flowerets from the main stalk and put them into a 6¼-cup hermetically sealable pickling jar. Using a stainless steel, glass, or enamel saucepan, bring to a boil the white wine or cider vinegar, peppercorns, and chilies and cook them for 30 seconds. Pour the vinegar mixture over the cauliflower flowerets in the pickling jar so that they are completely covered. Allow to cool and seal the jar tightly. Leave for 3 weeks in a cool, dark place.

VINEGARS

blackberry vinegar

Use in salad dressings or cooking.

Scant 2 cups blackberries
1 teaspoon mustard powder in a small cheesecloth bag
4 cups white wine vinegar

Wash the blackberries in cold water, trim away any stems and green parts, drain on paper towels, and place in a hermetically sealable pickling jar with the mustard. Pour over the white wine vinegar and seal the jar tightly. Leave for 2 weeks in a cool, dark place. Strain and bottle the vinegar.

raspberry vinegar

1½ cups raspberries
4 cups red wine vinegar

Put the raspberries in a hermetically sealable pickling jar. Pour over the red wine vinegar and seal the jar tightly. Leave for 2 months in a cool, dark place. Strain and bottle the vinegar, pressing the fruit to extract the juice.

borage leaves in vinegar

The leaves can be eaten on their own as a starter or added to salads or other dishes. The borage flowers give a blue color to the vinegar.

4 cups young borage leaves
A dash of white wine vinegar
scant ½ cup borage flowers
4 cups white wine vinegar (with 2 tablespoons salt added)

Rinse the borage leaves in a bowl of cold water with a dash of vinegar added. Place the leaves in a single layer on a clean, dry cloth and leave them to wilt for 8 hours. Place them in a 6¼-cup hermetically sealable pickling jar and add the borage flowers. Pour over the salted white wine vinegar and seal the jar tightly. Leave for 1 month in a cool, dark place.

tarragon vinegar

2 handfuls of fresh tarragon
10–12 very small pickling onions threaded onto toothpicks
A few borage flowers (optional)
4 cups white wine or cider vinegar

Put the tarragon into a hermetically sealable pickling jar with the onions and the borage flowers (if using). Pour over the white wine or cider vinegar and seal the jar tightly. Leave for 2 weeks in a cool, dark place.

shallot vinegar

4 cups white wine vinegar or cider vinegar
10 shallots
1 bay leaf
1 sprig of thyme
1 teaspoon black peppercorns

Pour the white wine or cider vinegar over the other ingredients in a hermetically sealable pickling jar. Seal the jar tightly. Leave for 2 weeks in a cool, dark place. Strain and bottle.

herb vinegar

4 cups red or white wine vinegar
1 sprig of tarragon
A few basil leaves
1 sprig of marjoram
1 sprig of thyme
1 clove (or a few juniper berries)
A few green and black peppercorns

Pour the vinegar over the other ingredients in a hermetically sealable pickling jar. Seal the jar tightly. Leave for 1 month in a cool, dark place. Strain and bottle.

amazingly aromatic vinegar

4 cups white wine or cider vinegar
2 handfuls of tarragon leaves and stems
2 handfuls of dill weeds
1 handful of fresh basil leaves
1 handful of fresh thyme
1 handful of marjoram
10–12 small shallots threaded onto toothpicks
1 red chili, whole (optional)

Pour the vinegar over the other ingredients in a hermetically sealable pickling jar. Seal the jar tightly. Leave for 2–3 weeks in a cool, dark place. Strain and bottle, leaving the thyme in the vinegar.

table mustard

2 tablespoons chopped parsley
2 tablespoons chopped chervil
2 tablespoons chopped chives
2 tablespoons chopped celery leaves
2 tablespoons chopped tarragon
2 tablespoons chopped thyme
1 clove of garlic
1 teaspoon salt
½ teaspoon black pepper
White wine vinegar (enough to cover the herbs)
Mustard powder
Olive oil

Blend the herbs, garlic, and salt and pepper. Transfer to a small, hermetically sealable pickling jar and add white wine vinegar to cover. Seal the jar tightly. Leave for 1 week in a cool, dark place. Add mustard powder to make a thick paste and olive oil to create a smooth consistency. Mix well and store in a sealed container in the refrigerator.

JELLY

physalis jelly

2¼ pounds physalis berries
Water
2¼ pounds sugar

Remove the berries from their parchment skins, wash, and cut them in half. Put them into a heavy-based saucepan, cover them with water, and simmer for 30 minutes. Blend the berry mixture, add the sugar, and return to the heat for 30 minutes. Store in tightly-sealed jars.

medicinal drinks, tinctures, and syrups

Infusions, decoctions, wines, liqueurs, tinctures, and syrups provide a valuable way of administering the active ingredients of various plants, herbs, and spices. Each of the following recipes is accompanied by the suggested dosage, a brief explanation of its properties (some of the terms used are explained in the glossary; pages 292–294), and the ailments or body systems that it is good for. See Chapter 2 for more information about specific ailments and their remedies. Most of the recipes give amounts for dried herbs. If you wish to substitute fresh herbs, use two to three times the given amount. Dried herbs can be bought from health stores and herbalists.

INFUSIONS

Infusions can be prepared one day in advance, stored in the refrigerator, and gently warmed when needed. They are relatively mild medicinal drinks and need to be taken frequently. Infusions made with lime flower, lemon balm, and camomile are recommended for children.

dandelion infusion

Dosage: ⅔ cup three times a day.
Properties: detoxifying, aids liver function.
Good for: bone and joint disorders, digestive system disorders, kidney and
        bladder disorders, eczema, high blood pressure.

4 cups boiling water
1 tablespoon dried dandelion root
1 tablespoon dried dandelion leaves

Pour the boiling water over the dandelion root and leaves, and cover. Leave to infuse for 10 minutes and then strain.

fennel infusion

Dosage: ⅔ cup three times a day. Alternatively, take a drop of fennel
        essential oil on a lump of sugar or in a teaspoon of honey.
Properties: antispasmodic, carminative, appetite and digestion stimulant.
Good for: digestive system disorders, women's health disorders, anemia,
        candida, polymyalgia rheumatica, Raynaud's disease.

⅔ cup boiling water
1 tablespoon fennel seeds

Pour the boiling water over the fennel seeds, and cover. Leave to infuse for 10 minutes and then strain.

raspberry-leaf infusion

Dosage: ⅔ cup of the warm infusion three times a day.
Properties: astringent.
Good for: fibrositis, menstrual cramp, polymyalgia rheumatica, pregnancy
        (especially the last few weeks).

⅔ cup boiling water
1 teaspoon dried raspberry leaves

Pour the boiling water over the raspberry leaves and cover. Leave to infuse for 5 minutes and then strain.

orange-zest infusion

Dosage: drink throughout the day instead of water.
Properties: stimulates the immune system.
Good for: blood and circulation disorders.

4 cups boiling water
1½ ounces orange zest
½ ounce bay leaves

Pour the boiling water over the orange zest and bay leaves, and cover. Leave to infuse for 20 minutes and then strain.

marjoram infusion

Dosage: drink throughout the day instead of water. For ease of use, mix the
        herbs together and store them in a jar.
Properties: aids digestion, antiseptic, antispasmodic.
Good for: respiratory system disorders, immune system disorders,
        insomnia, thrush.

1 teaspoon dried marjoram
1 teaspoon dried thyme
1 teaspoon dried mint
2 cups boiling water
Honey to taste

Pour the boiling water over the herb mixture and cover. Leave to infuse for a few minutes. Strain and add honey to taste.

lemon-balm and camomile infusion *(right)*

Dosage: ⅔ cup of the warm infusion two or three times a day. For ease of
     use, mix the herbs together and store them in a jar.
Properties: antispasmodic, sedative, detoxifying.
Good for: heart and circulation disorders, digestive system disorders,
     respiratory system disorders, nervous system disorders, women's
     health disorders, kidney stones, psoriasis, urticaria (hives).

3½ ounces dried lemon balm leaves
1 ounce dried camomile flowers
¾ ounce dried mint leaves
⅔ cup boiling water

Mix together the dried herbs. Pour the boiling water over 1 tablespoon of
the herb mixture, and cover. Leave to infuse for 10 minutes and then strain.

carrot-seed infusion

Dosage: ⅔ cup two or three times a day.
Properties: stimulates digestion, tonic, promotes bile flow, mild diuretic.
Good for: amenorrhea.

Scant ⅔ cup boiling water
1 tablespoon carrot seeds

Pour the boiling water over the carrot seeds, and cover. Leave to infuse for
10 minutes and then strain.

pear and apple infusion

Dosage: drink throughout the day instead of water.
Properties: diuretic, anti-inflammatory, detoxifying.
Good for: bone and joint disorders, kidney and bladder stones.

4 cups boiling water
2 cups pear leaves
1½ cups dried apple peel

Pour the boiling water over the pear leaves and apple peel and cover.
Infuse for 20 minutes and strain.

barley infusion

Dosage: drink throughout the day instead of water.
Properties: diuretic, calming, anti-inflammatory.
Good for: irritable bladder, prostatitis.

4 cups boiling water
½ cup barley grain

Pour the boiling water over the barley and cover. Leave to infuse for
3 hours and then strain.

elder and camomile infusion

Dosage: ⅔ cup of the warm infusion three or four times a day. This
     infusion can be given to young children.
Properties: promotes sweating, detoxifying, sedative, anti-inflammatory.
Good for: digestive system disorders, respiratory system disorders, nervous
     system disorders, immune system disorders, endometriosis,
     premenstrual syndrome, psoriasis.

1 cup boiling water
2 tablespoons dried elderflowers
1 tablespoon dried camomile flowers (or 1 camomile teabag)
Sugar to taste

Pour the boiling water over the elderflowers and camomile flowers and
cover. Leave to infuse for 10 minutes. Strain and sweeten with sugar.

sparkling lemon-balm infusion

Dosage: drink when desired. This recipe can be served as an aperitif for adults by replacing the sparkling water with sparkling wine.
Properties: refreshing, calming (excellent for children).
Good for: nervous system disorders, women's health disorders, angina, anxiety, cough, fear and nightmares in children, laryngitis, psoriasis, rhinitis, urticaria (hives).

For the infusion:
2¼ cups boiling water
45 fresh lemon balm leaves

For the drink:
2¼ cups sparkling mineral water—or wine if using
Juice of 1 orange
Juice of 1 grapefruit
Sugar to taste
1 fresh lemon balm leaf
1 slice of lemon

Pour the boiling water over the lemon balm leaves and cover. Leave to infuse until cold and then strain. Mix the infusion with the sparkling mineral water, or wine if using, orange and grapefruit juice. Add sugar to taste and serve in a frosted glass with the lemon balm leaf and a slice of lemon.

coriander seed infusion

Dosage: ⅔ cup of the warm infusion two or three times a day.
Properties: antispasmodic, carminative, stimulates the digestive system.
Good for: digestive system disorders, amenorrhea, menstrual cramp.

⅔ cup boiling water
1 tablespoon coriander seeds
Sugar to taste

Pour the boiling water over the coriander seeds and cover. Leave to infuse for 10 minutes. Strain and add sugar to taste.

ginger infusion

Dosage: ⅔ cup of the warm infusion four times a day or when desired.
Properties: stimulates digestive system, anti-emetic.
Good for: heart and circulation disorders, digestive system disorders, respiratory system disorders, nervous system disorders, digestive problems and morning sickness during pregnancy.

⅔ cup boiling water
2 tablespoons grated fresh ginger root
Sugar to taste

Pour the boiling water over the ginger and cover. Allow to infuse for 5 minutes. Strain and sweeten with a little sugar.

DECOCTIONS

As with infusions, decoctions can be prepared one day in advance, they are relatively mild, and should be taken frequently. Decoctions involve boiling the tough or woody parts of plants, such as stems, roots, seeds, and berries. Store decoctions in the refrigerator.

carrot-leaf decoction

Usage: apply to the skin two or three times a day.
Properties: promotes healing and regeneration of damaged skin, anti-inflammatory, analgesic.
Good for: chilblains.

1 handful of fresh carrot leaves
⅔ cup water
Carrot juice (extracted using a juicer)

In a saucepan, boil the carrot leaves in the water for 5 minutes. Strain and mix with an equal quantity of fresh carrot juice.

cherry-stem decoction

Dosage: ⅔ cup three or four times a day.
Properties: diuretic, detoxifying.
Good for: bone and joint disorders, measles, pleurisy, pneumonia.

1 ounce cherry stems
4 cups water

In a saucepan, boil the cherry stems in the water for 10 minutes and strain.

corn-hair and fennel-seed decoction

Corn hair consists of black, hair-like threads that surround the corn beneath the outer leaves. It is available in specialty herb stores or from herbalists.

Dosage: ⅔ cup of the warm infusion three times a day.
Properties: detoxifying, diuretic, anti-inflammatory, stimulates the digestive system.
Good for: kidney and bladder disorders, women's health disorders, chickenpox, prostatitis.

1 handful of dried corn hair
2 teaspoons fennel seeds
4 cups water

In a saucepan, bring the ingredients to a boil. Remove from heat, cover, and leave to infuse for 20 minutes. Strain.

lychee-seed decoction

Dosage: drink the warm decoction throughout the day.
Properties: analgesic, antispasmodic, astringent.
Good for: abdominal cramp and colic.

1 ounce lychee seeds
Zest of 1 lemon
1 tablespoon fennel seeds
2¼ cups water

In a saucepan, boil the ingredients in the water for 20 minutes, then strain.

physalis-berry decoction

Dosage: ⅔ cup four times a day.
Properties: diuretic, anti-inflammatory.
Good for: kidney and bladder disorders, prostatitis.

2 ounces physalis berries
4 cups water

In a saucepan, boil the berries in the water for 5 minutes. Allow to infuse for a further 10 minutes and strain.

cherry-stem and apple decoction

Dosage: ⅔ cup three times a day.
Properties: detoxifying, anti-inflammatory, diuretic.
Good for: arthritis (rheumatoid), chickenpox, measles.

1 handful of cherry stems
4 cups water
2 or 3 apples, sliced

In a saucepan, boil the cherry stems in the water for 10 minutes. Strain and pour the decoction over the apple slices. Cover and leave to infuse for 20 minutes. Strain, pressing the apple slices to extract all the juice.

lettuce-seed decoction

Dosage: 5 teaspoons three times a day.
Properties: calming, sedative, antispasmodic.
Good for: respiratory disorders, anxiety, kidney stones.

1 tablespoon lettuce seeds
1 cup water

In a saucepan, boil the lettuce seeds in the water for 10 minutes and then strain.

dill-seed decoction

Dosage: ⅔ cup of the warm infusion two or three times a day.
Properties: antispasmodic, carminative, stimulates the digestive system.
Good for: digestive system disorders, amenorrhea, menstrual pain.

1 tablespoon dill seeds
2¼ cups water
Sugar to taste

In a saucepan, boil the dill seeds in the water for 10 minutes. Strain and add sugar to taste.

fennel-seed decoction

Dosage: ⅔ cup of the warm infusion once a day.
Properties: antispasmodic, carminative, stimulates the digestive system.
Good for: digestive system disorders, women's health disorders, anemia, polymyalgia rheumatica, Raynaud's disease.

1 dessertspoon fennel seeds
⅔ cup water
Sugar to taste

In a saucepan, boil the seeds in the water for 5 minutes. Strain. Add sugar.

strawberry-leaf decoction

Dosage: drink throughout the day.
Properties: astringent, anti-inflammatory, detoxifying.
Good for: bone and joint disorders, heart and circulation disorders, respiratory system disorders, kidney and bladder disorders, prostatitis.

1 handful of fresh strawberry leaves
1 handful of fresh strawberry roots
4 cups water

In a saucepan, bring the ingredients to a boil. Remove from the heat and allow to infuse for 10 minutes. Strain.

cumin-seed decoction

Dosage: ⅔ cup of the warm infusion two or three times a day.
Properties: sedative, carminative, antiseptic.
Good for: digestive system disorders, women's health disorders.

1 teaspoon cumin seeds
⅔ cup water

In a saucepan, boil the cumin seeds in the water for 10 minutes. Strain.

barley water

Dosage: drink throughout the day.
Properties: diuretic, calming, anti-inflammatory.
Good for: heart and circulation disorders, digestive system disorders,
          kidney and bladder disorders.

4 cups water
1 ounce barley, germinated
Honey to taste

In a saucepan, bring the water and barley gently to a boil. Reduce and
simmer until the barley is cooked. Strain and add honey.

WINES AND LIQUEURS

Only small amounts of the following drinks need to be taken for medicinal
purposes. Wines should be stored in tightly corked bottles and kept for a few
weeks. When preparing liqueurs, use the strongest alcohol available to help
to extract the plants' active ingredients. Liqueurs can last for years. Store
away from bright light. Wines and liqueurs should not be given to children.

cinnamon wine *(right)*

Dosage: ¼ cup when desired.
Properties: tonic, aphrodisiac, antiseptic, aids digestion.
Good for: Raynaud's disease.

2 ounces cinnamon bark
¾ ounce vanilla beans
3 cups sweet red wine

Mix the ingredients together. Seal tightly and leave to macerate for 3 days.
Strain through cheesecloth and store in a tightly sealed bottle.

black currant wine

Dosage: ¼ cup a day.
Properties: tonic, astringent, laxative, improves vitality and digestion.
Good for: anemia, polymyalgia rheumatica, Raynaud's disease, ulcerative
          colitis.

1¾ cups black currants
3 cups dry white wine
¾ cup sugar
⅔ cup strong alcohol (vodka, eau de vie, or grappa)

Crush the black currants in a large bowl and pour over the dry white wine.
Seal the bowl with plastic wrap and refrigerate for a week. Press and strain
the mixture through cheesecloth. Add the sugar and over low heat, bring to
simmering point. Do not allow to boil. Cool and add the strong alcohol.
Store in a tightly sealed bottle and leave to age for several months.

artichoke-leaf wine

Dosage: ¼ cup morning and evening before meals.
Properties: detoxifying, improves liver function, stimulates the flow of bile.
Good for: ankylosing spondylitis, arteriosclerosis, cholecystitis, gallstones,
        hyperlipidemia.

2 ounces dried artichoke leaves, finely chopped
3 cups red wine

Add the artichoke leaves to the wine. Seal tightly and leave to macerate for 10 days. Strain through cheesecloth and store in a tightly sealed bottle.

cherry-leaf wine

Dosage: ¼ cup a day (dilute to taste).
Properties: diuretic, detoxifying.
Good for: bone and joint disorders.

80 cherry leaves
5 tablespoons sugar
3 cups red wine
⅖ cup kirsch

Add the cherry leaves and the sugar to the wine. Seal tightly and leave to macerate for 8 days. Remove the cherry leaves and add the kirsch.

blueberry wine

Dosage: 1 small glass a day.
Properties: tonic, aids digestion.

1¾ cups fresh blueberries
⅖ cup fresh raspberries or 1 cup black currants
Scant 3 cups dry white wine
¾ cup sugar
⅖ cup strong alcohol (such as vodka, eau de vie, or grappa)

In a large bowl, crush the fruit. Cover with the white wine, seal the bowl, and refrigerate for 1 week. Then press and strain the mixture, add the sugar to the liquid and, in a stainless steel pan, bring to slowly to simmering point. Cool and add the alcohol. Age in a tightly sealed bottle for several months.

juniper-berry wine

Dosage: ¼ cup a day.
Properties: tonic, diuretic, analgesic, aids digestion.
Good for: kidney and bladder disorders, diabetes mellitus.

¾ cup fresh juniper berries, crushed
¼ ounce lemon zest
3 cups white wine

Add the juniper berries and the lemon zest to the white wine. Seal tightly and leave to macerate in a cool, dark place for 1 week. Strain through cheesecloth and store in a tightly sealed bottle.

camomile and citrus wine

Dosage: ¼ cup when desired.
Properties: sedative, bitter tonic, stimulates digestion.
Good for: digestive system disorders, anxiety, endometriosis, insomnia.

2¼ cups camomile flowers
Zest of 1 unwaxed organic lemon
Zest of 1 unwaxed organic orange
1 teaspoon tea leaves (optional)
3 cups dry white wine
¼ cup sugar
⅔ cup strong alcohol (such as vodka or gin)

Mix all the ingredients together. Seal in an airtight container and leave to macerate in a cool, dark place for 1 week. Strain through cheesecloth and store in a tightly sealed bottle.

anisette

Dosage: 1 tablespoon (neat or diluted in 5 tablespoons water) when desired.
Properties: antispasmodic, carminative.
Good for: digestive system disorders, women's health disorders, headaches and migraine.

2 tablespoons green anise seeds or star anise
5½ teaspoons coriander seeds
Pinch of mace
Pinch of cinnamon bark
Scant 3 cups vodka
1¼ cups sugar
7 tablespoons water

Add the anise, coriander seeds, mace, and cinnamon bark to the vodka. Seal tightly and leave to macerate in a cool, dark place for 1 month. In a saucepan over low heat, completely dissolve the sugar in the water, then boil for 30 seconds. Allow to cool. Strain the vodka through cheesecloth, pressing the seeds to extract as much liquid as possible. Mix with the cooled syrup, store in a tightly sealed bottle, and keep in a cool, dark
place for 2 weeks before using.

camomile aperitif

Dosage: ¼ cup in the evening.
Properties: sedative, bitter tonic, enhances digestion and sleep.
Good for: endometriosis.

2¼ cups camomile flowers
3 cups white wine

Add the camomile flowers to the wine. Seal tightly and leave to macerate in a cool, dark place for 1 month. Strain through cheesecloth and store in a tightly sealed bottle.

lemon liqueur

Dosage: 5 teaspoons when desired.
Properties: carminative, aids digestion, astringent, aperitive.
Good for: cholecystitis, gallstones.

Zest of 3 organic lemons, cut into thin strips
½ cup almonds
1 small vanilla bean or cinnamon stick
Scant 3 cups strong vodka
1¼ cups sugar
⅔ cup water
1 almond or clove

Add the lemon zest, almonds, and vanilla to the vodka. Seal tightly and leave to macerate in a cool, dark place for 1 month. In a heavy-based pan, dissolve the sugar in the water completely and then boil for 30 seconds. Strain the infused alcohol and combine with the cooled syrup. Add an almond or clove and some of the original lemon zest to the mixture. Seal tightly and leave to mature for a few months.

basil liqueur *(far left)*

Dosage: 5 teaspoons when desired.
Properties: antiseptic, antispasmodic, stimulates appetite.
Good for: digestive system disorders, headaches and migraine.

80 fresh basil leaves
Scant 3 cups strong vodka
1¼ cups sugar
Water

Add the basil leaves to the vodka. Seal tightly and leave to macerate in a cool dark place for 1 month. In a heavy-based pan, dissolve the sugar over low heat in just enough water to make it wet. When all the crystals have dissolved, boil for 30 seconds. Mix the cooled syrup with the vodka, seal tightly, and leave for a further 3 weeks. To keep the green color of the liqueur remove some of the basil leaves (they can be used to make basil ice cream in an ice-cream maker).

quince liqueur

Dosage: ¼ cup when desired.
Properties: astringent.
Good for: digestive system disorders.

2¼ pounds quince, mashed
1 cup sugar
2 cloves
Pinch ground cinnamon
Vodka or brandy (see method for quantity)

Refrigerate the mashed quince for 48 hours, then press through cheesecloth to extract the juice. Add the sugar, cloves, and cinnamon and an equal volume of vodka or brandy. Seal tightly and leave to macerate for 2 months. Strain through cheesecloth and store in a tightly sealed bottle. Leave to age for a further 2 or 3 months.

TINCTURES

Tinctures are made with alcohol and provide a very concentrated way of taking the active ingredients of a plant. As with liqueurs, very strong alcohol should be used. Tinctures can have a lifespan of years. Store away from bright light.

artichoke-leaf tincture

Dosage: 30 drops in 5 tablespoons of water, morning and evening.
Properties: detoxifying, improves liver function, stimulates the flow of bile.
Good for: bone and joint disorders, cholecystitis, gallstones.

1¼ pounds dried artichoke leaves
3 cups strong alcohol (vodka, gin, or brandy)

Add the artichoke leaves to the alcohol. Seal tightly and leave to macerate in a cool, dark place for 3 weeks. Strain through cheesecloth and store in a tightly sealed bottle away from bright light.

aniseed tincture

Dosage: 20 drops in ⅖ cup of water one to three times a day.
        Or take 10 drops of tincture on a lump of sugar.
Properties: antispasmodic, carminative, stimulates the digestive system.
Good for: digestive system disorders, women's health disorders, headaches
        and migraine.

¾ cup aniseed (the seeds of the anise plant)
Scant 3 cups strong alcohol (vodka, eau de vie, or gin)

Add the aniseed to the alcohol. Seal tightly and leave to macerate in a cool, dark place for 1 month. Strain through cheesecloth and store in a tightly sealed bottle away from bright light.

coriander-seed tincture

Dosage: 15 drops in 5 tablespoons of water after a meal.
Properties: antispasmodic, carminative, aids digestion, aids lactation.
Good for: gastritis, amenorrhea.

1¾ ounces coriander seeds
2¼ cups strong alcohol (vodka, gin, or brandy)

Add the coriander seeds to the alcohol. Seal tightly and leave to macerate in a cool, dark place for 1 week. Strain through cheesecloth and store in a tightly sealed bottle away from bright light.

SYRUPS

The active ingredients of plants can be administered in the form of a syrup. Syrups should always be stored in a refrigerator and used within a few days (except crème de cassis, which will keep for several months).

The following test can help to determine the point during preparation at which a syrup should be removed from the heat: Take a teaspoon of the syrup and drop it into a glass of cold water; if it breaks into droplets, it needs further boiling; if it forms a single droplet, it is ready.

leek syrup

Dosage: 1 tablespoon three times a day.
Properties: soothing, expectorant, anti-inflammatory.
Good for: respiratory system disorders, fibrositis, polymyalgia rheumatica,
        sore throat, tonsillitis.

1 medium leek, chopped
4 cups water
¾ cup sugar

In a saucepan, simmer the leek in the water. When the water has reduced by approximately one-third, press the leek to squeeze out the juice. Remove the leek, add the sugar, and boil for a few more minutes. Allow to cool and pour into a sterilized bottle. Seal tightly and refrigerate.

peach syrup

Dosage: 3–4 tablespoons a day (2 tablespoons for children).
Properties: calming, laxative.
Good for: constipation in children.

⅖ cup boiling water
¾ ounce fresh peach flowers
Generous 1 cup honey

In a saucepan, pour the boiling water over the flowers, cover, and leave to infuse for about 6 hours. Strain through cheesecloth, add the honey, then bring to a boil, reduce the heat, and simmer for a few minutes. Allow to cool and pour into a sterilized bottle. Seal tightly and refrigerate.

black radish syrup

Dosage: 1 tablespoon three times a day.
Properties: soothing, anti-inflammatory, expectorant.
Good for: sore throat, tonsillitis, whooping cough.

1 black radish, peeled and sliced
Superfine sugar

Place the radish slices in a dish, covering each layer with plenty of sugar. Cover with plastic wrap and leave overnight. Press the radish slices to extract the syrup and strain into a sterilized bottle. Seal tightly and refrigerate.

mint syrup

Dosage: 1 teaspoon in a glass of water. Mint syrup can be added to water
or served with sorbet.
Properties: stimulates the digestive system, antispasmodic.
Good for: colitis, cough, endometriosis, food poisoning, rhinitis.

4 cups boiling water
3¾ cups fresh mint leaves
5 cups sugar

Pour the water over the mint leaves. Seal tightly and leave to infuse for
24 hours. Strain. In a pan, bring the infusion and sugar to a boil and simmer
for 3 minutes. Cool. Pour into a sterilized bottle. Seal tightly and refrigerate.

blackberry syrup *(right)*

Dosage: 1 tablespoon in ⅔ cup of water two or three times a day.
Properties: astringent.
Good for: diarrhea, dysentery.

6 cups blackberries
5 cups sugar
⅔ cup water

In a pan, bring the ingredients to a boil. Reduce the heat and simmer for
10 minutes. Cool. Pour into a sterilized bottle. Seal tightly and refrigerate.

crème de cassis

Dosage: take as desired. This vitamin C-rich syrup can be diluted with
water for children or added to dry white wine for adults.
Properties: tonic.
Good for: general well-being.

2 pounds 4 ounces black currants
2 pounds 4 ounces sugar

Fill up 2¼-pound jars with equal amounts of black currants and sugar in
thin, alternating layers. Seal the jars and leave in a cool, dark place for
6 months. Strain and pour into sterilized bottles. Seal tightly and refrigerate.

asparagus syrup

Dosage: 2 tablespoons morning and evening.
Properties: diuretic and sedative.
Good for: nervous system disorders, endometriosis, palpitations,
premenstrual syndrome, psoriasis.

Scant 1 cup asparagus tips juice (extracted using a juicer)
2 cups sugar

In a saucepan, boil the asparagus juice and sugar until a thick syrup forms.
Allow to cool and pour into a sterilized bottle. Seal tightly and refrigerate.

elderberry syrup

Dosage: 1 tablespoon every morning.
Properties: gentle laxative.
Good for: colic, constipation, irritable bowel syndrome (recommended for
elderly people).

13 cups fresh elderberries, slightly unripe (red rather than black), with the
stems cut off
⅔ cup water
1¾ cups sugar
¼ teaspoon cloves

In a saucepan, crush the berries and simmer them in the water for
30 minutes. Put the berry mixture in a piece of cheesecloth and allow
the juice to drip into a bowl overnight. In a nonreactive saucepan, bring
the juice, sugar, and cloves to a boil. Reduce the heat and simmer for
5 minutes. Allow to cool and pour into a sterilized bottle. Seal tightly
and refrigerate.

chapter four

diet in practice

Sometimes the best way to fortify the body against illness is to simplify the diet to a few basic ingredients that are easy to digest and assimilate. This enables the body to rid itself of toxins and emerge stronger and more resilient. The detoxification program on the following pages—a four-week prescription of healing foods, drinks, and exercise—is the ideal way to accomplish this and it can be followed successfully by most adults regardless of their level of health and fitness. This chapter also presents the vitamins, minerals, and other nutrients, such as antioxidants and essential fatty acids, that are needed for health, together with a selection of the foods in which they are found. There is also a short review of two basic elements of our everyday diet that have important health-giving properties but are often overlooked: culinary oils and bottled mineral waters.

the detox programme

In the past 50 years, there has been an increase in heart disease, cancer, and auto-immune or degenerative disorders such as rheumatoid arthritis. These illnesses may be directly or indirectly linked to toxicity in the body created during digestion. This toxicity is exacerbated by the excessive consumption of refined sugar, cereals, oils, meat, dairy products, and animal fat that characterizes the modern diet, by food processing and preserving methods, and by the buildup of toxins in the food chain owing to the use of hormones, chemical fertilizers, antibiotics, insecticides, and antifungal agents in farming.

During digestion, a series of complex processes involving a variety of secretions takes place in the digestive tract, each acting under a different pH (level of acidity). The result of these processes is the breakdown of food into nutrients that can be used by the body. However, if the pH in one section of the gut is wrong, digestion is impaired and fats, sugars, and proteins are only partially broken down. Food starts to putrefy in the gut and a pathogenic bacterial flora develops to the detriment of the beneficial flora. This can create toxicity in the body.

Both normal digestive processes and incomplete breakdown of animal proteins result in the production of acids. The body gets rid of a small amount of these acids rapidly via the lungs but denser acids, such as uric, phosphoric, and sulfuric acid, which are generated by the breakdown of animal protein, are eliminated slowly by the kidneys. If acid is not eliminated quickly enough, it too creates toxicity.

According to the late Dr. Kousmine, a nutrition and cancer specialist, acids that are not eliminated from the body during the day are stored in serous fluid (extra-cellular fluid) in the peritoneum (lining of the abdomen). At night when the body is resting the acids are filtered and disposed of. Over a period of time, however, acids build up in the body's tissues causing an accumulation of toxins. This can give rise to a variety of symptoms including fatigue, disturbed sleep, regurgitation, heartburn, lack of appetite or bulimia, diarrhea or constipation, migraine, bad breath, cold perspiration, lowered resistance to infections, muscular pain, rheumatism, bronchitis, and excessive mucus production resulting in chronic catarrh.

A detoxification diet can facilitate the rapid and efficient elimination of toxins and improve both short- and long-term health. The plan described here combines diet and exercise with herbal medicine and nutritional supplements. Although it is suitable for the majority of adults, it should not be followed by children, elderly people, or pregnant or breast-feeding women. If you are on long-term medication, such as hormone replacement therapy (HRT), or drugs for hypertension or thyroid problems, you should continue to take them throughout the program (consult your doctor if you are in any doubt about whether it is safe for you to follow a detox plan). It is useful to be aware of some possible side-effects of detoxification. These vary depending on the stage of the program but they tend to include mild headache, mood changes, and energy fluctuations. If side-effects do not abate after the first week, or you experience persistent or troublesome symptoms, consult your doctor.

Although the detox plan requires a few changes to your normal routine and some careful planning, it should be fairly easy to implement. Most people start to feel the benefits of detox about 10 days into the program.

week one

WHAT TO DO

During the first week you should eliminate all dairy and wheat-based products from your diet, reduce your salt intake, avoid meat and animal fat, tea, coffee, white sugar, candy, alcohol, and tobacco. Remember that foods such as pasta, cookies and bread all contain wheat; use rice, buckwheat, or quinoa as a substitute. Soy milk is available from most supermarkets and can be used as a replacement for cow's milk. In addition, you should:

● Drink 4–8 cups of mineral water every day; choose water that has a low mineral content (page 146).

● If you experience an excessive amount of abdominal gas and bloating, take two capsules of activated charcoal three times a day after meals.

- Eat a handful of fresh or dried blueberries every day.
- Drink herbal teas made from fennel, ginger, or camomile before and after your meals.
- Use plenty of herbs such as thyme, basil, rosemary, garlic, and shallots in your cooking.

HOW TO SUCCEED

- Revise your usual shopping list to include plenty of fresh fruit and vegetables, fish, rice, lentils, beans, millet, buckwheat flour, fresh herbs, and herbal teas such as ginger, peppermint, camomile, and fennel.
- Follow the recipes in this book and use a cook book with an emphasis on healthy food (Provençal and Mediterranean cooking are recommended).
- Start the day with a protein-based breakfast (mushrooms are a good source of protein) and eat well at lunchtime. This will provide you with enough energy to get through the day. In contrast, your dinner should be very light.
- Resist the temptation to have the occasional sugary snack, cup of tea or coffee, or alcoholic drink.

POSSIBLE SIDE-EFFECTS

You may experience mild headaches, bursts of energy alternating with fatigue, muscle aches and pains, sudden hunger, irritability, cravings for sweet foods, intestinal gas, abdominal distension, and regurgitation. These are most common during the first 48 hours. Side-effects vary from one person to another—you certainly won't experience all of these.

THE BENEFITS

Toward the end of week one, you may notice that your energy levels, appetite, and quality of sleep are improving.

week two

WHAT TO DO

Follow exactly the same guidelines as for week one but increase the percentage of raw fruit and vegetables so that they make up 70 per cent of your daily food intake. In addition, avoid eating after seven o'clock in the evening.

- To accelerate the detoxification process, drink ⅔ cup dandelion infusion (page 125), three times a day. Or drink ¼ cup artichoke-leaf wine (page 130) at lunchtime and early evening.
- Take propolis tablets to help reduce bacterial activity in the gut. Follow the dosage instructions on the package.

HOW TO SUCCEED

- Drink as much herbal tea as you like after seven o'clock in the evening.
- Try to go to bed earlier than usual—rest is an important aid to detoxification.
- Keep following the tips for success for week one.

POSSIBLE SIDE-EFFECTS

Cravings for candies and carbohydrates or feelings of hunger are common during week two. You may feel tired or cold immediately after you have had a meal and you may start to lose weight.

THE BENEFITS

Toward the end of week two you will start to feel more energetic both physically and mentally. Your digestion, breathing, and sleep patterns will be better and you may start to notice an improvement in chronic conditions, such as poor skin, eczema, rheumatism, or arthritis.

week three

WHAT TO DO

You should continue the program of diet and rest that you followed in week two but, to accelerate detoxification, you should build in a program of daily exercise. Do some low-intensity exercise for 45 minutes twice daily. The best types of exercise are brisk walking, cycling, or swimming.

You should also step up your intake of vitamins, minerals, and trace elements by drinking a glass of fruit or vegetable juice twice every day. Recommended fruit juices are blackberry, blueberry, cherry, or apricot. Good vegetable juice combinations include broccoli, green bean, and lemon juice or carrot, cabbage, and green or red bell pepper.

Before breakfast in the morning, drink the juice of half a lemon mixed with an equal amount of cold-pressed olive oil. This facilitates the emulsion and flow of bile into the digestive system. Other important dietary measures for week three are:

● Eat more of the following: rice, root vegetables such as carrot, celery root, Jerusalem artichoke and turnip, germinated legumes, green vegetables, raw apple, fig and Brazil nut.
● Eat fish at least twice a week.
● Drink 4–8 cups of mineral water every day; preferably with a medium to high mineral content (page 146).

HOW TO SUCCEED
● Drink some water or herbal tea before you exercise, but avoid exercising on a full stomach.
● Eat a light snack after exercise, but nothing too heavy.
● Keep following the tips for success for weeks one and two.

POSSIBLE SIDE-EFFECTS
Weight loss will continue as you burn calories during exercise. Exercise may also give rise to symptoms such as muscular aches (a recommended remedy for this is homeopathic arnica tablets of 30 or 200 potency; take when needed). However, if you experience a strong tightening or gripping pain in the center of your chest after a few minutes of exercise, you must rest immediately and consult your doctor. Any sharp pains in weight-bearing joints or your lower back, should also be reported to your doctor.

THE BENEFITS
You should continue to experience the benefits described in week 2. You will continue to feel more energetic, and your digestion, breathing, and sleep patterns will improve further.

week four
WHAT TO DO
Continue to follow a wheat- and dairy-free diet but reduce your raw fruit and vegetable consumption to 50 per cent of your total food intake. Start to eat lightly after 7 o'clock in the evening. Continue your twice-daily exercise program and keep taking the olive oil and lemon juice mixture before breakfast as in week 3. Drink fruit or vegetable juice twice a day and at least 6 cups of a mineral water that has a medium to high mineral content.

HOW TO SUCCEED
● Take a fish oil supplement every day for the next few weeks.
● Keep following the tips for success for weeks one to three.

POSSIBLE SIDE-EFFECTS
At this stage of your program, you should not experience any noticeable side-effects.

THE BENEFITS
You should be feeling really fit and healthy by week four. Your energy levels should be consistently high, you should be sleeping well, and any minor digestive problems should have completely disappeared. Chronic conditions such as eczema or rheumatism should be more manageable and may even have disappeared. Your immune system will be stronger and you will be more resistant to colds and influenza.

your diet after detox
Once you have completed your four-week detoxification program you can either follow the week-four guidelines for a further two weeks or you can return to a normal diet.

If you return to a normal diet, gradually reintroduce wheat products in the first week. If you experience any symptoms in response to them, eliminate wheat from your diet permanently. Dairy products should be reintroduced during the second week and any symptoms monitored. Again, if you have an adverse response, eliminate dairy products from your diet permanently.

Continue to practice as many aspects of the detox diet as you can and make sure that you apply the following principles to your long-term diet and lifestyle:
● Keep drinking plenty of water. Drink mineral water with a low mineral content (page 146), unless advised and supervised by a doctor or nutritionist.
● Eat meat and drink wine, coffee, and tea in moderation.
● Keep up your exercise program.
● Follow the detox program annually and repeat the first two weeks of the plan twice a year: once in the fall and once in the spring.

directory of vitamins, minerals, and other nutrients

THIS CHART LISTS VITAMINS, MINERALS AND OTHER NUTRIENTS THAT FORM AN IMPORTANT PART OF OUR DIET. THE BENEFITS OF EACH ARE GIVEN, AS WELL AS EXAMPLES OF FOODS THAT ARE PARTICULARLY GOOD SOURCES OF A NUTRIENT.

VITAMIN	BENEFITS	SOURCES
VITAMIN A (Retinol and Carotene)	Vitamin A is important for maintaining healthy skin. It also helps prevent frequent infections of the upper respiratory tract, such as colds and sore throats, and improves night vision. Retinol is found in animal products while carotenes are found in plant foods.	● carrot (pages 20–21) ● watercress (page 25) ● cabbage (pages 26–27) ● mango (page 38) ● melon (page 40)
VITAMIN B1 (Thiamine)	Vitamin B1 increases concentration. It is easily destroyed by cooking or exposure to ultraviolet light. A low intake of vitamin B1 can cause depression and irritability.	● watercress (page 25) ● cabbage (pages 26–27) ● zucchini (page 28)
VITAMIN B2 (Riboflavin)	Vitamin B2 is essential for the metabolism of fats, sugars, and proteins in the body.	● watercress (page 25) ● cabbage (pages 26–27) ● asparagus (page 31) ● milk (page 63)
VITAMIN B3 (Niacin)	Vitamin B3 reinforces the skin's natural protection against exposure to the sun. Deficiency can cause fatigue, depression, poor concentration, and dermatitis.	● cabbage (pages 26–27) ● zucchini (page 28)
VITAMIN B5 (Pantothenic acid)	Vitamin B5 is important for the health of the immune system and helps the body extract energy from food. Also called the stress vitamin.	● watercress (page 25) ● cabbage (pages 26–27) ● celery (page 28) ● avocado (page 31) ● strawberry (page 41)

VITAMIN	BENEFITS	SOURCES
VITAMIN B6 (Pyridoxine)	Vitamin B6 is necessary for healthy blood and for the metabolization of protein.	● onion (page 18) ● watercress (page 25) ● cabbage (pages 26–27) ● banana (page 38)
VITAMIN B12	Vitamin B12 is needed for the health of the nerves and to make red blood cells. Low intake can cause fatigue and dry skin.	● milk and cheese (page 63) ● egg (page 63)
BIOTIN	Biotin plays an important part in the metabolism of carbohydrate and fat.	● cabbage (pages 26–27) ● cherry (page 41) ● grapefruit (page 45) ● milk (page 63) ● egg (page 63)
FOLATE (folic acid; part of the vitamin B complex)	Folate is crucial for making genetic material and red blood cells. Women should take 400 mcg of folate daily during pregnancy.	● broccoli (page 24) ● cauliflower (page 24)
VITAMIN C	Vitamin C promotes tissue repair and wound-healing and is important for the general health of the immune system. It is an antioxidant and plays a major role in the absorption of iron and the formation of antibodies and collagen.	● broccoli (page 24) ● cabbage (pages 26–27) ● bell pepper (page 28) ● lemon (pages 46–47)
VITAMIN D (Calciferol)	Vitamin D is essential for healthy bones and skin. Sunlight is our main source of this vitamin. Some foods are fortified with vitamin D, and oily fish and dairy products are rich sources. When the skin is in contact with sunlight it manufactures its own vitamin D.	● egg (page 63) ● cheese (page 63) ● oily fish (page 64)
VITAMIN E (Tocopherol)	A powerful antioxidant, vitamin E prevents the degeneration of nerves and muscles. It helps keep the skin healthy and helps to prevent cardiovascular disease.	● wheat (page 35) ● peanut (page 49)

MINERAL	BENEFITS	SOURCES
CALCIUM	A major constituent of bone and teeth, calcium is also vital to nerve transmission, blood clotting and muscle function. It regulates the heartbeat and helps maintain a proper acid-alkaline balance. A good calcium intake is also important for healthy skin.	● broccoli (page 31) ● seaweed (page 40) ● almond (page 49) ● milk, cheese, butter, yoghurt (page 63)
COPPER	Copper is a trace element that is vital in forming connective tissue and for the growth of healthy bones. It helps the body absorb iron from food and is present in many enzymes, which protect against free radical damage.	● fig (page 38) ● sunflower seeds (page 59)
FLUORIDE	This mineral protects against tooth decay.	● asparagus (page 31)
IODINE	Iodine is required by the thyroid gland in order to produce the thyroid hormone, which regulates physical and mental development, including growth, reproduction and many other essential functions.	● seaweed (page 31) ● barley (page 35) ● shellfish (page 63) ● egg (page 63) ● milk (page 63)
IRON	Essential for the production of haemoglobin, the pigment in red blood cells that transports oxygen to every cell, iron also boosts energy levels, prevents anaemia and increases the body's resistance to disease.	● bean (page 32) ● lentil (page 32) ● prune (page 40) ● walnut (page 49) ● parsley (page 51)
MAGNESIUM	Magnesium is an important constituent of bones and teeth and is important for muscle contraction. It also calms the nervous system and regulates the heartbeat. It is required for normal calcium function.	● hazelnut (page 49) ● almond (page 49) ● pine nut (page 49) ● walnut (page 49)

MINERAL	BENEFITS	SOURCES
PHOSPHORUS	Phosphorus regulates protein activity and is essential for the release of energy in the body's cells. It also helps to form and maintain healthy bones and teeth and is necessary for the absorption of many nutrients.	● present in most foods
POTASSIUM	Potassium has a variety of functions: it regulates body fluids; it is essential for correct functioning of the cells and the transmission of nerve impulses; it keeps the heartbeat regular and maintains normal blood pressure.	● cauliflower (page 24) ● cabbage (pages 26–7) ● celery (page 28) ● mushroom (page 32)
SELENIUM	An antioxidant that protects from heart disease, some cancers and premature ageing, selenium is required for normal growth and fertility, thyroid action, proper liver function and healthy skin and hair.	● mushroom (page 32) ● buckwheat (page 33) ● walnut (page 49) ● shellfish (page 63) ● egg (page 63)
SILICA	Vital to the development of bones, silica also promotes healthy skin and connective tissues.	● leek (page 19) ● green bean (page 24) ● nettle (page 24) ● chickpea (page 33) ● strawberry (page 41)
SODIUM	Sodium regulates the balance of body fluids and controls levels of electrolytes in blood plasma. It is essential for nerve and muscle function. Most people in the Western world consume far more sodium than they need.	● seaweed (page 31) ● oat (page 35) ● grape and raisin (page 40)
SULPHUR	In its pure form sulphur works as an antifungal and antibacterial agent – it is used in creams for treating skin disorders such as acne. Sulphur also helps form proteins. It is present in every cell.	● radish (page 19) ● mango (page 38) ● horseradish (page 58) ● garlic (page 56) ● egg (page 63)
ZINC	Zinc benefits the reproductive system, fertility and the skin. It also helps wounds to heal and regulates the sense of taste. Zinc is required for a healthy immune system and good night vision and is vital for normal growth.	● lentil (page 32) ● nuts (page 49) ● red meat (page 63) ● shellfish (page 63) ● egg (page 63) ● wheatgerm (page 203)

OTHER NUTRIENTS	BENEFITS	SOURCES
ALLIUM COMPOUNDS	Allium compounds aid the proper function of the cardiovascular and immune systems.	● onion and shallot (page 18) ● leek (page 19) ● chive (page 52) ● garlic (pages 56–57)
ALPHA-LINOLEIC ACID	This is an essential fatty acid that is also known as omega-3 fatty acid. It has an anti-inflammatory effect that makes it good for rheumatoid arthritis, it helps to lower blood pressure and cholesterol, and reduce the likelihood of blood clots and heart attacks. It maintains cell membranes and transports fats around the body.	● walnut (page 49) ● oily fish (pages 64–65) ● flaxseed (page 198)
ANTHOCYANOSIDES	These antioxidants inhibit a variety of dangerous bacteria including E. coli.	● blueberry (pages 42–43)
BIOFLAVONOIDS	Bioflavonoids are antioxidants that facilitate the absorption of vitamin C. They strengthen the capillaries, which improves poor circulation and helps to prevent cardiovascular disease.	● blueberry (pages 42–43) ● mandarin and tangerine (page 45) ● grapefruit (page 45)
CAPSAICIN	An antioxidant, capsaicin can act as a pain reliever and anti-inflammatory agent. It also helps to reduce blood cholesterol and the risk of blood clots, aids digestion, and may kill harmful bacteria. Capsaicin may also prevent DNA damage.	● chili (page 55)
CAROTENOIDS (CAROTENE)	Carotenoids give the orange or yellow color to vegetables such as carrots. They have antioxidant properties that help to prevent cellular damage caused by free-radical attack. They also reduce the risk of cancer and cardiovascular disease. They are vitamin A precursors.	● carrot (pages 20–21) ● spinach (page 25) ● pumpkin (page 22-3) ● mango (page 38)

OTHER NUTRIENTS	BENEFITS	SOURCES
CHLOROPHYLL	Chlorophyll is the substance that gives plants their characteristic green color. It is thought to help keep blood healthy, promote wound healing, and kill bacteria. It may provide some protection against cancer and certain forms of radiation.	● green bean (page 24) ● dandelion (page 24) ● mâche (page 25) ● arugula (page 25) ● sorrel (page 53)
ELLAGIC ACID	A flavonoid found in fruits, ellagic acid appears directly to protect genes from attack by carcinogens.	● cherry (page 41)
GAMMA-LINOLEIC ACID (GLA)	By helping to keep the blood thin, gamma-linoleic acid contributes to the prevention of blood clots and blockages. It also reduces inflammation and relieves pain and improves nervous- and immune-system function.	● borage oil (page 53)
LINOLEIC ACID	This essential fatty acid is also known as omega-6 fatty acid. It can help to lower blood cholesterol.	● olive (pages 36–37) ● sunflower seed (page 59) ● walnut (page 49)
MALIC ACID	Malic acid makes it possible for the body to convert sugars and fats into energy.	● apple (page 45)
OLEIC ACID	High levels of oleic acid can lower cholesterol levels.	● olive (pages 36–37)
PECTIN	Pectin lowers blood pressure and blood cholesterol, softens stools to help prevent bulges in the colon and hemorrhoids, and reduces the risk of colon cancer.	● orange (page 41) ● apple (page 45) ● pear (page 45) ● persimmon (page 45) ● quince (page 45)
PHYTOESTROGEN	May help to alleviate menopausal symptoms and lower the risk of breast cancer. Mimics the activity of estrogen in the body.	● soy beans (page 33)

mineral water and culinary oils

water

Water is essential to life in any form. It makes up approximately two-thirds of the human body and is constantly being lost in the form of sweat, water vapor, urine, and feces. We need to replace this by drinking 4–8 cups of water every day.

Water varies greatly in content. The quality of drinking water in large urban areas is often poor. It may have been recycled three or four times and contain traces of hormones, nitrates, and metals such as lead (lead pipes are still common in many old houses). Bottled mineral water is significantly richer than tap water in a range of minerals including calcium, magnesium, potassium, bicarbonate, chloride, sulfate, silica, fluoride, zinc, manganese, selenium, and borate (check for these minerals on the label). Once opened, bottled water should be stored in the refrigerator and drunk quickly; it can rapidly become a breeding ground for bacteria. Some mineral waters are inappropriate for long-term daily use due to their high mineral content.

● Bottled waters with a low mineral content are excellent for everyday use and can be given to infants. They include Volvic and Evian.

● Bottled waters with a medium mineral content are beneficial when used every day for a limited amount of time. They include Vittel and Contrex. Mineral waters that are rich in calcium (San Pellegrino and Contrex) are recommended for the kidneys. Those rich in magnesium (Badoit and Hepar) are better for the liver.

● Bottled waters with a high mineral content, such as Vichy, have a strong therapeutic action and should be drunk occasionally or as part of the detox program (pages 136–139): They are diuretic, facilitate the elimination of toxins, strengthen teeth and bones, and improve kidney and liver function. They are effective for rheumatism and arthritis, circulatory disorders, hypertension, kidney problems, low immunity, and digestive and metabolic problems.

culinary oils

When selecting culinary oils try to choose cold-pressed ones, which are made by simple mechanical cleaning and crushing processes and which retain their nutritional and therapeutic properties. While industrially extracted oils keep for longer, they have lost most of their taste and therapeutic qualities. Industrial extraction is lengthy, complicated, and involves chemical processing and heating the oil to high temperatures. Recent research suggests that the industrial manipulation of fatty acids may make these oils detrimental to our health. The most common culinary oils are:

● Olive oil: In my opinion, this is the most nutritional and therapeutic type of oil (page 36).

● Sunflower oil: This is rich in vitamin E, oleic and linoleic acid. It can be used for cooking and in salads. Sunflower and walnut oil are excellent in combination—the sunflower oil moderates the strong taste of walnut and increases the shelf-life; the walnut oil supplies alpha-linoleic acid.

● Corn oil: This is rich in polyunsaturated fat (see Corn, page 33).

● Walnut oil: a mineral-rich, strong-tasting oil favored in south-west France. It is best diluted with sunflower or corn oil. A tablespoon can be added to vegetable juices to enhance their taste and therapeutic value.

● Hazelnut oil: This has a delicate taste, is very nutritious, and is best used in salads. Both hazelnut and walnut oils are traditionally given to children to support their growth and to treat mild digestive problems and worms, including tapeworm.

● Peanut oil: This can stand very high temperatures, which makes it good for frying. It is of little therapeutic or nutritional value. Organic peanut oil is difficult to find.

● Sesame oil: Widely used in Asian countries, this oil is comparable to olive oil in its therapeutic and nutritional value.

part two:
eat for immunity

kirsten hartvig

introduction

ABOUT PART TWO

Eat for Immunity gives you a strategy to maximize your self-healing potential and develop a better understanding of health and disease. It is divided into four chapters:

● Chapter Five, A Guide to the Immune System, explains the components of the immune system and how they work together to maintain health and combat disease.

● Chapter Six, Superfoods for the Immune System, looks in detail at 150 foods that support the immune system.

● Chapter Seven, Coping with Common Ailments, highlights some common ailments, and explains how you can use the foods described in Chapter Six to prevent illness and promote health.

● Chapter Eight, Immune Foods in Practice, shows you how to incorporate immune-enhancing foods into your daily diet with 180 recipes and a range of diet plans.

You don't need to read Eat for Immunity from cover to cover before using it. Keep it in the kitchen and use it as a reference source of good food and better health.

When making the recipes in Chapter Eight, choose organic ingredients whenever possible, since chemical farming involves the use of many different substances that are harmful to immunity. Eating organic is also the best way of avoiding genetically engineered foods, the long-term health effects of which are unknown.

food for life

Over the last 30 years, systematic scientific studies have confirmed that poor nutrition impairs the immune response, and that a diet based primarily on minimally processed and chemically unadulterated plant foods is the most effective way of enhancing immunity.

A recent global survey carried out by the World Cancer Research Fund together with the American Institute for Cancer Research concluded that plant-based diets protect against cancer. Hundreds of reliable studies show that fresh vegetables, fruits, nuts, grains and legumes are packed with immune-boosting phytochemicals.

Since the early 1960s, research has repeatedly confirmed that a diet high in natural fibre from vegetables, fruits and unrefined grains protects from a wide range of serious diseases.

Nutrition experts and scientists worldwide agree that high intakes of saturated fats from meat, dairy products, and convenience foods are linked with coronary heart disease, and that the activity of the immune system is improved by decreased total fat intake.

Large numbers of fish caught for human consumption have been shown to contain toxic heavy metals, hydrocarbons and radioactive contaminants, and those reared in fish farms are commonly dosed with antibiotics and treated with dyes. Oily fish contain unsaturated fatty acids that may protect against coronary thrombosis, but increasing fish oil intake without also reducing saturated fat intake is unlikely to have any significant effect on the development of coronary heart disease.

Taking fish oils in a concentrated form may cause excessive production of free radicals, which can interfere with immunity. Unlike fish oils, plant sources of polyunsaturated fatty acids are high in natural antioxidants, which combat the effects of free radicals.

Despite its reputation as a natural staple food, cow's milk may compromise immunity. Some people (particularly children) are allergic to milk protein and may develop eczema, hay fever or asthma as a result of consuming it, and people with mucus problems and allergy often experience substantial relief when they exclude milk products from their diet. Milk is also high in cholesterol and thus associated with an increased risk of heart problems.

Milk sugar (lactose) is digested in the stomach by an enzyme (lactase) which most humans stop producing at around the age of five, making it difficult to digest milk products efficiently. Contamination of milk products with hormones, antibiotics and other agricultural chemical residues may also produce unpredictable and unexpected adverse reactions.

Based on this overwhelming evidence, Eat for Immunity follows a plant-based approach to improving immunity that is relevant to every style of eating—carnivore, pescetarian, vegetarian and vegan. It is designed to help you tailor your personal food choices to the benefit of your immune system, increasing your intake of health-enhancing foods and cutting down on those that increase immune system workload.

dos and don'ts

Eat for Immunity can be used by nearly everyone, although people suffering from serious acute illness and young people under the age of eighteen are advised to follow the diet recommendations under the guidance of a suitably qualified medical practitioner. During pregnancy and while breast feeding, stringent diet regimes are not recommended, but eating a varied diet rich in fresh fruits, nuts, seeds, grains and vegetables is beneficial for both mother and baby.

The health suggestions in this book are intended to complement and enhance other treatments, not to replace them. Increasing your intake of some foods can change your body's reaction to medication (for example, cholesterol-lowering drugs), so if you are currently under medical treatment consult your practitioner before making any major dietary changes. If you are being treated for diabetes, you should follow your normal dietary guidelines and discuss the implications of change with your medical adviser.

side effects

The diet plans in Eat for Immunity are extremely unlikely to produce any unpleasant adverse reactions, but you may notice that withdrawal from tea, coffee, alcohol and smoking makes you feel more edgy, headachey, lethargic and short-tempered for a few days. An increase in fruit and vegetable intake may also make your bowels more loose, and the extra fibre may cause wind. Such symptoms soon pass, and are not a cause for concern.

As always, if you have any particular concerns or worries, or if you have any doubt about the suitability of the advice contained in this book in relation to your current situation, you should seek advice form your doctor (or, if he or she should feel unable to offer advice, from a registered naturopath or other suitably qualified medical practitioner).

Happy—and healthy—eating!

Kirsten Hartvig

a guide to
the immune system

A fully functioning immune system is one of the most vital aspects of a healthy body, helping to prevent and combat disease. However, for many people, the immune system does not function as effectively as it should. In some cases, the immune response fails to offer protection from disease, such as infection or cancer. In other cases, the immune system actively turns against its host, triggering a range of auto-immune and other disorders, such as rheumatoid arthritis, or allergies, that are increasingly prevalent in the modern world. Chapter Five explains how the immune system works, why it sometimes breaks down, and what you can do to strengthen it and keep it in tip-top condition.

NATURAL DEFENSE

When it comes to maintaining good health, the immune system is the body's most precious asset. By helping the body to resist infection and avoid cancer, it offers protection against many of the world's most widespread and deadliest diseases. Yet, despite modern scientific understanding and major advances in medical treatments, infection is still the commonest cause of illness and death worldwide. And cancer of the lung, stomach, breast, cervix, bowel, and prostate continue to be scourges of the modern world— responsible for over 2.5 million deaths worldwide per year.

What is going wrong? Why hasn't our detailed knowledge of the immune system enabled us to enhance our body's defense mechanisms in a sustainable way? In the process of developing ever more powerful means of attacking and destroying micro-organisms and cancer cells, have we lost sight of the need to strengthen our innate protective systems and nurture our inner environment?

In the early 1950s, with antibiotic therapy, general vaccination programs, radical cancer surgery, radiotherapy, and chemotherapy moving into the medical front line, it seemed clear to most people that scientific know-how was going to provide more effective solutions to disease than old-fashioned naturopathic methods designed to encourage the self-healing processes. Now, 60 years on, we are faced with the specter of malaria and tuberculosis on the rise once again, new strains of drug-resistant superbugs outwitting our most powerful technologies, vaccinations that sometimes harm as well as protect, a rising incidence of cancer, immunodeficiency syndromes such as A.I.D.S., and a rising tide of new influenza epidemics.

History suggests that, when things go wrong, human beings have a tendency to continue doing what doesn't work—only doing it harder. Despite valuable short-term tactical advances in the management of infectious disease and cancer, we are singularly failing in our strategic goal of improving world health in a sustainable manner. This is because we have attempted to usurp the power of the natural world, attacking it with crude weapons, and losing ourselves in a maze of technical detail, instead of working with nature and doing everything we can to enhance our natural powers of healing and self-defense.

Just as the pioneers of microbiology—Didier Bechamp, Claude Bernard, and Louis Pasteur—explained that micro-organisms should be thought of as agents of disease and not as causes, we need to understand that our detailed, valuable, and hard-won knowledge of the process of immunity is not the same as an understanding of its purpose. We have superimposed a dualistic, male-oriented, warlike model on to the remarkable scientific observations we have made, and are assuming that life is a battle between ourselves and the micro-organisms and cancer cells; that we inhabit a dog-eat-dog, kill-or-be-killed biological universe.

The effect has been to focus our attention on external factors, while neglecting an inward-looking, broader approach to healing that attempts to observe the interaction between the physical, mental, emotional, and spiritual aspects of self, and to understand how these affect health and our susceptibility to disease. As a result, we have developed a range of medical weapons that are becoming increasingly hazardous to use.

As a society, we seem to find it easier to spend our money on weapons and drugs rather than on good food, basic sanitation and clean water for those most at risk of disease. Therefore, we do not even keep faith with the knowledge that we do possess—*that immunity is profoundly compromised by malnutrition; that poverty and overcrowding creates the perfect environment for the spread of infectious disease; that the typical Western diet and lifestyle lead to cardiovascular problems and cancer; that fear and stress create an internal bodily environment that is prone to disease and degeneration because they suppress the immune system.*

This section is written in the knowledge that good health involves paying attention to body, mind, and spirit, that the immune response is the fundamental physical process of healing, and that health and healing are encouraged and enhanced by good food. On the following pages, we take a look at the history, mechanisms, language, and science of immunity, and explain how it operates both in health and disease, and how it can be influenced by diet and lifestyle. We hope you will use it as a reference as you explore other parts of the book, and as an aid to a better understanding of how the body heals and protects itself.

WHAT IS IMMUNITY?

At the beginning of the 18th century, Mary Pierrepont, an English noblewoman living in Constantinople, became interested in the local method for preventing smallpox, which involved taking scrapings from smallpox crusts and scratching them into the skin. This was an early form of vaccination. Although successful in some cases, the risk of actually developing smallpox from this procedure was very high, and her attempts to introduce inoculation into Britain were largely unsuccessful. However, with smallpox ravaging the 18th-century world (approximately 50 million people died from the disease in Europe between 1700 and 1800), the search for an effective preventative strategy continued.

Some years later, Edward Jenner, an English country doctor from the county of Gloucestershire, noticed that dairymaids who caught cowpox (a relatively minor condition causing spots on the hands) had a strong capacity to resist smallpox. In 1796, he inoculated a young boy with material taken from cowpox spots and then, in an experiment that caused much controversy at the time, inoculated the same boy several times with actual smallpox, without causing any ill effects! Not surprisingly, this dramatic demonstration led to large numbers of people visiting Jenner's country home seeking vaccination, and the success of his smallpox-prevention treatment paved the way for the development of the worldwide vaccination programs we see today.

However, at the time, Jenner's work did little to stimulate new thinking on the nature and causes of infectious disease. Since Roman times, doctors had been trying to discover the reason for the epidemics that decimated the population periodically, but the "germ" theory central to our current understanding of infection did not gain wide acceptance until the mid-19th century. It was then that an Italian, Agostino Bassi, proved that a disease of silkworms was caused by micro-organisms. Although not directly related to human health, his research formed the basis for later discoveries by the "giants" of microbiology—Pasteur, Robert Koch, Joseph Lister, and Paul Ehrlich—that revolutionized biomedicine.

Modern-day research into infectious disease follows two parallel tracks—the first investigating the form, nature, and lifestyle of pathogenic (or disease-causing) micro-organisms, and the chemicals that can be used to destroy them; the second looking into the nature of the body's inherent capacity to resist infection, and how this in-born immunity can be stimulated.

While this research has produced much valuable information and given us important new treatments, the commonly-held belief that germs are malign micro-foes, constantly out to get us—and that the best way of dealing with them is to zap them with increasing doses of powerful antibiotics—is, in fact, a misunderstanding of what the pioneers of microbiology and immunology were saying.

Pasteur, together with the other early holistic medical thinkers—Bechamp, Bernard, and Max von Pettenkofer—emphasized that microbes are only a part of the story, best thought of as agents of disease rather than the causes, their effects largely dependent on the nature of the bodily "terrain" they encounter. In other words, he understood that the state of the body's natural defense systems was paramount to the maintenance of good health.

what the immune system does

The immune system is the body's first line of defense against invasion by micro-organisms and "foreign" materials, and the basis for vaccination and the differences between blood groups. It also protects against the development of cancer by destroying mutant (abnormal) cells. However, immune reactions are not always helpful. If the immune system overreacts to the presence of harmless substances, it produces allergic conditions such as hay fever and asthma. When it is weakened and fails to protect us from infection, the body suffers from immunodeficiency states such as A.I.D.S. When it starts to attack its own body cells as if they were "foreign," the immune system causes autoimmune diseases such as rheumatoid arthritis and systemic lupus erythematosus (S.L.E.).

Thus, the immune system can help or harm the body, depending on the nature and strength of its reactions. There is no fundamental difference between the mechanisms underlying "protective" immunity and those that cause disorders such as allergy and autoimmunity. The part that the immune system plays in health and disease can be divided into two helpful effects—active and passive immunity —and two harmful effects—overactivity and underactivity:

● Active immunity involves the body's own defensive cells and chemicals, which act against bacteria, viruses, fungi, parasites, tumors, and foreign blood groups. Some forms of vaccination stimulate active immunity in the body.
● Passive immunity includes the antibodies acquired by a fetus from its mother, and also refers to vaccination with pre-formed antibodies taken from people or animals.
● Overactivity includes allergy and hypersensitivity to external substances, autoimmunity, and adverse blood transfusion reactions (rhesus incompatibility).
● Underactivity includes inherited immunodeficiency, and acquired immunodeficiency (for example, associated with H.I.V. infection, drugs, radiation, or environmental toxins).

components of the immune system

The immune system is an elaborate, interactive system of cells, chemicals, and tissues distributed throughout the body. When any of these components come into contact with any cells or substance to which they are programed to respond (such as bacteria, viruses, and pollen grains), a series of reactions is triggered that results in the "foreign invader" being destroyed or rendered harmless.

Any cell component or chemical substance that triggers a reaction by the immune system is known as an antigen. The reaction may be innate or adaptive (see page 160) and a property of adaptive immunity is that it is specific to the antigen that stimulated it. The cells and antibodies involved in an adaptive immune reaction to a particular antigen won't respond to any other antigen unless it is very similar indeed to the original.

Among the most important components of the immune system are white blood cells, such as lymphocytes, chemicals such as cytokines, antibodies, and the complement system, and tissues such as the lymph nodes. These form the "sharp end" of the immune system. They are the tools that the body uses to dismantle, destroy, and eliminate harmful antigens such as bacteria, viruses, and tumor cells. The way in which these various components interact determines how efficiently the immune system will function.

cells

The principal cells of the immune system are T cells, B cells, antigen-presenting cells (A.P.C.s), neutrophils and mast cells. All have clearly defined roles in the immune system.

● T cells are a type of white cell, or lymphocyte, found in the blood, bone marrow, and lymph nodes. They help to stimulate B cells (see below) to produce antibodies and act directly to destroy antigen-bearing organisms (such as viruses) that invade the body's own cells. T cells are divided into three groups, according to function—T helper cells, killer T cells, and regulatory T cells.

● B cells are another group of white cells, also found in the blood, bone marrow, and lymphoid tissues. When stimulated by contact with an antigen, they secrete antibodies, which enhance the body's response to a disease. Antibodies produced by any group of B cells react against only one specific antigen. After infection, some B cells remain in the circulation as "memory" cells, capable of recognizing the disease should it strike again. This function is described in more detail on page 163.

● Antigen-presenting cells are a group of cells (including dendritic cells, macrophages and activated B cells) found in the skin and throughout the lymphoid tissues. These process antigens to ensure the T cells recognize the presence of foreign cells and other substances as efficiently as possible, and do not confuse them with naturally occurring cellular material. Macrophages—a type of A.P.C. whose name means "big eaters"—are the waste-disposal units of the immune system, eating up all types of foreign matter and the debris that results from immune activity.

● Neutrophils are the commonest form of white blood cells. Like macrophages, they engulf bacteria and foreign matter.

● Mast cells are found throughout the body. When activated by antibodies during an immune reaction, they release chemicals (such as histamine) that trigger inflammation.

chemicals

Antibodies are also known as immunoglobulins (Ig). They are proteins secreted by B cells that activate enzymes and stimulate blood and tissue cells to destroy bacteria and other pathogens. There are five main classes of antibody:

● IgG is the most abundant immunoglobulin, found in the blood and throughout the body tissues. It activates the complement system (see below), and stimulates neutrophils and macrophages to destroy antigens.

● IgM is also found in the bloodstream. It, too, activates the complement system and is particularly important in the fight against bacteria.

● IgA is found in breast milk, tears, saliva, and the secretions from mucous membranes (such as the lining of the intestines and the respiratory and reproductive tracts) and so is one of the first lines of defense against invading micro-organisms. It helps resist gastro-intestinal infections, and maintains a healthy gut flora.

● IgE is found in the body tissues and can trigger allergic reactions, such as hay fever, by stimulating mast cells to release histamine.

Surface membrane molecules (also known as CD4 and CD8 molecules) are protein molecules found on the outer surface of T cells. They enhance the ability of T cells to trigger immune responses, and help them to recognize the difference between antigens and our own body cells. The number of T cells in the blood carrying CD surface molecules is important in the diagnosis of some diseases.

Cytokines are a group of chemicals secreted by white cells (including macrophages, T-helper cells, mast cells, and neutrophils). They help the cells of the immune system to communicate with each other and so improve the efficacy of the immune response. Three are particularly important:

● Interleukin 2 is secreted by killer T cells in response to the presence of antigens. It increases the rate of production of T cells.

● Tumor necrosis factor (T.N.F.). As the term "tumor necrosis" (tumor death) suggests, T.N.F. attacks and destroys tumor cells and can also kill virus-infected cells. It also plays a role in activating the immune response to disease, and can be responsible for a number of symptoms of illness (including fever, weight loss, and feeling generally unwell).

● Interferon gamma is produced by helper T cells (and other white blood cells). It encourages macrophage activity and has a strong anti-viral action. It also works with T.N.F. to destroy tumor cells and, like T.N.F., is responsible for some of the general symptoms of acute illness.

Complement is a group of proteins, made in the liver and found in the blood. When an immune reaction is triggered, antibodies start attaching themselves to antigens and this triggers a chain reaction by the complement enzymes that amplifies the immune response and produces the classic symptoms of inflammation—swelling, redness, and pain. The complement system also enhances the function of phagocytic cells, attacks the cell membrane of invading cells, and alerts other cells to the presence of foreign "invaders"

● M.H.C. markers were discovered in the latter half of the 20th century by scientists researching the phenomenon of transplant rejection. The scientists found a cluster of genes on chromosome six of human D.N.A. that they called the Major Histocompatibility Complex (M.H.C.). As well as containing the instructions for making some of the complement proteins, these "histocompatibility genes" are responsible for the presence of so-called M.H.C. "markers" on the surface of body cells. These markers identify cells as belonging uniquely to that body. They provide the means by which the immune system can distinguish between its "own" body cells and "foreign" cells (such as bacteria). The fact that M.H.C. molecules are genetically determined explains some of the variation in immune response shown by different individuals.

tissues

While many immune reactions happen in the bloodstream, there are other "lymphoid" tissues equally important to immunity—namely lymph nodes ("glands"), mucosa-associated lymphoid tissue (M.A.L.T.), the spleen, the bone marrow and the thymus.

● Lymph nodes are collections of lymphoid cells found throughout the body, including the neck, the armpits, and the groin. They are joined by a network of lymph-carrying vessels (the lymphatics), and are the main sites of storage, activation, and production of the lymphocytes. Lymph is a pale straw-colored fluid, similar to blood plasma, from which it is produced, but more watery and containing only lymphocytes plus some protein, fat, and salts. It circulates throughout the body via the lymphatics, and acts as a transport and communications medium for immune cells.

● M.A.L.T. is a diffuse collection of patches of lymphoid tissue found in many parts of the body, including the gastro-intestinal

tract lining, the appendix, the tonsils, the breasts, and the lungs. It contains clusters of B cells, T cells, and mast cells.

● The spleen, like other lymphoid tissues, contains B cells, T cells and macrophages. In the developing fetus, the spleen also produces red blood cells.

● The bone marrow is the main production site for red and white blood cells and is a constantly renewing reservoir of small, "primitive" immune system cells. Immature B cells leave the bone marrow to take up residence in the other lymphoid tissues. Immature T cells leave the bone marrow at an even earlier stage of development, and migrate to the thymus (hence the name "T" cell) where they are taught to recognize the difference between "self" (the body's own cells) and "other" (foreign cells and other material) before moving on to other lymphoid tissues. The thymus was named by the second-century physician Galen, who thought it looked like a bunch of thyme flowers. It is situated in the upper part of the chest and is crucial to the proper development of T cells and thus to the function of the immune system as a whole.

how the immune system works

We all have an innate, genetically determined ability to produce an immediate, non-specific immune response to disease-causing antigens that enter the body. The complement system, neutrophils, macrophages, and so-called "natural killer cells" combine to provide an initial defence against pathogens encountered by humans. However, there is such a wide variety of potentially pathogenic organisms in the world that we have also evolved a powerful system of adaptive immunity that enables us to mount a massive, specific defense against individual pathogens, and also protect us against future exposure to those same pathogens. This adaptive immune response is triggered by activation of the innate immune system and involves an interaction between antigen-presenting cells and T helper cells, which leads to the production of antibodies, cytokines, and cytotoxic T cells specifically directed against the particular strain of invading pathogen that is posing a threat.

The first time the immune system is exposed to a new antigen, the adaptive response takes about 10 days to reach full intensity, during which time the balance between resisting and succumbing to the disease can be very fine. Assuming we recover, the next time the immune system meets the same pathogen, the defensive response is powerful and immediate, giving us resistance to the disease.

recognition and defense

Innate or adaptive, our immune response is always a two-stage process. First, we have to recognize that a foreign, potentially harmful antigen has entered (or is trying to enter) the body. Second, we have to do something to defend ourselves from the invasion. In the process of recognition, we have to be sure as far as possible that we are not mistaking the surface characteristics of our own cells (or other harmless substances) for those of pathogens.

In the defense process, we have to be able to adapt and respond efficiently to a huge variety of potentially harmful antigens, yet without letting the intensity of the immune response cause damage to the body. And we have to do it fast enough to ensure that the invaders don't get the upper hand. Then we have to be able to remember past battles, in order to respond more quickly and effectively if faced with the same challenge in the future.

As well as the general and specific actions of the immune system, the body also has a number of non-specific protective mechanisms that amplify the effects of immunity, and which are triggered by immune activity. These non-specific responses can be grouped together under the general term "inflammation."

inflammation

This is one of the oldest recognized features of disease, first described by the Roman medical writer Celsus. It is the body's initial response to tissue or cell damage (internal or external), and the symptoms of heat, redness, swelling, and pain it causes are well known. Much orthodox medical treatment of illness is directed toward the suppression of inflammation, and in many cases (especially in chronic inflammatory conditions such as arthritis) this is both rational and humane.

However, the bad press that inflammation usually receives is misleading because, for most people, it is the process of inflammation that actually allows the immune system to do its work quickly and efficiently. To the naturopathic physician, inflammation is not an unwelcome event but the primary sign that the body is starting to heal itself. Naturopathic treatment seeks to keep the patient comfortable while allowing natural healing mechanisms to do their work unsuppressed.

The inflammatory process follows a set course. First, a cell or tissue is injured, or attacked by pathogens. As a result, chemicals are released from damaged cells or immune cells that cause blood vessels in the damaged area to widen, bringing more blood to the damaged area and slowing down the rate of blood flow. In addition, the blood vessels around the area become "leaky," allowing the free flow of immune cells and fluid into the tissues.

White cells in the blood line up along the blood vessel walls and pass into the damaged area. These cells come into contact with micro-organisms and foreign particles, triggering an immune reaction. Swelling caused by the fluid immobilizes and localizes the damage, and the other components of the immune system—including antibodies, cytotoxic T cells, and complement—then come into play and neutralize the antigens. The debris is swallowed up by macrophages and neutrophils.

control of immune reactions

With all this cellular and chemical firepower at its disposal, the immune system needs to include certain safeguards to ensure that its reactions do not get out of hand and start attacking healthy body cells. One simple control mechanism built into the system is that, because the intensity of the immune response depends on the amount of antigen present, as soon as immunity starts destroying antigen, the strength of the response fades naturally. This means that the immune response is inherently self-limiting.

As a further safeguard, when helper T cells are stimulated repeatedly during an immune reaction, some of

them turn into "regulating" T cells, which deactivate the immune system by producing inhibiting cytokines. Repeated activation of T cells ultimately leads to their death, making room for new T cells to protect against future infections. (In cases of deficient T-cell function, such as immunodeficiency states and malnutrition, this suppression function is lost, leading to an increase in allergic and autoimmune reactions; see pages 166–67.)

immune memory, tolerance, and vaccination

The capacity for immunological memory is one of the most important features of the immune system. When an immune response is triggered, a proportion of B and T cells form a "memory population" capable of multiplying rapidly and mounting a swift immune response if the body is exposed to the same antigen at a later date.

This response to the antigen may be so effective that the symptoms of disease are much milder than on the first occasion—or there may be no symptoms at all (in which case, the person is said to be immune to that disease). However, each antigen is recognized by its unique chemical characteristics, and immunological memory relates only to those antigens that have been encountered before. An individual who is immune to one kind of pathogen does not necessarily have immunity to other pathogenic organisms. The capacity for immunological memory underlies the concept of vaccination in its two forms— "active" and "passive." In active vaccination, immunity is induced artificially by exposing the body to small amounts of dead or inactivated micro-organisms, usually by injection. The protective response generated in the body by this form of vaccination can last for many years. However, for some diseases, it is not possible to produce a safe, active vaccine, but some measure of short-term protection can be given by passive vaccination—which involves injecting "ready-made" antibodies against the disease, usually derived from animals.

The debate over the safety and effectiveness of vaccination continues to smolder, with protagonists pointing to successes in the control of epidemic diseases such as smallpox, diphtheria, polio, and tuberculosis, and opponents claiming that it can cause brain damage and autism, and pointing to the increased incidence of allergy and autoimmune disease that has coincided with the widespread use of vaccination.

Whatever view you hold over the risks and benefits of vaccination, it is important to remember that vaccines necessarily contain antigens that have been altered from their original state, and that our understanding of the body's reactions to such antigens is far from complete.

Another extremely important property of the immune system is that, in general, it can distinguish between cells from its "own" body and "foreign" cells and antigens. As already explained, this is owing to the presence of "markers" on our body cells that signal "self" to the immune system.

In the developing fetus, these surface markers are "learned" by the immune system because the only cells passing through the unborn baby's lymphoid tissues are its own. In fact, if a newborn baby (whose immune system has not yet fully matured) is exposed to antigenic material there is a good chance that it will develop tolerance to the antigen rather than mount an immune response against it. (The same is true in some elderly people whose immune systems become progressively less efficient.) This means that it is ineffective to vaccinate very young babies, because their capacity to develop tolerance to antigens at this stage in life might leave them unprotected, despite the vaccination.

IMMUNITY AND DISEASE

For many years, it was thought that the symptoms and signs of infectious disease were caused by pathogens, and that the immune system was purely a protective shield, destroying microbes and eliminating dangerous toxins from the body. While the second part of this idea is still held to be true, it is now known that many of the unpleasant, painful, and damaging effects of infection are a direct result of the immune response itself, and that the protection we enjoy from the immune system carries a cost.

When it comes to infectious disease, most of us are happy to pay the price of short-term discomfort as long as we receive the longer-term benefit of recovering from the illness. If, on the other hand, the immune system begins to react to substances in the environment that would ordinarily pose no threat to health—or worse, starts attacking our own body tissues for no apparent reason—we get justifiably concerned. Before looking in detail at allergy and autoimmunity, it is helpful to look at the ways in which the immune system causes illness, and at what it is that makes us susceptible to immune-based diseases.

The following are important conditions caused by immune system activity:

● Heart—carditis in rheumatic fever, cardiomyopathy, and post-heart attack syndromes
● Lungs—alveolitis and asthma
● Gastro-intestinal and liver—celiac disease, ulcerative colitis, and some forms of hepatitis
● Skin—contact dermatitis, pemphigus, pemphigoid, and dermatitis herpetiformis
● Endocrine—Addison's disease, thyroiditis, and type I, insulin-dependent (early onset) diabetes mellitus
● Ear, nose, and throat—hay fever, otitis media ("glue ear")
● Eyes—uveitis, allergic conjunctivitis, and keratoconjunctivitis sicca
● Children—atopic eczema, milk allergy, food allergies, juvenile chronic arthritis, and Henoch-Schönlein purpura
● Blood—pernicious anemia, autoimmune hemolytic anemia, thrombocytopenia and blood transfusion reactions
● Reproductive—rhesus disease of newborn, and infertility
● Kidneys—glomerulolonephritis
● Joints—rheumatoid arthritis, S.L.E., and dermatomyositis
● Nerves—multiple sclerosis, myasthenia gravis, polyneuritis, polymyositis, post-vaccination/post-infection encephalitis
● Infections—immune activity is responsible for a variety of syndromes associated with tuberculosis, malaria, Chagas' disease, and leprosy
● General—anaphylaxis, graft rejection, serum sickness

immune-based disease

Anaphylactic (reaginic) immune reactions are caused by the release of histamine and other chemicals from mast cells, resulting in inflammation, edema, and contraction of smooth muscle. Anaphylaxis evolved to protect us against parasites, and to provide an immediate response to foreign antigens, but it is also responsible for allergic asthma, hay fever, atopic eczema, and food allergies. In its most severe form, acute anaphylaxis, reaction to an antigen causes a rapid onset of nausea, wheezing, itching, low blood pressure, abdominal pain, urticaria (hives), and loss of consciousness. Untreated, acute anaphylaxis can be fatal.

Cell reactive immune reactions involve antibodies sticking to the surface of body cells and triggering various inflammatory responses. Originally designed to destroy invading micro-organisms, these reactions are also responsible for blood transfusion incompatibility, rhesus disease of the newborn, acute graft rejection, and a variety of autoimmune conditions including hemolytic anemia, thyrotoxicosis, pemphigoid, and myasthenia gravis.

Immune complex reactions are caused by antibodies binding with soluble antigens (such as bacterial toxins) in the blood or body fluids. The resulting "immune complexes" are then deposited in the tissues, clogging small blood vessels, and triggering inflammation. Intended as a way of ridding the body of toxins, these reactions are a common cause of immune-related disorders including rashes, vasculitis, alveolitis, serum sickness, glomerulonephritis, rheumatoid arthritis, and systemic lupus erythematosus.

Cell-mediated reactions (or delayed hypersensitivity reactions) involve T cells and macrophages and offer protection against parasitic infection. They are also responsible for the clinical features of tuberculosis, leprosy, pernicious anemia, "contact" dermatitis, type I, insulin-dependent (early onset) diabetes mellitus, graft rejection and to "sensitization" to common substances (such as household chemicals and latex).

susceptibility to immune disease

One of the big unanswered questions in modern immunology is: "Why are some people more prone to immune-based diseases than others?" Research into this subject is ongoing but scientists have uncovered important clues that might point to possible answers. The first involves an immune phenomenon called "atopy." At least 5 per cent of the population have an inherited tendency to produce high levels of IgE, which reacts with common substances, such as pollen and food additives, to cause atopic allergic reactions—such as itching and sneezing. A popular but unproven theory suggests that children develop atopy because they are raised in oversanitized environments and eat "non-natural" diets (such as formula infant milks and convenience foods). The theory is that, because modern children are exposed to few disease microbes but are repeatedly in contact with artificial substances, the immune system directs too much of its attention toward harmless environmental antigens and hence lacks an adequate response to disease organisms. The allergic child, constantly suffering upper respiratory-tract infections, is an example of this mechanism at work.

There is some evidence that an inherited lack of some of the components of the complement system is responsible for the tendency to develop some immune disorders. Research has also shown that an individual's inherited M.H.C. type has a bearing on the development of a wide range of immunologically based diseases, including ankylosing spondylitis, celiac disease, Graves' disease, S.L.E., rheumatoid arthritis, and pernicious anemia.

Research in West Africa has shown an association between M.H.C. type and the capacity to resist malaria. Although useful in the diagnosis of some conditions, the reason for these associations is not yet clear.

allergy, autoimmunity, and immunodeficiency

Allergy (an unpleasant reaction to non-microbial, "harmless" environmental antigens) and autoimmunity (an immune response against one's own body tissues) are now major causes of illness, particularly in the Western world. Between them they are responsible for much of the daily workload of family doctors, and also generate a huge market for pharmaceutical products that control or suppress the immune response.

allergy

As we saw on page 164, allergic reactions fall into two categories: anaphylactic (or reaginic), rapid allergic responses caused by histamine released from mast cells; and cell-mediated, a slower response to environmental antigens involving T cells and macrophages. A significant proportion of the population have an inherited atopic tendency to anaphylactic allergic reactions of the skin, lungs, eyes, nose, and digestive tract causing conditions such as eczema, hay fever, conjunctivitis, asthma, and food allergy.

Celiac disease (an allergy to wheat gluten, which causes malabsorption), dermatitis herpetiformis (a blistering skin disease also caused by gluten), and allergic alveolitis (for example, farmer's lung, a potentially serious allergic lung inflammation usually caused by occupational exposure to molds) are other important conditions caused by allergy to environmental antigens. Allergic asthma is most often caused by tiny particles of antigenic material. Allergic rhinitis or hay fever is triggered by larger particles. The most common environmental antigens are: plant pollens, house dust mites, insect stings, pet dander (fur and feathers), fungal molds, food proteins, vaccines, drugs, household/industrial chemicals, latex, and heavy metals (especially chromium, cobalt, and nickel).

However, not all adverse reactions to environmental substances are caused by allergies. The term "allergy" is sometimes wrongly attached to any unpleasant reaction to a food or drug. Favism is a hemolytic anemia caused by an inherited lack of the enzyme glucose-6-phosphatase dehydrogenase, which is vital for the health of red blood cells. When a sufferer eats fava beans, inhales fava bean pollen, or takes certain drugs, including sulfonamide antibiotics and certain anti-malarial drugs, red blood cells are rapidly destroyed causing fever, abdominal pain and, in severe cases, coma and even death. The sensitivity of some asthma sufferers to drugs such as aspirin is more often a chemical, rather than an immunological, problem.

Orthodox treatment of allergy is a two-stage process. First, it involves reducing exposure to the allergen responsible (where possible) and, second, the use of drugs. Common drugs used for allergies include:

● Nasal sprays and inhalers (such as antihistamines and sodium cromoglycate), to inhibit the release of histamine from mast cells.

● Bronchodilators, to reduce muscle spasm in the lungs and open the airways.

● Corticosteroid drugs ("steroids"), which counteract inflammation.

autoimmunity

In normal circumstances, the immune system is able to distinguish clearly between "self" and "non-self." During their "education" in the thymus, developing T cells that may react to the body's own tissues are destroyed, and any self-reacting cells that do survive are suppressed by other cells in the immune system. However, for reasons not yet clearly understood, these safety mechanisms sometimes break down, resulting in an autoimmune disease.

Autoimmune diseases are usually chronic, and cause slow, progressive damage to organs and tissues. These conditions cover a spectrum ranging from "organ specific" disorders, in which only one "target" organ is damaged, to "multi-system" diseases involving a variety of body systems, and producing complex patterns of symptoms and signs.

Organ-specific autoimmune disease include:

● Thyroid—Hashimoto's thyroiditis, and Graves' disease

● Adrenal gland—Addison's disease

● Pancreas—Type I (early onset) diabetes mellitus

● Nerves and muscles—multiple sclerosis, and myaesthenia gravis

● Skin—pemphigus, pemphigoid, and vitiligo

● Kidney—Goodpasture's syndrome

● Liver—primary biliary cirrhosis

● Stomach—pernicious anemia

● Hair—alopecia

● Ovaries—premature ovarian failure

● Uterus—endometriosis.

Autoimmune disease is growing increasingly common, so the search for a cause is generating an enormous research effort. This research has uncovered important clues suggesting possible trigger mechanisms for autoimmune reactions. It seems, for example, that certain infections (particularly viruses), vaccinations, and environmental factors can cause subtle changes in lymphocyte function that lead to a break down in self-recognition by the immune system.

Some microbes even stimulate B cells to produce "auto-antibodies" directly, by mimicking the actions of T helper cells, and it is possible that other micro-organisms contain proteins that closely resemble those of human tissues. If the immune system makes antibodies to such micro-organisms, it will unwittingly produce antibodies that damage the body's own cells as well.

Many of those suffering from autoimmune diseases have an inherited immunological instability that affects their ability to control immune responses. In particular they may lack T regulating cells, which normally keep stray "auto-reactive" T helper cells under control.

immunodeficiency

In order to cope with the huge diversity of potentially harmful micro-organisms (and other antigens) that we are exposed to in life, the immune system has evolved into a highly complex system of many inter-related components. Although this gives a wide repertoire of immune responses, it also means that damage or deficiency in any part of the system makes us susceptible to illness.

Immunodeficiency is now an increasingly common cause of disease worldwide. The basic feature of immunodeficiency is the tendency to suffer more frequent and more serious infection than normal, often from micro-organisms not usually considered dangerous.

Immunodeficiency can be divided into two categories: primary—a genetic defect involving the lack of a vital immune system component; and secondary—the direct result of another disease process, or the consequence of exposure to drugs, chemicals, or ionizing radiation. Primary immunodeficiency is usually diagnosed early in life (most often in a child suffering frequent ear, nose, throat, and chest infections), and in some cases (such as in severe combined immunodeficiency—S.C.I.D.) it may lead to early death. When primary immunodeficiency is owing to a lack of B cells (such as X-linked hypogammaglobulinemia—Bruton's disease), lifelong injections of immunoglobulin are necessary to maintain health. Deficiency of complement proteins can also be managed with drugs and enzyme injections.

Secondary immunodeficiency is more common than the primary type, and has a wide variety of possible causes. The commonest are leukemia, Hodgkin's lymphoma, myeloma, burns, severe kidney disease, Down's syndrome, chronic inflammation, chronic infection (such as malaria and leprosy), congenital rubella (German measles), surgery/radiation of lymphoid tissues, drug therapy (especially corticosteroids and anti-cancer drugs), and poverty.

Of these, poverty is probably the most common cause of immunodeficiency worldwide. Protein-energy malnutrition causes decreased cellular immunity, atrophy of lymph nodes, a reduction of T cells, and an overall decrease in the capacity of the immune system to deal with infection.

H.I.V. and A.I.D.S.

Of all the possible causes of immunodeficiency, in the last 30 years the most important has undoubtedly been acquired immune deficiency syndrome (A.I.D.S.). This is a slow, progressive deterioration of immune function and to date has been responsible for more than 25 million deaths worldwide since 1981, with the brunt of the disease borne by the populations of sub-Saharan Africa, south and south-eastern Asia, and South America. A.I.D.S. is now probably responsible for more deaths per year than malaria, and is a major factor in the re-emergence of tuberculosis as a world health problem.

As in other immunodeficiency states, the central problem faced by the A.I.D.S. sufferer is susceptibility to severe infections by viruses, bacteria, fungi, and parasites. The other important feature of full-blown A.I.D.S. is the development of tumors such as lymphoma (cancer of

lymphoid tissue) and Kaposi's sarcoma (a type of skin tumor).

The commonest A.I.D.S.-related infections are Herpes simplex, Herpes zoster, cytomegalovirus (C.M.V.), tuberculosis, salmonella, toxoplasma, cryptosporidium, giardia, pneumocystis, cryptococcus, histoplasma, candida, and strongyloides.

A.I.D.S. is caused by infection with the H.I.V.1 virus, one of a family of "retro viruses" thought to have originated in primates. It causes immunodeficiency by affecting T helper cells, macrophages, and dendritic cells, and by affecting the pattern of cytokine release.

The fact that the H.I.V. virus is able to fuse with immune system cells and commandeer their internal workings—and that it is capable of assuming a wide range of antigenic forms during the course of the disease—enables it to evade the body's protective immune response, and makes the development of effective treatments very difficult.

Combination antiretroviral drug therapy is the main type of treatment for H.I.V. and A.I.D.S.. It is not a cure, but can keep the amount of H.I.V. in the body low, stop the weakening of the immune system, and allow recovery from previous damage caused by the virus. Antibacterial and antifungal drugs are also used to treat infections. Health education programs about the need for safer sex, safe blood transfusion procedures, and reducing shared-needle use by intravenous drug users are the mainstays of prevention, and much research is being devoted to the development of a safe and effective vaccine.

Given the close link between nutrition and immunity, it is not surprising that diet and the treatment of H.I.V. infection are also intimately related. It has been shown that good nutrition greatly improves the outcome of drug therapy and chances of long-term survival. Maximizing the quality of the diet can also play a major role in improving the quality of life of A.I.D.S. sufferers (see page 240–41).

IMMUNITY AND FOOD

Like the lungs, the gastro-intestinal tract is a major "meeting place" in which the body comes into contact with the outside world. All food and drink has to pass through it before being absorbed and used for nutrition, and its lining is rich in lymphoid tissue called Peyer's patches.

The challenge for the immune system is that it has to be tolerant of the wide variety of "foreign" food proteins that we consume habitually, while at the same time being able to recognize and destroy potentially harmful micro-organisms that might contaminate our food and water.

It manages this by suppressing the production of any IgG and IgM antibodies that might react against food protein molecules, and by increasing the amount of IgA antibody in gut secretions. IgA has the ability to bind directly to pathogenic micro-organisms, and to neutralize them without activating the complement system or causing inflammation.

However, when the immune system is combating an infection elsewhere in the body, gastro-intestinal lymphoid tissue can get caught up in the action and start attacking harmless food antigens. This in turn causes inflammation and damage to the lining of the gastro-intestinal tract. Severe malnutrition can also damage the lining of the intestines and disturb the pattern of immune responses.

allergy or intolerance?

Sometimes—and especially in those with a family tendency to atopic conditions such as eczema, asthma, and hay fever —the immune system reacts against certain foods. In addition to triggering general allergic symptoms, this causes inflammation of the intestinal lining and increased contraction of intestinal muscle, leading to abdominal discomfort, diarrhea, wind, and poor absorption of nutrients. Deficiencies of vitamins, minerals, and other nutrients can, in turn, affect the immune system. For example:

● Essential fatty acid deficiency causes atrophy of lymphoid tissues and decreased ability to produce antibodies.

● Vitamin A and E deficiency affects the immune defenses of skin and mucous membranes, decreases T cell activity and antibody production, and so increases infection risk.

● Vitamin B6, folate and pantothenate deficiency decreases T and B cell activity.

● Iron deficiency (or excess iron) increases infection risk.

● Zinc deficiency causes atrophy of lymphoid tissue, decreases B and T cell responses and inhibits development of the immune system in the fetus.

There is a tendency these days to label all unpleasant reactions to food as "food allergy," but for accurate diagnosis and effective treatment, it is necessary to classify such reactions under their correct headings: food intolerance; food allergy; and psychological intolerance.

Food intolerance is a general term covering all negative reactions to foodstuffs, including those caused by inherited enzyme deficiencies, interactions with drugs and medicines, and chemical irritations (for example, by chilli pepper).

Food allergy means that a particular food is triggering a specific immune response. True food allergy is more common in children, and can express itself in a variety of ways including eczema, asthma, urticaria, mood disturbance, severe anaphylactic reactions, epilepsy, poor growth, diarrhea, vomiting, and gastro-intestinal bleeding. (The association between childhood hyperactivity and food allergy is not clearly established.)

Food allergy in adults tends to cause urticaria, asthma, migraine, or "irritable bowel syndrome"-type symptoms such as nausea, bloating, abdominal pain, and alternating constipation and diarrhea. There is also some evidence implicating food allergy in arthritis and depression. Accurate diagnosis of food allergy is time-consuming and usually involves elimination diets followed by "challenges" with the suspect food(s). Patch and scratch tests, cytotoxic blood testing, hair analysis, applied kinesiology, vega testing, and iridology are also used, with varying degrees of success.

Psychological intolerance means reacting to a food which, although causing unpleasant symptoms when eaten in a recognizable form, causes no reaction when it is disguised or made unrecognizable by mixing with other foods. Generally speaking, orthodox medical practitioners tend to over-diagnose psychological intolerance, whereas complementary therapists tend to under-diagnose it.

cow's milk allergy

Despite its status as a staple food in the West, cow's milk is a common cause of food allergy in children and is responsible for a variety of symptoms—including eczema, asthma, diarrhea, vomiting, and malabsorption of nutrients causing slow growth.

The allergen responsible is beta-lactoglobulin, a protein that forms part of milk whey, and most children (and many adults) have antibodies in their blood to milk protein. Babies can become sensitized to milk protein via the breast milk if the mother's diet contains cow's milk and milk products. Although the majority of children have developed "tolerance" to cow's milk by about one year old, the lining of the intestine continues to show abnormalities. Excluding cow's milk from the diet resolves the problem.

Allergy to cow's milk is not the same as lactose intolerance, another common cause of gastro-intestinal upset in children. Babies and young children produce the enzyme lactase, which can digest lactose, a sugar found in breast milk. Production of this enzyme drops sharply after weaning and in most races (except Western Caucasians) is practically non-existent in adults. If an individual with lactase "deficiency" drinks cow's milk, the lactose will not be digested and so will pass into the colon, causing diarrhea, wind, and abdominal discomfort. Lactose intolerance is a common cause of "unexplained" abdominal pain in children and is also common after bouts of gastroenteritis.

celiac disease

Celiac disease is another immune-related gastro-intestinal condition, in which eating wheat gluten causes inflammation and damage to the lining of the small intestine. This leads to severe malabsorption of important nutrients resulting in multiple health problems including diarrhea, weight loss, flatulence, edema, anemia, muscle wasting, bone problems, and disturbance of heart rhythm. The exact nature of the immune reaction that causes celiac disease is unclear, but it is known that people with the condition have an inherited genetic susceptibility, and that the components of gluten that cause the problem are called gliandins. Although potentially serious, celiac disease can be managed by eating a gluten-free diet. This means avoiding wheat, barley, rye, and, usually, oats—for life. However, rice, maize, and soy products are safe, and not everyone with the disorder is sensitive to oats.

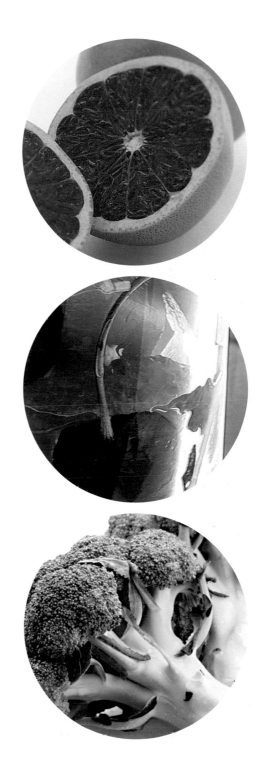

IMPROVING IMMUNITY

Immunity that harms and immunity that heals are both caused by the same basic mechanisms, so knowing which nutritional and lifestyle factors influence immunity gives us a powerful way of enhancing personal health, and of coping with many common ailments that have immune disturbance at their root. A healthy immune system is the basis of well-being, so making it more efficient, and avoiding anything that might compromise or weaken it, are the fundamental steps to life-long health.

Later sections of this book look in detail at how you can select the right foods to optimize immune function, but clinical experience and modern research also show that other factors have powerful effects on immunity, particularly stress, environmental pollution, alcohol, cigarettes and recreational drugs, medical interventions, obesity, lack of exercise, and age factors.

managing stress

Chronic stress causes the adrenal glands to secrete higher levels of corticosteroids, which depress immune function. In acute stress reactions, high epinephrine levels also decrease T-helper-cell activity, increase T suppressor cell activity and lead to degeneration of lymphoid tissues. Changes in mood alter the amount of IgA present in secretions from mucous membranes, and depression interferes with T and B cell function. Therefore, chronic stress is a major risk factor for illness, particularly cancer and heart disease, and making the lifestyle changes necessary to reduce its impact on our lives is a vitally important preventative health strategy. Stress-management techniques such as yoga, deep breathing, meditation and autosuggestion can also have a significant effect on immune function and reduce our susceptibility to disease.

avoiding pollution

Environmental pollutants are broadly divided into three categories:
● Radiation—from microwave appliances, mobile phones, television and radio transmitters, television and computer screens, high tension overhead electricity cables, and nuclear installations and reprocessing plants.
● Chemicals—including garden and agricultural pesticides and herbicides, aerosols, industrial emissions, engine exhaust fumes,

smoke, paints, fungicides, and household products such as air fresheners, detergents, and furniture polish.
● Biological—such as house dust and dust mites, pet dander, and molds.

All of these can compromize immunity. Minimizing the use of household chemicals, buying organic produce, using dust-covers on mattresses, exchanging carpets for wood or tiled flooring, avoiding smoking and smokers, ensuring good ventilation in the house, limiting the amount of time spent in front of television screens and computer monitors, and household maintenance to avoid damp and mold formation are all achievable ways of improving immune-system health.

avoiding alcohol, cigarettes, and drugs

In many parts of the world, alcohol is one of the most important controllable risk factors for serious illness. It depresses the immune response and is clearly associated with heart disease, hypertension, stroke, gastritis, pancreatitis, peptic ulcers, serious liver damage, and deterioration of mental function. As with hard-drug use, it is a major cause of poor nutrition, which further damages immune competence. Tobacco smoke contains high concentrations of dangerous chemicals including benzene, carbon monoxide, and cadmium (a powerful immuno-suppressant also found in fungicides, fertilizers, and rubber tires). Cannabis inhibits both T cell and macrophage activity. Put simply, drinking, smoking, and recreational drug use are not compatible with a healthy immune system.

taking treatment —with caution!

Medicinal remedies used to control the symptoms of allergic reactions—antihistamines, bronchodilators, decongestants, sodium cromoglycate, corticosteroids—are designed to dampen immune system activity, but many other drugs— including anti-inflammatories, blood thinners, oral contraceptives, hormone replacement therapy (H.R.T.),

antibiotics, and anti-cancer drugs—can cause unintentional suppression of normal immune responses. Diagnostic and therapeutic X-rays and other ionizing radiations also carry a risk of immune-system damage. Informed and appropriate use of medical drugs, plus avoidance of unnecessary high-energy imaging procedures, should form part of any strategy for immune health.

controlling weight

Obesity is a global epidemic, which is clearly related to the increasing occurence of type 2 diabetes, and the high incidence of coronary heart disease worldwide. Obesity is also strongly implicated as a risk factor for cancer, especially of the breast, uterus, cervix, and ovary in women, the prostate in men, and the colon and rectum in both sexes. As immunity plays a major role in protecting against cancer, and as it is proven that obese people are more likely to die earlier than the non-obese, maintaining a healthy body weight is a common sense way of encouraging long-term immune health, as well as improving general well-being.

taking exercise

Research confirms that regular moderate exercise enhances immune function and protects against cancer, heart disease, and osteoporosis, as well as being an effective way to relieve stress. Three or more 30-minute exercise sessions a week, such as brisk walking, jogging, cycling, or swimming, are ideal for optimizing immunity, but beware over-exertion— it suppresses T cell function and other immune responses.

for young and old

At both extremes of age, the immune system is less efficient, so paying special attention to the above factors is particularly important for children and the elderly. As far as children are concerned, breastfeeding, avoiding cow's milk, allowing minor illnesses to take their course without suppressing the symptoms with drugs, and eliminating unnecessary exposure to environmental antigens, are the basics of healthy immune system development.

chapter six

superfoods
for the immune system

The medicinal value of food for warding off illness has been acknowledged for thousands of years. More recently, scientific research has discovered hundreds of beneficial nutrients in the foods we eat. By applying our knowledge of these nutrients and of how they work to our diet, we can eat foods that boost our immune system and so help protect ourselves against a host of ailments.

This chapter presents profiles of 150 foods packed with disease-fighting nutrients, including eleven "star foods," such as beet and shiitake mushrooms, that are particularly effective in boosting the body's natural defenses.

fruits and vegetables

ROOTS AND BULBS

CARROT

★ VITAMIN A; CAROTENOIDS; FIBER; DAUCARIN

✔ ANTI-AGING, ANTI-CANCER, ANTIOXIDANT, GOOD FOR SKIN
   AND EYES

! HIGH CARROT INTAKE CAUSES ORANGE/YELLOW SKIN COLORING;
   THIS EFFECT IS HARMLESS AND GOES ONCE INTAKE IS REDUCED

Carrots (*Daucus carota*) support the immune system, help
circulation, aid wound healing and promote healthy skin. Carrot
purée can be used to treat child and infant diarrhea, and chronic
viral infections such as herpes simplex. Carrots help prevent the
formation of cancer cells and can protect against heart disease
and arthritis. They play a role in regulating blood-sugar levels and
thus may help protect against diabetes.

*RECIPES carrot 'n' beet salad (page 260), carrot and lemon with
garlic (page 275), healing soup (page 280)*

SWEET POTATO

★ VITAMINS A, B3, C, E, FOLATE; CAROTENOIDS (IN YELLOW VARIETY);
   COMPLEX CARBOHYDRATES, FIBER, SUGARS

✔ ANTIOXIDANT, ANTIVIRAL (YELLOW VARIETY), ENERGY-BOOSTING

There are two varieties of sweet potato (*Ipomoea batatas*)—yellow
and white. The yellow variety contains high levels of vitamin A and
carotenoids, which enhance the immune response and help the
body deal with viral infections and cancer. Both varieties boost
resistance to infection and help maintain optimum energy levels.
They are useful in convalescence, and they nourish the nervous
system, help maintain healthy muscles, and keep skin and mucous
membranes in good condition.

*RECIPES nettle and sweet potato mash (page 187), sweet potato
curry (page 272), vegetable kebabs (page 263)*

YAM

★ VITAMINS A, B1; CAROTENOIDS (IN YELLOW YAM); COMPLEX
   CARBOHYDRATES, FIBER, PROTEIN

✔ ANTIOXIDANT, ANTIVIRAL (YELLOW YAM), ENERGY-BOOSTING

There is a yellow and a white variety of yam (*Dioscorea spp.*). The
yellow kind aids immunity and inhibits cancer growth. Both kinds
help maintain a healthy heart, nerves, muscles, and metabolism.

RECIPES use as sweet potato

ONION

★ VITAMINS B1, B6; SULFUR COMPOUNDS

✔ ANTI-ASTHMATIC, ANTIBACTERIAL, ANTI-CANCER, ANTISEPTIC,
   DIURETIC, LOWERS BLOOD FAT AND CHOLESTEROL

! MAY CAUSE INDIGESTION IN THOSE WITH GASTRO-INTESTINAL
   DISORDERS

Onion (*Allium cepa*) is a useful remedy against arthritis and gout. A
natural antibacterial, it also helps lower blood cholesterol, blood fat
and blood sugar. Onions decrease the formation of blood clots,
too. They inhibit the activity of *Helicobacter pylori* (thought
responsible for gastritis and stomach ulcers), and may protect
against stomach cancer by decreasing the conversion of nitrates
to nitrites in the stomach. Onion syrup (prepared like garlic
oxymel—page 285) is a useful remedy for colds and coughs.

*RECIPES french onion tart (page 271), samosa parcels (page 264),
tofumasalata (page 264)*

POTATO

★ VITAMINS B COMPLEX, C; POTASSIUM; IRON; SOLANIDINE
   ALKALOIDS; FIBER, COMPLEX CARBOHYDRATES, PROTEIN

✔ ANTIOXIDANT, ENERGY-BOOSTING, NUTRITIONAL VALUE

! GREEN AND DAMAGED POTATOES HAVE AN INCREASED ALKALOID
   CONTENT THAT MAKES THEM TASTE BITTER, AND WHICH CAN BE
   TOXIC IN LARGE AMOUNTS

Potatoes (*Solanum tuberosum*) boost energy and strengthen
immunity. They lower blood-fat levels, improve tissue oxygenation,
promote a healthy nervous system, and improve wound healing.
They help the body absorb and use other nutrients and alleviate
stomach ulcer, digestive and malabsorption disorders. For most
benefit, eat in their skins. Hot potato water and raw potato juice
are traditional remedies for arthritis and gout.

*RECIPES shepherdess' pie (page 262), Hasselbach potatoes
(page 272), welsh leek and potato soup (page 274)*

VEGETABLE FRUITS

BUTTERNUT SQUASH

★ VITAMINS A, E; MAGNESIUM; CAROTENOIDS

✔ ANTI-CANCER, ANTIOXIDANT

Butternut squash (*Curcubita sp.*) helps protect against cancer, heart disease, and mental dysfunction. It aids normal blood cell function and encourages healthy skin, muscles, and nerves.

RECIPES butternut squash with bell pepper and tomato (page 269)

OKRA

★ VITAMIN C; FOLATE; CALCIUM, MAGNESIUM, IRON, ZINC; FIBER

✔ ANTIDEPRESSANT, IMMUNO-STIMULANT

Okra (*Ablemoscus esculenta*) helps protect against colon cancer and other disorders related to low fiber intake, such as diverticulitis. It strengthens the immune system by supporting lymphatic tissue and white blood cells, aids the development and maintenance of a healthy nervous system, and reduces the risk of heart disease.

RECIPES okra in sweet and sour tamarind sauce (page 272)

PUMPKIN

★ VITAMINS A, E; CAROTENOIDS

✔ ANTIOXIDANT, ANTI-CANCER

Like butternut squash, pumpkin (*Curcubita maxima*) helps prevent the formation of cancer cells and promotes healthy skin.

RECIPES pumpkin soup (page 261)

RED BELL PEPPER

★ VITAMINS A, C, B6, FOLATE; CAROTENOIDS; FIBER, BIOFLAVONOIDS

✔ ANTIOXIDANT, ANTI-CANCER, SUPPORTS NERVES

❗ ONE OF SOLINACEAE FAMILY OF VEGETABLE FRUITS AND MAY CAUSE ADVERSE REACTIONS IN THOSE WITH FOOD ALLERGIES OR ARTHRITIS

Red bell pepper (*Capsicum sp.*) has a very high vitamin-C content and it contains powerful, protective antioxidants that increase the defence against degenerative disease. It helps prevent A.M.D. (Age-related Macular Degeneration), boosts immunity and helps protect against cancer. It helps maintain normal blood-fat levels, and production of hemoglobin by red blood cells.

RECIPES broiled bell peppers (page 263), catalan salad (page 276), vegetable kebabs (page 263), paella (page 268)

TOMATO

★ VITAMINS A, C, E; LYCOPENE; FIBER

✔ ANTI-CANCER, ANTIOXIDANT, ANTIVIRAL

❗ ONE OF SOLINACEAE FAMILY OF VEGETABLE FRUITS — MAY CAUSE ADVERSE REACTIONS IN THOSE WITH FOOD ALLERGIES OR ARTHRITIS

Tomatoes (*Lycopersicon sp.*) are packed with antioxidants. They improve the immune response while also helping to maintain energy levels. This combination makes tomatoes a useful addition to the diet of those suffering from energy-compromising conditions. They are used in prostate cancer and heart disease; and they boost resistance to infectious disease, encouraging wound healing and keeping the skin and mucous membranes in good condition.

RECIPES baked tomatoes on toast (page 258), beans and tomatoes on toast (page 258), cool tomato soup (page 260), tomato and cucumber canapés (page 266), tomato cocktail (page 267), tomato salsa (page 274), tomato ketchup (page 283)

beet

BEET HAS BEEN USED AS A FOOD AND A MEDICINE SINCE EARLY
TIMES. ITS UNIQUE MIXTURE OF MINERALS AND PHYTOCHEMICALS
RESISTS INFECTION, BOOSTS CELLULAR INTAKE OF OXYGEN, AND
TREATS DISORDERS OF THE BLOOD, LIVER, AND IMMUNE SYSTEM.

The origin of beet

A native of southern Europe, beet (*Beta vulgaris rubra*) is now
cultivated worldwide. It is derived from the sea beet, which grows
wild around the Mediterranean. Beet has an unmistakable sweet
flavor that is strongest when the food is eaten raw. Its leaves taste
like spinach and, as with spinach, can be cooked, or eaten raw in
salads. Modern Western medicine makes little use of the healing
power of beet, but the vegetable is held in high regard by
practitioners of natural medicine all over the world.

Beet was prized in ancient Greece, where people would offer
it up to the god Apollo. Legend has it that Aphrodite ate beet to
retain her beauty. In the old English medical tradition, beet was
regarded as an important remedy for blood ailments. Herbalists
and naturopaths of today still use beet as an effective treatment
for disorders of the blood and the immune system, and often refer
to it as "the vitality plant."

Beet's immune-boosting properties

Beet stimulates the immune system by improving cell
respiration and tissue oxygenation. It does this by
encouraging the production of new red blood cells
(a process called *erythropoiesis*). The enhanced cell respiration
helps keep the heart, muscles, and nerves in good condition.
There is evidence that eating beet causes cancer cells to either
revert to normal or die, by altering their rate of cell respiration.
This may not cure the disease, but may help to boost the length
and quality of life of sufferers. Beet also helps stabilize the
body's pH (acid–alkaline balance). This is important for
immunity because bacteria thrive when the body's pH is disturbed.
Beet can be used to treat chronic infections, cancers (particularly
leukemia), skin problems, M.E., inflammatory bowel disease, liver
disease, and in the prevention and treatment of heart disease and
rheumatoid arthritis. It also aids fat metabolism and liver function.

Using beet

Beet has no harmful side effects and is well tolerated by most
people. It needs to be eaten over a relatively long period of time
to improve general health and vitality in all cases of chronic illness.
The average dose is one medium-size beet per day. Beet is just
as effective cooked or baked as it is eaten raw or juiced. Try this
recipe for a blood-purifying drink:
juice equal amounts of beet,
carrot, celery, tomato, and
a lemon. Drink 1 to 2
wineglassfuls per day
for three weeks.

IMMUNE-BOOSTING PROFILE

★ FOLATE; MANGANESE, POTASSIUM; IRON; BETANIN, MALONIC ACID, PHYTOSTEROL, SAPONIN; FIBER, PROTEIN, SUGARS

✔ ANTI-CANCER, ANTI-INFLAMMATORY, ANTIOXIDANT, DETOXIFYING, IMMUNO-STIMULANT, BOOSTS CELL OXYGENATION, REJUVENATING

! BETANIN, THE PIGMENT IN BEET, MAY COLOR FECES AND URINE RED; THIS IS HARMLESS AND THE EFFECT DISAPPEARS ONCE YOU STOP EATING THE VEGETABLE

! THE LEAVES CONTAIN OXALIC ACID AND SHOULD BE AVOIDED BY PEOPLE SUFFERING FROM KIDNEY STONES OR ARTHRITIS

baked beet salad *(above)*

2 beets, washed but not peeled	1 bunch of watercress, finely chopped
1 scallion, finely chopped	1 tablespoon balsamic vinegar
	2 tablespoon safflower oil

Dry the beets gently and rub in a little oil. Bake in a medium hot oven (350°F) for about an hour. Cool under running water, peel and chop into sticks. Place in a salad bowl and mix with the rest of the ingredients.

beet and horseradish salad

3 beets, grated	4 tablespoons fresh mint, finely chopped
1 cup plain soy yogurt	
1 tablespoon horseradish, grated	Salt to taste

Mix the yogurt, horseradish, and salt. Gently fold the beet into the dressing and garnish with mint.

scandinavian beet burgers

3 cups white rice, well cooked	1 tablespoon marjoram
4 ounces firm tofu, grated	Salt and pepper to taste
2 beets, grated	
2 tablespoons breadcrumbs	Flour for dipping
1 tablespoon balsamic vinegar	Oil for frying
1 tablespoon olive oil	

Mix the rice, tofu, beet, breadcrumbs, vinegar, oil and marjoram in a bowl. Season and shape into flat cakes. Dip in flour and fry at high temperature for 2 minutes on each side. Turn down the heat and continue frying for about 5 minutes on each side. Serve in burger buns, with salad, slices of tomato, cucumber, raw onion, and mustard and tomato ketchup (*see page 267*).

LEAVES AND FLOWERS

AMARANTH LEAVES

★ VITAMINS A, C, B2, FOLATE; CALCIUM, MAGNESIUM, MANGANESE, PHOSPHORUS, POTASSIUM; IRON; FIBER, PROTEIN

✔ ANTI-ALLERGIC, ANTI-CANCER, ANTIOXIDANT, ENERGY-BOOSTING

! AMARANTH HAS A HIGH PROTEIN CONTENT, WHICH MAY MAKE IT HARDER FOR CHILDREN TO DIGEST LARGE AMOUNTS.

The leaves of amaranth (*Amaranthus candatus*) are high in protein and a good source of energy. Amaranth leaves aid liver function and wound healing, help regulate blood-fat levels, and are good for the digestion. They may also help protect against heart disease, cancer, and rheumatoid arthritis. The leaves can be used like other greens in salads, or steamed or creamed like spinach. Amaranth tisane is taken to treat bronchitis and irritable bowel syndrome.

RECIPES amaranth and tofu puffs (page 268)

ASPARAGUS

★ VITAMINS B1, B3, E, FOLATE; POTASSIUM; ZINC; RUTIN, SAPSONIN, TANNIN; ASPARAGINE, PURINES; FIBER, PROTEIN

✔ ANTISPASMODIC, DIURETIC, GENTLY LAXATIVE, SOOTHING TO THE URINARY TRACT, WOUND HEALING

Asparagus (*Asparagus officinalis*) is a gentle diuretic that is used to stimulate urine flow and hence alleviate water retention, urinary tract problems, and arthritis. As a general tonic, it helps maintain the health of skin, mucous membranes and blood vessel walls. It may have a role in regulating blood cholesterol levels and inhibiting the growth of cancer cells. Asparagus is also a good food to relieve constipation.

RECIPES asparagus with ravigote (page 258), asparagus asian-style (page 262), catalan salad (page 269), pasta salad (page 276), scrambled tofu (page 276)

BELGIAN ENDIVE

★ FOLATE; IRON; PROTEIN; BITTER PRINCIPLE; FIBER

✔ ANTI-ALLERGIC, ANTI-STRESS, DIGESTIVE

Belgian endive (*Chichorium intybus*) has a delicate, slightly bitter taste that is popular in France. It stimulates the liver and digestion, and helps to regulate and maintain energy levels. Endive is also

good for the health of the skin and mucous membranes.

RECIPES broiled endive and brazil nut salad (page 191), grapefruit salad (page 201)

BROCCOLI (GREEN- AND PURPLE-SPROUTING)

★ VITAMINS A, C, E, B3, B5, FOLATE; CALCIUM, PHOSPHORUS, POTASSIUM; IRON, ZINC; GLUCOSINOLATES; CAROTENOIDS; PROTEIN

✔ ANTI-CANCER, ANTIOXIDANT, ANTI-STRESS, ENERGY-BOOSTING

💡 SEE GLOSSARY FOR INFORMATION ON GLUCOSINOLATES

Broccoli (*Brassica oleracea var.*) is very nutritious and high in vitamin C. It is a useful aid to detox and is good for the heart, skin (especially acne), nerves, and muscles, anemia, and fatigue. It helps prevent cancer (especially colon), block genetic damage, and avoid birth defects.

RECIPES sweet potato curry (page 272)

BRUSSELS SPROUTS

★ VITAMINS C, B1, B5, B6, PHOSPHORUS, POTASSIUM; GLUCOSINOLATES; FIBER, PROTEIN, SUGARS

✔ ANTI-ALLERGIC, ANTIOXIDANT, ANTI-STRESS

💡 SEE GLOSSARY FOR INFORMATION ON GLUCOSINOLATES

Brussels sprouts (*Brassica oleracea gemmifera*) are high in vitamin

C. They strengthen immunity and the skin, nerves, and mucous membranes. They help maintain energy and blood-fat levels, and may protect against asthma, migraine, depression, and cancer.

RECIPES serve steamed or boiled as side dish

BUTTERHEAD LETTUCE

★ VITAMINS A, FOLATE; CALCIUM, IRON, POTASSIUM, ZINC; FIBRE

✔ ANTI-CANCER, ANTIOXIDANT, LOW-CALORIE

Butterhead lettuce (Lactuca sativa sp.) improves oxygen transport, liver function, and wound healing. It helps to regulate blood-fat levels and is good for the heart, nerves, and muscles.

RECIPES provençal mesclun salad (page 275)

CAULIFLOWER

★ VITAMINS C, B3, B5, B6; PHOSPHORUS, POTASSIUM; ZINC; GLUCOSINOLATES; FIBER, PROTEIN

✔ ANTI-ALLERGIC, ANTI-CANCER, ANTIOXIDANT, ANTI-STRESS

💡 SEE GLOSSARY FOR INFORMATION ON GLUCOSINOLATES

Cauliflower (Brassica oleracea botrytis) encourages antibody and hemoglobin production and protects against allergy, asthma, migraine, and depression. It improves skin health and mucous membranes, helps maintain energy levels, and regulates blood fats.

RECIPES creamy cauliflower soup (page 261), green lentil salad (page 276)

DANDELION LEAF

★ VITAMINS A, C, K; CALCIUM, IRON, MAGNESIUM, MANGANESE, CAROTENOIDS; CHOLINE; GLYCOSIDES, BITTER PRINCIPLE

✔ ANTI-RHEUMATIC, DETOXIFYING, DIGESTIVE STIMULANT; DIURETIC, LAXATIVE, LIVER TONIC

Dandelion (Taraxacum officinale) is a powerful diuretic, which doesn't cause loss of potassium, unlike many diuretic medicines. It also stimulates bile flow and suports normal liver function.

RECIPES eat raw in salads

FLORENCE FENNEL

★ POTASSIUM; ZINC; VOLATILE OILS, BITTER PRINCIPLES; FIBER

✔ ANTI-INFLAMMATORY, CARMINATIVE, DIURETIC, DIGESTIVE AID

Fennel (Foeniculum vulgare dulce) helps relieve colic, wind and bloating and regulate blood-fat levels .

RECIPES florence fennel salad (page 261), green party (page 276), black-eye pea and wild marjoram soup (page 280)

GLOBE ARTICHOKE

★ VITAMINS B3, B5, BIOTIN, FOLATE; BITTER PRINCIPLE; PROTEIN

✔ ANTI-ALLERGIC, ANTI-STRESS, DIGESTIVE STIMULANT, LIVER TONIC DETOXIFYING, DIURETIC

Globe artichoke (Cynara scolymus) stimulates the appetite, enhances liver function and increases bile flow. It helps lower blood cholesterol and blood-fat breakdown. it may relieve hang-overs.

RECIPES artichoke hearts, fava beans and shiitake (page 268), paella (page 268), artichoke salad (page 275)

MUSTARD CRESS

★ VITAMINS A, C, B3, FOLATE; CALCIUM; IRON; GLUCOSINOLATES, SULFUR, VOLATILE OIL; PROTEIN; FIBER

✔ ANTIBACTERIAL, ANTI-CANCER, ANTI-CATARRHAL, ANTIOXIDANT, CIRCULATORY STIMULANT

💡 SEE GLOSSARY FOR INFORMATION ON GLUCOSINOLATES

Mustard cress (Brassica hirta) improves iron absorption, oxygen transport, and wound healing, and helps balance blood-fat levels. It also contains mustard oil, which is good for colds, nasal catarrh and sinusitis, and to stimulate circulation (also locally).

RECIPES provençal mesclun salad (page 275)

NASTURTIUM

★ VITAMIN C; GLUCOSINOLATES, VOLATILE OIL

✔ ANTIBACTERIAL, ANTIMICROBIAL, ANTIOXIDANT, ANTISEPTIC, ANTIVIRAL

💡 SEE GLOSSARY FOR INFORMATION ON GLUCOSINOLATES

Nasturtium (Tropaeolum majus) leaves and flowers are powerful natural antibiotics, and are particularly useful for loosening phlegm and relieving respiratory-tract infections such as bronchitis.

RECIPES toasted tempeh with herb salad (page 264), tropical sunshine salad (page 277), green leafy salad (page 183)

RADICCHIO

★ VITAMINS B2, B3; POTASSIUM; ANTHOCYANIN, BITTER PRINCIPLES; FIBER

✔ ANTI-CANCER, ANTI-INFLAMMATORY, ANTIOXIDANT, DIGESTIVE AID, MILD LAXATIVE

Eating radicchio (Cichorium var.) helps the body maximize energy release from food, to lower blood-sugar and cholesterol levels and the formation of blood clots. It also relieves indigestion, and soothes heartburn and reflux.

RECIPES orange mango salad (page 276)

curly kale

CURLY KALE IS A MEMBER OF THE BRASSICA FAMILY, WHICH INCLUDES CABBAGE, BROCCOLI, AND BRUSSELS SPROUTS. IT IS PACKED WITH VITAMINS, MINERALS, AND PHYTOCHEMICALS THAT GUARD AGAINST BACTERIAL AND VIRAL INFECTION, HEART DISEASE, AND CANCER.

The origin of curly kale

Curly kale (*Brassica oleracea acephala*) is also known as "Borecole," from the Dutch word "Boerenkool" meaning "peasants' cabbage." It is derived from the wild cabbage (*Brassica oleracea*), which is a native of southwestern Europe and the Mediterranean region and grows on seaside cliffs. Opinions differ over when the wild cabbage was first cultivated (estimates range from a few hundred to thousands of years ago!) but it has been developed into a number of edible varieties.

Other members of the cabbage family form "heads" but curly kale retains its ancestral shape—leaves set loosely on a stem. The leaves are blue-green and, as the name implies, curly and crimped. Although kale and the other edible brassicas originated in temperate zones, they are now cultivated all over the world.

A characteristic of the brassicas is that they hold a lot of water in their leaves, making them fleshy and succulent foods. Like other members of the family, curly kale is a biennial—it grows for two years, storing a large amount of nutrients in its leaves. We can benefit from this nourishment only if the leaves are harvested during its first year. In its second (final) year, the plant will use the stored nutrients to produce flowers and seed.

Immune-boosting properties

Curly kale is a valuable winter vegetable, with an extremely high content of vitamins A, C, and K, as well as minerals and protective phytochemicals. It is one of the tastiest of the cabbage family and easily overwinters to provide important nutrients when little else is growing in temperate regions. Its phytochemicals facilitate oxygen transport to the tissues, support immunity, aid liver function, and play a part in controlling blood-fat levels, and helping the body to release and utilize the energy in food. Curly kale thus promotes the health of the heart, nerves, and muscles and protects against high blood pressure, vascular disease, and rheumatoid arthritis.

Curly kale is good for the skin, encourages wound healing and the maintenance of healthy cell membranes, and may protect against estrogen-linked cancers such as those of the breast and ovaries. It helps regulate protein and fat metabolism and, because of its vitamin K content, encourages normal blood clotting. It also improves iron absorption from food and facilitates the production of hemoglobin and red blood cells. It may offer protection against asthma, migraine, and depression, and aid the nervous system.

Packed with protection

Curly kale contains three important groups of protective phytochemicals: glucosinolates, bioflavonoids, and sterols (phenylpropanoids). Glucosinolates include indoles, dithiolthiones, sulphoraphane, and isothiocyanates. Indoles, in particular, protect against various carcinogens. They also help reduce the activity of estrogen in the body and therefore have a dual role in protecting against estrogen-related cancers.

Bioflavonoids stimulate the immune system. They chelate (combine with) metals and make blood platelets less sticky, thus protecting against abnormal blood clotting and preventing heart disease.

Sterols influence the absorption of cholesterol from food and its metabolism in the body. They also affect the production of steroid hormones.

IMMUNE-BOOSTING PROFILE

★ VITAMINS A, C, E, K, B2, B6, FOLATE; CALCIUM, COPPER, IRON,
MAGNESIUM, MANGANESE, POTASSIUM; BIOFLAVONOIDS,
GLUCOSINOLATES, KAEMPFEROL STEROLS; FIBER, PROTEIN

✔ ANTI-ALLERGIC, ANTI-CANCER, ANTIOXIDANT, DETOXIFYING,
IMMUNO-STIMULANT

💡 SEE GLOSSARY FOR INFORMATION ON GLUCOSINOLATES

curly kale parcels *(above)*

1 pound fresh curly kale, chopped	1 onion, finely chopped
2 tablespoons olive oil	1 teaspoon turmeric
8½ ounces tempeh, cut into small cubes	1 teaspoon cumin
	Pinch of cayenne
1 tablespoon soy sauce	Salt and pepper to taste
2 garlic cloves, finely chopped	1 packet phyllo pastry

Stir-fry the curly kale in the oil for 2 minutes. Add the other ingredients
one by one, stirring in between. Add a little water and simmer gently for
5 minutes (until the kale goes soft). Open out sheets of phyllo pastry
(as many as you have filling for), brush with oil and place a generous
portion of the filling in the middle of each one. Fold each sheet into a
parcel. Brush each parcel with oil and bake at 425°F until golden.

curly kale, tomato, and fava beans

3 tablespoons olive oil	4 garlic cloves, finely chopped
1 red onion, chopped	Salt and pepper to taste
2 pounds fava beans, shelled	2 tablespoons lemon juice
1 pound curly kale, chopped	2 scallions, chopped
1 pound tomatoes, in wedges	

Heat the oil gently in a deep saucepan. Sauté the onion for 2 minutes,
add the beans and cook for 5 minutes. Add the curly kale and the
tomatoes and stir-fry for 2 minutes, then add the garlic, salt and
pepper. Add enough water to cover, bring to the boil and simmer for
30 minutes (or until all the liquid is reduced). Add lemon juice, check
seasoning, garnish with scallions and serve with couscous.

green leafy salad

1 handful of fresh curly kale, finely chopped	1 small handful of fresh mint, finely chopped
1 handful of iceberg lettuce, shredded	1 small handful of nasturtium flowers and calendula (pot marigold) petals (optional)
1 handful of lamb's lettuce	Lemon tahini dressing
1 small handful of parsley sprigs, finely chopped	(see page 267)

Mix the green leaves in a bowl. Garnish with the flowers. Pour the
dressing over and mix gently. Serve with bread or cooked bulgur.

 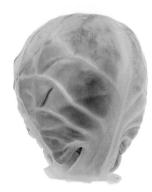 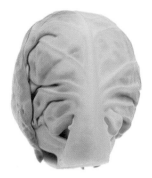

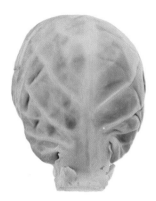  

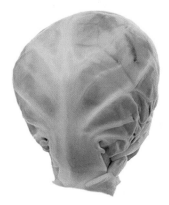  

ARUGULA

★ VITAMINS A, C; BITTER PRINCIPLE, VOLATILE OIL; FIBER

✔ ANTI-CANCER, ANTISCORBUTIC, ANTIOXIDANT, CIRCULATORY STIMULANT, DIGESTIVE

Arugula (*Eruca sativa*) contains mustard oil, which gives it a peppery flavour and stimulates circulation. It stimulates the liver and aids digestion, especially of fatty foods. It also helps improve immunity and wound healing.

RECIPES arugula salad (page 275), sweetcorn and sun-dried tomato salad (page 276), green party (page 280), vegetable cocktail (page 283), shiitake salad (page 221)

SAVOY CABBAGE

★ VITAMINS A, C, B3, FOLATE; CALCIUM, POTASSIUM; IRON; GLUCOSINOLATES; FIBER, PROTEIN

✔ ANTI-CANCER, ANTIOXIDANT, ENERGY-BOOSTING

♀ SEE GLOSSARY FOR INFORMATION ON GLUCOSINOLATES

Savoy cabbage (*Brassica oleracea capitata*) aids detoxifying and improves oxygen transport in the blood. It is a good source of vitamin B3, which boosts energy and strength, and helps keep the heart, muscles, skin, mucous membranes, and nerves healthy.

RECIPES garlic and savoy cabbage (page 215)

SPINACH

★ VITAMINS A, C, E, B2, B6, FOLATE, K; CALCIUM, MAGNESIUM, MANGANESE, POTASSIUM; IRON; CAROTENOIDS, OXALIC ACID; FIBER, PROTEIN

✔ ANTI-CANCER, ANTIOXIDANT, ANTIVIRAL, IMMUNO-STIMULANT

! FOODS CONTAINING OXALIC ACID ARE BEST AVOIDED IF YOU SUFFER FROM KIDNEY OR BLADDER STONES, OR RHEUMATOID ARTHRITIS

Spinach (*Spinacea oleracea*) is high in folate, making it important for women before and during pregnancy. It is also rich in vitamins A, C, and K, helping to protect the skin and stimulate the immune system. The carotenoids are powerful antioxidants, protecting against cancer, particularly of the lung, breast, and cervix, and protecting the eyes. It is a good source of energy, aids liver function, regulates blood-fat, and protects against heart disease.

RECIPES spinach bouillabaisse (page 271), sweet potato curry (page 272), tomato cocktail (page 283)

SPRING GREENS

★ VITAMINS A, C, K, B2, B3, B5, FOLATE; CALCIUM, PHOSPHORUS, POTASSIUM; IRON, ZINC; GLUCOSINOLATES; PROTEIN, FIBER

✔ ANTI-ALLERGIC, ANTI-CANCER, ANTIOXIDANT, ANTI-STRESS, DETOXIFYING, ENERGY-BOOSTING, WOUND HEALING

♀ SEE GLOSSARY FOR INFORMATION ON GLUCOSINOLATES

Spring greens (*Brassica oleracea var.*) have a particularly high content of vitamins A and C, and of carotenoids, which help protect eyesight. They support the liver's detoxifying action, and help boost immunity, especially against cancerous cell degeneration.

RECIPES spring greens and macadamia nuts (page 274)

STEVIA

★ GLUCOSIDES (STEVIOSIDE)

✔ HYPOGLYCEMIC, HYPOTENSIVE, CALORIE-FREE SWEETENER

Stevia (*Stevia rebaundia*) is up to 300 times sweeter than sugar. It is a useful sugar substitute in the treatment of obesity and high blood pressure, and for diabetics. It can lower blood glucose and enhance glucose tolerance.

RECIPES use as a sugar alternative in baking. As a guide: for 1 cup sugar use 1 tbsp stevia; for 1 tbsp sugar use ½ tsp stevia, and for 1 tsp sugar use a pinch stevia.)

SWISS CHARD

★ VITAMINS A, C, FOLATE; MAGNESIUM, MANGANESE, POTASSIUM; IRON

✔ ANTI-CANCER, ANTIOXIDANT

Swiss chard (*Beta vulgaris cycla*) increases natural resistance by supporting oxygen transport via the blood to nerves, muscles, and liver, and helps in the regulation of blood-fat levels.

RECIPES swiss chard and juniper berries (page 275)

WATERCRESS

★ VITAMINS A, C, E, K, B1, B2, B3, B6; CALCIUM, MANGANESE; IRON; GLUCOSINOLATES, VOLATILE OIL; PROTEIN, FIBER

✔ ANTI-CANCER, ANTIOXIDANT, ANTISCORBUTIC, EXPECTORANT

! EXCESSIVE INTAKE OF WATERCRESS MAY CAUSE KIDNEY PROBLEMS, AND SHOULD BE AVOIDED IN THOSE WITH KIDNEY DISEASE

♀ SEE GLOSSARY FOR INFORMATION ON GLUCOSINOLATES

The main medicinal use of watercress (*Nasturtium officinale*) is to relieve arthritic conditions and upper respiratory-tract congestion. Watercress stimulates the immune and lymphatic systems.

RECIPES avocado, watercress, and cumin salad (page 197), grapefruit salad (page 191), baked beet salad (page 139), green lentil salad (page 276), chinese salad (page 276)

nettle

THE NETTLE MAY JUST BE A HUMBLE WEED, BUT IT IS PACKED WITH NUTRIENTS THAT STRENGTHEN THE IMMUNE SYSTEM AND FORTIFY THE BODY AGAINST DISEASE. THIS VERSATILE PLANT CAN ALSO ENRICH AND PURIFY THE BLOOD TO HELP ALLEVIATE CIRCULATORY DISORDERS.

The origin of the nettle

The nettle (*Urtica dioica*) is one of the world's commonest weeds. It quickly colonizes any piece of reasonably fertile and well-watered land, and is found in fields, gardens, woodland, and wasteground throughout the world's temperate zones. Being a "greedy" plant, the nettle stores up large quantities of vital nutrients that promote health and restock depleted tissues and body systems. This makes nettle a fortifying remedy that strengthens the whole body.

Immune-boosting properties

In immunodeficiency states, chronic degenerative diseases, and cancer, nettle has a unique ability to revitalize and replenish, helping the body to cope better in difficult circumstances, and providing many of the building blocks necessary for health and healing. As a gentle but efficient diuretic, nettle can be very effective in the management of disorders of the heart and circulation, helping to rid the body of excess fluid while toning up blood-vessel walls. It has a beneficial effect on the kidneys, enhancing their ability to excrete uric acid and so relieving gout (which is caused by excess uric acid in the tissues and joints). The nettle's ability to cleanse the body of accumulated waste also promotes the healing of chronic skin problems such as eczema. Being rich in iron, nettle is a useful treatment for anemia.

Using nettle

Nettle tea has been used for centuries as a blood purifier and "spring tonic," and is an excellent aid during convalescence from illness. As both a circulatory stimulant and a diuretic, it is a powerful aid to detox and thus useful in the management of arthritis, urinary-tract problems, and skin problems such as psoriasis. Cold nettle tea is a useful external remedy for the relief of burns and minor wounds. The green tips of the plant can be used fresh or dried. For drying, it is best to pick the young shoots on a fine morning, after the sun has dried the dew. The young tips can be harvested almost all year round to provide a nutritious, healing, and tasty addition to any diet. Pick and wash the nettle tops. Boil them in a little water for about 10 minutes, then remove them with a slotted spoon (preserve the liquid for use as a bouillon or a medicine). Chop finely and use with other vegetables in soups, stews, and pasta sauces. As a side dish, precooked nettles are delicious stir-fried with leeks, garlic, salt, and pepper. They can also be used as a substitute for spinach (although they need a little more cooking water). Cooked nettles have a surprisingly full-bodied flavor. Try nettle lasagne, which uses cooked nettles and lentils for the filling instead of meat.

IMMUNE-BOOSTING PROFILE

★ VITAMINS A, C, K, B1, B2, B3, B5; CALCIUM, MAGNESIUM, PHOSPHATE, PHOSPHORUS, POTASSIUM; BORON, BROMINE, COPPER, IRON, SELENIUM, SILICA, ZINC; ACETYLCHOLINE, CHLOROPHYLL, FORMIC ACID, LYCOPENE, GLUCOQUINONE, HISTAMINE, SEROTONIN, TANNIN; FIBER, OMEGA-3, -6, AND OLEIC FATTY ACIDS

✓ ANTI-CANCER, ANTI-INFLAMMATORY, ANTIOXIDANT, ASTRINGENT, CIRCULATORY STIMULANT, DETOXIFYING, DIURETIC, LOWERS BLOOD SUGAR, TONIC

! USE GLOVES WHEN HANDLING THE FRESH PLANT; NETTLE SHOULD NOT BE EATEN UNCOOKED

nettle and sweet potato mash *(above)*

1 pound sweet potatoes, peeled and chopped
8½ ounces fresh nettle tips
3 tablespoons olive oil
1 red onion, sliced
6 ounces green peas
Salt and pepper to taste

Pick and wash the nettles (wearing gloves). Boil the sweet potatoes in lightly salted water until soft. Mash and set aside. Boil the nettles in a little water until soft. Remove from water and chop. Heat the oil in a pan or wok and stir-fry the onion until soft. Add the peas, then the nettles and the sweet potato. Mix well, season, and serve hot.

spiced nettle soup

8 ounces fresh nettle tips
2 tablespoons olive oil
½ teaspoon cayenne
1 teaspoon turmeric
1 bay leaf
1 garlic clove, chopped
1 leek, chopped
2 potatoes, chopped into cubes
1 carrot, chopped
1 parsley root or parsnip, chopped
2 tablespoons flour
7½ cups basic vegetable bouillon (see page 260)
Salt and pepper to taste

Pick and wash the nettles (wearing gloves). Steam in a little water until soft, then chop finely. Heat the oil gently in a big saucepan. Add the spices, stir for ½ minute, then add the vegetables. Stir-fry for a few minutes, but don't let them brown. Sprinkle with the flour at low heat, mix well and add the bouillon. Bring to the boil and simmer for 10–15 minutes, then add the nettles (together with their cooking water). Heat through and simmer for another 5 minutes. Season and serve.

nettle and lime tisane

2 fresh nettle tips or 1 teaspoon dried nettle
1 thick slice of lime
1 cup boiling water

Wearing gloves, place the nettle in a tea filter in a large cup or mug. Add the boiling water and the lime. Leave to infuse, covered with a lid, for 5 minutes.

SWEET FRUITS

APPLE

★ VITAMIN C; POTASSIUM; MALIC ACID, TANNIN, VOLATILE OIL; FIBER, PECTIN, SUGARS

✔ DETOXIFYING, LOWERS CHOLESTEROL

Apples (*Malus domestica*) stimulate the secretion of digestive juices and aid protein digestion. They contain pectin, which binds with cholesterol and bile acids, enhancing their excretion from the body. The pectin makes apples a remedy for simple diarrhea. Apples protect the body against the effects of some environmental toxins.

RECIPES yogurt with fruit (page 259), baked apples (page 278), beet and apple (page 280), guava and apple (page 282)

APRICOT (FRESH AND DRIED)

★ VITAMINS A, C, E, B2, B3, B5; CALCIUM, MAGNESIUM, POTASSIUM; COPPER, IRON, ZINC; FIBER, SUGARS

✔ ANTIOXIDANT, DETOXIFYING, IMMUNO-STIMULANT

❗ BRIGHT ORANGE DRIED APRICOTS HAVE BEEN TREATED WITH SULFUR AND SHOULD BE AVOIDED

Apricots (*Prunus armeniaca*) promote detoxification and waste elimination. They also contribute to efficient antibody production. Apricots help stabilize blood-sugar levels, keep muscles, nerves, enzymes, and hormones working properly, facilitate the release of energy from food and tissue stores, and enhance the transport of oxygen in the blood.

RECIPES fruity pancakes (page 259), muesli (page 259), apricot and ginger (page 280), nirvana (page 283), soft tutti fruity (page 283)

BANANA

★ VITAMINS C, B3, B5, B6, BIOTIN; MAGNESIUM, MANGANESE, POTASSIUM; FIBER, SUGARS

✔ ANTI-STRESS, ENERGY-BOOSTING, DIGESTIVE STIMULANT

Bananas (*Musa cavendishii*) help prevent high blood pressure, heart disease, cancer, and rheumatoid arthritis. They enhance the metabolism of protein, carbohydrate, and fats, stabilize blood-sugar levels, and promote healthy skin, hair, nerves, and bone marrow. Easy to digest, they are useful in the management of gastro-intestinal disorders.

RECIPES baked apples (page 278), blackberry cream (page 280), caribbean smoothie (page 280), creamy mango (page 280)

CANTALOUPE MELON

★ VITAMINS A, C, B3, B6, FOLATE; POTASSIUM; CAROTENOIDS; SUGARS

✔ ANTIOXIDANT

With its high levels of vitamins A and C, and carotenoids, cantaloupe melon (*Cucumin melo*) may inhibit cancer cells. It aids wound healing, and helps maintain the health of all body tissues. It also enhances release of energy from other foods.

RECIPES: ruby red melon salad (page 258), mint and melon soup (page 261), melon and orange (page 282)

GRAPE

★ VITAMINS C, K, B1, B2, B6, BIOTIN; MAGNESIUM, MANGANESE, PHOSPHORUS; COPPER, IRON; ANTHOCYANIN, TARTARIC ACID; SUGARS

✔ ANTI-INFLAMMATORY, ANTIOXIDANT, DETOXIFYING

Fresh grapes (*Vitis vinifera*), and dried grapes (sultanas, raisins, and currants), are "biological response modifiers"—inhibiting the action of allergens, viruses, and carcinogens. They also act as free radical scavengers, making them ideal detoxifiers (See page 289.)

RECIPES fresh fruit salad (page 258), grape and raisin smoothie (page 283), oatmeal with dried fruit and quinoa (page 258)

GUAVA

★ VITAMINS A, C, B2, B3, B5, B6, FOLATE; COPPER, MAGNESIUM, MANGANESE, POTASSIUM, FIBER, SUGARS

✔ ANTIOXIDANT, DETOXIFYING, IMMUNO-STIMULANT

Guava (*Psidium guajava*) has a very high vitamin-C content and is an excellent natural antioxidant, mopping up free radicals. It has a major role in serious immunodeficiency disorders, heart disease, and cancer, and reduces the severity of auto-immune diseases.

RECIPES fruity pancakes (page 259), guava and apple (page 282)

KIWI (CHINESE GOOSEBERRY)

★ VITAMINS C, E, K, B6, FOLATE; COPPER, MAGNESIUM, MANGANESE, POTASSIUM, FIBER, SUGARS

✔ ANTIOXIDANT

An advantage of kiwi fruit (*Actinidia deliciosa*) is that it keeps well for a long time after harvesting with little loss of its nutritional value—even after 6 months' storage, 90 per cent of the vitamin C is still intact. Kiwi fruits encourage the health and repair of all body tissues, and promote the release of the energy from other foods.

RECIPES fresh fruit salad (page 258), tropical fruit salad (page 279)

MANGO

★ VITAMINS A, C, FOLATE, B3; POTASSIUM; CITRIC ACID, PAPAIN; FIBER, SUGARS

✔ ANTI-ALLERGIC, ANTIBIOTIC, ANTI-CANCER, ANTIOXIDANT, DETOXIFYING, ENERGY-BOOSTING, IMMUNO-STIMULANT

! IN RARE CASES, MAY CAUSE DERMATITIS

Mango (*Magnifera indica*) stimulates the immune system and helps protect mucous membranes from pathogens. Papain is a protein-digesting enzyme that may help anyone suffering gluten intolerance or wheat allergy.

RECIPES creamy mango (page 280), mango and lime (page 282)

PAPAYA (PAW-PAW)

★ VITAMINS A, C; CAROTENOIDS, PAPAIN; FIBER, SUGARS

✔ ANTI-ALLERGIC, ANTIBACTERIAL, ANTIOXIDANT, DETOXIFYING

The papain in papaya (*Asimina triloba*) promotes the breakdown of protein and can play an important role in alleviating digestive disorders and detoxifying the body. Papaya can help prevent skin disorders, gastro-intestinal ulcers, pancreatic disorders, cancer, and other conditions related to dysfunctional immunity.

RECIPES fresh fruit salad (page 258), papaya power (page 283)

PASSION-FRUIT

★ VITAMINS A, C, B2, B3; MAGNESIUM, PHOSPHORUS; IRON, ZINC; CITRIC ACID; FIBER, SUGARS

✔ ANTI-ALLERGY, ANTI-CANCER, ANTIOXIDANT

Passion-fruit (*Passiflora incarnata*) helps ensure healthy nerves, skin, and mucous membranes, boosts energy levels, relieves muscle cramps, and alleviates insomnia and depression.

RECIPES passion-fruit sorbet (page 278), height of passion (page 282), passion and lime (page 283)

PINEAPPLE

★ VITAMINS C, B1, B6; COPPER, MANGANESE, BROMELAIN, CITRIC ACID; FIBER, SUGARS

✔ ANTI-CANCER, ANTI-INFLAMMATORY

Pineapple (*Ananas comosus*) modifies the body's inflammatory response, speeds up tissue repair and alleviates fluid retention. It aids digestion, helps prevent blood clots and atherosclerosis, relieves angina, and lowers blood pressure.

RECIPES pina colada (page 283), pink pineapple (page 283)

grapefruit

GRAPEFRUIT IS A POWERFUL DETOXIFIER, HELPING TO RID THE BODY
OF HARMFUL MICROBES AND STRENGTHENING THE IMMUNE SYSTEM
AGAINST FURTHER ATTACK. IT MAY ALSO AID TISSUE REPAIR AND
HELP RESIST THE GROWTH OF TUMORS.

The origin of grapefruit

Grapefruit (*Citrus paradisi*) is thought to have originated in Jamaica,
possibly as a mutation of the pummelo (*Citrus maxima*), or as a
hybrid between the pummelo and the sweet orange (*Citrus
sinensis*). By 1750 it had become popular throughout the West
Indies, and its fame then spread rapidly to the American mainland
and the rest of the world. Depending on the variety, grapefruits are
lemon-yellow or orange-yellow when ripe, with a juicy, fragrant,
light yellow, pink, or ruby-red pulp, and a distinct sweet-sharp acid
flavor. When buying grapefruits, choose ones that feel heavy for
their size, with firm, shiny skin. Avoid very soft or dull-colored fruits.
The nutritional content varies with type and color. Fruits with ruby-
red and pink pulp contain more vitamin A than the yellow variety.

Immune-boosting properties

Grapefruit is a natural detoxifier, acting on the digestive system
and liver. Its detoxifying action, combined with a strong growth-
inhibiting effect on bacteria, fungi, parasites, and viruses, means
that grapefruit can be beneficial in immunodeficiency states, as
well as for colds and flu. Grapefruit contains a wealth of protective
phytochemicals that enhance immunity and wound healing, and
may inhibit tumor growth. Although citrus fruits in general are best
avoided by those suffering from auto-immune disorders, there is
evidence that grapefruit improves some inflammatory conditions.

Grapefruit is an effective pick-me-up when stress takes its toll
on energy levels. It also aids healing by strengthening bones, blood
vessels, and other tissues. The soluble fiber in grapefruit helps
lower blood cholesterol (and other blood fats) by binding with

excess cholesterol and bile acids and promoting their excretion
from the body. This makes it useful in the prevention and treatment
of heart and artery disease and gallstones. By aiding digestion and
waste elimination, grapefruit relieves constipation. The fruit also
inhibits the formation of calcium oxalate kidney stones, by reducing
the amount of calcium salts in the urine.

Grapefruit boosts fat metabolism, which explains its popularity
as a "fat burning" aid in weight-loss diets. An average serving of
grapefruit is less than 100 calories and yet its high fiber content
helps satisfy hunger. Its bitter principles aid the digestion of other
foods, thus enabling dieters to gain maximum nutritional value
from their meals while keeping their appetite under control.

Citricidal—grapefruit seed extract—is a natural, broad-spectrum
antimicrobial agent active against streptococci, staphylococci,
salmonella, mycobacteria, and other pathogens. Grapefruit oil is
a powerful astringent and antiseptic that can
be used to cleanse oily skin and
as a gentle treatment for
acne and other minor
skin conditions.

★ VITAMINS A, C, FOLATE; POTASSIUM; BITTER PRINCIPLE,
  BIOFLAVONOIDS, CITRIC AND PHENOLIC ACIDS, LYCOPENE; FIBER,
  PECTIN, SUGARS

✔ ANTI-ALLERGIC, ANTI-CANCER, ANTIMICROBIAL, ANTIOXIDANT,
  LOWERS BLOOD PRESSURE, LOWERS CHOLESTEROL LEVELS,
  DETOXIFYING, DIGESTIVE STIMULANT, IMMUNO-STIMULANT

❗ GRAPEFRUIT JUICE MAY INTERACT WITH SOME PRESCRIBED DRUGS
  SO CHECK WITH YOUR MEDICAL PRACTITIONER IF YOU ARE TAKING
  ANY MEDICINES

stuffed grapefruit *(above)*

2 grapefruits, halved, flesh
  removed, and chopped
1 avocado, stoned and peeled, in
  cubes
1-in cube fresh ginger root, finely
  chopped

1 pear, core removed, in cubes
1 small green bell pepper,
  deseeded, finely chopped
2 black olives, stoned
2 tablespoons fresh lemon balm,
  finely chopped

Mix the grapefruit flesh with the avocado, ginger, pear, and green bell
pepper. Divide the filling between the two half shells. Garnish with
olives and lemon balm.

grapefruit and peppermint fizz

1 bunch of fresh peppermint
2½ cups boiling water
2 tablespoons maple syrup

2 ruby-red grapefruits
1 lime
Ice cubes

Put the mint in a teapot or bowl, pour the boiling water over and
leave to infuse for 5 minutes. Add the maple syrup and leave to cool.
Squeeze the grapefruit and the lime and divide the juice between four
tall glasses. Add the peppermint infusion when cool. Serve with ice.

grapefruit salad

1 grapefruit, peeled and
  cut into segments
1 avocado, peeled, stoned
  and sliced
1 endive, thinly sliced

2 stalks celery, thinly
  sliced
3½ ounces bean sprouts
1 bunch of watercress
Lime dressing (*see page 267*)

Combine all the ingredients in a salad bowl. Add some dressing,
garnish with watercress and serve immediately.

CITRUS FRUITS

LEMON

★ VITAMIN C, CITRIC ACID; FIBER

✔ ANTI-ALLERGIC, ANTIBACTERIAL; ANTIOXIDANT

Lemons (*Citrus lemon*) contain high levels of vitamin C, which boosts the body's resistance to infection, as well as enhancing iron absorption, aiding efficient wound healing, and strengthening cell membranes. Lemons also lower blood-fat levels, and help maintain the health of the heart, nerves, and muscle tissue.

RECIPES guacamole (page 266), lemon tahini dressing (page 267), carrot and lemon with garlic (page 280), cold buster (page 284)

LIME

★ VITAMIN C, CITRIC ACID, FIBER

✔ ANTI-ALLERGIC, ANTIBACTERIAL, ANTIOXIDANT

Like lemon, lime (*Citrus aurantifolia*) improves the health of all body tissues and enhances iron absorption. It may speed up wound healing and increase the efficiency of the immune system. It therefore has a role in the prevention and treatment of cancer.

RECIPES lime dressing (page 267), mango and lime (page 282), passion and lime (page 283), pina colada (page 283), tempeh kebabs (page 209), nettle and lime tisane (page 187)

ORANGE

★ VITAMINS C, B1, FOLATE; POTASSIUM; BETA-SITOSTEROL; FIBER, SUGARS

✔ ANTIOXIDANT, ANTI-STRESS, LOWERS CHOLESTEROL

! ORANGES CAN TRIGGER MIGRAINE ATTACKS IN SOME CASES

! IT MAY BE BEST TO AVOID ORANGES IN YOUR DIET IF YOU SUFFER FROM RHEUMATOID ARTHRITIS

The high vitamin C content in oranges (*Citrus sinensis*) helps to maintain healthy blood cells, and increases resistance to infections. Oranges also lower blood cholesterol, and may protect against cancer, improve iron absorption and wound healing. Eating oranges helps to maintain optimum energy levels, keeps skin and mucous membranes in good condition, aids antibody production, and protects against high blood pressure and allergy.

RECIPES orange mango salad (page 276), melon and orange (page 282), pink pineapple (page 283), sunrise (page 283), oriental salad with tempeh (page 209)

BERRIES

BILBERRY (BLAEBERRY, WHORTLEBERRY, WINBERRY)

★ VITAMIN C; ANTHOCYANIN; FIBER, SUGARS

✔ ANTIBACTERIAL, ANTI-INFLAMMATORY, ANTIOXIDANT, ANTISEPTIC, TONIC

Bilberries (*Vaccinium myrtillus*) help to treat rheumatoid arthritis. They improve micro-circulation, strengthen blood capillaries, tone up the cardiovascular system, and help prevent blood clots. Bilberries can be used to stop diarrhea, to soothe throat infections, and to improve night vision and prevent cataracts.

RECIPES use in place of blackberries, raspberries, or cranberries

BLACKBERRY

★ VITAMINS C, E, K, B3, FOLATE; COPPER, MANGANESE; CITRIC ACID; FIBER, SUGARS

✔ ANTIOXIDANT, TONIC

Blackberries (*Rubus ulmifolius or R. alleghanensis*) improve iron absorption, increase energy release from food and enhance oxygen transport to the tissues. They aid liver function, speed up protein and fat metabolism, help regulate blood-fat levels, and encourage wound healing. They may also offer some protection against heart disease and some cancers.

RECIPES blackberry crumble (page 279), blackberry cream (page 280), yogurt with fruit (page 259)

SWEET CHERRY

★ VITAMIN C, POTASSIUM; ANTHOCYANIN, MALIC ACID; FIBER, SUGARS

✔ ANTI-INFLAMMATORY, ANTIOXIDANT, DETOXIFYING, REJUVENATING

♡ TISANES MADE FROM CHERRY STALKS ARE A TRADITIONAL REMEDY FOR CYSTITIS

Cherries (*Prunus avium*) boost energy and are beneficial to the heart, muscles and nerves. Eating cherries can lower uric acid levels in the blood and so is a traditional way of avoiding gout. They reduce platelet "stickiness" and help prevent blood clots, and can help relieve the symptoms of rheumatoid and osteoarthritis.

RECIPES ruby red melon salad (page 258)

CRANBERRY

★ VITAMIN C E, K; MANGANESE, ANTHOCYANIN, BENZOIC, CITRIC AND QUINIC ACIDS; TANNIN; FIBER; SUGARS

✔ ANTI-CANCER, ANTIOXIDANT

The juice of cranberries (*Vaccinium vitis-idaea*) prevents harmful bacteria from sticking to the bladder wall, and has long been used to relieve urinary-tract infections. Cranberry juice has powerful antioxidant effects that improve cardiovascular health and help prevent cancer. It may also reduce kidney stones.

RECIPES cranberry spritzer (page 280)

ELDERBERRY

★ VITAMINS A, C, B1, B2, B3, B6, BIOTIN; CALCIUM, IRON, PHOSPHORUS, POTASSIUM; ANTHOCYANINS, TANNIN; SUGARS

✔ ANTI-ALLERGIC, ANTI-CANCER, ANTIOXIDANT, ASTRINGENT, DIURETIC, ENCOURAGES SWEATING, LAXATIVE

Elderberries (*Sambucus nigra*) are an effective remedy for disorders of the upper respiratory tract, such as excess mucus, colds, and influenza, and can be used to relieve all types of inflammation, including rheumatic complaints. They improve iron absorption from food and aid hemoglobin production, benefit blood-fat levels, and fat metabolism, aid liver function, and boost energy.

RECIPES elderberry cordial (page 284)

HAWTHORN

★ VITAMIN C; ANTHOCYANIN, GLYCOSIDES, SAPONINS, TANNIN

✔ ANTI-INFLAMMATORY, ANTIOXIDANT, LOWERS BLOOD PRESSURE, TONIC

Hawthorn berries (*Crataegus monogyna*) benefit the whole cardiovascular system. They are gentle in action and can help support the heart in heart failure, as well as being used to treat hypertension, arteriosclerosis, and angina. They reduce the "stickiness" of blood platelets and may help prevent thrombosis (abnormal blood-clot formation). They may also inhibit the growth of some cancers, especially of the lung, skin, and esophagus.

RECIPES circulation booster (page 284)

MULBERRY

★ VITAMINS C, E, K, B2, B3, BIOTIN, FOLATE; MANGANESE, POTASSIUM; IRON; ANTHOCYANIN, CITRIC ACID; FIBER, SUGARS

✔ ANTIOXIDANT

! UNRIPE MULBERRIES CAN BE TOXIC AND SHOULD NOT BE EATEN

Mulberries (*Morus nigra*) boost energy and strength, support nerve, heart, liver, muscle, and bone marrow function, and help to keep cell membranes healthy. They enhance iron absorption, reduce

blood-fat levels, improve oxygen transport to the tissues, and aid protein and fat metabolism. They may also protect against heart disease, cancer, and rheumatoid arthritis.

RECIPES use in place of blackberries in recipes

RASPBERRY

★ VITAMINS C, E, K, B3, B5, BIOTIN, FOLATE; IRON, MAGNESIUM, POTASSIUM; TANNINS, CITRIC ACID, SALICYLIC ACID; FIBER, SUGARS

✔ ANTIOXIDANT, DETOXIFYING, LAXATIVE, TONIC

♀ RASPBERRY LEAVES ARE ALSO USED MEDICINALLY TO HELP ENSURE HEALTHY PREGNANCY AND BIRTH

Raspberries (*Rubus idaeus*) activate the body's natural self-cleansing ability, and improve the health of the skin, hair, sweat glands, nerves, liver, bone marrow, and mucous membranes. They enhance wound healing and have powerful antioxidant properties. Raspberries boost the body's energy levels, and also encourage efficient protein and fat metabolism.

RECIPES raspberry gateau (page 278), raspberry sorbet (page 279), fruity pancakes (page 259)

ROSEHIP

★ VITAMIN C; CAROTENOIDS, TANNIN; PECTIN

✔ ANTI-ALLERGIC, ANTIOXIDANT, HEALING, MILD LAXATIVE

Rosehips (*Rosa canina*) are rich in vitamin C and improve immunity to infections, especially colds. They boost energy levels, help maintain healthy mucous membranes, enhance wound healing, and help prevent heart disease and the formation of cancer cells.

RECIPES pick-me-up (page 286), rosehip syrup (page 286), tea for ear infections (page 287)

STRAWBERRY

★ VITAMINS C, K, FOLATE; MAGNESIUM, MANGANESE, POTASSIUM; ANTHOCYANINS, TANNINS; CITRIC ACID; FIBER, SUGARS

✔ ANTI-INFLAMMATORY, ANTIOXIDANT, ASTRINGENT, DIURETIC, LAXATIVE

Strawberries (*Fragaria* x *ananassa*) can be used to treat fever and to relieve the symptoms of rheumatoid arthritis. Good for the health of the skin and mucous membranes, strawberries improve wound healing, encourage iron absorption, and reduce blood-fat levels. They may help prevent high blood pressure, atherosclerosis, allergy and acne, and protect against age-related loss of vision.

RECIPES fruity pancakes (page 259)

raspberry

BOTH RASPBERRY FRUIT AND LEAVES HAVE BEEN USED AS
MEDICINE FOR CENTURIES. IN BOTANICAL TERMS, THE RASPBERRY
IS CONSIDERED TO BE AN "AGGREGATE FRUIT" RATHER THAN A TRUE
BERRY, CONSISTING OF NUMEROUS "DRUPELETS" ARRANGED AROUND
A CENTRAL CORE THAT IS LEFT BEHIND ON THE PLANT WHEN THE
FRUIT IS PICKED.

The origin of raspberries

Wild raspberries are forest plants native to North America,
Europe, and Northern Asia. The American raspberry (*Rubus
strigosus*) and European raspberry (*Rubus idaeus*) are closely
related, and most modern commercial raspberries are hybrids
of the two. The name *idaeus* refers to Mount Ida near Troy,
where the ancient Greeks picked raspberries to use both as a
food and a medicine. However, it was the Romans who spread
raspberries throughout Europe.

There are many references in old pharmacopeia as to the
ability of raspberry fruit "to strengthen the heart." During the
cholera epidemic that hit Europe in the 19th century, the leaves
formed part of an herbal mixture that effectively treated the
life-threatening diarrhea by combating fluid loss and
replacing potassium.

Raspberries as a cure

Raspberry fruits contain polyphenols, which have an
anti-inflammatory and antibiotic effect, and which also
decrease the rate of cancer-cell proliferation. They can be
used to help relieve symptoms of coughs, colds, flu, and
arthritis and may be useful in the management of allergies,
cancer, and diabetes.

The tannins in raspberry leaves have astringent qualities,
making them useful in the treatment of diarrhea, mouth ulcers,
cold sores, bleeding gums, and as part of a gargle mixture
to relieve sore throats. Raspberry leaf tea can be used as an
eyewash in cases of mild conjunctivitis.

Raspberry leaf tea has also been used for centuries as an
aid to natural childbirth. Drunk every day during the last two
months of pregnancy, it can help ease the birth process and
ensure that the uterus gets back into shape afterwards. Many
herbalists recommend the tea to ease period pain, lighten
heavy periods, and—together with sage leaves—to reduce the
severity of menopausal symptoms.

Oil extracts from raspberry seeds can be used as a potent
skin-healing and moisturising salve, high in vitamin C and E,
and in omega-3 and omega-6 fatty acids. Raspberry vinegar
is a traditional remedy against fever, sore throats, and chest
complaints (see recipe, opposite). Add 1 to 2 tbsp. to a glass
of still or sparkling water and drink two or three times a day.

IMMUNE-BOOSTING PROFILE

★ FRUIT: VITAMINS A, B2, B3, C, K, THIAMINE; IRON, CALCIUM, POTASSIUM, MANGANESE; PROTEIN, FIBER; GLUCOSE, FRUCTOSE, XYLITOL; CITRIC ACID, MALIC ACID, PECTIN, POLYPHENOL
LEAVES: TANNINS, POLYPEPTIDES, FLAVONOIDS

✔ ASTRINGENT, TONIC, ANTISPASMODIC, COOLING, ANTI-INFLAMMATORY

! RASPBERRIES ARE FRAGILE AND WILL KEEP ONLY FOR A FEW DAYS IN THE REFRIGERATOR. IT IS BEST NOT TO RINSE THEM, BUT IF THEY DO NEED RINSING, PLACE THEM IN A COLANDER AND DIP THEM CAREFULLY IN COLD WATER JUST BEFORE USE.

quick raspberry purée *(above)*

2 cups raspberries
½ cup sugar
1 teaspoon lemon juice

Mash or blend together the raspberries, sugar, and lemon juice. Serve with ice cream or pancakes, or on toast instead of jam.

raspberry vinegar

1½ cups white vinegar
2 cups raspberries
½ cup cane sugar

Put all of the ingredients in a stainless steel pan over a low heat and warm through until the sugar fully dissolves. Do not let the mixture boil. Strain, then transfer to a clean bottle. Store in the refrigerator.

raspberry smoothie with peach and vanilla

1 cup raspberries, plus extra to decorate
1 peach
1 banana
¾-in piece of vanilla bean
scant ½ cup plain soy yogurt
1 squeeze of orange juice
1 teaspoon maple syrup (optional)
2 thin slices of lime, to decorate

Blend the raspberries, peach, banana, and vanilla bean in a food processor. Add the yogurt, orange juice, and maple syrup and blend until smooth. Pour into a tall glass, decorate with the lime slices and a few extra raspberries, and serve.

avocado

AVOCADO IS PACKED WITH ENERGY AND IMMUNE-BOOSTING
PHYTOCHEMICALS. IT CAN HELP TO GUARD AGAINST CANCER, STROKE,
AND HEART DISEASE, AND HAS STRONG ANTI-INFLAMMATORY AND
ANTI-FUNGAL PROPERTIES. THIS AMAZING FRUIT ALSO STABILIZES
BLOOD SUGAR AND BLOOD FATS, AND HELPS TO MAINTAIN HEALTHY
BLOOD PRESSURE.

The origin of avocado

The avocado pear is thought to have originated in Central America,
where it was an important component of the diet of the native
Aztec people. It was discovered by the Spanish conquistadors in
the 16th century, but was little-known to the rest of the world until
the early 20th century. Avocados are now popular all over the
world and grown commercially in many tropical and subtropical
regions, mainly in Australia, Brazil, USA, Israel, Mediterranean
Europe, South Africa, and southeast Asia.

The avocado grows on an evergreen tree (*Persea americana*)
with small green-yellow flowers. The tree starts producing fruit
when it is three years old. A mature tree can display one million
flowers on its branches, of which only 100 to 400 will set fruit.
Healthy avocado trees can continue to produce
fruit for hundreds of years. Avocados are
normally picked before they are fully
ripened. On average, an avocado
takes about a week to ripen
at room temperature.
The process can be
accelerated by
placing the

unripe avocado in a paper bag along with an apple. The flesh of
the fruit discolors easily when exposed to the air. You can prevent
this by rubbing lemon juice on to the exposed surface of the flesh.

Immune-boosting properties

The avocado is a highly nutritious fruit that can be used to
replenish vitamin and mineral loss, especially of potassium. It
contains more potassium than banana, as well as several other
important nutrients and powerful antioxidants that mop up free
radicals—the destructive molecules known to trigger the
development of cancer and heart disease. In particular, it can help
prevent and treat cancer of the mouth and throat, prostate and
breast. The phytochemicals in avocado have strong anti-
inflammatory and antifungal properties. They work by inhibiting the
germination of fungal spores, and so make avocado useful in the
treatment of internal and external yeast infections.

The particular combination of nutrients and micro-nutrients
found in the avocado stimulates the immune system, enhances
antibody production and acts as a mild vasodilator, relaxing the
muscles surrounding blood vessels, reducing blood pressure and
the risk of stroke. Eating avocado helps protect the skin from the
effects of ageing, and maintains hair, mucous membranes, sweat
glands, nerves, muscles, and bone marrow in good condition. New
research suggests that avocados can improve sperm health.

Energy-rich

Avocados differ from other fruits in being extremely high in fat
(75 per cent), most of which is monounsaturated oleic acid. There
are many health benefits associated with eating a diet high in
monounsaturated fat such as this. In particular, such fats reduce
levels of L.D.L. cholesterol in the blood, and have a beneficial effect
on the composition of blood fats in general. Monounsaturated fat
also helps to stabilize blood-sugar levels. Most of the rest of the fat

found in avocados is polyunsaturated. As the fruit ripens, the small amount of saturated fat it contains steadily turns into polyunsaturated fat. Avocados also contain phytochemicals called beta-sitosterols, which reduce the absorption of cholesterol from food (these chemicals are widely used in the manufacture of blood-cholesterol-lowering drugs).

IMMUNE-BOOSTING PROFILE

★ VITAMINS C, E, K, B1, B2, B3, B5, B6, BIOTIN, FOLATE; MAGNESIUM, MANGANESE, POTASSIUM, ZINC; BETA-SITOSTEROLS, CAROTENOIDS, GLUTATHIONE; FIBER; OLEIC ACID, OMEGA-3 AND -6 FATTY ACIDS

✔ ANTI-CANCER, ANTIFUNGAL, ANTI-INFLAMMATORY, ANTIOXIDANT

! PEOPLE WHO ARE ALLERGIC TO NATURAL RUBBER (LATEX) HAVE A ONE IN TWO CHANCE OF BEING ALLERGIC TO AVOCADO

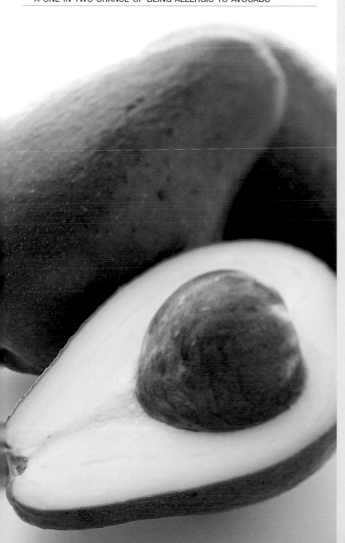

filled avocados *(above)*

2 avocados, halved, stone removed	1 tablespoon tarragon vinegar (or wine vinegar)
2 ripe tomatoes, finely chopped	4 tablespoons sunflower oil
½ cucumber, finely chopped	1 garlic clove, crushed
1 bunch of chives, finely chopped	½ teaspoon soy sauce
	½ teaspoon tabasco

Place the avocado halves on separate plates. Gently mix the tomato, cucumber, and chives, and divide on top of the avocado halves. Beat the dressing ingredients together and drizzle over the avocados. Serve with French bread.

avocado smoothie

1 avocado, peeled and chopped	1 teaspoon finely chopped fresh ginger root
1 pear, peeled, deseeded, and chopped	½ cup soy milk
¼ grapefruit, squeezed	4 tablespoons plain soy yogurt

Blend all the ingredients. Serve immediately in a glass.

avocado, watercress, and cumin salad

2 teaspoons cumin seeds	thinly sliced
1 bunch of watercress, chopped	Lemon tahini dressing
3 large ripe avocados,	(see page 267)

Roast the cumin seeds in a dry skillet. Remove and crush. Place the watercress on a large plate. Arrange the avocado on top. Sprinkle with dressing and garnish with the roasted cumin.

nuts and seeds

ALMOND

★ VITAMINS E, B2, B3, B5, BIOTIN, FOLATE; CALCIUM, MAGNESIUM, MANGANESE, PHOSPHORUS, POTASSIUM; BORON, COPPER, IRON, ZINC; STEROLS; FIBER, PROTEIN, MONOUNSATURATED FAT, OMEGA-6

✔ ANTIOXIDANT, LOWERS CHOLESTEROL, NUTRIENT-RICH

! BEWARE BITTER-TASTING ALMONDS—THEY CAN BE TOXIC

Almonds (*Prunus dulcis*) help maintain healthy blood-sugar and blood-fat levels, strengthen the cardiovascular system, and reduce the risk of coronary heart disease and stroke. They may also lower blood pressure and strengthen cell membranes.

RECIPES *muesli (page 259), toasted nuts and seeds (page 264)*

CASHEW

★ VITAMINS K, B1, B5, B6, BIOTIN; MAGNESIUM, MANGANESE, PHOSPHORUS, POTASSIUM; BORON, COPPER, IRON, SELENIUM, ZINC; FIBER; PROTEIN; OLEIC ACID, OMEGA-3 AND OMEGA-6

✔ ANTIOXIDANT, LOWERS CHOLESTEROL AND LDL FAT LEVELS

Cashews (*Anacardium occidentale*) help to maintain healthy blood pressure and blood-fat levels, aid hemoglobin production and fat metabolism, ease stress, and help keep skin, hair, glands, nerves, mucous membranes, blood cells, and bone marrow healthy.

RECIPES *toasted nuts and seeds (page 264), paella (page 268)*

FLAXSEED (LINSEED)

★ VITAMINS B1, B2, B3, B5, B6; CALCIUM, MAGNESIUM, PHOSPHORUS, POTASSIUM, IRON, ZINC; GLYCOSIDES; FIBER, MUCILAGE, OMEGA-3 AND -6

✔ ANTI-COUGH, LOWERS CHOLESTEROL, IMMUNO-STIMULANT, LAXATIVE

Flaxseeds (*Linum usitatissimum*) can help treat coughs, bronchitis, chronic constipation, and psoriasis. They also help lower blood sugar and cholesterol levels, and protect against certain cancers.

RECIPES *muesli (page 259)*

HAZELNUT

★ VITAMINS E, C, K, B1, B6, BIOTIN, FOLATE; CALCIUM, MAGNESIUM, MANGANESE, PHOSPHORUS, POTASSIUM, BORON, COPPER, IRON, ZINC; FIBER, PROTEIN, STEROLS, OLEIC ACID, OMEGA-3 AND -6

✔ ANTIOXIDANT, LOWERS LDL AND CHOLESTEROL, ANTI-CANCER

! SOME PEOPLE ARE ALLERGIC TO HAZELNUTS

Hazelnuts (*Corylus avaellana*) help regulate blood fats and aid cell renewal and repair. They help protect cells against free radical damage and benefit skin, hair, nails, glands, nerves, bone marrow, and mucous membranes.

RECIPES *toasted nuts and seeds (page 264)*

MACADAMIA NUT (QUEENSLAND NUT)

★ VITAMINS B1, B3, B5, B6, BIOTIN; MAGNESIUM, MANGANESE, PHOSPHORUS, COPPER, IRON, ZINC; FIBER, PROTEIN, UNSATURATED FAT

✔ ANTIOXIDANT, LOWERS CHOLESTEROL, GOOD FOR SKIN

Macadamia nuts (*Macadamia ternifolia*) reduce oxidative stress, lower blood cholesterol, and benefit the cardiovascular system. They are a favorite ingredient in skin restorative preparations.

RECIPES *spring greens and macadamia nuts (page 274)*

MELON SEED

★ VITAMINS B2, B3, FOLATE; CALCIUM, MAGNESIUM, MANGANESE, POTASSIUM; COPPER, IRON, ZINC; PROTEIN, UNSATURATED FAT

✔ ANTIOXIDANT, LOWERS CHOLESTEROL

Melon (*Cucmis melo*) seeds support the immune and cardiovascular systems, help regulate healthy blood-fat levels, and provide the nutrients necessary to aid wound healing and help maintain healthy skin, nails, and nerves.

RECIPES *toasted nuts and seeds (page 264)*

PECAN NUT

★ VITAMINS E, B1, B2, B6; CALCIUM, MAGNESIUM, MANGANESE, PHOSPHORUS, POTASSIUM, COPPER, SELENIUM, ZINC; FIBER, PROTEIN, STEROLS, OLEIC ACID, OMEGA-3 AND -6

✔ ANTIOXIDANT, LOWERS CHOLESTEROL

! SOME PEOPLE ARE ALLERGIC TO PECAN NUTS

Pecan nuts (*Carya illinoinensis*) help prevent heart disease and cancer (particularly of the breast and prostate). Eating pecans regularly lowers blood cholesterol and improves blood lipid balance, and has also been shown to reduce benign prostate enlargement.

RECIPES *muesli (page 259)*

PISTACHIO

★ VITAMINS E, B1, B2, B3, FOLATE; CALCIUM, MAGNESIUM,
PHOSPHORUS, POTASSIUM; COPPER, IRON, SELENIUM, ZINC;
FIBER, PROTEIN, STEROLS, POLY- AND MONOUNSATURATED FATS,
OMEGA-6

✔ ANTIOXIDANT, LOWERS CHOLESTEROL

Pistachio (*Pistacia vera*) nuts protect against heart disease and
some cancers, aid liver function and metabolism, boost energy,
and improve neurological health and function of blood cells,
muscles, nerves, mucous, membranes, and skin.

RECIPES muesli (page 259), toasted nuts and seeds (page 264)

PINE NUTS INE NUT (PINE KERNELS)

★ VITAMINS E, K, B1, B2, B3, FOLATE; MAGNESIUM, MANGANESE,
POTASSIUM; COPPER, IRON, ZINC; FIBER, PROTEIN,
UNSATURATED FAT, STEROLS, OMEGA-6

✔ ANTI-INFLAMMATORY, ANTIOXIDANT

Pine (*Pinus spp.*) nuts help protect against heart disease,
rheumatoid arthritis, diabetes, epilepsy and some cancers. They
aid metabolism and bone health.

RECIPES pasta, pesto, and shiitake (page 221)

PUMPKIN SEED

★ VITAMINS B1, B2, B3; MAGNESIUM, PHOSPHORUS, POTASSIUM;
COPPER, IRON, SELENIUM, ZINC; FIBER, OMEGA-3, PROTEIN,
UNSATURATED FAT

✔ ANTI-INFLAMMATORY, ANTIOXIDANT, DETOXIFYING, IMMUNO-STIMULANT

Pumpkin (*Cucurbita maxima*) seeds are highly nutritious, and help
prevent and treat cardiovascular, immunodeficiency, and
autoimmune disorders. They can also benefit the prostate gland.

RECIPES carrot 'n' beet salad (page 275)

SESAME SEED/TAHINI

★ VITAMINS E, B1, B2, B3, B6, FOLATE; CALCIUM, MAGNESIUM,
MANGANESE, PHOSPHORUS; COPPER, IRON, ZINC; STARCH, FIBER,
PROTEIN, POLY- AND MONOUNSATURATED FATS, OMEGA-6,
STEROLS, PHYTOESTROGENS

✔ ANTI-CANCER, ANTIOXIDANT, LOWERS CHOLESTEROL, NUTRIENT-RICH

Sesame (*Sesamum indicum*) seeds aid tissue repair and renewal,
and help the body cope with stress. Tahini is ground sesame paste.

*RECIPES oriental salad with tempeh (page 209), lemon tahini
dressing (page 267), green lentil salad (page 276)*

SUNFLOWER SEED

★ VITAMINS E, B1, B2, B3, B5, B6, FOLATE; CALCIUM, MAGNESIUM,
MANGANESE, PHOSPHORUS, POTASSIUM; COPPER, IRON, SELENIUM,
ZINC; FIBER, PROTEIN, POLY- AND MONOUNSATURATED FATS,
STEROLS, OMEGA-6

✔ ANTI-CANCER, ANTIOXIDANT, LOWERS CHOLESTEROL,
NUTRIENT-RICH

Sunflower (*Helianthus annuus*) seeds help regulate blood-fat levels,
improve the skin, and aid tissue repair. They may help treat eczema.

RECIPES muesli (page 259), toasted nuts and seeds (page 264)

SWEET CHESTNUT (SPANISH CHESTNUT)

★ VITAMINS B3, B5, B6; MAGNESIUM, MANGANESE, PHOSPHORUS,
POTASSIUM; COPPER, ZINC; COMPLEX CARBOHYDRATES, FIBER,
SUGARS, PROTEIN

✔ ENERGY-BOOSTING, IMMUNO-STIMULANT, NUTRIENT-RICH

Sweet chestnuts (*Castanea sativa*) are versatile and nutritious.
Their energy is released slowly and steadily in the body, helping
to stabilize blood-sugar levels and boosting energy and strength.

RECIPES sweet chestnuts and kumquats (page 273)

WALNUT

★ VITAMINS E, B1, B2, B3, B5, B6, BIOTIN, FOLATE; CALCIUM,
MAGNESIUM, MANGANESE, PHOSPHORUS, POTASSIUM; COPPER,
IRON, SELENIUM, ZINC; FIBER, PROTEIN, STEROLS, OMEGA-3 AND 6

✔ ANTIOXIDANT, ANTI-INFLAMMATORY, LOWERS CHOLESTEROL

Walnuts (*Juglans sp.*) reduce the risk of heart disease and cancer,
benefit blood cells, muscles, and nervous system, aid brain
function, boost energy and strength, and help us cope with stress.

RECIPES florence fennel salad (page 275), arugula salad (page 276)

brazil nut

THIS DELICIOUS SOUTH AMERICAN KERNEL IS ONE OF THE RICHEST
NATURAL SOURCES OF SELENIUM AND VITAMIN E—POWERFUL
ANTIOXIDANTS WITH ANTI-AGEING PROPERTIES THAT CAN HELP GUARD
AGAINST MANY DISORDERS INCLUDING HEART DISEASE AND CANCER.

The origin of the Brazil nut

The Brazil nut, also called the para nut, cream nut and castanea,
is the edible seed of a giant tree (*Bertholletia excelsa*) that grows in
the Amazon rainforest. It is an important source of nutrition—and
income—to the local population. Most Brazil nuts are collected
from wild trees. They grow in clusters of 8 to 24 nuts enclosed in
a woody, fibrous fruit capsule that looks like a cross between a
coconut and a cooking pot with a lid. The nut is enclosed in a
hard, dark-brown, wedge-shaped shell. From January to June,
the capsules ripen and fall to the ground, where they are collected.
The kernels are taken out, sun-dried and washed before being sold
and exported, mainly to North America and Europe. (After the nuts
have been removed, the dried capsules are used as animal traps,
a practice that has given them the name "monkey-pots.")

Immune-boosting properties

The Brazil nut is extremely nutritious with high levels of protein,
unsaturated fat, selenium, zinc, and other minerals, plus substantial
quantities of vitamins E and B1. It is the combination of vitamin E
with selenium that gives the Brazil nut its special immune-
enhancing properties. These two important antioxidants work

synergistically, each improving the performance of the other to
boost immune-system function. Antioxidants prevent cell damage
by mopping up free radicals and thus preventing the "oxidative"
chain reactions that can damage DNA. Some oxidation is normal
and vital for health (the immune system actually uses oxidative
reactions to destroy micro-organisms), but if the level of oxidation
outstrips the body's own defensive capabilities, the resulting
excess of free radicals can cause cellular damage.

Accumulated damage by free radicals is known to be an
important factor in ageing and disease, and the role of antioxidants
in the prevention and treatment of illness is well recognized.
Antioxidants play a preventative role in many conditions including
asthma, heart disease, immunodeficiency disorders, and cancer.

Selenium enhances immunity by activating an enzyme in the
body called glutathione peroxidase, which inhibits the formation
of free radicals and suppresses tumor growth. Infection depletes
the body's selenium levels. This, in turn, suppresses the immune
system because a low level of selenium affects the normal antibody
response to infection and cell damage. Thus even a moderate
increase in selenium intake is beneficial to the body's self-defense
mechanisms, and can help to reduce the risk of cancer, heart
disease, and fungal infections such as candidiasis. However,
it is possible to get too much of a good thing.
Taking excess selenium as a food
supplement can result in selenium
toxicity, which causes hair loss,

dizziness, fatigue, and skin problems. Fortunately, the Brazil nut–selenium "package" provides a natural safety limit because brazil nuts satisfy hunger long before selenium intake reaches toxic limits. Many other foods of plant origin also contain selenium—the amount depending on the plant's ability to absorb it from the soil. Unfortunately, in many parts of the world, modern agricultural practices have depleted the soil of selenium, providing yet another good reason for preserving the Amazon rainforest—Brazil nuts.

IMMUNE-BOOSTING PROFILE

★ VITAMINS E, B1, BIOTIN; CALCIUM, MAGNESIUM, MANGANESE, PHOSPHORUS, POTASSIUM; COPPER, SELENIUM, ZINC; FIBER, POLY- AND MONOUNSATURATED FATS, OMEGA-6

✔ ANTI-CANCER, ANTIOXIDANT, IMMUNO-STIMULANT, LOWERS CHOLESTEROL

! SOME PEOPLE ARE ALLERGIC TO BRAZIL NUTS

! GENETICALLY MODIFIED SOY BEANS MAY CONTAIN GENES FROM BRAZIL NUTS, AND SO MAY TRIGGER AN ALLERGIC REACTION

brazil nuts and sun-dried tomatoes with beans (above)

7 ounces Brazil nuts, chopped	1 pound French beans, topped and tailed
3½ ounces sun-dried tomatoes, sliced	1 tablespoon olive oil salt and pepper

Steam the beans till tender. Place the rest of the ingredients in a bowl, add the beans while still hot, mix well, and serve.

broiled endive and brazil nut salad

4 endives, halved lengthwise	Salt and pepper
3 tablespoons olive oil	2 ounces Brazil nuts

Brush the endives with olive oil, then broil a few minutes on each side until they begin to char and soften. Brush with more oil as you turn them, if necessary. Place on a serving dish, scatter with Brazils nuts and serve with vinaigrette.

spicy brazil nut pâté

2 ounces Brazil nuts, roughly chopped	Pinch of cayenne 1 teaspoon thyme
Soy sauce	3 tablepoons olive oil
1 pound 2 ounces mushrooms, chopped	Salt and pepper to taste
7 ounces tofu, crumbled	2 tbs fresh parsley
2 garlic cloves, chopped	
1 teaspoon garam masala	

Roast the Brazil nuts in a dry skillet, add a little soy sauce, stir, and remove from the pan. Sauté the mushrooms and the tofu in the oil with the garlic, thyme, and the spices until soft. Blend all the ingredients (except the parsley) to a coarse paté. Place in a serving dish, garnish with parsley, and serve.

grains

BULGUR WHEAT

★ VITAMINS B1, B2, B3, B5, B6; MAGNESIUM, MANGANESE, PHOSPHORUS, POTASSIUM, COPPER, IRON; COMPLEX CARBOHYDRATES, PROTEIN

✔ EASILY DIGESTIBLE, ENERGY-BOOSTING, LOW-FAT, LOW-GI

! AVOID IF ALLERGIC OR SENSITIVE TO GLUTEN IN WHEAT

Bulgur is the cracked kernels of boiled and dried durum wheat (*Triticum durum*). Use fine grains for saladscover with boiling water and leave for a few minutes to expand and soften. Cook larger grains like rice, but for less time and with less water.

RECIPES bulgur wheat salad (page 275)

MUESLI (SWISS STYLE, NO ADDED SUGAR)

★ VITAMINS E, B1, B2, B3, B5, B6, BIOTIN, FOLATE; CALCIUM, MAGNESIUM, PHOSPHORUS, POTASSIUM; SELENIUM, IRON, ZINC; COMPLEX CARBOHYDRATES, FIBER, PROTEIN, SUGARS

✔ ANTI-CANCER, ANTIOXIDANT, ANTI-STRESS, LOWERS CHOLESTEROL

Muesli contains a potent mixture of highly nutritious, vitality-enhancing ingredients.

RECIPES muesli (page 259)

OATS

★ VITAMINS B1, B2, B3, B5, E; MAGNESIUM, MANGANESE, PHOSPHORUS, POTASSIUM, IRON, SELENIUM, ZINC; COMPLEX CARBOHYDRATES, FIBER, PROTEIN, OMEGA-6

✔ ANTI-CANCER, ANTI-STRESS, LOWERS CHOLESTEROL, ENERGY-BOOSTING

Oats are high in protein, iron, and soluble fiber. They lower blood cholesterol, ease stress, and soothe tired nerves.

RECIPES muesli (page 259), oatmeal with dried fruit and quinoa (page 258), blackberry crumble (page 279), pick-me-up (page 286)

PASTA (MADE FROM DURUM WHEAT)

★ VITAMINS B1, B2, B3, FOLATE; MAGNESIUM, MANGANESE, PHOSPHORUS, POTASSIUM; IRON, SELENIUM, ZINC; COMPLEX CARBOHYDRATES, FIBER, PROTEIN

✔ ENERGY-BOOSTING

! AVOID IF ALLERGIC OR SENSITIVE TO GLUTEN IN WHEAT

Durum wheat (*Triticum durum*) is high in protein. When ground to flour and mixed with water, it is ideal for rolling into pasta shapes.

RECIPES pasta, pesto, and shiitake (page 221)

QUINOA

★ VITAMINS E, B1, B2, B3, B5, B6, FOLATE; CALCIUM, MAGNESIUM, MANGANESE; PHOSPHORUS, POTASSIUM; COPPER, IRON, SELENIUM, ZINC; SAPONINS; COMPLEX CARBOHYDRATES, FIBER, PROTEIN, OMEGA-6

✔ ANTI-CANCER, ANTIOXIDANT, GOOD FOR BREASTFEEDING, ENERGY-BOOSTING, GOOD FOR HEART AND CIRCULATION, COMPLETE PROTEIN, LOWERS CHOLESTEROL, WEIGHT LOSS

♡ CONTAINS NO GLUTEN

Quinoa (*Chenopodium quinoa*) is arguably the most nutritious of all grains. It is rich in protein and minerals, and can be used to add nutritional value to breakfast cereals, biscuits, and casseroles.

RECIPES porridge with dried fruit and quinoa (page 258), curried quinoa and vegetable soup (page 205) quinoa tabouleh (page 205)

RICE

★ VITAMINS B1, B3, B5, B6; MAGNESIUM, MANGANESE, PHOSPHORUS; COPPER, IRON, SELENIUM, ZINC; COMPLEX CARBOHYDRATES, FIBER

✔ ENERGY-BOOSTING, LOWERS CHOLESTEROL

♡ CONTAINS NO GLUTEN

Brown rice (*Oryza sativa*) is a rich source of energy, fiber, protein, and B vitamins. It helps protect the cardiovascular system, nerves, digestion, muscles, mucous membranes, skin, hair, glands, and bone marrow. Rice milk is a good alternative to cow's milk—good for those with irritable bowel syndrome.

RECIPES rice: paella (page 268), kichuri—rice with lentils (page 273), rice milk: heart chai (page 283), muesli (page 239)

WHEATGRASS

★ VITAMINS A, E; ZINC; CHLOROPHYLL; ESSENTIAL FATTY ACIDS, FIBER, PROTEIN

✔ ANTIOXIDANT, DETOXIFYING

Wheatgrass (*Triticum sp.*) comes from young, newly sprouted wheat kernels. It is a highly concentrated source of immune-enhancing nutrients, and is a powerful liver detoxifier. It stimulates hemoglobin production, lowers cholesterol, and helps regulate blood-fat levels.

RECIPES grow your own to eat in sandwiches or salads, or, buy wheatgrass juice, or add wheatgrass powder to other juices

CORN (SWEETCORN, MAIZE)

★ VITAMINS C, B1, B3, B5, FOLATE; MAGNESIUM, PHOSPHORUS, POTASSIUM, MANGANESE; STARCH, SUGAR, FIBER, PROTEIN

✔ ANTI-STRESS, AIDS DIGESTION

💡 CORN SILK (FINE THREAD ON FRESH CORN COBS) CAN BE USED IN A TISANE TO SOOTHE IRRITATIONS OF THE BLADDER AND URETHRA

Corn (*Zea mays*) aids wound healing, strengthens immunity by boosting antibody production, and keeps the skin and mucous membranes in good condition. It helps the body cope with stress, stabilizes blood sugar, and maintains a healthy level of blood fats.

RECIPES sweet potato curry (page 272), tempeh kebabs (page 209)

WHEAT BRAN

★ VITAMINS B1, B2, B3, B5, B6, FOLATE; MAGNESIUM, MANGANESE, PHOSPHORUS, POTASSIUM; COPPER, IRON, SELENIUM, ZINC; FIBER

✔ ANTIOXIDANT, DETOXIFYING, LAXATIVE

❗ THE PHYTATES IN BRAN INHIBIT ABSORPTION OF NUTRIENTS INCLUDING IRON, CALCIUM, AND ZINC; HOWEVER, AS BRAN ALSO CONTAINS LARGE AMOUNTS OF THESE MINERALS, THE NET EFFECT OF EATING IT IN MODERATE AMOUNTS IS STILL HIGHLY BENEFICIAL

❗ ALWAYS DRINK PLENTY OF FLUIDS WHEN EATING BRAN TO AVOID INTESTINAL BLOCKAGE

Wheat bran, the outer layer of wheat (*Triticum sp.*) grain, is the richest source of insoluble fiber. It absorbs large amounts of water and increases in bulk, aiding the passage of waste through the bowel and relieving constipation. This helps prevent diseases such as diverticulitis and bowel cancer. Bran also helps regulate blood-fat and blood-sugar levels.

RECIPES muesli (page 259)

WHEAT GERM

★ VITAMINS E, B1, B2, B3, B5, B6, BIOTIN, FOLATE; MAGNESIUM, MANGANESE, PHOSPHORUS, POTASSIUM; COPPER, IRON, SELENIUM, ZINC; COMPLEX CARBOHYDRATES, FIBER, PROTEIN, SUGARS, POLYUNSATURATED FAT, OMEGA-6

✔ ANTIOXIDANT, ANTI-STRESS

❗ AVOID IF ALLERGIC OR SENSITIVE TO GLUTEN IN WHEAT

The inner layer of wheat (*Triticum sp.*) grain, wheatgerm is a natural source of zinc, vitamin E and B-complex vitamins. It helps to boost energy levels, enhances fat metabolism, and helps protect against heart disease, immunodeficiency disorders, and some cancers.

RECIPES muesli (page 259), try sprinkling on salads and desserts

WILD RICE

★ VITAMINS B1, B2, B3, B5, B6, FOLATE; MAGNESIUM, MANGANESE, PHOSPHORUS, POTASSIUM; IRON, ZINC; COMPLEX CARBOHYDRATE, FIBER

✔ ENERGY-BOOSTING, LOWERS CHOLESTEROL

💡 WILD RICE IS A NATIVE AMERICAN GRASS, UNRELATED TO COMMON RICE BUT EQUALLY NUTRITIOUS

Wild rice (*Zizania aquatica*) aids metabolism and helps maintain energy levels. It enhances the health of nerves, muscles, skin, and mucous membranes, and helps prevent cardiovascular disease.

RECIPES provençal-style kidney beans (page 271), sweet chestnuts and kumquats (page 273), wild rice salad (page 277)

quinoa

QUINOA IS A TASTY, VERSATILE GRAIN-LIKE SEED. IT IS EASY TO COOK AND HAS A TEXTURE AND APPEARANCE SIMILAR TO COUSCOUS—ALTHOUGH QUINOA IS MUCH MORE SUBSTANTIAL AND NUTRITIOUS.

The origin of quinoa

Quinoa is a "pseudocereal" (that is, grain-like, but not a grass) originating in the South American Andes and grown for its edible seeds. Closely related to beetroot and spinach, its leaves are also edible. It is an undemanding, altitude-tolerant plant that can be cultivated up to about 13,000ft., and archaeological evidence from Lake Titicaca in Bolivia shows that quinoa has been cultivated in the region for at least 9,000 years. The Incas referred to quinoa as "the mother of all grains," and they held it to be a sacred gift from the gods.

Sixteenth-century Spanish colonists actively suppressed Andean quinoa cultivation, replacing it with their own foods. This contributed to the collapse of the Inca civilization as the population suffered severe malnutrition and infant mortality. Happily, quinoa was "rediscovered" in the 1970s when two American students of a Bolivian spiritual leader were encouraged to consume quinoa to help them develop deeper spiritual sensitivity. Quinoa was unavailable outside South America, so the two founded the *Quinoa Corporation* in Colorado, and quinoa's popularity as a source of high-quality nutrition has been growing ever since.

Therapeutic properties

Quinoa is arguably the most nutritious of all the grains. It has a very high protein content (18 per cent) and—unlike many other grains—is rich in the amino acids lysine, methionine, and cystine, giving it the same protein value as cow milk. It is also high in polyunsaturated fat and contains less carbohydrate than other grains. It is gluten-free, a good source of fiber, and rich in vitamins E, B1, B2, B6, and folate, as well as phosphorus, calcium, magnesium, selenium, zinc, iron, and antioxidants.

The Incas were famed for their physical endurance, and quinoa's high protein, complex-carbohydrate, vitamin, and mineral content makes it a perfect endurance food. They also found it beneficial for pregnant women and nursing mothers, helping to keep them well nourished and produce healthy milk.

The nutrients in quinoa may help control weight and reduce the risk of cardiovascular disease, diabetes, colon cancer, and breast cancer.

Using quinoa

Quinoa is gluten-free and easy to digest, which makes it an ideal staple for those who cannot eat wheat and other gluten-containing grains. Try putting cooked quinoa "oatmeal" in a clean dish towel or muslin cloth and using it as a compress on bruises to relieve pain and reduce coloration. This compress can also help soothe cuts and grazes. Quinoa has a high calcium content, which reflects its reputation as a bone healer. The Incas treated broken bones by eating extra quinoa and using plaster casts made from quinoa "oatmeal."

The Incas also used quinoa to treat urinary tract infections, tuberculosis, and liver problems, and today it is still used as a remedy for altitude and motion sickness.

IMMUNE-BOOSTING PROFILE

★ VITAMINS E, B1, B2, B6, FOLATE; CALCIUM, IRON, MAGNESIUM, PHOSPHATE, SELENIUM, ZINC; COMPLEX CARBOHYDRATES, CYSTINE, FIBER, LYSINE, METHIONINE, PROTEIN, POLYUNSATURATED FATTY ACIDS; ANTIOXIDANTS

✔ EASES ALTITUDE AND MOTION SICKNESS, ANTI-DIABETIC, ANTI-CANCER, CARDIOVASCULAR TROPHORESTORATIVE, LACTATIVE AND NOURISHING FOR PREGNANT WOMEN AND NURSING MOTHERS, SLIMMING AID, URINARY DISINFECTANT, BONE HEALING

♀ PERFECT ENDURANCE FOOD; CONTAINS NO GLUTEN

! QUINOA SHOULD BE SOAKED IN WATER FOR 15 MINUTES BEFORE COOKING TO GET RID OF THE OUTER COATING OF SAPONIN, WHICH HAS A BITTER TASTE. DRAIN AND RINSE AGAIN BEFORE COOKING IN FRESH WATER (SEE RECIPES)

! THE LEAVES ARE DELICIOUS AND YOU CAN EAT THEM LIKE SPINACH. ALSO LIKE SPINACH, HOWEVER, THEY CONTAIN OXALIC ACID—EAT THEM ONLY IN SMALL AMOUNTS IF YOU SUFFER FROM RHEUMATIC COMPLAINTS OR KIDNEY STONES

curried quinoa and vegetable soup *(above)*

1 tablespoon olive oil
1 onion, chopped
2 carrots, diced
2 red bell peppers, halved, seeded, and chopped
1 handful green beans, chopped
4 tablespoons curry paste
1 cup quinoa, rinsed and soaked in cold water for 15 minutes, then drained
1¾ cups coconut milk
salt and pepper

Heat the oil in a large saucepan over a medium-low heat. Sauté the onion, then add the vegetables one at a time. Add the curry paste and a splash of water. Bring to the boil, then reduce the heat to low and simmer uncovered for 5 minutes, stirring occasionally, until the vegetables begin to soften. Add the quinoa, followed by the coconut milk and 2½ cups hot water. Bring to the boil, then reduce the heat to low and simmer gently for 10 minutes, until the quinoa is cooked. Check the seasoning and serve with warm tortillas, chapatis, or naan bread.

quinoa tabouleh

Tabouleh is a Lebanese salad, traditionally served on a bed of lettuce leaves that are used to scoop up the grains.

1 cup quinoa, rinsed and soaked in cold water for 15 minutes, then drained
1 small head of lettuce, rinsed but leaves kept whole
4 tomatoes, chopped
½ cucumber, chopped
1 red bell pepper, halved, seeded, and chopped
2 scallions, thinly sliced
2 tablespoons chopped mint
1 small bunch flat-leaf parsley, chopped
¼ cup Kalamata or other black olives
juice of 1 lemon
2 tablespoons extra virgin olive oil
2 tablespoons tamari soy sauce
2 garlic cloves, minced

Put the quinoa and 2 cups water in a saucepan and bring to the boil. Reduce the heat to low and simmer gently for 10 minutes, until the water is absorbed. Take off the heat, transfer to a clean dish, then set aside to cool.

Make a bed of lettuce leaves in a big salad bowl. In another bowl, toss the cooked quinoa with the rest of the ingredients until they are evenly distributed. Arrange on top of the lettuce leaves and serve.

legumes

ADUKI BEAN

★ VITAMINS B1, B2, B3, B5, B6, FOLATE; MAGNESIUM, MANGANESE, PHOSPHORUS, POTASSIUM; COPPER, IRON, ZINC; COMPLEX CARBOHYDRATES, FIBER, PROTEIN

✔ HEALING, ENERGY-BOOSTING

Aduki beans (*Phaseolus angularis*) help release energy from food and keep skin and mucous membranes in good condition.

RECIPES add to stews, casseroles and salads

BLACK-EYE PEA (BLACK-EYE BEAN, COWPEA)

★ VITAMINS B1, B2, B3, B5, B6, BIOTIN, FOLATE; CALCIUM, MAGNESIUM, MANGANESE, PHOSPHORUS, POTASSIUM; COPPER, IRON, SELENIUM, ZINC; COMPLEX CARBOHYDRATES, FIBER, PROTEIN

✔ AIDS DIGESTION, LOWERS CHOLESTEROL, IMMUNO-STIMULANT.

Black-eye peas (*Vigna sinensis*) have a savory flavor and are used like haricot and lima beans. Full of energy and micro-nutrients, they enhance the body's ability to make amino acids and DNA.

RECIPES beans and tomatoes on toast (page 258), black-eye pea and wild marjoram soup (page 261)

BUTTERBEAN

★ VITAMINS K, B1, B2, B3, B5, B6, FOLATE; CALCIUM, COPPER, POTASSIUM, PHOSPHORUS, MAGNESIUM, MANGANESE; IRON, SELENIUM, ZINC; COMPLEX CARBOHYDRATES, FIBER, PROTEIN

✔ ANTI-STRESS, LOWERS CHOLESTEROL

Butterbeans (*Phaseolus vulgaris sp.*) help the body release energy from food and protect the immune and nervous systems. They also help maintain healthy skin, glands, hair, and bone marrow.

RECIPES italian butterbean soup (page 268)

FAVA BEAN

★ VITAMINS C, K, B1, B2, B3, B5, B6, BIOTIN, FOLATE; CALCIUM, MAGNESIUM, MANGANESE, PHOSPHORUS, POTASSIUM; COPPER, IRON, SELENIUM, ZINC; COMPLEX CARBOHYDRATES, FIBER, PROTEIN

✔ ANTI-STRESS, LOWERS CHOLESTEROL, DETOXIFYING

The high level of vitamin B5 and folate in fava beans (*Vicia faba*) makes them a useful support for the body's defense against stress.

RECIPES artichoke hearts, fava beans, and shiitake (page 261)

GARBANZO BEAN

★ VITAMINS E, B2, B3, B5, K, FOLATE; CALCIUM, MAGNESIUM, MANGANESE, PHOSPHORUS, POTASSIUM; IRON, SELENIUM, ZINC; COMPLEX CARBOHYDRATES, FIBER, PROTEIN, OMEGA-6

✔ ANTI-CANCER, ANTIOXIDANT, ANTI-STRESS, LOWERS CHOLESTEROL

Garbanzos (*Cicer arietinum*) aid the absorption of nutrients and protect the cells from free radical damage. They support the function of nerves, muscles, enzymes, and hormones and may help protect the body against heart disease and cancer.

RECIPES spicy moroccan soup (page 262), hummus with crudités and warm pitta bread (page 262), winter hot pot (page 272)

HARICOT BEANS/GREEN BEAN

★ VITAMINS A, C, K, B1, B2, B3, FOLATE; MAGNESIUM, MANGANESE, POTASSIUM, IRON; FIBER

✔ ANTI-CANCER, ANTIOXIDANT, LOWERS CHOLESTEROL

Haricot beans and green beans (*Phaseolus vulgaris sp.*) help keep cells well oxygenated and in good condition. They also enhance energy levels, support the nervous system, and aid liver function.

RECIPES beans and tomatoes on toast (page 258); okra in sweet and sour tamarind sauce (page 272), salad niçoise (page 275)

LENTIL

★ VITAMINS B1, B2, B3, B5, B6, FOLATE; MAGNESIUM, MANGANESE, PHOSPHORUS, POTASSIUM; COPPER, IRON, SELENIUM, ZINC; COMPLEX CARBOHYDRATES, FIBER, PROTEIN

✔ ANTIOXIDANT, ENERGY-BOOSTING, LOWERS CHOLESTEROL

Lentils (*Lens esculenta sp.*) are an excellent source of antioxidants, and so can protect against heart disease and cancer. They improve the function of red blood cells and the integrity of cell membranes, and also help regulate blood-fat levels.

RECIPES spicy moroccan soup (page 262), casserole de puy (page 268), shepherdess' pie (page 272), winter hot pot (page 272), khichuri—rice with lentils (page 273), green lentil salad (page 276)

MANGETOUT PEA

★ VITAMINS A, C, K, B1, B2, BIOTIN, FOLATE; MAGNESIUM, MANGANESE, PHOSPHORUS, POTASSIUM; ZINC; IRON; FIBER, PROTEIN

✔ ANTI-CANCER, ANTIOXIDANT

Mangetout peas (*Pisum sativum sp.*) are good for the skin, hair, glands, nerves, and muscles. They aid metabolism, liver function, and antibody production, and help maintain energy levels.

RECIPES chinese salad (page 276)

MUNG BEAN SPROUTS

★ VITAMINS C, K, B2, FOLATE; PHOSPHORUS; IRON; FIBER, PROTEIN, STEROLS

✔ ANTI-STRESS, LOWERS CHOLESTEROL

Mung bean sprouts (*Phaseolus aureus*) help the body maintain optimum energy levels during stressful situations. They also aid antibody production and enhance liver function.

RECIPES asparagus asian-style (page 269), carrot 'n' beet salad (page 275), chinese salad (page 276), grapefruit salad (page 191), oriental salad with tempeh (page 209)

PINTO BEAN

★ VITAMINS K, B1, B2, B3, B5, B6, FOLATE; CALCIUM, MAGNESIUM, MANGANESE, PHOSPHORUS, POTASSIUM; COPPER, IRON, SELENIUM, ZINC; COMPLEX CARBOHYDRATES, FIBER, PROTEIN

✔ ANTIOXIDANT, ENERGY-BOOSTING, LOWERS CHOLESTEROL

Pinto beans (*Phaseolus vulgaris sp.*) help keep the skin, mucous membranes, and muscles (including the heart) in good condition, maintain optimum energy levels, and aid the nervous system.

RECIPES spicy moroccan soup (page 262)

SOY BEAN

★ VITAMINS K, B2, B1, B3, B5, B6, BIOTIN, FOLATE; CALCIUM, MAGNESIUM, MANGANESE, PHOSPHORUS, POTASSIUM; COPPER, IRON, SELENIUM, ZINC; ISOFLAVONES, PROTEASE INHIBITORS, SAPONINS; COMPLEX CARBOHYDRATES, FIBER, PROTEIN, OMEGA-3 AND -6

✔ ANTI-CANCER, ANTIOXIDANT, ENERGY-BOOSTING, LOWERS CHOLESTEROL, NUTRIENT-RICH

! SOME PEOPLE ARE ALLERGIC TO SOY

! MUCH OF THE WORLD'S SOY CROP HAS BEEN GENETICALLY MODIFIED: BUY ORGANIC

! SOME GENETICALLY MODIFIED SOY BEANS CONTAIN GENES FROM BRAZIL NUTS, AND SO MAY TRIGGER AN ALLERGIC REACTION

Nutritious and versatile, soy beans (*Glycine max*) can be eaten sprouted or cooked, and as tempeh, tofu, soy milk, flour, yogurt, sauce, or miso. They contain numerous phytochemicals beneficial to human health, some of which halt the growth of hormone-sensitive tumor cells. In particular, soy bean products are believed to reduce the risk of prostate and breast cancer, and can help both prevent and treat cardiovascular disease. Soy milk, which is made from soy beans, is a nutritious alternative to dairy milk.

RECIPES see tofu (below) and tempeh (page 208)

SOY YOGURT

★ AS FOR SOY BEAN, PLUS LACTOBACILLI

✔ ANTI-CANCER, ANTIOXIDANT, IMMUNO-STIMULANT, LOWERS CHOLESTEROL

! AS FOR SOY BEAN

Live yogurt contains lactobacilli, beneficial bacteria that help prevent the colonization of the gut by harmful micro-organisms. Live yogurt is especially helpful after antibiotic treatment (which kills off beneficial bacteria in the digestive tract). It also helps in the treatment of urinary-tract infections, gastroenteritis, infection by *helicobacter pylori* (the bacterium that causes stomach ulcers), inflammatory bowel disease, and colon cancer.

RECIPES yogurt with fruit (page 259), potato salad (page 276), raspberry gateau (page 278), blackberry cream (page 280), passion and lime (page 283), avocado smoothie (page 185)

TOFU (BEANCURD)

★ FOLATE; CALCIUM, MAGNESIUM, MANGANESE, PHOSPHORUS, POTASSIUM; COPPER, IRON, SELENIUM, ZINC; ISOFLAVONES, SAPONINS; PROTEIN, OMEGA-6

✔ ANTI-CANCER, LOWERS CHOLESTEROL, CALCIUM-RICH

! AS FOR SOY BEAN

Tofu is an extremely versatile food that is made from soy beans (*Glycine max*) in a process similar to cheese-making. It is high in protein, free from saturated fat, easy to digest and, like all soy products, has many health benefits. Soft tofu has a delicate texture and is generally mixed with other ingredients before being used in recipes. Firm tofu can be cut, sliced, chopped, or crumbled and added to a wide variety of dishes. Both soft and firm types have a neutral taste and absorb flavors readily when marinated or cooked with herbs and spices. See also tempeh (page 208).

RECIPES scrambled tofu (page 258), tofumasalata (page 264), tofu balls (page 266), amaranth and tofu puffs (page 268), spicy tofu burgers (page 273)

tempeh

TEMPEH IS A VERSATILE AND NUTRITIOUS PRODUCT MADE FROM SOY BEANS. PACKED WITH PHYTOCHEMICALS, IT IS ONE OF THE BRIGHTEST STAR FOODS FOR BOOSTING IMMUNITY, AND PREVENTING CANCER, HEART DISEASE, AND HORMONE-RELATED PROBLEMS.

The origin of tempeh

Tempeh is a form of beancurd, originally produced in Indonesia but now popular all over the world. It is a near-perfect source of protein. Unlike animal meat, it contains no saturated fats, and it is also one of the few vegetable products to contain vitamin B12.

Tempeh is made by mixing dehulled, split, and precooked soy beans (*Glycine max*) with a yeast culture in a process similar to cheese-making. The beans are packed tightly into perforated containers (traditionally banana leaves, but nowadays usually plastic bags) and molded into flat cakes or sausages. These are set to incubate, in ovens or in the sun, at a temperature of 60–100°F until the process of fermentation transforms the mixture into a tight lump. The finished product is delicious, with a nutty taste resembling chicken or fish. Tempeh can be sliced and fried, or cut into cubes and added to stews and other dishes. The fermentation process initiates the partial breakdown of the beans, which makes tempeh easier to digest than other cooked beans, with less tendency to cause flatulence.

Immune-boosting properties

Tempeh is packed with health-enhancing carbohydrates, fiber, and protein and also contains a wealth of minerals, B vitamins, phytoestrogens (isoflavonoids), protease inhibitors and saponins that have anti-microbial and anti-cancer properties. Phytoestrogens are active against viruses, and are known to inhibit the growth of cancers and halt the spread of malignant cells into surrounding tissues, reducing the risk of breast and prostate cancers in particular. They also appear to be protective against many other hormone-related health problems, such as fibrocystic breast disease, osteoporosis, endometriosis, and uterine fibroids.

Protease inhibitors are believed to prevent cancer-causing agents from entering cells and so help to keep cellular DNA intact. They have also been found to inhibit the growth of some cancers and to stop the spread of tumor cells. Saponins support the immune system, reduce the growth rate of some cancer cells, and help control blood cholesterol. Tempeh protein improves the efficiency of cell-mediated immunity.

Heart protector

Heart disease is much less common in regions where soy bean protein is eaten in preference to animal protein. Like other soy products, tempeh helps lower blood cholesterol. It contains a protein that inhibits intestinal absorption of dietary cholesterol and helps remove cholesterol from the blood, thereby reducing the risk of cardiovascular disorders. Tempeh also contains antioxidants, which may help prevent cardiovascular disorders such as atherosclerosis.

The nutrients in tempeh boost energy levels and make the body better able to cope with stress by supporting both the nervous and immune systems. They also keep hair, glands, blood cells, bone, bone marrow, skin, and mucous membranes in good condition, and act as building blocks for proteins, carbohydrates and fats. The nutrients in tempeh aid in the production of hemoglobin (the chemical that transports oxygen in the blood), as well as supporting liver function and fat metabolism, and may also protect against high blood pressure, allergy, asthma, migraine, depression, and prostate disorders.

IMMUNE-BOOSTING PROFILE

★ VITAMINS B2, B3, B6, B12, BIOTIN; CALCIUM, MAGNESIUM, MANGANESE, PHOSPHORUS, POTASSIUM; COPPER, IRON, ZINC; ISOFLAVONES, PROTEASE INHIBITORS, SAPONINS; COMPLEX CARBOHYDRATES, FIBER, PROTEIN

✔ ANTI-CANCER, ANTI-STRESS, ANTI-VIRAL, LOWERS CHOLESTEROL, ENERGY-BOOSTING, IMMUNO-STIMULANT

! SOME PEOPLE ARE ALLERGIC TO SOY PRODUCTS

! MUCH OF THE WORLD'S SOY BEAN CROP HAS BEEN GENETICALLY MODIFIED: BUY ORGANIC

oriental salad with tempeh

1-in piece fresh ginger root, finely chopped
1 garlic clove, finely chopped
4-in stalk of lemongrass, finely chopped
4 tablespoons lemon juice
1 tablespoon balsamic vinegar
1 tablespoon maple syrup
½ cup orange juice
4 tablespoons soy sauce

8 tempeh rashers, cut into chunks
1 tablespoon sesame oil
1 bunch of scallions, thinly sliced
8 baby corns, steamed
3½ ounces bean sprouts
6 leaves of chinese cabbage, shredded
salt and pepper
2 tablespoons sesame salt

Mix the ginger, garlic, lemongrass, lemon juice, vinegar, maple syrup, orange juice, and soy sauce in a bowl. Add the tempeh and leave to marinate for 1 hour. Remove the tempeh (keeping the marinade in the bowl), and fry it in the oil. Sprinkle with salt. Mix the scallions, baby corns, bean sprouts and chinese cabbage in a salad bowl, mix in the marinade, add the tempeh and sprinkle with sesame salt.

tempeh kebabs *(above)*

7 ounces tempeh, cubed
1 zucchini, in thick slices
1 lime, in wedges
8 garlic cloves
2 corns, cut into chunks
16 cherry tomatoes
1 eggplant, diced
1 pound small new potatoes, cooked

For the marinade:
2 tablespoons lemon juice
2 tablespoons sherry
2 tablespoons olive oil
1 tablespoon soy sauce
2 garlic cloves, crushed
4 tablespoons tomato sauce

Place the kebab ingredients in a bowl. Add the marinade ingredients and mix well. Leave covered for a couple of hours, stirring occasionally. Divide the different ingredients between 8 barbecue skewers. Brush with the leftover marinade and place on a hot barbecue for about 10 minutes, turning from time to time.

herbs and spices

HERBS

BORAGE (BEEPLANT, TALEWORT)

★ VITAMINS A, B3, C; CALCIUM, MAGNESIUM, PHOSPHORUS, POTASSIUM; ZINC; MUCILAGE, SAPONINS, TANNIN, VOLATILE OIL, OMEGA-6 (GLA)

✔ ANTI-INFLAMMATORY, ANTIOXIDANT, DIAPHORETIC, EXPECTORANT

The leaves of borage (*Borago officinalis*) can be used to treat inflammation, fevers, and coughs, and help the body recover from the effects of stress. They taste like cucumber and are delicious chopped finely and added to salads.

RECIPES immuni-tea (page 285), stress relief (page 286), tea for fever (page 287), tea for glands (page 287), cough mixture (page 284)

CATNIP (CATMINT, CATNEP)

★ CALCIUM, MAGNESIUM, PHOSPHORUS, POTASSIUM; ZINC; BITTER PRINCIPLE, TANNIN, VOLATILE OILS

✔ ANTISPASMODIC, ASTRINGENT, CIRCULATORY AND DIGESTIVE STIMULANT, DIAPHORETIC, FEBRIFUGE

Catmint (*Nepeta cataria*) leaves and flowering tops are particularly useful in treating childhood fevers and respiratory-tract infections, and help settle stomach upsets and diarrhea.

RECIPES sleepy time (page 286), tea for fever (page 287)

CAMOMILE (CHAMOMILE—WILD, GERMAN, ANNUAL)

★ COUMARINS, MUCILAGE, RUTIN, SALICYLIC ACID, TANNIN, VALERIANIC ACID, VOLATILE OIL

✔ ANTI-ALLERGIC, ANTI-INFLAMMATORY, ANTISPASMODIC, SEDATIVE

Camomile (*Matricaria recutita*) flowers relieve restlessness and tension, and are useful for headache, anxiety, and sleeplessness. They also help relieve digestive upsets, and are particularly suitable for children.

RECIPES calming tea (page 284), hay fever relief (page 284), sleepy time (page 285), tea for fever (page 286), camomile tonic (page 287)

CLEAVERS (CLIVERS, GOOSEGRASS)

★ BIOFLAVONOIDS, CITRIC ACID, COUMARINS, GLYCOSIDES, TANNIN

✔ ANTI-CANCER, ANTI-INFLAMMATORY, DETOXIFYING

Cleavers (*Galium aparine*) is a tonic for the lymphatic system, useful for treating swollen glands, eczema, psoriasis, joint problems, edema, ulcers, tumors, infections of the urinary tract, and urinary stones.

RECIPES immuni-tea (page 285), tea for ear infections (page 287), tea for glands (page 287), tea for the skin (page 287)

ECHINACEA

★ ECHINACEIN, GLYCOSIDE (ECHINACOSIDE), RESIN, VOLATILE OIL

✔ ANTI-ALLERGIC, ANTI-CANCER, ANTI-INFLAMMATORY, ANTIMICROBIAL, ANTISEPTIC, IMMUNO-STIMULANT.

Echinacea (*Echinacea angustifolia*) enhances the body's natural resistance to infection by stimulating the immune system. It is one of the most important natural remedies against colds and influenza and other infectious diseases (including H.I.V.) and cancer.

RECIPES tea for fungal infections (page 287), hay fever relief (page 285), immuni-tea (page 285), tea for glands (page 287)

ELDERFLOWER

★ CHOLINE; BIOFLAVONOIDS (INCLUDING RUTIN AND KAEMPFEROL), CYANOGLYCOSIDE; MUCILAGE, OMEGA-3 AND -6, PECTIN, TANNIN, VOLATILE OIL

✔ ANTI-MUCUS, ANTI-INFLAMMATORY, CIRCULATORY AND IMMUNE STIMULANT, DIAPHORETIC, EXPECTORANT

Elderflower (*Sambucus spp*) enhances natural resistance to disease and promotes perspiration—excellent for colds, influenza and high temperature, as well allergic symptoms and mucus.

RECIPES cold buster (page 284), elderflower spritzer (page 284), hay fever relief (page 285), lung-cleansing tea mix (page 286), tea for ear infections (page 287)

FEVERFEW (MIDSUMMER DAISY)

★ BITTERS, VOLATILE OIL

✔ ANTI-INFLAMMATORY, DIGESTIVE STIMULANT, PAINKILLING,

VASODILATOR

! CHEWING FRESH FEVERFEW LEAVES MAY CAUSE MOUTH ULCERS

! STIMULATES UTERUS AND SO BEST AVOIDED DURING PREGNANCY

The leaves of fresh feverfew (*Tanacetum parthenium/ Chrysanthemum parthenium*) are used to relieve headache. They offer an effective way of preventing migraine, and can help relieve the pain of rheumatoid arthritis.

RECIPES tea for headache (page 287)

LAVENDER

★ TANNIN, VOLATILE OIL

✔ ANTIDEPRESSANT, ANTISPASMODIC, RELAXING, SEDATIVE

Lavender (*Lavendula angustifolia*) is an effective treatment for headaches, and for nervous exhaustion, depression, and skin irritations. Soothing and relaxing, it promotes healing by bringing body and mind into balance.

RECIPES calming tea (page 284), pick-me-up (page 286), sleepy time (page 286), stress relief (page 286)

LEMON BALM

★ BITTERS, ROSMARINIC ACID, TANNIN, VOLATILE OIL

✔ ANTI-DEPRESSANT, ANTI-VIRAL, LOWERS BLOOD PRESSURE, MILD SEDATIVE, RELAXANT

Lemon balm (*Melissa officinalis*) is a sweet-tasting herb that can help prevent and treat cold sores, and is thought to reduce the growth rate of tumors. It has a calming effect on the nerves and the digestion, and is useful in the management of heart problems.

RECIPES calming tea (page 284), immuni-tea (page 285), pick-me-up (page 286), stress relief (page 286)

CALENDULA (MARIGOLD)

★ VITAMIN C; BITTERS, CAROTENOIDS, LUTEIN, LYCOPENE, QUERCETIN, MUCILAGE, RESIN, RUTIN, SALICYLIC ACID, SAPONINS, VANILLIC ACID

✔ ANTI-MICROBIAL, ANTI-INFLAMMATORY, ANTIOXIDANT, WOUND HEALING

Calendula or marigold (*Calendula officinalis*) flowers are a natural antibacterial, antifungal, and antiviral treatment for mouth and skin infections, inflammation, and ulcers (both internal and external). Calendula helps relieve gall-bladder disorders, and may have a role in the management of cancer.

RECIPES tea for fungal infections (page 287), tea for ear infections (page 287), tea for glands (page 287), tea for the skin (page 287)

PEPPERMINT

★ VITAMINS A, C, B2, B3, FOLATE; CALCIUM, MAGNESIUM, MANGANESE, POTASSIUM; COPPER IRON; BITTERS, PECTIN, RUTIN, STEROLS, TANNIN, VOLATILE OILS (INCLUDING MENTHOL)

✔ ANTI-CANCER, ANTIMICROBIAL, ANTIOXIDANT, ANTISEPTIC, ANTISPASMODIC, CARMINATIVE, COOLING, DIGESTIVE, STIMULANT

Peppermint (*Mentha x piperita*) is an effective treatment for colds and coughs, helping to clear airways and make breathing easier. It also stimulates the secretion of digestive juices and helps to relieve symptoms of indigestion, ulcerative colitis, and Crohn's disease.

RECIPES mint and melon soup (page 261), nectarine surprise (page 279), green tea with mint (page 285), lung-cleansing tea mix (page 286), grapefruit and peppermint fizz (page 191)

ROSEMARY

★ VITAMINS A, C, FOLATE; CALCIUM, MAGNESIUM, MANGANESE; IRON, ZINC; BIOFLAVONOIDS, BITTERS, SAPONINS, STEROLS, VOLATILE OILS (INCLUDING CAMPHOR)

✔ ANTI-MICROBIAL, ANTIOXIDANT, ANTISPASMODIC, ASTRINGENT, CARMINATIVE, CIRCULATORY AND DIGESTIVE STIMULANT, TONIC

Rosemary (*Rosmarinus officinalis*) stimulates the circulation and the nervous system. It is a traditional tonic for the heart, and it has a calming effect on the digestion. It is also an effective treatment for tension headaches.

RECIPES scrambled tofu (page 258), pick-me-up (page 286), tea for aches and pains (page 287), tea for headache (page 287)

SAGE (RED, GARDEN)

★ VITAMIN A; CALCIUM, MAGNESIUM, MANGANESE, POTASSIUM; ZINC; BIOFLAVONOIDS, GLYCOSIDES, PHYTOESTROGENS, SAPONINS, TANNIN, VOLATILE OIL

✔ ANTI-MICROBIAL, ANTIOXIDANT, DIGESTIVE, DRYING AND PERIPHERAL VASODILATOR

! AVOID DURING PREGNANCY

Sage (*Salvia officinalis*) is an antiseptic herb that improves the health of mucous membranes. It can also reduce perspiration.

RECIPES mushrooms with sage and thyme stuffing (page 272), eucalyptus mixture (page 285), sage mix for sore throats (page 286)

ST. JOHN'S WORT (HYPERICUM)

★ VITAMIN C; BIOFLAVONOIDS, CAROTENOIDS, GLYCOSIDES, PECTIN, RESIN, TANNIN

✔ ANTIDEPRESSANT, ANTISEPTIC, ASTRINGENT, ANTI-INFLAMMATORY, ANTIOXIDANT, EXPECTORANT, HEALING, PAINKILLING

! MAY INHIBIT THE EFFECT OF PRESCRIPTION DRUGS: IF RECEIVING MEDICATION, SEEK YOUR DOCTOR'S ADVICE BEFORE TAKING

St. John's wort (*Hypericum perforatum*) is helpful in the management of post-viral disorders. It is an effective remedy for mild depression and can also be used as a mild painkiller.

RECIPES calming tea (page 284), tea for aches and pains (page 287), tea for joints (page 287)

THYME (COMMON, GARDEN)

★ VITAMIN A, C, B2, B6; CALCIUM, MAGNESIUM, MANGANESE, COPPER, IRON; BITTERS, BIOFLAVONOIDS, RESIN, VOLATILE OIL (INCLUDING THYMOL AND CAMPHOR); OMEGA-3 AND -6

✔ ANTIMICROBIAL, ANTIOXIDANT, ANTISEPTIC, ANTISPASMODIC, ASTRINGENT, CARMINATIVE, EXPECTORANT

Thyme (*Thymus vulgaris*) contains the volatile oil thymol, a powerful antiseptic and one of the most effective of all herbal antibiotics. It is particularly useful in the treatment of respiratory-tract infections, such as bronchitis, laryngitis, and whooping cough, and helps relieve the symptoms of asthma. Thyme is also beneficial in the treatment of gastro-intestinal disorders including colic and diarrhea.

RECIPES beans and tomatoes on toast (page 258), italian butterbean soup (page 261), marinated olives (page 264), mushrooms with sage and thyme stuffing (page 272), catalan salad (page 276), cough mixture (page 284), eucalyptus mix (page 285)

VIOLET (BLUE, SWEET)

★ ALKALOID, METHYL SALICYLATE, RUTIN, SAPONINS, VOLATILE OIL

✔ ANTI-CANCER, ANTI-INFLAMMATORY, EXPECTORANT

Violet (*Viola odorata*) leaves and flowers have a role in the management of malignant tumors and may help inhibit the spread of cancer. They are also useful in the treatment of chronic bronchitis, chronic nasal mucus, skin problems, and arthritis.

RECIPES yogurt with fruit (page 259), lung-cleansing tea mix (page 286), tea for the skin (page 287), cough mixture (page 284)

WILD MARJORAM (EUROPEAN OREGANO)

★ VITAMIN A, C, K; CALCIUM, MAGNESIUM, MANGANESE, PHOSPHORUS, POTASSIUM; COPPER, IRON, ZINC; BIOFLAVONOIDS, BITTERS, STEROLS, TANNINS, VOLATILE OILS; OMEGA-3, -6 AND OLEIC ACID

✔ ANTIMICROBIAL, ANTIOXIDANT, DIAPHORETIC, EXPECTORANT, STIMULANT, WARMING

Wild marjoram (*Origanum vulgare*) is an excellent warming remedy for coughs (including whooping cough), colds, and influenza. It can also be used to relieve headache and indigestion.

RECIPES black-eye pea and wild marjoram soup (page 261), cold buster (page 284), tea for headache (page 287), cough mixture (page 284), scandinavian beet burgers (page 179)

YARROW (MILFOIL)

★ BIOFLAVONOIDS, BITTERS, RESIN, SALICYLATES, TANNIN, VOLATILE OILS (INCLUDING CINEOL, AZULENE AND CAMPHOR)

✔ ANTI-INFLAMMATORY, ANTISEPTIC, ASTRINGENT, BLOOD PRESSURE LOWERING, DIAPHORETIC, DIGESTIVE TONIC, PERIPHERAL VASODILATOR

! EXCESS YARROW INTAKE CAN CAUSE HEADACHE

Yarrow (*Achillea millefolium*) has a long tradition as a remedy for colds and influenza but in fact this versatile herb has a multitude of beneficial effects on health. As an anti-inflammatory and diaphoretic it helps to relieve mucus, bronchitis, cystitis, and gastro-intestinal inflammation, and enables the body to deal more effectively with infections. As a cardiovascular restorative, it improves peripheral circulation and lowers blood pressure. As an external remedy, it has a longstanding reputation for stopping bleeding and healing wounds.

RECIPES circulation booster (page 284), cold buster (page 284), cystitis relief (page 284), tea for ear infections (page 287)

garlic

THIS AROMATIC HERB DOESN'T JUST KEEP VAMPIRES AT BAY! GARLIC PROTECTS AGAINST A WIDE RANGE OF BACTERIAL, FUNGAL, AND VIRAL INFECTIONS. IT ALSO STRENGTHENS THE HEART AND BLOOD VESSELS AND HELPS PREVENT CANCER.

The origins of garlic

Garlic (*Allium sativum*) is a plant so ancient that no one is really sure of its origins. It is thought to have evolved from the wild garlic of central Asia (*Allium longicuspis*), and is known to have been cultivated in Egypt and Mesopotamia before 2000BCE. According to Pliny, it had a semi-divine status in the ancient world, and was called upon in the swearing of oaths. Now one of the world's most popular herbs, it is cultivated and used worldwide as both a food and medicine.

Immune-boosting properties

Garlic grows best where warm and dry summers prevail, and is itself a warming and drying herb. It is also one of the most effective natural anti-microbials, stimulating the production of white blood cells and acting against a wide range of bacteria, fungi, parasites, and viruses. Even with the development of modern antibiotics and a more sophisticated understanding of microbiology, garlic is still regarded by many health practitioners as first-line treatment for infectious disease. Garlic fights various gastro-intestinal infections and infestations such as dysentery, typhoid, threadworm, and tapeworm. It contains a volatile oil that is mostly excreted through the lungs, making it an excellent remedy for respiratory disorders such as bronchitis, mucus, influenza, and whooping cough. This oil is also active against tuberculosis, and plays a role in the management of asthma. Garlic combats fungal

infections such as yeast infections, athlete's foot, and ringworm, and is a standard ingredient in anti-candida diets, encouraging the growth of beneficial bacteria and inhibiting pathogens. It may also reduce the virulence of the H.I.V. virus.

One of the most popular modern uses for garlic is in dealing with cardiovascular disease. It acts on the circulatory system to reduce the level of blood fat and cholesterol, and decreases the tendency of the blood to clot.

Over time, garlic will also lower blood pressure significantly, It prevents the formation of atheroma (fat deposits on artery walls), and studies have also shown that garlic reduces the arteriosclerotic changes (hardening of arteries) that appear with age. These changes are accelerated by smoking, and eating a typical Western diet high in saturated fats and sugar.

Alliin is one of the active ingredients responsible for garlic's ability to suppress the formation of cancer cells and enhance the immune system's ability to slow the spread of malignant tumors. This corresponds with epidemiological findings that cancer is less common in areas with high garlic consumption.

Even the idea that garlic keeps vampires away may be based on fact, not fiction. In Central Asia, a rare variety of the disease porphyria was once relatively common. Symptoms included extreme paleness and a complete intolerance to sunlight. Relief from some of these might have been found in garlic's medicinal properties.

IMMUNE-BOOSTING PROFILE

★ VITAMIN C, B1, B6; CALCIUM, MANGANESE, PHOSPHORUS, POTASSIUM; COPPER, IRON, SELENIUM, ZINC; BIOFLAVONOIDS, GLUCOKININ, MUCILAGE, PHYTOHORMONES, VOLATILE OILS (INCLUDING ALLICIIN)

✔ ANTIBACTERIAL, ANTICOAGULANT, ANTI-MUCUS, ANTIOXIDANT, ANTISEPTIC, DETOXIFYING, EXPECTORANT, LOWERS BLOOD PRESSURE AND CHOLESTEROL

! THE SULFUR COMPOUNDS IN GARLIC CAN IRRITATE ULCERS

! HIGH DOSES OF GARLIC CAN EXAGGERATE THE EFFECTS OF ANTICOAGULANT AND BLOOD-PRESSURE-LOWERING DRUGS

♡ EAT WITH PARSLEY TO AVOID GARLIC ON THE BREATH

tomato, wild marjoram, and garlic salad (above)

2 pounds ripe tomatoes, sliced
4 tablespoons fresh wild
  marjoram, chopped
2 garlic cloves, finely chopped
6 tablespoons olive oil
2 tablespoons balsamic vinegar
Salt and pepper to taste

Arrange the tomatoes on a large plate and sprinkle with marjoram, garlic, oil, and vinegar, and salt and pepper.

garlic and savoy cabbage

3 tablespoons olive oil
1 teaspoon curry powder
1 tablespoon black mustard
  seeds
1 medium savoy cabbage,
  finely shredded
3 garlic cloves, finely chopped
2 tablespoons desiccated
  coconut
1 tablespoons maple syrup
2 tablespoons lemon juice
Salt and pepper to taste

Heat the oil in a large skillet or wok. Add the spices and stir-fry until the mustard seeds begin to pop. Add the cabbage and the garlic and stir-fry until the cabbage begins to wilt. Add the coconut and stir-fry for 1 minute more, then add the maple syrup and lemon juice. Mix well and season with salt and pepper. Serve hot.

rich garlic dressing

4 tablespoons balsamic vinegar
1 tablespoon maple syrup
1 tablespoon Dijon mustard
2 garlic cloves, crushed
Salt and pepper to taste
½ cup olive oil (approximately)

Whisk or hand-blend the vinegar, maple syrup, mustard, garlic, salt, and pepper with a little oil. Add the oil very slowly, a little at a time until the dressing starts to emulsify. Then add more oil, still a little at a time, until the taste is right. Adjust seasoning.

SPICES

BLACK CUMIN

★ VITAMINS A, B1, B2, B3; CALCIUM, MAGNESIUM, PHOSPHORUS, POTASSIUM; COPPER, IRON, ZINC; OMEGA-3 AND -6

✔ ANTI-ALLERGIC, ANTI-INFLAMMATORY, ANTIMICROBIAL, ANTIOXIDANT

Black cumin (*Nigella sativa*) is a useful remedy for allergy, eczema and upper respiratory tract disorders such as asthma and bronchitis. It may also help in the prevention of immunodeficiency disorders.

RECIPES beans and tomatoes on toast (page 258), spicy moroccan soup (page 262), baba ganoush (page 262), garlic oxymel (page 285), heart chai (page 285)

CARAWAY

★ VITAMINS B1, B2, B3, B6; CALCIUM, MAGNESIUM, MANGANESE, PHOSPHORUS, POTASSIUM; COPPER, IRON, ZINC; BIOFLAVONOIDS, STEROLS, VOLATILE OIL, OMEGA-3

✔ ANTIBACTERIAL, ANTISPASMODIC, CARMINATIVE, EXPECTORANT

Caraway (*Carum carvi*) seeds are used to alleviate upper respiratory tract problems such as asthma and bronchitis and in a gargle to treat laryngitis. They can also be chewed to alleviate gastro-intestinal disorders, including indigestion, colic, diarrhea, and trapped gas.

RECIPES healing soup (page 260), spicy moroccan soup (page 262), pan bread (page 274), spicy chai (page 286)

CAYENNE

★ VITAMINS A, C, E, K, B2, B3, B6; CALCIUM, MAGNESIUM, MANGANESE, PHOSPHORUS, POTASSIUM; IRON, ZINC; BIOFLAVONOIDS, STEROLS, VOLATILE OIL, OMEGA-3

✔ ANTIBACTERIAL, ANTI-CANCER, ANTI-INFLAMMATORY, ANTI-MUCUS, DIAPHORETIC, STIMULANT, TONIC

! CAYENNE IRRITATES MUCOUS MEMBRANES: HANDLE WITH CARE, AND AVOID IN CASES OF GASTRITIS OR STOMACH ULCER.

Cayenne (*Capsicum annuum*) is a powerful circulatory stimulant that increases the blood supply to all parts of the body, thus creating a feeling of heat. It is useful for preventing colds, and to deal with general debility in convalescence.

RECIPES spicy moroccan soup (page 262), cold buster (page 284), heart chai (page 285), tea for fever (page 287)

CELERY SEED

★ VITAMIN B6; CALCIUM, MAGNESIUM, MANGANESE, PHOSPHORUS; COPPER, IRON, ZINC; BIOFLAVONOIDS, VOLATILE OIL

✔ ANTIOXIDANT, DETOXIFYING, DIGESTIVE TONIC, URINARY ANTISEPTIC

! SHOULD BE AVOIDED DURING PREGNANCY

Celery (*Apium graveolens*) seeds enhance the elimination of uric acid from the body making them useful in arthritic conditions, particularly gout. They also help in the treatment of urinary-tract infections and stones.

RECIPES tea for joints (page 287)

EUCALYPTUS

★ BIOFLAVONOIDS, VOLATILE OIL

✔ ANTIBACTERIAL, ANTIFUNGAL, ANTIOXIDANT, ANTISEPTIC, ANTISPASMODIC, EXPECTORANT, FEBRIFUGE, STIMULANT

Eucalyptus (*Eucalyptus globulus*) is a well-known ingredient in cough remedies, and is useful in treating upper respiratory tract infections in general. It also acts against urinary-tract infections, and has broad-spectrum antibiotic properties.

RECIPES eucalyptus mix (page 285), lung-cleansing tea mix (page 286)

GINGER

★ MAGNESIUM, POTASSIUM, COPPER; MUCILAGE, PHENOLS, RESIN, VOLATILE OILS

✔ ANTISEPTIC, ANTISPASMODIC, CARMINATIVE, DETOXIFYING, DIAPHORETIC, EXPECTORANT, VASODILATOR

Ginger (*Zingiber officinale*) is a warming and comforting remedy for colds and chills. It stimulates peripheral circulation and helps the body rid itself of toxins.

RECIPES korean kimchi-style salad (page 263), apricot and ginger (page 280)

HORSERADISH

★ VITAMIN C, FOLATE; ASPARAGIN, RESIN, VOLATILE MUSTARD OIL

✔ ANTI-ALLERGIC, ANTIBACTERIAL, ANTI-CANCER, ANTIOXIDANT, ANTISEPTIC, DETOXIFYING, DIAPHORETIC, EXPECTORANT, TONIC

! AVOID IN CASES OF UNDERACTIVE THYROID

Horseradish (*Armoracia rusticana*) is a circulatory stimulant, useful for chronic rheumatic conditions, urinary-tract infections, and respiratory tract disorders, such as asthma, bronchial mucus, whooping cough, and hay fever. It also stimulates digestion.

RECIPES beet and horseradish salad (page 179)

JUNIPER

★ BITTER PRINCIPLES, GLYCOSIDE, TANNIN, VOLATILE OIL

✔ ANTIBACTERIAL, ANTI-MUCUS, ANTIFUNGAL, CARMINATIVE, DIURETIC, URINARY ANTISEPTIC

! SHOULD BE AVOIDED DURING PREGNANCY AND BY THOSE WITH KIDNEY DISEASE

A digestive stimulant, juniper (*Juniperus communis*) helps detoxify the body and relieves arthritis and gout. It is also used to treat urinary-tract disorders.

RECIPES swiss chard and juniper berries (page 275)

LICORICE ROOT

★ BIOFLAVONOIDS, TANNIN, BITTER PRINCIPLES, COUMARINS, GLYCOSIDES, GLYCYRRHIZIN, PHYTOESTROGEN, VOLATILE OILS

✔ ANTI-INFLAMMATORY, ANTIOXIDANT, ANTISPASMODIC, ANTI-STRESS, EXPECTORANT, GENTLE LAXATIVE, IMMUNO-STIMULANT

! MAY CAUSE POTASSIUM LOSS AND RAISE BLOOD PRESSURE

Licorice (*Glycyrrhiza glaba*) helps the body to cope better in stressful conditions, and has a beneficial effect on the adrenal glands (useful for recovery after steroid therapy). It also relieves bronchial mucus and coughs, and is a specific treatment for gastro-intestinal ulcers. It has been found to inhibit tumor growth.

RECIPES licorice mix (page 286), immuni-tea (page 285), lung-cleansing tea mix (page 286), cough mixture (page 284)

MUSTARD SEED (BLACK)

★ VITAMINS B1, B2, B3; CALCIUM, MAGNESIUM, PHOSPHORUS, POTASSIUM; IRON, ZINC; MUCILAGE, SINIGRIN, VOLATILE OIL

✔ CARMINATIVE, DIAPHORETIC, DIURETIC, STIMULANT, TONIC

! MUSTARD SEED CAN CAUSE IRRITATION — USE SPARINGLY

Black mustard (*Brassica nigra*) stimulates the circulation and relieves colds, bronchitis, fevers, and influenza.

RECIPES sweet potato curry (page 272), tea for joints (page 287)

TURMERIC

★ VITAMIN C, B3; POTASSIUM, MAGNESIUM, MANGANESE; COPPER, IRON, ZINC; CURCUMINOIDS, STEROLS, VOLATILE OIL, OMEGA-6

✔ ANTIBACTERIAL, ANTI-INFLAMMATORY, ANTIOXIDANT

Turmeric (*Curcuma longa*) aids immunity by enhancing the health of the liver. It also mops up free radicals and so helps fight degenerative diseases.

RECIPES casserole de puy (page 268), paella (page 268)

other foods and drinks

EVENING PRIMROSE OIL

★ VITAMIN E; STEROLS; OMEGA-6 (GLA)

✔ ANTI-INFLAMMATORY, HEALING, IMMUNO-STIMULANT, MILD ANTI-
  COAGULANT, LOWERS CHOLESTEROL

! CAN CAUSE HEADACHES AND INTERACT WITH PRESCRIPTION DRUGS

Evening primrose (*Oenothera biennis*) oil improves the health of all
body cells, and promotes tissue and nerve repair. It treats acne,
eczema and psoriasis, and auto-immune conditions, especially
multiple sclerosis, lupus and rheumatoid arthritis. It normalizes
prostaglandins and may reduce P.M.T. and incidence of breast
cysts. It may help guard against breast cancer and heart disease.

RECIPES use in marinades and dressings, or sprinkle on food

GREEN TEA

★ BIOFLAVONOIDS, CATECHINS, THEOPHYLLINE

✔ ANTI-ALLERGIC, ANTI-ASTHMATIC, ANTIOXIDANT, LOWERS BLOOD
  FATS, LOWERS BLOOD PRESSURE, PREVENTS ABNORMAL CLOTTING

! GREEN TEA CONTAINS CAFFEINE

Green tea is made from the fresh leaves of the tea bush (*Camellia
sinensis sp*). Unlike black tea, it is unfermented and does not
contain the tannins and polyphenolic compounds that inhibit
absorption of micronutrients such as iron.

RECIPES green tea with mint (page 285), heart chai (page 285)

MISO

★ VITAMINS B2, B3, FOLATE; CALCIUM, MAGNESIUM, PHOSPHORUS;
  COPPER, IRON, ZINC

✔ ANTIOXIDANT, HEALING, LOWERS BLOOD FATS

Miso is a paste made from fermented soy beans, used as the
basis of stews, soups, marinades, and sauces. It helps keep heart,
nerves, and muscles healthy, aids liver and red blood cell function,
and regulates blood-fat levels.

RECIPES shiitake mushroom soup (page 261)

OYSTER MUSHROOM

★ VITAMINS B1, B2, B5; PHOSPHORUS, POTASSIUM, COPPER; IRON

✔ ANTI-INFLAMMATORY, ANTIOXIDANT

Oyster mushroom (*Pleurotus ostreatus*) enables the body to make
full use of the energy stored in the tissues, and helps red blood
cells to function properly. It aids liver function, and may help
protect against heart disease, cancer, and rheumatism.

RECIPES use in recipes in place of shiitake or button mushrooms

POLENTA

★ VITAMINS B1, B3; MAGNESIUM, PHOSPHORUS; IRON, ZINC; COMPLEX
  CARBOHYDRATES, FIBER, OMEGA-6, PROTEIN

✔ ANTIOXIDANT, ENERGY-RICH

Polenta is an important energy-rich savory cornmeal that boosts the body's natural healing capacity. It can taste rather bland on its own, but is an excellent accompaniment to many Mediterranean dishes and a familiar ingredient in Italian country cooking. It is particularly popular as polenta cakes. To make, add boiling water, *herbes de Provence*, sea salt and pepper to pre-cooked polenta to form a stiff dough. Shape the dough into small patties and fry in olive oil until golden brown.

RECIPES *serve as an accompaniment in place of potatoes or rice*

SAFFLOWER AND SUNFLOWER OILS

★ VITAMIN E; STEROLS; OMEGA-6

✔ ANTIOXIDANT, HEALING, IMMUNO-STIMULANT

Safflower (*Carthamus tinctorius*) and sunflower (*Helianthus annuus*) oils enhance the body's ability to react to injury and repair tissue damage. The omega-6 fatty acids and vitamin E they contain are important for healthy cell membranes and skin. They also have a beneficial effect on blood pressure, ensure normal blood-clotting, and help lower blood-cholesterol levels.

RECIPES *tropical sunshine salad (page 277), baked beet salad (page 179), samosa parcels (page 264), hasselbach potatoes (page 274), carrot 'n' beet salad (page 275), raspberry gateau (page 278), filled avocados (page 197)*

SEA VEGETABLE (HIJIKI, IZIKI)

★ VITAMINS A, B2, B12, FOLATE; CALCIUM, MAGNESIUM, MANGANESE,
  SODIUM; COPPER, IODINE, IRON

✔ ANTIOXIDANT, IMMUNO-STIMULANT

♀ IODINE IN THE DIET PROTECTS AGAINST THE ABSORPTION OF
  RADIOACTIVE IODINE FROM THE ENVIRONMENT

Most of the iodine in the body is found in the thyroid gland. It is an essential component of thyroid hormones, which influence nearly all biochemical reactions in the body and regulate growth, metabolic rate, and tissue health. The most reliable sources of iodine in the diet come from the sea, and one of the easiest to use (and most tasty) of the edible seaweeds is sea vegetable, which is also known as hijiki, or iziki.

RECIPES *shiitake with sea vegetable (iziki) (page 221)*

SUN-DRIED TOMATO

★ VITAMINS A, E; POTASSIUM; COPPER, IRON, ZINC; LYCOPENE;
  ESSENTIAL FATTY ACIDS, PROTEIN, SUGARS

✔ ANTI-CANCER, ANTIOXIDANT

Sun-dried tomatoes (*Lycopersicon esculentum*) promote the health of all body cells (especially the nerves, muscles, skin, and mucous membranes). They help prevent the formation of cancer cells and protect against heart disease.

RECIPES *sweetcorn and sun-dried tomato salad (page 276), brazil nuts and sun-dried tomatoes with beans (page 201)*

VEGETABLE MARGARINE

★ VITAMIN E; PHYTOSTEROLS; ESSENTIAL FATTY ACIDS

✔ ANTIOXIDANT, LOWERS BLOOD PRESSURE, LOWERS CHOLESTEROL

! CHOOSE UNSATURATED, NON-HYDROGENATED PLANT MARGARINES

Like the oils it is made from, vegetable margarine helps keep cell membranes healthy, lowers blood cholesterol, and has a beneficial influence on blood pressure.

RECIPES *scrambled tofu (page 258), welsh leek and potato soup (page 262), french onion tart (page 271), pear tart (page 279)*

WHEATGERM OIL

★ VITAMIN E; PHYTOSTEROLS; OMEGA-3 AND -6

✔ ANTIOXIDANT, HEALING, LOWERS CHOLESTEROL

Wheatgerm (*Triticum sp.*) oil increases the efficiency of the immune response and helps to prevent the immune system from over-reacting to allergens. It increases the health of all cell membranes and may protect against heart disease and cancer. It is also good for skin problems and rheumatoid arthritis.

RECIPES *use in salad dressings, and as a replacement for butter or margarine on vegetables*

YEAST EXTRACT

★ VITAMIN B1, B2, B3, B6, B12, FOLATE; CALCIUM, MAGNESIUM,
  PHOSPHORUS, POTASSIUM; IODINE, IRON, SODIUM, ZINC

! SOME YEAST EXTRACTS ARE HIGH IN SALT

Yeast extract is a concentrated source of minerals and vitamins, particularly B vitamins. It can help the body to maintain optimum energy levels and improve the health of the blood, bone marrow, nervous system, skin, muscles, mucous membranes, and heart. It can be spread on bread or added to soups and stews.

RECIPES *italian butterbean soup (page 261)*

★shiitake mushroom

DELICIOUS AND NUTRITIOUS, SHIITAKE MUSHROOMS HAVE LONG BEEN PRIZED IN THE EAST FOR THEIR ABILITY TO COMBAT INFECTION AND PROTECT AGAINST HEART DISEASE. NOW THE WEST IS DISCOVERING THE AMAZING PROPERTIES OF THIS "FOOD OF EMPERORS".

The origin of shiitake

Shiitake mushrooms (*Lentinus edodus*) are native to Japan, China, and Korea. Shiitake has a long history of medicinal use in the East, useful in the prevention and treatment of infectious diseases and gastro-intestinal problems, and as a remedy to improve circulation and increase vitality. In China, shiitake mushrooms were once reserved for the emperor and his family. Today, shiitake is one of the most widely produced edible mushrooms in the world.

Immune-boosting properties

As well as being delicious, shiitake mushrooms are an excellent source of immune-boosting minerals and vitamins, essential amino acids, and enzymes. They are particularly high in vitamin B5, also called "the stress vitamin," because it enhances our ability to cope with stress and the ageing process, and it keeps our nervous system healthy. Modern scientific research has concentrated on shiitake's immune-stimulating properties, but Japanese studies have long confirmed its beneficial properties against other common health problems such as atherosclerosis and cancer. Shiitake's ability to stimulate resistance to disease and enhance the immune response is thought to be owing to the fact that the fungus causes the release of interferon and, at the same time, increases the number of macrophages in the blood, enhances phagocytosis, and increases the activity and number of blood lymphocytes. (Lymphocytes and macrophages are two of the most important blood cell types involved in immunity—see page 158.) This combination of actions means that shiitake strengthens the body's first line of defense against infection, by encouraging blood cells to destroy harmful organisms and share information about them with the rest of the immune system, and to clear up cellular debris and waste. In particular, eating shiitake increases resistance to viral infection.

Shiitake's powerful stimulation of immune reaction has kindled interest in the West because of its potential use in the treatment of H.I.V. infections and A.I.D.S. Research suggests that shiitake increases resistance to H.I.V. by blocking initial stages of infection. It is also active against viral encephalitis infection.

The polysaccharide compound lentinan in shiitake lowers blood pressure and blood cholesterol, and benefits the whole cardiovascular system, making shiitake a useful remedy in the prevention and treatment of heart disease. It has a strong tendency to inhibit the growth of tumor cells, and to prevent the spread of metastases (secondaries). Rather than attacking tumors directly, it works by stimulating the immune system, and boosting the body's own ability to inactivate and eliminate malignant cells.

Shiitake mushrooms are widely available, and can be bought fresh, dried, or pickled. Fresh or pickled shiitake are prepared and eaten in the same way as white mushrooms. Dried mushrooms should be rinsed and then soaked for half an hour before use. Remove the stems before cooking.

IMMUNE-BOOSTING PROFILE

★ VITAMINS B2, B3, B5, B6; COPPER, MANGANESE, SELENIUM, IRON; BIO-ACTIVE ENZYMES; LENTINAN (POLYSACCHARIDE), PROTEIN

✔ ANTIBACTERIAL, ANTI-CANCER, ANTIVIRAL, ANTI-STRESS, LOWERS CHOLESTEROL, IMMUNO-STIMULANT

! SHIITAKE MAY CAUSE DIARRHEA IF EATEN IN LARGE QUANTITIES

shiitake with sea vegetable *(above)*

½ breakfast cup dried sea vegetable (iziki)
1 bunch of scallions
3 tablespoons olive oil
8 ounces fresh shiitake mushrooms, cut into strips
4 ounces asparagus

4 carrots, cut into julienne strips
1 cup vegetable bouillon
1 tablespoon dry sherry
2 tablespoons soy sauce
2 tablespoons toasted sesame seeds

Rinse the iziki, soak in warm water for 30 minutes, then rinse again. Finely chop the scallions. Heat the oil in a wok, add the iziki, then the mushrooms, asparagus, carrots, and scallions. Stir-fry for a few minutes, then add the bouillon, sherry and soy sauce. Simmer gently for 10 minutes. Top with toasted sesame seeds. Season to taste.

shiitake salad

9 ounces smoked tofu, cubed
3 tablespoons olive oil
8 ounces fresh shiitake
2 tablespoons fresh tarragon, finely chopped

1 tablespoons lime juice
Salt and pepper to taste
1 little gem lettuce
1 handful arugula
1 handful sorrel leaves

Stir-fry the tofu in oil for a few minutes. Add the shiitake; fry till tender. Add tarragon and lime juice; season. Serve on a bed of green leaves.

pasta, pesto, and shiitake

14 ounces pasta spirals
4 carrots, finely chopped
Kernels of 2 corns
4 tablespoons green peas
10 ounces fresh shiitake, halved
1 teaspoon soy sauce
4 tablespoons lemon juice

For the pesto:

4 tablespoons pine nuts, ground
2 garlic cloves, crushed
1 bunch fresh basil, chopped
1 teaspoon coarse sea salt
4 tablespoons olive oil

Mix the pesto ingredients and set aside. Cook the pasta in salted water and a splash of oil. After 5 minutes, add the carrots, kernels and peas and cook for 2 more minutes. Drain, place in a bowl and mix in the pesto. Fry the shiitake until golden; add a little soy sauce as you turn off the heat. Add the mushrooms to the bowl and mix. Sprinkle with lemon juice and freshly ground black pepper.

chapter seven

coping with
common ailments

Making the right food choices not only keeps your immune system in optimum condition but also helps you target specific diseases. The following pages feature some of the common ailments that can develop when the immune system is operating below par, and the steps you can take to avoid or manage such disorders. There is advice on which superfoods to include in your meals, along with page references directing you to mouthwatering recipes that present these foods at their best. There is also advice on problematic products you should avoid, and other simple ways to ensure your immune system is ready for anything that the modern world might have in store.

colds and flu epidemics

SUPERFOODS FOR COLDS AND FLU EPIDEMICS: BLACKCURRANT, BORAGE, CATMINT, CAYENNE, CAMOMILE, ECHINACEA, ELDERBERRY AND FLOWERS, GARLIC, GINGER, GRAPEFRUIT, GUAVA, HORSERADISH, LEMON, NASTURTIUM, ORANGE, PEPPERMINT, RASPBERRY, ROSEHIP, WILD MARJORAM, YARROW

Cold and influenza (flu) are viral infections. Both can cause runny nose, sore throat, headache, fever, and general malaise. Cold symptoms are usually mild at first and develop relatively slowly. In contrast, flu symptoms start abruptly and include aching joints and limbs, high fever, shivering, severe headache, and often a persistent dry cough. Most flu symptoms last only a few days, but a cough may persist, and depression, lethargy, and tiredness often follow and may be long-lasting. Flu can be accompanied by secondary bacterial infections, such as bronchitis or pneumonia, which take advantage of the body's weakened state (especially among the elderly).

Flu epidemics

The flu virus is highly infectious and causes seasonal outbreaks of moderate to severe illness lasting one to two weeks. In modern times, increased international travel has allowed outbreaks to spread rapidly, leading to global pandemics.

The flu virus affects animals and birds (particularly intensively reared pigs and poultry), as well as humans, and can change its form in unpredictable ways. As a result, immunity to older strains of the virus may not protect from newer, mutated strains. When a new strain crosses over from animals or birds to humans, it may spread quickly to large numbers of people.

Worldwide flu outbreaks have occurred several times in history, and there have been (on average) three major

pandemics per century over the past 300 years. The Spanish flu of 1918–19 killed over 100 million people. It was caused by the influenza A (H1N1) virus and was so aggressive that many people died just a few days after becoming infected. Although flu normally affects the most vulnerable (such as children and the elderly), Spanish flu also affected the strongest—nearly half its victims were young, healthy adults.

Since the Spanish flu catastrophe, there have been two more major pandemics, Asian flu in 1957–58 and swine flu in 2009. Asian flu began in China in 1956 and originated in wild ducks when a mutated avian flu virus combined with a human virus strain. It spread around Asia and continued to North America and the rest of the world, killing around 2 million people. Although a vaccine developed in 1957 helped contain the outbreak, a further mutation of the avian flu virus (H3N2) was responsible for the milder pandemic in 1968–69.

In 2009, a new strain of influenza A (H1N1/09)—otherwise known as swine flu or Mexican flu—caused a new pandemic. Existing flu vaccines provided no protection, and children had no immunity to the new strain, but adults, particularly those over 60, were not as badly affected.

H1N1/09 has proved more contagious than seasonal flu, spreading from person to person via droplets from coughs and sneezes. Those infected are contagious for several days after the fever subsides, and although the symptoms are usually quite mild compared to seasonal flu, the swine flu virus can infect cells much deeper in the lungs, destroying alveoli and causing severe respiratory symptoms in certain individuals, and even acute respiratory distress syndrome, which can be fatal. Ordinary seasonal flu vaccines are ineffective against swine flu and resistance is developing against Tamiflu. The other available anti-viral vaccine, called Relenza, is still effective.

Another flu strain causing concern to health professionals and governments is the H5N1 influenza A virus, also known as "bird flu." It first appeared in Asian birds and has spread globally, killing tens of millions of wild birds and resulted in the culling of hundreds of millions of factory farmed birds. Thankfully, transmission from birds to people is not common, and only a few people (mostly those known to have handled infected birds) have caught the infection. H5N1 is a very virulent virus, however, and it has killed 60 percent of infected people.

Cold and flu prevention

Although flu vaccines are available, flu vaccination is a much-debated topic. While there is evidence that vaccination against seasonal flu has benefit for the long-term health of high-risk groups, it is important to understand that the emergence of new mutant flu virus strains is unpredictable and that vaccines can be made only against virus strains that already exist. Flu vaccination is only partially effective because the vaccine does not give resistance to all possible strains of the virus, and adverse reactions to the vaccine are relatively common. It is therefore very important to take a "prevention is better than cure" attitude toward flu (and colds), doing everything possible to maintain a strong immune system through good diet and healthy lifestyle.

We are constantly surrounded by cold and flu viruses. To strengthen your resistance to colds and flu, ensure good nutrition, manage your stress levels, and try to avoid alcohol, tobacco, recreational drugs, chemicals, excess sugar intake, high levels of dietary cholesterol and other fats, dehydration, and over-exposure to hot or cold. Flu is highly infectious and usually occurs in epidemics that peak in winter.

Cold and flu management

Support the body and let the infection take its course rather than suppressing symptoms that show the body's defences are at work. The best treatment in the acute phase is sleep and rest, eating very little, and drinking lots of liquids in the form of water, weak herbal tea, and soup.

Good hydration creates a less favourable environment for the virus while improving the function of the immune system. Because of their natural sugar content, fruit juices and sweetened drinks are not beneficial once the disease gets hold, but thanks to their high antioxidant content, fruit juices are excellent cold and influenza preventives. Dairy products are "mucus forming" and should be avoided altogether.

SUGGESTED RECIPES FOR COLDS AND FLU EPIDEMICS

Raspberry vinegar (page 195), cool tomato soup (page 260), mint and melon soup (page 261), spicy moroccan soup (page 262), autumn fruit juice (page 280), sunrise—left (page 283), cold buster (page 284), cough mixture (page 284), elderberry cordial (page 284), eucalyptus mix (page 285), immuni-tea (page 285), lung-cleansing tea mix (page 286), sage mix for sore throats (page 286), si c (page 286), tea for joints (page 287), tea for fever (page 287), tea for headache (page 287).

Cold remedy (tea mixture): Infuse 1 teaspoon each of elderflowers and camomile flowers in 1¼ cups boiling water for 10 minutes.

ear, nose, and throat infections

SUPERFOODS FOR E.N.T. INFECTIONS: BEET, BILBERRY, BLACK MUSTARD SEED, BLACKBERRY, CARROT, CHERRY, CLEAVERS, ECHINACEA, ELDERFLOWER, EUCALYPTUS, GARBANZOS, GARLIC, GRAPEFRUIT, GRAPES, GUAVA, HORSERADISH, LEEK, LEMON, MANGO, MARIGOLD, NETTLE, ONION, PEPPERMINT, PUMPKIN, SAGE, SHIITAKE, STRAWBERRY

The ear, nose, and throat are closely linked by a labyrinth of tubes and passages. This allows infection to spread quickly from one to another. Common ear, nose, and throat (E.N.T.) disorders include middle ear and throat infections (including tonsillitis) and sinusitis.

Middle ear infection (otitis media) is especially common in children and often follows colds, flu, tonsillitis, or childhood fevers. It can lead to a build-up of fluid that puts pressure on the eardrum, causing severe earache. The eardrum may perforate, which relieves pressure and pain. Recurrent middle ear infection can lead to glue ear, a chronic condition causing deafness and learning difficulties.

Sinusitis is inflammation of the cavities in the bones around the nose, causing headache, facial pain, and stuffy nose. It is a common complication of colds and flu, and may also be caused by allergy, injury, tooth infection, or poor drainage of the sinuses.

Throat infection can be viral or bacterial, and cause fever, malaise, sore throat, and difficulty swallowing associated with inflammation of the lymphoid tissues (tonsils and adenoids) at the back of the throat. Swollen adenoids can cause difficulty breathing, and a tendency to repeated ear or upper respiratory tract infection.

Prevention

The best way to prevent ear, nose, and throat infections is to strengthen the immune system by eating lots of vegetables and fruit—particularly those high in vitamins A and C, bioflavonoids, and zinc. Avoid common allergens, such as dairy foods (including cow's milk in baby formulas), eggs, shellfish, wheat, and peanut butter. Avoid repeated upper respiratory tract infections by following the guidelines on page 224. If you do catch a cold or suffer a bout of influenza, take plenty of time to convalesce after the symptoms subside, and do not go out and about too early.

Management

Seek professional help in cases of suspected middle ear infection or if a nose or throat disorder leads to breathing difficulties. Drink lots of fluids (water, herb tea, diluted vegetable juices, and soups). Get plenty of rest, including bed rest if necessary. Avoid suspected allergens and concentrated sources of sugar such as dried fruit, honey, syrups, and concentrated fruit juice. Gentle facial massage helps alleviate sinusitis. Herbal gargles can ease throat infections.

SUGGESTED RECIPES FOR E.N.T. INFECTIONS

Ear infections: green leafy salad (page 183), shiitake mushroom soup (page 261), beet and apple (page 280), green party (page 280), grape and raisin smoothie (page 283), cold buster (page 284), tea for ear infections (page 287).

Sinusitis: beet and horseradish salad (page 179), spiced nettle soup (page 187), carrot and lemon with garlic (page 280), elderflower spritzer (page 284), eucalyptus mix (page 285)

Throat infection: mint and melon soup (page 261), pumpkin soup (page 261), welsh leek and potato soup (page 262), cool cucumber (page 280), garlic oxymel (page 285), sage mix for sore throats (page 286), si c (page 286), tea for glands (page 287) .

Sinusitis remedy (horseradish poultice): Grate fresh horseradish root into a portion of oatmeal, wrap the mixture in a tea towel and place the compress over the nose, cheeks, and forehead (taking care to avoid the eyes).

childhood fevers

SUPERFOODS FOR CHILDHOOD FEVERS: BORAGE, CARROT, CATNIP, CLEAVERS, ECHINACEA, ELDERBERRIES AND FLOWERS, GARLIC, GINGER, GRAPEFRUIT, GUAVA, LEMON, ONION, ORANGE, PEPPERMINT, ROSEHIP, STRAWBERRIES, SWEET POTATO, WILD MARJORAM, YARROW

Childhood fevers are common, especially those arising from colds and other simple respiratory tract infections. They are part of the immune system's natural development and should be managed rather than suppressed. While most childhood fevers resolve quickly, it is vital to exclude serious disorders such as meningitis, so never hesitate to seek medical help in cases of high fever, or if you are worried about a child's condition.

The diseases chickenpox, rubella (German measles), measles, mumps, and whooping cough are also common causes of fever in childhood. Chickenpox causes sore throat, headache, and a spotty rash. Rubella causes runny nose, sore throat, swollen lymph nodes (glands), rash, and sometimes joint pain. (Rubella infection during pregnancy may lead to birth-defects.) Measles causes sore eyes, runny nose, dry cough, white spots in the mouth, and rash. It may be complicated by middle ear infection, bronchitis, pneumonia, or, less commonly, febrile convulsions (fits). Mumps causes sore throat and painful swelling of the salivary glands. Whooping cough causes distressing bouts of coughing.

Prevention

A healthy diet aids the proper development and functioning of the immune system and is the mainstay of prevention of childhood fevers. Encourage your children to eat fresh and dried fruit, carrot and cucumber sticks, grapes, tomatoes, grains, nuts, and seeds, and restrict the availability of candies, sodas, burgers, and other junk foods. Give children the chance to eat organic foods whenever possible.

Management

During the acute phase of the fever, bed rest, tender loving care, and plenty of fluids (water and weak herbal teas) are the most important steps. Use catmint to help control the fever. When the child's appetite starts to return, offer freshly prepared juices (diluted with water). During convalescence, fruit salads and soups are beneficial, and children love pasta dishes. Avoid sugar, dairy produce, and junk foods, as well as common allergens (wheat, eggs, peanut butter, additives).

SUGGESTED RECIPES FOR CHILDHOOD FEVERS

scandinavian beet burgers (page 179), raspberry vinegar (page 195), fresh fruit salad (page 258), fruity pancakes (page 259), yogurt with fruit (page 259), mint and melon soup (page 261), black-eye pea and wild marjoram soup (page 261), italian butterbean soup (page 261), tibetan dumpling soup (page 262), raspberry gateau (page 278), tropical fruit salad (page 279), apricot and ginger (page 280),blackberry cream (page 280), caribbean smoothie (page 283), cool cucumber (page 280), creamy mango (page 280), nirvana (page 283), pink pineapple (page 283), soft tutti fruity (page 283), cough mixture (page 284), elderberry cordial (page 284), si c—*left* (page 286), sleepy time tea (page 286) tea for fever (page 287).

bronchitis and pneumonia

SUPERFOODS FOR BRONCHITIS: BLACK MUSTARD SEED, BLACKBERRY, BLACKCURRANT, BORAGE, CARAWAY, CARROT, CAMOMILE, CHERRY, CLEAVERS, CURLY KALE, ECHINACEA, ELDERFLOWER, EUCALYPTUS, GARLIC, GRAPE, GRAPEFRUIT, GUAVA, HORSERADISH, LEEK, LEMON, LICORICE ROOT, MANGO, NASTURTIUM, NETTLE, ONION, PEPPERMINT, SWEET POTATO, THYME, SWEET VIOLET, WATERCRESS, WILD MARJORAM, YARROW

BRONCHITIS

Bronchitis is an inflammation of the lining of the bronchial tubes in the lungs. The acute form of bronchitis is usually caused by a viral or bacterial infection and often follows a bout of cold or influenza. The symptoms are cough (initially harsh and dry, later with yellow or green sputum), shortness of breath, and fever. Pneumonia is a potentially serious complication of bronchitis and is particularly dangerous for elderly people. Chronic bronchitis causes persistent or recurrent cough and breathing difficulties. It is most common in people with lowered immune function, particularly smokers, drug and alcohol abusers, patients taking immuno-suppressive drugs, and those suffering immunodeficiency disorders and cancer. Chronic bronchitis goes hand in hand with structural damage within the lungs called emphysema, which decreases the amount of lung tissue available to absorb oxygen and get rid of carbon dioxide and other waste products. The lungs also develop a rough, thickened lining, making breathing very difficult.

Prevention

The most important step you can take to avoid chronic bronchitis is to quit smoking—or not start in the first place. Keep your weight within optimum limits and eat plenty of foods rich in vitamins A and C, bioflavonoids, and zinc to enhance your immune function. Avoid noxious fumes and immuno-suppressive drugs wherever possible, and breathe fresh air every day. Avoid eating dairy products, which encourage the production of excess mucus.

Management

Drink large amounts of fluids (water, herbal tea, soup), and juices rich in vitamin C—the immune system needs a lot of this nutrient when fighting infection. Garlic, onion, and leek have natural antibacterial properties and help prevent complications such as pneumonia from developing (see below). Limit your sugar consumption, particularly added sugar, carbonated drinks, concentrated fruit juices, and sweets, and cut out dairy products altogether. Try to avoid suppressing the cough. Herbal expectorants make the cough more "productive" and make it easier to get rid of excess mucus from the airways. A warm poultice (see opposite) applied to the chest eases breathing. Rest is important but avoid lying flat in bed, which may make breathing more difficult and exacerbate the cough. Use extra pillows or a bolster to prop up your head and upper body.

PNEUMONIA

Pneumonia is a common illness affecting all age groups and is a major cause of death worldwide, especially in the elderly and the very young.

Bacteria, viruses, fungi and parasites, as well as injury to the lungs from accidental inhalation of a chemical or liquid are all causes, but in some cases the cause remains a mystery. Symptoms include cough, chest pain, fever, night sweats, and difficulty breathing.

Pneumonia occurs mainly during the winter months when the body's resistance is low and infectious diseases flourish. Research shows that underlying illnesses such as flu, emphysema, alcoholism, or immune deficiency heighten the risk, and low vitamin-D levels also seem to increase susceptibility, as does long-term immobility.

The disease can be very serious and medical help should always be sought if pneumonia is suspected, especially in children and older people. Between 20 and 40 per cent of pneumonia sufferers will need hospital treatment and, of these, 5 to 10 per cent will die. Before the advent of antibiotics, a third of pneumonia sufferers died from the infection.

Prevention

Anyone with a chronic respiratory disease, such as asthma, and anyone with long-term health problems, such as diabetes, heart disease, or kidney problems, should be considered at risk of contracting pneumonia. Those with a previous history of the disease are also more susceptible.

Natural prevention includes taking proper care when suffering from colds, flu, and other respiratory illnesses and taking time to convalesce before resuming normal activities (something that is increasingly difficult in modern society). Good nutrition, minimal stress, a steady blood sugar level, and avoiding over-exposure to hot or cold helps keep the immune system strong. Smoking should be avoided. Vaccines are available against both bacterial and viral pneumonia.

Management

The treatment of pneumonia varies with the cause, but antibiotics are effective against only bacterial pneumonia. It is important, therefore, to seek qualified professional advice in all suspected cases. Whatever the cause, there are a number of things you can do to aid a speedy and full recovery:

- Drink as many fluids as possible—especially water, diluted fruit juices, herbal teas, and clear soups
- Avoid dairy products to minimize mucus production in the respiratory tract
- Apply a hot water bottle to your chest and upper back for half an hour daily. Put a few drops of eucalyptus oil on a cloth between the hot water bottle and your skin for enhanced effect
- Use echinacea to boost the immune system

SUGGESTED RECIPES FOR BRONCHITIS AND PNEUMONIA

Green leafy salad (page 181), nettle and sweet potato mash (page 265), yogurt with fruit (page 243), basic vegetable soup (page 244), tropical sunshine salad (page 261), blackberry cream (page 264), carrot and lemon with garlic (page 264), cold buster (page 268), cough mixture (page 268), garlic oxymel (page 269), lung-cleansing tea mix (page 270), spicy chai (page 270), si c (page 270), tea for fever (page 271).

Cough remedy: Pour 1 cup boiling water over 2 to 3 teaspoons of flaxseeds and leave to infuse for 10 to 15 minutes.

Inhalation: Add 1 tablespoon each of chamomile, thyme, eucalyptus, and wild marjoram to 2½ cups boiling water and infuse for 5 minutes, covered. Wrap a blanket around yourself and put a big towel over your head. Take the lid off the infusion and gently inhale the steam for about 10 minutes. Splash your face with cool water.

Mustard poultice: Mix 5 teaspoons of crushed black mustard seeds with a large portion of hot oatmeal. Wrap the mixture in a clean dish towel and put this on the chest for 20 minutes; make sure it is not so hot as to cause discomfort and check from time to time that the mustard is not causing skin irritation.

cystitis

SUPERFOODS FOR CYSTITIS: ASPARAGUS, BEET, BLACK CURRANT, CARROT, CELERY SEEDS, CHERRIES, CLEAVERS, CRANBERRY, CURLY KALE, EUCALYPTUS, GARLIC, GRAPES, GUAVA, HORSERADISH, JUNIPER, MANGO, MARIGOLD, QUINOA, RICE, SOY YOGURT, THYME, YARROW

Cystitis is inflammation of the bladder, most often caused by an infection. The disorder triggers various symptoms including lower abdominal pain, painful and frequent urination, a feeling of urgency to urinate and that the bladder is never completely empty. The urine smells fishy and looks cloudy (maybe with traces of blood).

Cystitis is more common in women than in men (possibly because the urethra—the tube that carries urine out of the body—is shorter in women and close to the openings of the vagina and anus, making infection more likely). Cystitis is often associated with pregnancy, sex, sensitivity to cold, and mechanical injury (such as medical catheterization).

Classical cystitis is caused by bacterial infection, but other organisms, such as chlamydia, are frequently involved. However, many people suffer recurrent symptoms of cystitis without any obvious infective cause, and are given a diagnosis of "urethral syndrome." Some cases of urethral syndrome can be explained by an allergy or sensitivity to materials such as nylon, washing powder, soaps, and bubble baths. In bacterial cystitis, serious complications can occur if the infection spreads to the kidneys including acute glomerulonephritis (the symptoms of which are severe malaise, high fever, and intense back pain), and chronic reflux nephropathy, which can cause permanent kidney damage.

Prevention

Eat plenty of fresh foods, mainly of plant origin, and avoid eating too much sugar or drinking too much alcohol or coffee. Keep your meat and dairy intake to a minimum, and avoid junk food and food additives altogether. Include foods that contain plenty of vitamins A and C, and bioflavonoids and zinc. Garlic also has natural antibiotic properties and helps the body to deal with urinary-tract infections. In severe cases, try the detox diet on page 272.

Above all, avoid dehydration and get plenty of rest. Replace coffee and tea with lots of herbal teas, and water. Avoid acidic foods and drinks (including citrus fruits). Pay attention to personal hygiene, and make sure that you are not allergic to the soaps or soap powders you are using. Avoid douches and intimate deodorants, because they may disrupt the natural bacterial flora and allow harmful micro-organisms to flourish. If you have a tendency to cystitis, it is also important to empty your bladder and wash your genitals before and after sex.

Management

Cranberry juice can be a highly effective treatment for cystitis. Otherwise, the conventional treatment for cystitis is a course of antibiotics together with high fluid intake, regular bladder emptying, and scrupulous hygiene. However, many cases do not respond to this regimen, and repeated or long-term use of antibiotics can bring other problems (such as candidiasis and disturbance of intestinal flora). If you do take antibiotics it is important to allow the body to rebuild its natural defenses afterward. Eating live yogurt helps the bowel to recolonize with beneficial micro-organisms. Antioxidants including vitamins A, C, and E, and zinc, selenium, and bioflavonoids help to restore immune function.

SUGGESTED RECIPES FOR CYSTITIS

Beet and horseradish salad (page 179), nettle and sweet potato mash (page 187), avocado smoothie (page 197), pasta, pesto, and shiitake (page 221), ruby red melon salad (page 258), yogurt with fruit (page 259), asparagus with ravigote (page 262), korean kimchi-style salad (page 263), tzaziki (page 267), asparagus asian-style (page 269), mushrooms with sage and thyme stuffing (page 272), swiss chard and juniper berries (page 275), cranberry spritzer (page 280), vegetable cocktail (page 283), cystitis relief (page 284), immuni-tea (page 285).

fungal infections

SUPERFOODS FOR FUNGAL INFECTIONS: AVOCADO, BEET, BRAZIL NUT, CALENDULA, CARROT, CAMOMILE, CINNAMON, ENDIVE, EUCALYPTUS, FAVA BEAN, GARLIC, GINGER, GRAPEFRUIT, LEEKS, LEMON BALM, LENTILS, LIVE SOY YOGURT, PAPAYA, PSYLLIUM SEEDS, PUMPKIN, RASPBERRY, RICE, SPINACH, SPRING GREENS, SWISS CHARD, THYME,

Common fungal infections include candidiasis or "thrush" (yeast infection caused by *Candida albicans*); athlete's foot (*Tinea pedis*); and ringworm (*Tinea corporis*). There are two forms of candidiasis—oral and genital. Oral thrush produces thin, white, moist, cottage-cheesy plaques inside the mouth, which rub off to leave red, sore patches. It mainly affects sick babies, the immuno-compromised and the elderly. Vaginal thrush causes abnormal vaginal discharge, irritation, and soreness. In managing the disease it is important to treat sexual partners to avoid a cycle of re-infection. Candida is a common yeast that forms part of our normal gut flora. Drugs (particularly antibiotics and steroids), stress, and poor diet can lead to candida overgrowth that affects absorption of nutrients as well as general health, and can lead to serious illness if it spreads to the rest of the body.

Fungal skin infections affect warm, damp places, such as groin creases, and produce clearly demarcated, moist, itchy dark red patches with a few smaller lesions scattered around. Infected finger nails appear thick and brownish. Ringworm appears as a scaly, red patch that enlarges and becomes a raised, scaly circle with a pale center. It looks as though it has been caused by a burrowing worm, hence the name. It may spread and form more circles, and can cause bald patches if it affects the scalp. Athlete's foot often develops between the fourth and fifth toes with the skin becoming itchy, pale, damp, flaky, cracked, and mushy.

Prevention and management

Factors that suppress immunity can increase the risk of fungal infections. These include a diet high in sugar and saturated fat, drugs (antibiotics, steroids, chemotherapy, oral contraceptives, anti-ulcer medication), environmental chemicals, alcohol, and stress. Avoiding these is the mainstay of prevention. Papaya contains enzymes that can inhibit yeast proliferation. Cut down on dairy products and, if you have to take antibiotics, eat live yogurt to help restore a healthy balance of intestinal flora. To manage fungal infection, take plenty of rest. Avoid known food allergens, alcohol, dairy products, and foods high in refined sugar, such as sucrose, fructose, syrup, fruit juice, honey, and dried fruits. Take a teaspoon of psyllium seeds in a glass of water after meals.

SUGGESTED RECIPES FOR FUNGAL INFECTIONS

Baked beet salad (page 179), green leafy salad (page 183), stuffed grapefruit (page 191), avocado smoothie (page 197), spicy brazil nut paté (page 201), korean kimchi-style salad (page 263), guacamole (page 266), tzaziki (page 267), chinese salad (page 276), apricot and ginger (page 280), carrot and lemon with garlic—above (page 280), calming tea (page 284), eucalyptus mix (page 285), spicy chai (page 286), khichuri—rice with lentils (page 273), stress relief (page 286), tea for fungal infections (page 287).

herpes simplex

SUPERFOODS FOR HERPES SIMPLEX: ADUKI BEAN, AVOCADO, BEET, BRAZIL NUT, CARROT, GARBANZOS, GARLIC, HAZELNUT, LEMON BALM, LENTILS, LICORICE ROOT, MACADAMIA NUT, MARIGOLD, MUESLI, PINE NUTS, PUMPKIN SEEDS, SHIITAKE, SPINACH, ST. JOHN'S WORT, SUN-DRIED TOMATOES, SUNFLOWER AND SAFFLOWER OILS, SWEET POTATO, TEMPEH, TOFU, TOMATO, WALNUT, WHEAT GERM, YAM

Herpes simplex is a virus that causes blisters on skin and mucous membranes known as cold sores. The sores commonly appear on the face, fingers, mouth, lips, and genitals, and are often accompanied by swollen lymph nodes, itching, stinging pain, fatigue, and fever. The virus is transmitted through direct contact with an active cold sore, for example via saliva or sexual fluids.

After the initial infection, the virus lies dormant and may remain unnoticed for long periods of time, until the body's resistance is lowered by colds (hence the name) and other infections, stress, trauma, menstruation, or exposure to sun. Cold sores recur near or at the primary site of infection whenever the body is feeling run down, and last for one or two weeks. Men are generally more prone to cold sores than women.

Herpes simplex infection is a common cause of genital ulcers, but it is important to exclude other, more serious causes such as syphilis and lymphoma. Genital cold sores are also associated with an increased risk of developing cervical dysplasia (abnormal changes in cervical cells that may be a prelude to cancer). The herpes virus is not a direct cause (cervical cancer is known to be caused by the papilloma virus) but rather simply a symptom of a run-down immune response failing to keep cell changes in check.

Prevention

The best way to avoid infection is to avoid direct contact with active cold sores. The likelihood of infections and the frequency of recurrence are both reduced by maintaining good general health. Resistance to infection depends on having a strong immune system, which in turn depends on good nutrition and having sufficient rest, fresh air, and exercise. People suffering from immunodeficiency syndromes, or whose immunity is suppressed by drugs, stress, poor nutrition, or chronic disease, are at greater risk of infection. People with eczema are also more susceptible to cold sores and other viral skin conditions.

Management

Eat foods containing vitamins A and C, and bioflavonoids and carotenoids, which all enhance resistance and inhibit viral attack. Foods rich in zinc reduce the time it takes for sores to heal. Vitamin E-rich foods speed up healing and help reduce pain. Foods with anti-viral properties, such as shiitake, garlic, lemon balm, calendula (marigold), St. John's wort, spinach, sweet potato, tempeh, yam, and tomato should also be included in the diet. Following a detox diet (see page 288) is a good way to help the body avoid recurring cold sores. Managing stress, avoiding exposure to allergens and limiting refined carbohydrate intake are also important factors.

Carrot, beet, and licorice root and lemon balm are all efficient anti-cold-sore remedies. Licorice root reduces the cell damage caused by herpes simplex infection, and inhibits the growth of the sores. A tisane made of licorice root and lemon balm may decrease the severity and duration of an outbreak if taken regularly (3–4 cups per day) as soon as the first signs of a sore appear. However, licorice causes an increase in the rate at which potassium is eliminated from the body. So, when taking licorice, you should also include in your diet plenty of foods that are high in potassium, such as banana, avocado, sweet potato, dried apricot, beans and peas, and green leaves.

SUGGESTED RECIPES FOR HERPES SIMPLEX

Green leafy salad (page 183), oriental salad with tempeh (page 209), shiitake salad (page 221), oatmeal with dried fruit and quinoa (page 258), muesli (page 259), tofumasalata (page 264), pan amb oli (page 267), winter hot pot (page 272), sweet potato curry (page 272), carrot 'n' beet salad (page 275), blackberry crumble (page 279), calming tea (page 284), pick-me-up (page 286), tea for glands (page 287).

eczema

SUPERFOODS FOR ECZEMA: ASPARAGUS, BEANS, BELL PEPPER, BILBERRY, BUTTERNUT SQUASH, CAMOMILE, CARROT, CLEAVERS, CURLY KALE, ECHINACEA, ELDERBERRY, EVENING PRIMROSE OIL, FLAXSEED, GRAPEFRUIT, GRAPES, HAWTHORN, LENTILS, MANGO, NETTLE, PEAS, PINE NUTS, PUMPKIN SEEDS, SPINACH, SUNFLOWER OIL AND SEEDS, SWEET POTATO, VIOLET, SWISS CHARD, TEMPEH, TOFU, WALNUT OIL

Eczema (also called dermatitis) is a very common skin condition characterized by red, itchy, weeping skin patches, which are prone to infection. As time goes by, the skin becomes progressively harder, drier, and more brittle because of repeated scratching.

Atopic eczema causes an itchy, sometimes weeping and scaly rash on the face, and in body creases. It is common in infants and tends to run in families—two-thirds of eczema sufferers have a family member with the condition, and many also develop hay fever and/or asthma. There is also an increased susceptibility to skin infections, including cold sores and warts. Seborrheic eczema causes a crusty rash on hairy skin—especially in the armpits and groin creases and on the face in men. When it occurs on the scalp in babies it is called "cradle cap."

Irritant eczema is caused by direct contact with strong chemicals and usually develops within 24 hours of initial exposure. It causes redness, blisters, and cracks in the skin, but does not spread beyond the area exposed to the irritant. Allergic contact dermatitis develops after a second exposure to an allergen such as lanolin, skin cream additives, antibiotic ointments, and nickel in jewelery or buttons. The rash is most prominent over the area of initial contact, but can spread all over the body.

Prevention

Food allergy is a common cause of eczema, and dairy products are the most likely culprits. Stress is also a common factor, and tension can provoke itching. Identifying and eliminating allergens, and dealing with stress, are thus the mainstays of prevention.

Management

It is necessary to eliminate known food allergens. Animal fats and dairy products should be limited in the diet until symptoms subside. Deficiency of essential fatty acids is sometimes a factor in the development of eczema and can be avoided by eating more polyunsaturated oil. Walnut oil is particularly useful because it is both anti-inflammatory and anti-allergic. Evening primrose oil, sunflower oil and seeds, and flaxseed also help dampen inflammation. Foods containing bioflavonoids are important for controlling inflammation and allergic reactions and enhance the action of vitamin C. Foods containing high levels of zinc and vitamin A are excellent for skin healing and repair.

SUGGESTED REMEDIES FOR ECZEMA

Grapefruit salad (page 191), fresh fruit salad (page 258), spicy moroccan soup (page 262), toasted nuts and seeds (page 264), tofu balls (page 266), tomato and cucumber canapés (page 266), asparagus asian-style (page 269), spinach bouillabaisse (page 271), spring greens and macadamia nuts (page 274), arugula salad (page 275), orange mango salad (page 276), natural beauty (page 282), calming tea (page 252), licorice tea mix (page 286), tea for the skin (page 287).

Steroid creams and tablets are common orthodox treatments for eczema, but can carry a risk of side effects after prolonged use. Try a calendula (marigold) ointment or make this compress to reduce inflammation. Pour 1 pint boiling water on to 3 tbs calendula flowers. Cover and allow to cool. Strain and use the liquid to soak a compress before placing it on the affected area. Keep the compress moist and leave in place for 1 hour.

Detoxifying herbs such as nettle, cleavers, violet, camomile, and echinacea aid the digestive system and are an important part of the treatment. Oily ointments can ease discomfort, and barrier creams and gloves can prevent contact with allergens.

psoriasis

SUPERFOODS FOR PSORIASIS: APPLE, AVOCADO, BANANA, BEANS, BEET, BELGIAN ENDIVE, BERRIES, BRAZIL NUTS, BROCCOLI, CAMOMILE, CARROT, CLEAVERS, CURLY KALE, DRIED FRUIT, GLOBE ARTICHOKE, GRAPES, GREEN LEAVES, LENTILS, LICORICE ROOT, MELON, MUSHROOMS, NETTLE, NUTS, OKRA, PAPAYA, PARSNIP, PEAS, PINEAPPLE, PUMPKIN, SPINACH, SQUASH, SWEET POTATO, SUN-DRIED TOMATOES, WHEATGRASS

Psoriasis is a relatively common skin condition that tends to run in families. It is characterized by red, silvery, scaly "plaques" of thickened skin, especially on the scalp, and on the outside of the knees and elbows. These are caused by skin cells dividing at a much faster rate than normal. The scaly plaques can be itchy and may join up to cover large areas of skin. Some sufferers also develop arthritis. The condition seems to run in families, and problems with protein digestion, impaired liver function, smoking, excess alcohol and animal fats consumption, and psychological trauma may be associated with the development of psoriasis.

Prevention and management

Both ultraviolet light (from sunlight) and seawater are beneficial—so relaxing on a sunny beach is an excellent preventative and curative measure. Protein digestion can be enhanced by eating foods containing digestive enzymes and vitamin A, such as papaya and pineapple. Detoxing is also important, and is encouraged by eating plenty of fruits and vegetables, and foods that encourage liver function such as beet, globe artichoke, belgian endive, turmeric and wheatgrass. Foods high in the trace elements chromium and zinc are beneficial. Chromium helps regulate blood-sugar levels and zinc is necessary for skin repair. Foods high in vitamins A, E, folate, and selenium are helpful too. Essential fatty acids found in flaxseeds, walnuts and walnut oil, fatty fish, and fish oil inhibit production of inflammatory leukotrienes in the skin. However, avoid animal fats, found in dairy products and meat, which contain substances, such as arachidonic acid that increase leukotriene production. Avoid alcohol and high-protein foods, limit sugar intake and try excluding gluten (found in wheat, barley, rye, and oats).

Exercise improves circulation and contributes to detoxing. A warm flaxseed poultice may help. Mix a portion of crushed seeds with hot water to make a mushy paste. Spread the paste on to folded muslin or a thin flannel. Wrap the material well around the paste to stop it oozing out. Place the poultice on the affected area and cover with a piece of plastic to keep the moisture in. Leave it in place until it no longer feels pleasantly warm.

SUGGESTED RECIPES FOR PSORIASIS

Nettle and sweet potato mash (page 187), broiled endive and brazil nut salad (page 201), spicy brazil nut paté (page 201), spicy moroccan soup (page 262), tomato and cucumber canapés (page 266), casserole de puy (page 268), butternut squash with bell pepper and tomato (page 269), okra in sweet and sour tamarind sauce (page 272), beet and apple—*left* (page 280), papaya power (page 283), pink pineapple (page 283), calming tea (page 284), immuni-tea (page 285), tea for the skin (page 287).

Remedy: Pour a cup of boiling water on to 2 to 3 tsp of flaxseeds; leave to infuse for 10 minutes. Drink a cup morning and evening.

hay fever

SUPERFOODS FOR HAY FEVER: ARTICHOKE, AVOCADO, BEANS, BEET, BELL PEPPER, BERRIES, BROCCOLI, BUTTERNUT SQUASH, CARROT, CAULIFLOWER, CORN, GREEN TEA, GUAVA, HORSERADISH, LENTILS, MARIGOLD, MUSTARD CRESS, OKRA, PAPAYA, SEA VEGETABLE, SHIITAKE, SPINACH, SUN-DRIED TOMATOES, SWEET POTATO, SWISS CHARD, TEMPEH, VEGETABLE OIL, WHEAT GERM OIL, YEAST EXTRACT

Hay fever is an allergic condition that causes inflammation of the mucous membranes lining the nasal cavity. It is often seasonal. Allergy to tree pollen is worst in spring, allergy to grass and weed pollen is worst in the summer, and allergy to molds occurs mainly in the fall. Allergy to dust mites and animal dander tends to be worse in the winter when sufferers spend more time indoors with the windows closed. The tendency to develop hay fever often runs in families. When inhaled antigens come into contact with the mucous membranes of the upper respiratory tract, the immune system releases histamine and other chemicals that cause a variety of unpleasant symptoms. These include runny nose, sneezing, and itchy eyes. It is also common to feel lethargic.

Allergic reactions are much more frequent and severe if you are over-tired, under stress, recovering from infection, or your immune system is compromised. Common food allergens (such as dairy foods) can lower the threshold for developing hay fever symptoms.

Prevention

To prevent attacks, aim to strengthen and detoxify the immune system, and minimize exposure to allergens. It is beneficial to avoid additives, such as colorings and preservatives, and common food allergens including eggs, fish, shellfish, nuts (especially peanuts), dairy products, chocolate, wheat, and citrus fruits. At the same time you should include some of the foods and herbs listed above in your daily diet. For the prevention to be effective, start at least a month before the season that your hay fever symptoms occur.

Management

Eat lots of foods containing vitamins B5, B6, B12 and E, trace elements such as selenium and magnesium, and bioflavonoids and carotenoids. Follow an elimination diet (see page 288) to discover which foods and drinks aggravate your allergy. Avoid dairy products altogether. To strengthen and detoxify your immune

system, avoid coffee, tea, chocolate, and refined sugar, and limit your intake of potatoes and citrus fruits. Consider excluding wheat during the hay fever season.

Keep your house as dust-free as possible. Consider having wooden or tiled floors with rugs instead of carpets, which trap dust and animal dander. Exclude pets from bedrooms. Wash all bedding regularly, using washing powder or perfume-free washing liquid, and choose non-feather and low-allergy mattresses, duvets, and pillows. Open the windows at least once a day in winter.

SUGGESTED RECIPES FOR HAY FEVER

beet and horseradish salad (page 179), artichoke hearts, fava beans and shiitake (page 268), okra in sweet and sour tamarind sauce (page 272), provençal mesclun salad (page 275), green lentil salad (page 276), tropical sunshine salad (page 277), height of passion (page 282), elderberry cordial (page 284), elderflower spritzer—above (page 284), green tea with mint (page 285), hay fever relief (page 285), immuni-tea (page 285), syrup of onion (see recipe for garlic oxymel—page 285), pick-me-up (page 286).

asthma

SUPERFOODS FOR ASTHMA: AVOCADO, BEANS, BEET, BELL PEPPER, BERRIES, BLACK CUMIN, BROCCOLI, BUTTERNUT SQUASH, CARAWAY, CARROT, CAULIFLOWER, CAYENNE, CORN, CURLY KALE, DRIED FRUIT, EUCALYPTUS, GARLIC, GREEN TEA, GUAVA, HORSERADISH, LENTILS, LICORICE ROOT, NETTLE, OKRA, ONION, PAPAYA, POTATO, SEA VEGETABLE, SHIITAKE, SORREL, SWEET POTATO, TEMPEH, THYME, YARROW

Asthma is a common respiratory disorder causing wheezing, difficulty breathing, and dry cough. It is caused by a narrowing of the airways in the lungs as a result of spasm in the bronchial tubes and excess production of thick, sticky mucus. There are two main types: one begins in childhood (especially in families with a history of asthma or allergy) and often clears up with age; the other starts later in life and is often preceded by infection. "Late onset" asthma tends to be chronic and is often harder to treat. Asthma attacks can be triggered by an allergic reaction to dust, pollen, foods, drugs, and bacteria, and by exhaustion, excitement, tension, anxiety, exercise, over-exposure to cold air, colds and influenza, or certain drugs (such as beta-blockers). In cases of mild asthma, sufferers usually have no breathing problems between attacks. However, those who have frequent, severe attacks over many years can suffer from constant breathing difficulty. During an attack it takes tremendous effort to breathe, and severe, prolonged attacks can be fatal unless treated with bronchodilators, steroids, oxygen, and, if necessary, artificial ventilation. During an attack, most sufferers find they can breathe more easily when sitting up rather than lying down.

Prevention

Finding and avoiding the underlying causes and trigger factors is the most important preventative measure. For example, keeping the home as dust-free as possible and washing bedding regularly in perfume-free detergents can help eliminate house-dust mites. Elimination diets are useful for identifying potential food allergens and avoiding them. The most common offenders are: eggs, fish, shellfish, nuts (especially peanuts), milk, chocolate, wheat, citrus fruits, apples, and food additives and coloring such as tartrazine, benzoates, sulfur dioxide, and sulfites.

Management

Exclude all meat, fish, eggs, and dairy products from the diet, as elimination of animal products has been shown to significantly reduce susceptibility to attacks. Other potential trigger factors that should be avoided include known allergens such as food additives, and also aspirin and other non-steroidal anti-inflammatory drugs, chlorinated tap water, and coffee, tea, refined sugar, and added salt. Limiting the amount of grains in the diet can also be beneficial. Eat plenty of foods containing vitamins B5, B6, B12, C, and E, magnesium, trace elements such as selenium, and carotenoids.

SUGGESTED RECIPES FOR FOR ASTHMA

Beet and horseradish salad (page 179), curly kale parcels (page 183), curly kale, tomato and fava beans (page 183), nettle and sweet potato mash (page 187), filled avocados (page 197), shiitake with sea vegetable (page 221), casserole de puy (page 268), butternut squash with bell pepper and tomato (page 269), italian butterbean soup (page 261), potato salad (page 276), salad with sorrel and tempeh (page 277), eucalyptus mix—*above* (page 285), lung-cleansing tea mix (page 286).

migraine

SUPERFOODS FOR MIGRAINE: ADUKI BEAN, BRAZIL NUT, CALENDULA FLOWERS, CAMOMILE, CAYENNE, CORN, FAVA BEAN, FEVERFEW, GARLIC, LAVENDER, MELON SEED, MUESLI, MUSHROOM, OATS, OKRA, ONION, PASSION FLOWER, PEAS, RICE, ROSEMARY, SWISS CHARD, TAHINI, TEMPEH, WALNUTS AND WALNUT OIL, WILD MARJORAM

Migraine is a recurrent and intense form of headache, often accompanied by visual and gastro-intestinal disturbances. Symptoms occur when sudden changes in the neurotransmitter serotonin within the brain affect other neurotransmitters. The pain always begins on one side of the head, and attacks may start with a visual "aura". Subsequent dilation of the blood vessels causes a characteristic throbbing headache, often accompanied by nausea, vomiting, and sensitivity to light. Migraine often runs in families, and may be associated with a childhood tendency to symptoms such as stomach ache, colic, vomiting, dizziness, or travel sickness. Migraine is more common in women than men, and can be triggered by many factors including food allergy. Chronic stress is thought to cause changes to the nervous system that make attacks more likely. Hormonal changes associated with menstruation and the menopause may be a factor. Musculoskeletal disorders such as whiplash injury may be other important triggers.

Prevention

It may help to keep a diary and make a note of any factors that seem to be linked to an attack, such as particular foods and your emotional state just prior to an attack. Identifying and avoiding allergens can often reduce the number and severity of migraines you suffer. Common offenders include red meat (especially pork), dairy products, wheat, chocolate, eggs, cheese, alcohol (especially red wine, sherry, and port), tobacco, coffee, strong tea, tomato, oranges, white sugar, shellfish, and food additives (such as nitrates, benzoic acid, tartrazine, and monosodium glutamate).

Eating a leaf of fresh feverfew each day over a long period of time may reduce the frequency and/or intensity of the attacks. However, some people are sensitive to the bitter principles in feverfew and can develop small blisters in the mouth after eating the fresh leaves. If you are susceptible to this problem, you can take feverfew in the form of a tisane (place a couple of fresh leaves

in a cup, pour boiling water over the top and leave to infuse). Calendula (marigold) flowers offer some protection from the effects of food allergens because they contain quercetin, which dampens down the body's responses to allergens. Foods containing vitamin B3 (niacin) may also be useful in preventing migraine attacks. These include soy products such as tempeh and tofu, muesli, fava beans, brown rice, aduki beans, corn, and mushrooms.

Management

Many people find the condition is improved by a change of diet such as a reduction in intake of animal produce and increased consumption of fresh fruits and vegetables. Important foods and drinks to eliminate are those containing alcohol, caffeine, cheese, chocolate, shellfish, and oranges. Vegetable oils (particularly walnut), cayenne, garlic, and onion are all beneficial. Foods high in magnesium (such as Brazil nuts, okra, melon seeds, tahini paste, Swiss chard, and brown rice) may also help in the longterm treatment of migraines.

SUGGESTED RECIPES FOR MIGRAINE

Green leafy salad (page 183), nettle and sweet potato mash (page 187), spicy brazil nut paté (page 201), muesli (page 259), khichuri —rice with lentils (page 273), florence fennel salad (page 276), tea for aches and pains (page 287). tea for headache (page 287).

Following a detox and elimination diet (see page 288) can be very useful for identifying and avoiding some of the causes of migraine attacks. After completing the diet, alcohol, cheese, oranges, and shellfish should still be avoided until symptom-free for six months. Foods high in animal fats should be kept to a minimum; vegetable oils, garlic, and onion should form a regular part of the diet.

rheumatoid arthritis

SUPERFOODS FOR ARTHRITIS: ADUKI BEAN, ALFALFA, ASPARAGUS, BEET, BELGIAN ENDIVE, BERRIES, CARROT, CELERY, CLEAVERS, CURLY KALE, FENNEL, FEVERFEW, GARLIC, GRAPES, HARICOT BEANS, HAWTHORN, JUNIPER, LENTILS, LICORICE ROOT, MANGO, NETTLE, NUTS, ONION, PAPAYA, PEAS, PINEAPPLE, RICE, SEA VEGETABLE, SUNFLOWER SEEDS AND OIL, SWISS CHARD, TAHINI, TEMPEH, VIOLET

Rheumatoid arthritis is a chronic, generalized inflammatory disease that attacks the membranes surrounding joints and tendons, causing pain, swelling, stiffness, and loss of movement. It mostly affects adults but can occur in childhood. It commonly begins with weeks of feeling generally unwell, perhaps with weight loss, mild fever, stiffness, and pain. The joint symptoms often start in the hands or feet, and are worse in the morning. The inflammation may spread to affect all of the joints, leading to increased pain, swelling, stiffness and—in severe cases—deformity. Most sufferers also have some degree of anemia and vitamin C deficiency.

The condition is an auto-immune disease in which antibodies attack the lining of the joints. What triggers the process is unclear, although it may be associated with genetic factors, nutrition, and lifestyle. There is also an association with poor digestion and waste elimination, which can lead to an accumulation of antigenic toxins.

SUGGESTED RECIPES FOR ARTHRITIS

curly kale parcels (page 183), nettle and sweet potato mash (page 187), spiced nettle soup (page 187), broiled endive and brazil nut salad (page 201), garlic and savoy cabbage (page 215), yogurt with fruit (page 259), toasted nuts and seeds (page 264), toasted tempeh with herb salad (page 264), artichoke hearts, fava beans, and shiitake (page 268), asparagus asian-style (page 269), swiss chard and juniper berries (page 275), spring greens and macadamia nuts (page 274), florence fennel salad (page 276), tropical sunshine salad (page 277), heart warmer (page 282), green tea with mint (page 285), immuni-tea (page 285), licorice mix (page 286), tea for joints (page 287).

Prevention and management

Rheumatoid arthritis is virtually non-existent in cultures where the diet consists mainly of fresh, unadulterated fruits, vegetables, nuts, and grains. However, it is relatively common in communities that eat a diet high in sugar, meat, dairy products, saturated fat, and refined carbohydrates. Different fats influence inflammation in different ways. Arachidonic acid (from meat and dairy products) increases inflammation but a diet high in polyunsaturated fats and low in saturated fat inhibits inflammation and improves symptoms.

Free radicals are responsible for much of the inflammatory damage caused in arthritis. So eating foods high in antioxidants can be beneficial. Improving digestion with foods such as papaya and pineapple, which contain proteolytic enzymes, alleviates the effect of food allergy and reduces the inflammatory process in the joints. Bioflavonoids block release of histamine and leukotrienes, which are both active inflammatory agents. Foods containing copper reduce arthritic inflammation. Foods high in niacin and tryptophan (components of vitamin B3) dampen arthritic pain.

To aid the elimination of toxins, include natural diuretics in the diet (celery seeds, nettle, and cleavers), and support the liver with foods containing bitter principles (globe artichoke, endive, and chicory). Taking psyllium seeds helps detoxify the gut and a traditional grape fast (see page 273) can aid general detoxification. Eliminating food allergens can have a beneficial effect on rheumatoid arthritis. Common offenders are dairy products, red meat, pork, wheat, vegetables of the solinacea family (tomato, eggplant, pepperfruits, tobacco—although potatoes are usually fairly well tolerated), shellfish, alcohol (especially red wine and port), oranges, and coffee. Other foods to avoid are strawberries, sorrel, currants (red and black), rhubarb, beet leaves, and spinach.

inflammatory bowel disease

SUPERFOODS FOR I.B.D.: APPLE, AVOCADO, BANANA, BILBERRY, BORAGE, BUTTERNUT SQUASH, CAMOMILE, CARAWAY, CARROT, FLAXSEED, FLORENCE FENNEL, GRAPEFRUIT, LAVENDER, LEMON BALM, LENTIL, LICORICE ROOT, MANGO, MUESLI, OATS, OKRA, PAPAYA, PEAS, PEPPERMINT, PINEAPPLE, POTATO, RICE, ROSEMARY, LIVE SOY YOGURT, SWEET POTATO, TAHINI

Inflammatory bowel disease (I.B.D.) is a general term for two important digestive disorders, ulcerative colitis and Crohn's disease. Ulcerative colitis involves recurrent inflammation of the large intestine. There is ulceration, leading to bouts of profuse and bloody diarrhea, fever, abdominal pain, dehydration, and often weight loss. There is a risk of life-threatening perforation of the bowel. Crohn's disease involves chronic patchy inflammation of the bowel resulting in diarrhea (without blood) and fever. It may lead to abscesses, poor absorption of nutrients, bowel obstruction, and perforation. I.B.D. may develop at any age, but most often starts between the ages of 15 and 35. Ulcerative colitis is currently the more common of the two, but the incidence of Crohn's disease is rising. The cause is not well understood, but the Western lifestyle and diet, infection, allergy, auto-immune disorders, and heredity, psychosomatic, and emotional factors have all been implicated.

Prevention and management

A balanced diet containing sufficiently good quality calories is one of the most important factors in the prevention and management of I.B.D. The diet should include foods high in calcium, magnesium, potassium, and trace elements such as zinc and iron. Folate and vitamin B12 are important for the health of the intestinal mucosa and vitamins A, C, and E are powerful antioxidants able to inhibit inflammation. Bioflavonoids found in most medicinal herbs have a powerful effect on enzymes involved in the inflammatory response. Inflammation can also be reduced by cutting consumption of animal fats in favor of omega-3 oils found in walnut oil, flaxseed oil and fish oils. Aim to re-establish the natural gut flora by adding live soy yogurt and complex carbohydrates to the diet. But avoid wheat bran, sugar, and refined carbohydrates, and common food allergens such as wheat, corn, and dairy products.

SUGGESTED RECIPES FOR INFLAMMATORY BOWEL DISEASE

Avocado smoothie (page 183), oatmeal with dried fruit and quinoa (page 258), muesli (page 259), yogurt with fruit (page 259), healing soup (page 260), pumpkin soup (page 261), tzaziki (page 267), winter hot pot (page 272), khichuri—rice with lentils (page 273), lemon rice (page 273), carrot 'n', beet salad (page 275), florence fennel salad (page 276), green lentil salad (page 276), wild rice salad (page 277), baked apples (page 278), tropical fruit salad (page 279), caribbean smoothie (page 280), creamy mango (page 280), stress relief (page 286), papaya power (page 283), calming tea (page 284), green tea with mint (page 285), pick-me-up (page 286), spicy chai—*left* (page 286). Steam or bake vegetables to make them easier to digest.

H.I.V. AND A.I.D.S.

SUPERFOODS FOR H.I.V. AND A.I.D.S.: BEANS, BEET, BELL PEPPER, BLACK CUMIN, BORAGE, BROCCOLI, BUTTERNUT SQUASH, CALENDULA, CARROT, CATECHIN, CITRUS FRUITS, CURLY KALE, ECHINACEA, EVENING PRIMROSE OIL, GARBANZOS, GRAPEFRUIT, GREEN LEAVES, GREEN TEA, GUAVA, LENTILS, LICORICE ROOT, MANGO, MUESLI, NETTLE, NUTS, OKRA, PAPAYA, PASTA, PEANUT BUTTER, PUMPKIN SEED, SAFFLOWER AND SUNFLOWER OILS, SEA VEGETABLE, SEEDS, SHIITAKE, SPINACH, STRAWBERRY, SWEET POTATO, TEMPEH, TOFU, TOMATO, YAM

Acquired immune deficiency syndrome (A.I.D.S.) is a group of disorders related to previous infection by the human immunodeficiency virus (H.I.V.). Blood, vaginal fluid, semen and breast milk of people infected by H.I.V. contain enough virus to infect others. Everyone is potentially at risk of infection, therefore the most vulnerable groups are people with multiple sexual partners, intravenous drug users who share needles and syringes, and recipients of blood products in countries that do not employ scrupulous screening procedures. The incubation period is 1 to 6 months after infection by the virus. Progression from infection to being "antibody positive" is not fully understood. The infection is divided into four groups:

● primary H.I.V. infection;
● asymptomatic phase;
● persistent generalized lymph node enlargement (P.G.L.);
● full-blown A.I.D.S., involving opportunistic lung infections, skin cancer (Kaposi's sarcoma), and lymphatic cancer.

Prevention

The most important preventative measure you can take is to use safer sexual practices if your partner's sexual history is unknown to you. This involves taking steps to prevent contact with sexual fluids—for example, by using condoms or avoiding penetrative sex. Intravenous drug users should never share injecting materials. When traveling in developing countries, it is advisable to carry disposable syringes and needles with you, in case of emergency.

Your diet should include plenty of foods that help prevent viral infection, such as garlic, Brazil nut, and echinacea, and that strengthen the immune system, such as shiitake and beet.

Management

A.I.D.S. is a serious problem all over the world and, although a cure remains elusive, there are simple nutritional and lifestyle changes that are proven to make life easier for sufferers. H.I.V. infection, nutritional status and immune function are intimately connected. The relationship between H.I.V. infection and food is important because strategies that improve nutritional status have a beneficial effect on the course of the disease. The outcome with drug therapy is less hopeful in people with compromised nutrition, whereas good nutrition greatly improves the chances of longer survival.

In Africa, A.I.D.S. was first known as "slim disease" because the condition caused rapid weight loss, leading to early death. The wasting associated with A.I.D.S. is caused by inefficient absorption of food, excessive loss of nutrients (mainly through chronic diarrhea), and less efficient use of nutrients that are absorbed. Once the disorder has been diagnosed, it is possible to maintain the weight of the patient through intensive feeding regimes. When the condition has been stabilized, patients can regain some of the weight they have lost and start to build up the reserves that will make it easier to cope with the condition. Avoiding, reversing, or delaying the wasting process requires adopting measures involving all the ways in which food is converted into energy and body mass.

Food intake H.I.V.-positive individuals often have a poor appetite, because of inefficient absorption of nutrients, secondary infections, the side effects of certain drugs, fungal infections of the mouth or esophagus (which makes eating and swallowing difficult), and enlargement of the liver or spleen (which gives a false feeling of fullness). Depression may also be a factor. Therefore, the quality of the food that the sufferer eats is of vital importance to compensate for the lack of quantity.

Absorption The food we eat is broken down in the small intestine, and nutrients are absorbed through the gut wall. This important process can be hampered by H.I.V. infection, and is also disturbed by diarrhea, which causes food to pass through the digestive system too quickly. Antibiotics used to destroy harmful bacteria may also kill friendly bacteria that live in the gut and support the digestive process by aiding absorption and manufacturing vitamins.

To boost nutrient absorption, it is best to avoid dairy produce and include foods such as apple, grapefruit, garbanzos, amaranth leaves, potatoes, fennel, arugula, globe artichoke, Belgian endive, and the medicinal herbs peppermint, thyme, catnip, and calendula.

Metabolism Our metabolic rate determines how quickly we expend the energy we obtain from food. It is often raised in H.I.V. infection and is responsible for much of the fatigue and lethargy felt by people with A.I.D.S. H.I.V. infection alters metabolism, with less protein being manufactured by the liver and more being broken down and used for energy. The result is muscle wasting and a decline in "lean body mass." To maintain energy and stabilize metabolism, the diet should be high in complex carbohydrates, vegetable proteins, and fiber, and low in fat. All produce should be fresh, organic, and unprocessed.

Foods rich in zinc, vitamins A and C, and bioflavonoids are beneficial because they inhibit the activity of viruses and bacteria. Licorice root and echinacea both support the immune system and enhance many aspects of immune function, as well as inhibiting the spread of viral infection. Grapefruit, pumpkin seed, Brazil nut, nettle, black cumin, borage, sweet potato, yam, tomato, and shiitake act specifically against immunodeficiency. Important immuno-stimulants include okra, beet, spinach, curly kale, guava, safflower and sunflower oil, evening primrose oil, sea vegetable, peanut butter, and marigold.

The stress factor

The psychological and emotional stress following a diagnosis of H.I.V. may contribute to the progression of the disease because negative emotions have a detrimental effect on the immune response. However, positive emotions enhance appropriate immune responses, so involvement in pleasurable, creative activity, and spending more time in the company of close friends and loved ones are both positive ways of improving immune function.

SUGGESTED RECIPES FOR H.I.V. AND A.I.D.S.

nettle and lime tisane (page 187), nettle and sweet potato mash (page 187), grapefruit and peppermint fizz (page 191), grapefruit salad (page 191), avocado smoothie (page 197), avocado, watercress, and cumin salad (page 197), brazil nuts and sun-dried tomatoes with beans (page 201), broiled endive and brazil nut salad (page 201), shiitake salad (page 221), healing soup (page 260), tofu balls (page 266), artichoke hearts, fava beans, and shiitake (page 268), okra in sweet and sour tamarind sauce (page 272), shepherdess' pie (page 272), carrot 'n' beet salad (page 275), tropical sunshine salad (page 277), wild rice salad (page 277), heart warmer (page 282), vegetable cocktail—*above* (page 283), immuni-tea (page 285), stress relief (page 286).

stress and chronic fatigue syndrome

SUPERFOODS FOR STRESS: BEANS, BORAGE, BROCCOLI, CABBAGES, CARROTS, GRAPEFRUIT, GREEN LEAVES, LAVENDER, LEMON BALM, LENTILS, LICORICE ROOT, MANGO, MUESLI, NUTS, OATS, ORANGE, PAPAYA, RICE, STRAWBERRY, TEMPEH, TOFU
SUPERFOODS FOR C.F.S.: AVOCADO, BANANAS, BEANS, BEET, BELL PEPPER, BLACK CURRANT, BORAGE, CAMOMILE, CLEAVERS, ECHINACEA, GRAPEFRUIT, GREEN LEAVES, LICORICE ROOT, LIVE SOY YOGURT, MUESLI, NUTS, OKRA, PAPAYA, PEAS, RICE, TEMPEH, TOFU, WHEATGRASS

STRESS

The relationship between stress and ill health is well documented, but stress levels vary enormously from person to person, as does each individual's ability to cope. To deal effectively with stress, it is necessary to take account of these variations, and to remember that the immune system does not work in isolation. It is affected by thoughts, actions, and emotional responses as well as by disease, environment, general lifestyle, age, and genetic predisposition.

Stress hormones such as epinephrine and cortisol enable the body to cope with stressful situations, but if they are released in excess or over too long a period, they inhibit (and can damage) the immune response. This means that during periods of chronic stress, exposure to pathogens is more likely to cause disease.

Prevention and management

Like rest and relaxation, good nutrition can reduce the effects of stress in our lives and enhance immune function. Foods high in vitamins A and C, and zinc and selenium are particularly helpful. Other foods and herbs for stress relief include Belgian endive, cauliflower, artichoke, banana, sesame seed, oats, corn, wheat germ, borage, lemon balm, lavender, and licorice root.

CHRONIC FATIGUE SYNDROME (C.F.S.)

This poorly understood syndrome is also known as myalgic encephalomyelitis (ME) or post-viral syndrome, and may relate to the immune system's difficulty in handling viral infections when already overburdened by "environmental" stress. It does not seem to be related to any specific viral infection, but can persist for months or even years. Common symptoms include severe fatigue after minimal exertion that is not relieved by rest, generalized aches and pains, depressed mood, recurrent sore throats, swollen lymph nodes, headache, mild fever, difficulty adjusting to changes in temperature, and gastro-intestinal disturbance. There may also be a variety of inexplicable neurological symptoms.

Prevention and management

In addition to the stress prevention strategies above, the best way to prevent or manage C.F.S. is through detoxification and following a diet rich in foods that enhance resistance to disease and support immunity. To boost the immunity drink plenty of pure water and eat a variety of fresh fruit and vegetables. Choose foods rich in vitamins B5 and C, essential fatty acids, calcium, magnesium, and zinc.

SUGGESTED RECIPES FOR STRESS AND C.F.S.

Stress: spiced nettle soup (page 187), brazil nut salad (page 201), scrambled tofu (page 258), muesli (page 259), creamy cauliflower soup (page 261), samosa parcels (page 264), toasted nuts and seeds (page 264), amaranth and tofu puffs (page 268), artichoke hearts, fava beans and shiitake (page 268), broiled endive and provençale-style kidney beans (page 271), blackberry cream (page 280), creamy mango (page 280), stress relief (page 286).

C.F.S.: grapefruit salad (page 191), shiitake with sea vegetable (page 221), sweet chestnuts and kumquats (page 273), carrot 'n' beet salad (page 275), tomato cocktail (page 283), immuni-tea (page 285), sleepy time (page 286).

depression and anxiety

SUPERFOODS FOR DEPRESSION: AVOCADO, BANANA, BEANS, BORAGE, ENDIVE, GREEN LEAVES, LICORICE ROOT, MANGO, MUESLI, PEAS, RED PEPPER, RICE, SOYA PRODUCTS, TAHINI, YEAST EXTRACT; SUPERFOODS FOR ANXIETY: APRICOT, ARTICHOKE, BEANS, BUTTERNUT SQUASH, CAULIFLOWER, CAMOMILE, GRAPEFRUIT, GREEN LEAVES, LAVENDER, LEMON BALM, OATS, OKRA, PASSION FLOWER, POTATO, RED PEPPER, ROSEMARY, ST JOHN'S WORT, SWEET POTATO, TEMPEH, TOFU, WALNUT, YEAST EXTRACT

DEPRESSION

There are two forms of depression: psychotic and reactive. Those suffering bi-polar disorder also experience periods of depression. Psychotic depression is a severe emotional disturbance more common in middle age. The sufferer may become agitated, or profoundly withdrawn and lethargic, and may experience hallucinations and delusions. There are disturbances in bowel habit, appetite and sleep, and a real risk of suicide. Reactive depression is a reaction to traumatic events such as bereavement and may be accompanied by anxiety, and disturbed appetite and sleep. The underlying causes are not completely understood but contributing factors include physical disorder (such as underactive thyroid), diet, food allergy, smoking, drugs and lifestyle.

Prevention and management

Measures to prevent or manage depression include taking regular exercise; avoiding cigarettes, alcohol and drinks containing caffeine; using alternatives to oral contraception; eliminating food allergens and additives (particularly aspartame); and eating regular meals with plenty of fresh fruits and vegetables (to stabilize blood-sugar levels). To optimize your nutritional state, eat foods high in B and C vitamins, and magnesium and tryptophan. St John's wort is an effective herbal antidepressant, and herbs that support the adrenals, such as borage and licorice root, are also valuable.

ANXIETY

Anxiety states are dominated by fast pulse, sweating, butterflies in the stomach, light headedness, and feelings of apprehension and fear. Chronic anxiety takes a toll on the immune system and can lead to physical illness, such as irritable bowel syndrome. The cause can be hormonal, or linked to overactive thyroid and premenstrual syndrome, or a traumatic event. It can also be a symptom of psychiatric illness, such as depression or dementia.

Prevention and management

Once hormonal imbalance has been ruled out, anxiety can often be managed with foods that strengthen the nervous system, such as oats, potato, sweet potato, butternut squash, okra, red pepper, Brussels sprouts, cauliflower, artichoke, spring greens, curly kale, apricot, grapefruit, walnut, tempeh, butterbeans, haricot beans, pinto beans and yeast extract. Herbs to calm the nerves include camomile, lemon balm, rosemary, lavender and passion flower.

SUGGESTED RECIPES FOR DEPRESSION & ANXIETY

Depression: pasta, pesto and shiitake (page 221), italian butterbean soup (page 261), hummus with crudités and warm pitta bread (page 262), baba ganoush (page 264), paella (page 268), chinese salad (page 276), baked apples (page 278), calming tea (page 284), licorice mix (page 286), pick-me-up (page 286), stress relief (page 286).

Anxiety: curly kale parcels (page 183), ruby red melon salad (page 258), porridge with dried fruit and quinoa (page 258), creamy cauliflower soup (page 261), spicy moroccan soup (page 262), rocket salad (page 275), apricot and ginger (page 280), camomile tonic (page 284), sleepy time (page 286).

attention-deficit hyperactivity disorder

SUPERFOODS FOR ADHD: AVOCADO, BANANA, BEANS, BEET, BORAGE, CARROTS, CAMOMILE, CHICKPEAS, CRANBERRY, FENNEL, KALE, LAVENDER, LENTILS, MINT, OATS, PAPAYA, PINEAPPLE, POTATO, PUMPKIN, QUINOA, RED PEPPER, ROSEMARY, ST JOHN'S WORT, SESAME SEEDS, SPINACH, TEMPEH, WALNUTS

ADHD is a developmental disorder defined as "the coexistence of attention problems and hyperactivity, with each behavior occurring infrequently alone." It is a chronic disability affecting as many as 10 per cent of boys and 4 per cent of girls. Children in North America and Europe are more likely be affected than those in Africa and the Middle East. Half of all sufferers continue to have symptoms as adults.

The causes of ADHD are not certain, but consensus is that it affects specific areas of the brain, making problem solving, planning ahead, understanding other people's actions, and self control more difficult. Symptoms typically start before the age of seven and include exaggerated inattention, hyperactivity, and impulsiveness. The child is easily distracted, forgetful, and frequently switches from one activity to another, finding it difficult to focus on any one thing and becoming quickly bored.

Affected children may suffer from learning difficulties (despite above-average intelligence) and be prone to self-destructive behavior. Recent research suggests that children with ADHD move around incessantly because it helps them concentrate.

Most children exhibit some ADHD-like symptoms from time to time as part of the normal process of growing up.

Before making a diagnosis of ADHD, therefore, it is important to consider social causes (such as bereavement or parental divorce) for persistently difficult behavior. In addition, there may be certain physical causes, such as chronic ear infection that causes hearing loss; epilepsy; specific learning difficulties; anxiety or depression; and drug or alcohol use.

Unrecognized, ADHD often leads to a chaotic adult life, involving drug and alcohol abuse and severe psychiatric illness, including depression, anxiety, and bipolar disorder.

Risk factors

There are a number of factors thought to contribute to the development of ADHD. Drinking alcohol and smoking during pregnancy; premature birth; and infections during pregnancy, at birth, and in early childhood are all linked to higher risk of a child being born with ADHD. It is also thought that some genetic defects may cause a decrease in the production of the brain's neurotransmitters dopamine and serotonin, and thus increase the likelihood of developing the condition.

In addition, studies show that food allergies and allergies to specific food additives increase the level of hyperactivity in some children. Addiction to sugar—combined with an inability to maintain balanced blood-sugar levels—may also contribute. Researchers also report that overexposure to computers, television, and other screens seems to increase symptoms; other research suggests that exposure to Wi-Fi frequencies can trigger hyperactivity and attention deficit.

Management

Stimulant medication (which, paradoxically, calms the symptoms of ADHD) has been used for some years with varying success, but recent studies suggest that drug treatment is no better than other forms of therapy in the long term. A combination of medication, behavior modification, lifestyle change, and counseling forms the mainstay of conventional treatment, but natural approaches also have an important role to play.

Artificial additives, especially sunset yellow FCF, quinoline yellow, carmoisine, allura red, tartrazine, and ponceau 4R, have been shown to exacerbate ADHD behavior in children. These are found in many convenience foods, drinks, candies, and cookies. Food allergy to peanuts, shellfish, cow milk, chocolate, oranges, wheat, corn, yeast, soy, and eggs may also play a role. It can help to avoid foods and drinks containing natural salicylates. These include: apples, apricots, blackberries, currants, cherries, grapes and raisins, gooseberries, raspberries, strawberries, nectarines, peaches, plums and prunes, oranges, cucumber, tomatoes (including ketchup), and almonds. (Note that aspirin contains salicylates, too.)

As with all food sensitivities and allergies, it's rarely necessary or appropriate to apply a blanket exclusion of a whole range of foods, and a simple exclusion diet (see pages 288–9), followed by reintroduction of suspect foods one by one is usually enough to identify particular culprits.

If your child has ADHD, give them plenty of fresh, organic fruit and vegetables and include as many organic whole grains as possible. Use non-hydrogenated, unsaturated fats, and offer foods containing omega-3 fatty acids (oily fish, nuts, seeds), but limit those containing saturated fats and trans fats. Also steer clear of foods with a high GI count (see page 253). Read labels and avoid food additives. Limit your child's sugar intake and check for food intolerance, especially to wheat or dairy.

SUGGESTED RECIPES FOR ADHD

Oatmeal with dried fruit and quinoa (page 258), beans on toast (page 258), yogurt with fruit (page 259), healing soup (page 260), pumpkin soup (page 261), shiitake mushroom soup (page 261), welsh leek and potato soup (page 262), hummus with crudités (page 262), grilled red peppers (page 263), baba ganoush (page 264), toasted tempeh (page 264), marinated olives (page 264), artichoke hearts, fava beans and shiitake (page 268), asparagus asian style (page 269), spinach bouillabaisse (page 271), winter hot pot (page 272), khichuri (page 273), lemon rice (page 273), hasselbach potatoes (page 274), spring greens with macadamia nuts (page 274), swiss chard and juniper berries (page 274), carrot and beetroot salad (page 275), provençal mesclun salad (page 275), catalan salad (page 276), chinese salad (page 276), florence fennel salad (page 276), green lentil salad (page 276), salad with sorrel and tempeh (page 276), tropical sunshine salad (page 277), passion fruit sorbet (page 278), nectarine surprise (page 279), tropical fruit salad (page 279), caribbean smoothie (page 280), carrot and lemon with garlic (page 280), cranberry spritzer (page 280), heart warmer (page 282), height of passion (page 282), papaya power (page 283), piña colada (page 283), calming tea (page 284), green tea with mint (page 285), pick-me-up (page 286), stress relief (page 286).

cancer

SUPERFOODS FOR CANCER: AVOCADO, BEET, BEANS, BELL PEPPER, BERRIES, BRAZIL NUT, BROCCOLI, BUTTERNUT SQUASH, CABBAGE, CALENDULA, CARROT, CELERY SALT, CLEAVERS, CURLY KALE, ECHINACEA, GARBANZOS, GARLIC, GRAPEFRUIT, GRAPES, GRAPESEED, GREEN LEAVES, GUAVA, LEMON, LENTILS, MANGO, MUNG BEAN SPROUTS, NETTLE, NUTS, OLIVES, ORANGE, PAPAYA, PASTA, POTATOES, PULSES, RICE, VEGETABLE OILS, SEEDS, SHIITAKE, SPICES, SUN-DRIED TOMATOES, SWEET POTATO, TEMPEH, TOFU, VIOLET, WHOLEMEAL BREAD, WILD RICE

Research into the nature of cancer has not yet clarified exactly what it is that turns a normal cell into a cancer cell. Although we know that carcinogens such as chemicals, radiation, tobacco, asbestos, and viruses can cause tumors, it is not known precisely how or why. But there is growing evidence that nutritional, social psychological, and environmental factors play a role in cancer.

Evidence linking food and nutrition to cancer risk is growing and has been collected over a number of years by comparing different diets with cancer rates. There are big differences in incidence and death from cancer in different parts of the world, but specialists have identified general patterns. Developing countries tend to have high rates of cancers of the upper digestive tract, liver and cervix, whereas developed countries have relatively high rates of hormone-related cancers, and cancers of the colon and rectum.

There is great variation in the length and intensity of exposure to particular environmental carcinogens that will trigger cancerous changes. It is also possible that simultaneous exposure to a combination of carcinogens produces cancer where one alone would have been relatively harmless, and that exposure to stress may alter the body's response to different carcinogens. Genetic factors play a role in some cancers, and some carcinogens—such as free radicals—can originate within the body. Some tumors are benign (non-spreading), but malignant tumors invade surrounding tissues and spread via blood and lymph to form metastases

(secondary tumors). There is increasing understanding surrounding the role of viruses in cancer formation. In other mammals (such as chickens, rabbits, mice, and cats) several tumors are known to be caused by viruses, but the picture in humans is less clear. However, there is good evidence that viruses cause cancers in humans (including cervical and liver cell cancer, lymphoma, and leukemia).

There are many different types of cancer, each one with its individual features, but all cancers sooner or later disturb normal body function. The danger signals for malignant disease include a change in bowel or bladder habit, sores that won't heal, unusual bleeding or discharge, newly discovered lumps, obvious changes in skin moles or warts, a persistent cough and/or hoarseness, coughing up blood, and, very importantly, loss of appetite and unexplained weight loss.

Prevention

It has been estimated that in the U.S. 30 per cent of all cancer deaths are related to dietary factors, and that 30 to 40 per cent of cancer cases throughout the world are potentially preventable with simple changes to diet and lifestyle. It is now beyond doubt that the most effective way to reduce cancer risk is to stop smoking, eat plenty of fresh fruit and vegetables, and limit exposure to occupational and environmental carcinogens. Environmental carcinogens are usually man-made and fall into five distinct groups—additives, dyes and coal tar, pollutant chemicals, fumes, and radiation. Not all of these will inevitably trigger cancer in all cases, but it is worth remembering that many carcinogens cause damage by weakening the immune system and so may be indirectly responsible for causing cancerous changes. Therefore, in cancer prevention and management it is very important to keep the immune system as strong as possible by adopting a healthy lifestyle, and eating a diet rich in energy and vital nutrients.

For cancer prevention, choose a plant-based diet that includes a rich variety of vegetables, fruits, nuts, legumes, and minimally processed starchy foods. Eat at least five portions of seasonal, organic fresh fruit and vegetables daily, all year round, and at least five portions a day of grains, legumes, roots, and tubers. Use modest amounts of vegetable oils (mainly olive, walnut, grapeseed, and safflower and sunflower oils), and avoid animal fats altogether. Use herbs, spices, celery salt, and soy sauce to season foods, and limit consumption of salted and pickled foods and table salt.

Choose organic foods free of additives, pesticides, and other chemicals. Avoid alcohol, meat, and dairy products, and if animal protein is eaten, choose fish, organic poultry, or meat from non-domesticated animals. Choose minimally processed foods and limit your consumption of refined sugar. Avoid being over- or underweight, stop smoking and take an hour's exercise daily.

Immune system boosters to guard against cancer include garlic, beet, grapefruit, curly kale, nettle, avocado, Brazil nut, cleavers, calendula, violet, echinacea and shiitake mushroom,

among many others. Also important are foods that contain vitamins A (sweet potato, carrot, red bell pepper, green leaves, mango, papaya, butternut squash), C (guava, red and green bell peppers, green leaves, black currants, papaya, mango, lemon, orange, cabbage, broccoli), E (avocado, nuts, sun-dried tomatoes, sweet potato, sunflower seeds), zinc (aduki beans, tofu, tempeh, lentils, muesli, garbanzos, tahini, pumpkin seeds) and selenium (beans, Brazil nuts, lentils, pasta, sunflower seeds, mushrooms, wholemeal bread), carotenoids (yellow and orange fruits and vegetables), bioflavonoids (especially anthocyanin in dark-colored berries such as red grapes, blueberries, cranberries, and hawthorn berries, and quercetin in calendula) and the fatty acids found in walnuts.

Management

In the early stages of cancer, the most effective dietary approach is to detoxify the system (see detox diet page 288). Later on in the course of the disease, freshly made juices, smoothies, and tisanes are particularly helpful because they contain a high concentration of nutrients (together with antioxidants and other immune system boosters), but are nevertheless easy to digest. Half of the diet should be fresh fruits, especially grapes, which are detoxifying and also contain immune-enhancing anthocyanin. The diet should also be rich in complex carbohydrates—for example, from potatoes, sweet potatoes, rice, and wild rice, and essential fatty acids, such as from walnuts. Good sources of protein are legumes, mung bean sprouts, tofu, mushrooms (especially shiitake), and tempeh.

SUGGESTED RECIPES FOR CANCER

Green leafy salad (page 183), nettle and lime tisane (page 187), spiced nettle soup (page 187), grapefruit salad (page 191), avocado smoothie (page 197), oriental salad with tempeh (page 209), baked tomatoes on toast (page 258), black-eye pea and wild marjoram soup (page 261), shiitake mushroom soup (page 261), guacamole (page 266), tofu balls (page 266), tomato and cucumber canapés (page 266), artichoke hearts, fava beans, and shiitake (page 268), casserole de puy (page 268), arugula salad (page 275), carrot 'n' beet salad (page 275), wild rice salad (page 277), tropical fruit salad (page 279), green party (page 280), caribbean smoothie (page 280), greek casserole (page 271).guava and apple—left (page 282), tea for glands (page 287), tea for the skin (page 287).

ischaemic (coronary) heart disease

SUPERFOODS FOR ISCHEMIC HEART DISEASE: ALFALFA, ALMOND, APRICOT, BELL PEPPER, BLACK-EYED PEA, BRAZIL NUT, BROCCOLI, BUTTER BEAN, CANTALOUPE MELON, FLAXSEED, GARBANZOS, GARLIC, GINGER, GREEN LEAVES, GUAVA, HARICOT BEANS, HAWTHORN BERRIES, HAZELNUT, LEMON, LENTILS, MACADAMIA NUT, MANGETOUT PEAS, MANGO, MELON, MUESLI, OKRA, ONION, ORANGE, PAPAYA, PINEAPPLE, PINE NUT, PINTO BEAN, PUMPKIN SEED, RICE, SESAME SEED, SOY BEAN, SUNFLOWER SEED, SWISS CHARD, TAHINI, TEMPEH, TOFU, YAM

Ischemic heart disease is the partial blockage of the coronary arteries by atherosclerosis and thrombosis, leading to poor blood supply to the heart muscle. It is one of the commonest causes of illness and disability and the main cause of death in the Western world. Its major symptom is angina, and the worst outcome is myocardial infarction (heart attack).

Risk factors include smoking, high blood pressure, high blood cholesterol, a diet high in saturated fats and salt and low in fiber, obesity, diabetes, gout, emotional stress, lack of exercise, social deprivation, oral contraception, genetic predisposition, and age.

Prevention

Avoid smoking, alcohol, and coffee completely. Daily gentle exercise, such as walking, is beneficial. Stress is dangerous and should be avoided where possible (or counteracted with plenty of relaxation). High blood cholesterol, triglyceride (fat) and low- and very low-density lipoproteins (L.D.L.s and V.L.D.L.s) are associated with the build-up of fatty deposits in the blood vessels that can lead to coronary artery blockage. Saturated fats (such as animal fats) make things worse, but monounsaturated (mostly oleic acid

from olive oil) and polyunsaturated fats (from nuts, seeds, and kernels) are associated with more favorable blood-fat levels and thus reduced risk of heart disease. "Trans-fats" have the same negative effect on blood-fat levels as saturated fats. Obesity, alcohol, and refined sugar also contribute to raised blood-fat levels.

Avoiding red meat, eggs, milk, and cheese is desirable, and a decrease in overall fat intake by avoiding "table fats" (such as butter) and foods containing invisible fat (such as mayonnaise, cakes, and rich sauces and soups) can make a major contribution to long-term cardiac health. The diet should be high in complex carbohydrates and fiber with plenty of fresh fruit and vegetables.

The risk of heart attack is also reduced by high levels of the antioxidant glutathione which plays a significant role in blood fat metabolism, the regulation of blood pressure and the control of inflammation. Since it can only be made within the body, the way to ensure adequate glutathione is to eat foods containing the "precursors" from which it is made, particularly the amino acid cysteine. It is found red pepper, garlic, onions, broccoli, brussels sprouts, oats, wheatgerm and most animal foods. Silymarin from milk thistle also helps replenish body glutathione.

Management

Angina and heart attack are serious conditions that require professional medical attention. Orthodox management is to encourage gentle exercise and maintain a normal lifestyle while reducing relevant risk factors, and taking drugs such as oral nitrates, beta-blockers, and nifedipine. People at high risk of myocardial infarction may be offered a coronary bypass operation.

The therapeutic goal is to improve blood supply and nutrition to the heart muscle. Healthy eating plays a vital role in the management of heart disease. The aim is to create a diet that provides beneficial nutrients without clogging up the tissues and blood vessels with sugars, fats, and additives. Fresh fruits, vegetables, nuts, seeds, pulses, and whole grain foods reduces

SUGGESTED RECIPES FOR HEART DISEASE

Baked beet salad (page 179), brazil nuts and sun-dried tomatoes with beans (page 201), oriental salad with tempeh (page 209), oatmeal with dried fruit and quinoa (page 258), muesli (page 259), italian butterbean soup (page 261), shiitake mushroom soup (page 261), spicy moroccan soup (page 262), paella (page 268), french onion tart (page 271), okra with sweet and sour tamarind sauce (page 272), provençal mesclun salad (page 275), chinese salad (page 276), orange mango salad (page 276), baked apples (page 278), tropical fruit salad (page 279), mango and lime (page 282), papaya power (page 283), vegetable cocktail (page 283), circulation booster (page 284), green tea with mint—*above* (page 285), heart chai (page 285), si c (page 286).

blood-cholesterol levels and improves the blood-fat balance. Alfalfa sprouts and leaves decrease blood-cholesterol levels and reduce fatty plaque formation in blood vessels. Bromelain from pineapple inhibits blood clot formation and also breaks down fatty plaques in the arteries. Onions, garlic, and ginger have the same effect, and ginger and garlic also lower levels of blood cholesterol and fat. Magnesium deficiency causes coronary artery spasm and irregular heart beat. Good sources of this mineral include Brazil nuts, okra, melon and sunflower seeds, tahini, Swiss chard, brown rice, muesli, tempeh, tofu, and other soy bean products.

Carnitine is a vitamin-like compound made in the liver, kidney, and brain. It is made from the amino acid lysine (with the help of iron and vitamin C), and is effective in treating heart disease because of its ability to boost the metabolism of saturated fats and cholesterol. The heart normally stores more carnitine than it needs but lack of oxygen in ischemic heart disease causes depletion of carnitine stores. Foods rich in lysine and iron (such as tempeh, lentils, muesli, peas, tahini, garbanzos, beans, nuts, and seeds) help to replenish carnitine. Good sources of vitamin C include guava, bell pepper, green leaves, mangetout peas, broccoli, papaya, mango, and citrus fruits.

People with heart disease often have a deficiency of coenzymes because their nutritional intake does not keep pace with the increased needs of their tissues. Coenzymes CoA and Q10 are particularly beneficial to the heart because they are involved in the transport of fatty acids to and from cells and in the conversion of fat into energy. Coenzymes have many components in their structure that cannot be synthesized in the body, and which must therefore be supplied in the diet. B-complex vitamins are particularly important in this regard, and good sources of B vitamins include muesli, yeast extract, beans, peas, tahini, soy products such as tempeh, and green leaves.

Hawthorn berries and flowering tops are valuable herbal remedies for heart and circulation disorders. They strengthen the heart muscle and lower blood pressure and blood cholesterol levels. They contain anthocyanoid bioflavonoids, which relax the smooth muscle of the artery walls, thus dilating the blood vessels that feed the heart muscle, and increasing the supply of nutrients and oxygen. Garlic is an excellent blood cleanser and thinner, and, if used regularly over a period of time, guards against the formation of fatty deposits in the blood vessels. It can also help to keep blood-cholesterol levels under control.

obesity

SUPERFOODS FOR OBESITY: AMARANTH LEAVES, APPLE, APRICOT, ARUGULA, ASPARAGUS, AVOCADO, BANANA, BEANS, BEET, BELGIAN ENDIVE, BERRIES, BUTTERNUT SQUASH, CARAWAY, CARROT, CAULIFLOWER, CELERY SEEDS, CAMOMILE, CUCUMBER, CURLY KALE, FENNEL, GARLIC, GINGER, GREEN TEA, GRAPE, GRAPEFRUIT, KIWI, LEMON, LENTILS, LETTUCE, MANGO, MELON, MUESLI, NETTLE, ONION, PAPAYA, PEPPERMINT, PINEAPPLE, QUINOA, RED PEPPER, SPINACH, TOMATO, WATERCRESS, WILD RICE, YEAST EXTRACT

According to the World Health Organisation (WHO), there are more than a billion overweight adults in the world—at least 300 million of whom are clinically obese (that's three times more clinically obese people than in 1980). Particularly worrying is an increasing trend in childhood obesity: being overweight increases the risk of serious chronic disease and disability.

The WHO guidelines break down clinical obesity into class one, class two, and class three, allocated according to your Body Mass Index (BMI). The BMI is a measure that relates your weight to your height. It is calculated by dividing your weight by the square of your height. So: your weight in pounds times 703 divided by the square of your height in inches. For example, if a person weighs 165 pounds and is 68 inches tall, their BMI is 165 x 703 / (68 x 68), giving 25. A BMI over 30 is considered obese. From 30 to 34.9 is class one obesity, from 35 to 39.9 is class two, and a BMI of more than 40 is class three.

Obesity is a complex condition caused by overconsumption of energy-dense, nutrient-poor foods high in saturated fats and sugars (such as burgers and fries), combined with a lack of physical activity. As with many other chronic conditions, it does not go away by itself, and there is no quick fix available.

Many experts believe that the profound changes seen in society, local communities, and individual families over recent decades have given rise to the current obesity epidemic.

Prevention during childhood

Children need to learn to care about what they eat and to know what is in the food they consume, where it comes from, and why it is considered good or bad for health. Taking time to prepare meals together brings an added benefit: children who learn to cook are more likely to cook for themselves in adulthood rather than relying on ready-made and fast food.

Making some form of exercise, dance, or sport a daily family activity is good for bonding and well-being, and it helps establish a healthy habit of physical activity. Having less weight to carry makes exercise increasingly enjoyable and helps provide further motivation to eat lighter meals.

Gentle weight-loss guidelines

To be sustainable, weight loss needs to be part of an integrated approach to daily eating habits and behavior patterns. The easiest way to begin is to make positive changes to your diet. First, look at what you eat, instead of how much you eat. Switching from energy-dense, fat filled, low-nutrition foods to lighter, fiber-containing, vegetable-based, nutrient-rich foods provides plenty of energy and nourishment to help your body detox, digest, and function better—which will help you lose weight. Eat six small meals a day, rather than three big meals and three snacks (see box, opposite).

Try to base your diet on fresh, unprocessed fruit and vegetables, nuts, and whole grains—you can eat as many of these as you like. Cut down the amount of fatty, sugary foods you eat—no more cakes, candy, cream, desserts, white bread, cornflakes, sugary breakfast cereals, French fries, potato chips, fast foods, and so on. A good idea is to wean yourself off sugar gradually—eat a little less each day until you are down to no added sugar or sugary snacks at all. Move away from eating foods that contain saturated animal-based fats. Instead opt for unsaturated vegetable-oil-based fats. Try to eat no more than two eggs a week, and steer clear of alcohol until you reach your target weight. This has more to do with how it affects your mood and motivation, rather than its empty calories.

However, for sustained weight management, your diet has to be something you can stick to in the long term, so on special occasions (and certainly no more than once a week), treat yourself to something from the forbidden list. If you feel you're denying yourself everything, you won't keep to your healthy eating plan.

In addition, try to keep your blood-sugar levels stable. Dips in blood sugar cause energy slumps—and these often send you reaching for a sweet, quick-fix snack. Choose foods with a low GI count (see pages 253–5) and eat six, smaller regular meals to make sure you keep your energy steady. Be prepared for hunger attacks and cravings in the early stages of weight loss and keep rice cakes, raw carrots, or fresh fruit on hand.

SUGGESTED DIET PLAN FOR OBESITY

The following suggested daily diet plan provides proven, effective suggestions for meals that help you achieve lasting weight change. Remember: the key is to eat more, smaller meals with no snacks in between, instead of fewer, bigger meals with lots of snacks.

ON WAKING

A glass of cold water.

BREAKFAST

1 glass of freshly squeezed grapefruit juice; 1 portion of sugar-free muesli with probiotic plain yogurt (dairy or soy); 1 banana; 1 big portion of fresh or frozen berries; 1 hot drink (tea, coffee, or herbal tea, such as ginger tea with a slice of lemon).

MID-MORNING MEAL

1 glass of cold water, 1 small cup of fennel tea, followed by a cup of regular tea or coffee, if desired; 2 pieces of fresh fruit (such as apple, orange, apricot, banana, or a small bunch of grapes); 1 handful of nuts and seeds (such as almonds, Brazil nuts, hazelnuts or pumpkin seeds); 1 crispbread with vegetable margarine, marmite, vegetable sandwich spread, or honey; 1 small piece of dark chocolate.

LUNCH

1 glass of cold water; 1 piece of grapefruit; 1 big portion of seasonal salad or steamed vegetables; 1 piece of wholemeal bread or 1 portion of rice; 1 small portion of fish, poultry, or seared tofu; 2 or 3 pieces of fresh fruit; coffee, tea, or herbal tea (such as nettle tea with slice of lemon), if desired.

AFTERNOON MEAL

1 glass of cold water; 1 small cup of fennel tea, followed by a cup of regular tea or coffee, if desired; 1 piece of fresh fruit; 3 pieces of raw food (eg. carrot, celery, fennel, tomato, radish, cucumber, cauliflower); 1 small handful of nuts or seeds; crispbreads or sugar-free crackers with or without vegetable margarine, marmite, or honey.

APERITIF

1 glass of water; 1 vegetable juice or smoothie (see recipes, pages 280–83); rice cakes.

DINNER

1 glass of water; 1 generous portion of vegetable soup (see recipe, page 260; you can make a large batch and refrigerate it for several days); 1 generous portion of steamed or grilled vegetables, with a small portion of steamed or grilled fish, meat, or vegetarian/vegan alternative; 1 small piece of dark chocolate.

BEFORE BEDTIME

1 cup of camomile tea; 1 or 2 rice cakes.

diabetes

SUPERFOODS FOR DIABETES: AVOCADO, BLUEBERRY, BROCCOLI, GREEN VEGETABLES, HAWTHORN, LEGUMES, MINT, MISO, NUTS AND SEEDS, OATS, ONION, PUMPKIN, QUINOA, RASPBERRY, RED PEPPER, ROOT VEGETABLES, ROSEHIPS, SHIITAKE MUSHROOMS, TEMPEH, TOMATO, WHEATGERM AND BRAN, WHEATGRASS, WHOLE GRAINS, YARROW.

Diabetes mellitus (sugar diabetes) is a metabolic disorder in which either the body doesn't make enough of the hormone insulin (type 1 diabetes), or body cells do not respond to the insulin that the body does produce (type 2 diabetes). Insulin ensures that your body's cells take up blood sugar (from the carbohydrates you eat) in order to create energy. If your cells do not absorb enough blood sugar, it accumulates in your blood, causing hyperglycaemia—or high blood sugar—which in turn causes a range of health problems. (A third type of diabetes, known as "gestational diabetes," affects some women during pregnancy—even those without a history of the condition.)

Approximately 85 percent of people with diabetes are type 2. Around 90 percent of those are also obese or overweight. Obesity causes insulin insensitivity because the fat cells of obese people appear to have fewer insulin "receptors" than those who are not overweight.

Both type 1 and type 2 diabetes result in an inability to control carbohydrate metabolism properly. Increased blood sugar levels can cause excess thirst, "acetone breath" (the breath smelling sweet and fruity), and a host of long-term health problems, including heart and circulation problems, eye disease, kidney damage, neuromuscular symptoms, and increased susceptibility to viral, bacterial, and fungal infections.

Prevention

Usually present from childhood, type 1 diabetes is an auto-immune disorder, and may be the result of a genetic predisposition plus the effects of a non-specific viral infection, causing the immune system to attack and destroy the body's insulin-producing cells. Breastfeeding seems to help prevent an infant from developing type 1 diabetes. You can reduce the risk of developing type 2 diabetes by eating healthily and exercising.

Management

Type 1 and type 2 diabetes are chronic conditions requiring medical supervision. Weight loss and lifestyle changes can reverse type 2 diabetes in the early stages, and medication can restore blood-sugar control. Since the 1921 discovery of insulin, type 1 diabetes has been manageable with daily injections.

Diabetics can help manage the disease through diet. Low-GI foods, which release their sugars slowly (see page 255), help keep blood sugar stable. Raw and unprocessed foods are among the best because in these foods the cell walls have not been broken down by cooking or processing so they take longer to release their sugar into the blood. It's important to eat foods that are rich in fiber (particularly soluble fiber), antioxidants, magnesium, and zinc, too. Wholegrain bread and rye instead of wheat can help keep blood sugar stable. Limit your salt intake to less than ¾ teaspoon (1.5g) per day, and restrict your intake of saturated fat and alcohol. Eat three well-balanced meals each day and three healthy snacks in between.

SUGGESTED RECIPES FOR DIABETES

Muesli (page 259), shiitake mushroom soup (page 261), spicy moroccan soup (page 261), korean kimchi-style salad (page 263), casserole de puy (page 268), khichuri (page 273), kale and macadamia nuts (page 274), carrot and beet salad (page 275), bulgur wheat salad (page 275), provençal mesclun salad (page 275), green lentil salad (page 276), cool cucumber (page 280), green party (page 280), heart warmer (page 282), tomato cocktail (page 283), sunrise (page 283), vegetable cocktail (page 283), circulation booster (page 284), green tea with mint (page 285), heart chai (page 285), pick-me-up (page 286).

the glycemic index

DEVELOPED BY DR. DAVID JENKINS AND OTHERS IN TORONTO IN 1981, THE GLYCEMIC INDEX RANKS FOODS ACCORDING TO HOW QUICKLY THEY ARE DIGESTED AND HOW QUICKLY THE CARBOHYDRATES IN THEM ARE ABSORBED INTO THE BLOODSTREAM FROM THE DIGESTIVE TRACT.

The Glycaemic Index (GI) ranks carbohydrate-containing foods on a scale from 0 to 100, according to how much they raise your body's blood-sugar levels after you have eaten them. The higher the number on the GI scale, the faster your body digests and absorbs the food, resulting in bigger fluctuations in blood-sugar levels (the energy highs and lows we experience over the course of a day). Choosing low-GI carbohydrates causes less fluctuation in blood-glucose and insulin levels, which is beneficial in the management of diabetes and the prevention of heart disease, and when you're trying to lose weight sustainably. For single foods, a low GI value is associated with improved blood-sugar control (to keep energy levels balanced), increased insulin sensitivity, and a reduction in fat levels (cholesterol) in the bloodstream. Low-GI foods will also help prolong physical endurance, giving you power for longer, which also helps with weight management.

FOODS WITH HIGH GI: > 70

fastfoods, snacks, and sweets

	GI		GI		GI		GI		GI
scone, plain	92	sugar (sucrose)	84	jelly bean	80	doughnut	76	cinnamon–raisin bread	71
fruit bar	90	chocolate power bar	83	licorice, soft	78	waffle	76	melba toast	70
popcorn	89	pizza, cheese and		english muffin	77	cupcake, iced	72		
pretzel	84	tomato	80	vanilla wafer	77	corn chips, plain salted	72		

bread, breakfast cereals, grains, rice, noodles, and pasta

	GI		GI		GI		GI		GI
pancake, buckwheat	102	muesli	86	pancake, wheat	80	wheat flake cereal	75	wholegrain cereal rings	74
middle eastern		shredded wheat		water cracker	78	grapenut	75	bread, wholewheat	72
flatbread	97	cereal	83	baguette, white, plain	78	bread, spelt	74	bread, white wheat	71
amaranth, popped	97	wheat noodles, fresh	82	cocoa-covered rice		bran flakes	74	crispbread	71
bagel	95	puffed rice breakfast		cereal	77	cornflakes	74		
tapioca, boiled	93	cereal	82	oatmeal	76	white rice, boiled	72		

fruit and vegetables

	GI		GI		GI		GI		GI
potato, white without skin,		charlotte potato,		potato, mashed	83	sweet potato, boiled	77	rutabaga, boiled	72
baked	98	boiled	92	potato, microwaved	82	pumpkin, boiled	75	watermelon	72
potato, white, boiled	96	potato, red, boiled	89	fava bean, boiled	79	yam, boiled	74		

dairy products and dairy alternatives

	GI		GI
ice cream (vanilla/chocolate)	80	rice milk	79

drinks

	GI		GI
carbonated glucose drink	95	weight-management drink	89

No measure is perfect, however, and if you are eating a normal, varied diet, you need to consider the total amount of carbohydrate you consume (GI values don't take into account the amount of carbohyrdrate in a food), as well as the GI of individual foods, and the extra potential nutritional benefits or hazards of some foods with a higher GI. Some high-fat foods, for example, turn out to have a low GI, but may have a negative impact on your heart and circulation, and some foods (such as bread and potatoes) have health benefits that outweigh their relatively high GI.

For those with diabetes, it is usually possible to maintain good blood-sugar control as long as carbohydrates provide less than 50 percent of total dietary calories, and those carbohydrates come from "complex" sources (such as whole grains), which are also good sources of soluble fiber and resistant starch. Dietary soluble fiber, in particular, aids sugar and fat metabolism and reduces fasting blood-glucose levels. Eating plenty of raw vegetables is the easy way to get enough soluble fiber without having to eat too much carbohydrate.

To switch from high-GI carbohydrates to low-GI carbohydrates means eating breakfast cereals based on oats, barley, and bran instead of rice and corn; eating wholegrain breads; reducing the amount of potatoes in your diet; and switching from white, parboiled rice to brown or basmati, and

FOODS WITH MEDIUM GI: 56–69

fastfoods, snacks, and sweets

	GI		GI		GI		GI		GI
wholewheat cracker	69	hamburger	66	corn syrup	63	muesli bar	61	blueberry muffin	59
wheat thin	67	fillet-o-fish burger	66	wholegrain bar	62	rice cake	61	fruit bread	57
chocolate and		chickenburger	66	hamburger bun	61	potato chips	60		
caramel bar	68	shortbread cookie	64	fruit finger, kids'	61	veggie burger	59		

bread, breakfast cereals, grains, rice, noodles, and pasta

	GI		GI		GI		GI		GI
rice, risotto, boiled	69	barley, rolled	66	fruit and fiber breakfast		rice pudding, baby	59	pumpernickel bread	56
gnocchi	68	couscous, rehydrated	65	cereal	61	rice, basmati, white,		rice, long grain, white,	
pitta bread	68	muesli	64	chapati	60	organic, boiled	57	boiled	56
bread, buckwheat	67	buckwheat	63	corn flour	59	bread, rye, whole kernel	57		
bread, garbanzo flour	67	pasta, white	61	noodles, buckwheat,		oats, rollled	57		
croissant	67	noodles, rice	61	instant	59	pastry, puff	56		

fruit and vegetables

	GI		GI		GI		GI		GI
pineapple	66	apricot, canned in		fig, dried	61	haricot bean,		kiwi fruit	58
pumpkin, boiled	66	syrup	64	papaya	60	pressure cooked	59	apricot, fresh	57
cantaloupe melon	65	cherry	63	corn, boiled	60	peach, canned in		lychee	57
raisin	64	banana	62	mango	60	syrup	58		

dairy products and dairy alternatives

	GI		GI
yogurt with fruit	64	ice cream	57

soups

	GI
chicken and mushroom	
soup	69
lentil soup	57

drinks

	GI		GI
carbonated orange drink	68	cranberry juice drink	56
beer	66	lemonade	54
carbonated cola drink	63		

from white pasta and noodles to wholegrain pasta and noodles and quinoa. Eating plenty of salad vegetables also reduces the GI load because most vegetables (apart from the starchy ones) have a zero GI value. Eggs, fish, and meat also have no GI rating because they contain no carbohydrate.

The tables on pages 253–255 list some of the most popular foods in a Western diet, ranked according to their GI values from high to low. All the foods listed are uncooked or raw, unless otherwise stated. For a full GI list, see the database compiled by the University of Sydney: www.glycemicindex.com

FOODS WITH LOW GI: < 56

fastfoods, snacks, and sweets

	GI		GI		GI		GI		GI
oatmeal cookie	55	danish pastry	50	granola bar	46	chocolate and nut spread	30	omega bar	21
rich tea cookie	55	chocolate, plain	49	hazelnut and apricot bar	42	apricot and apple fruit		mixed nuts and raisins	21
maple syrup	54	orange marmalade	48	tropical dried fruit snack	41	strip	29	peanut	7
french fries	54	banana cake	47	tortilla	38	sausage	28	hummus	6
chocolate chip muffin	53	chocolate pudding	47	fish finger	38	raspberry fruit spread	26		
honey	52	chocolate cookie	46	carrot cake	36	cashew nut	25		
strawberry jam	51	sponge cake	46	apricot and almond bar	34	chocolate, dark	23		

bread, breakfast cereals, grains, rice, noodles, and pasta

	GI		GI		GI		GI		GI
high-fibre wheat bran cereal	55	toasted wheat flake breakfast cereal	54	rice, brown, steamed	50	ravioli, meat-filled, boiled	46	fettucine, egg, boiled	32
lasagne sheet, boiled	55	quinoa, cooked	53	bread, buckwheat	47	barley, pearl, boiled	35	wheat, whole kernels	30
sugared cornflakes	55	bread, barley flour	53	soba noodles, instant, rehydrated	46	spaghetti, wholegrain, boiled	32	cannelloni, spinach and ricotta filled, boiled	15
bread, spelt multigrain	54	bread, wholegrain	52	bulgur, boiled	46				

fruit and vegetables

	GI		GI		GI		GI		GI
green pea	54	date	45	great northern bean	36	peach	28	kidney bean	19
blueberry, wild	53	pineapple, canned in juice	43	lentils, steamed	35	apple	28	carrot, raw	16
parsnip, boiled	52	orange	40	pear	33	mung bean sprout	25	soy bean, dried, boiled	15
butternut squash, boiled	51	baked beans	40	pinto bean, steamed	33	yellow split pea, boiled	25	garbanzo, dried, boiled	10
grape	49	strawberry	40	carrot, boiled	33	grapefruit	25		
potato, new	47	blackeyed pea	38	apricot, dried	30	plum	24		
peach, canned in juice	46	bean, dried, boiled	37	prune	29	cherry, sour	22		
				apple, dried	29	black bean, cooked	20		

dairy products and dairy alternatives

	GI		GI
soy yogurt	50	milk, 2% fat, organic	34
yogurt, probiotic	45	milk, whole, organic	34
soymilk, organic	43	fromage frais	20
yogurt, plain	35		

soups

	GI
tomato soup	52
chicken soup	43
vegetable soup	20

drinks

	GI		GI
orange juice	53	carrot juice	43
fruit juice, unsweetened	45	banana smoothie	30
apple juice, unsweetened	44	tomato juice	23

immune
foods in practice

Eating is not only the most important route to good health, it is highly enjoyable, too! The most nutritious plant foods are usually also the tastiest. On the following pages we have created a host of delicious recipes that you can enjoy for breakfast, dinner, supper, or as tasty snacks. They comprise foods that are packed with vitamins, minerals, and other vital nutrients, combined in ways that maximize their health-giving properties. Choose organic whenever possible.

breakfasts

baked tomatoes on toast

4 large ripe beefeak tomatoes
3½ ounces mushrooms, finely chopped
2 garlic cloves, crushed
1 bunch of fresh basil, finely chopped
Breadcrumbs
Sea salt and freshly ground pepper
Olive oil
4 thick slices of bread, toasted

Preheat the oven to 350°F. Cut off the bottom of the tomatoes and scoop out the flesh into a bowl. Mix with the mushrooms, garlic, and basil. Add enough breadcrumbs to make the mixture hang together. Season with salt and pepper. Fill the tomato shells with the mixture. Sprinkle with a little olive oil. Bake in the oven for about 20 minutes, until the tomatoes are quite soft. Spread a little olive oil on each slice of toast, place a tomato on each and serve immediately.

scrambled tofu

8 ounces marinated tofu
4 tablespoons soy milk
Sea salt and freshly ground pepper
1 ounce polyunsaturated vegetable margarine
4 slices of wholemeal bread, toasted
Fresh chopped rosemary

Crumble the tofu and mix with the milk. Add salt and pepper to taste. Melt the margarine gently in a saucepan, add the tofu and stir continuously over a low heat until you have a thick, creamy consistency. Meanwhile make the toast. Divide the scrambled tofu on each piece, garnish with rosemary. Serve immediately.

ruby red melon salad *(far right)*

2 cantaloupe melons, peeled and deseeded
1 pink grapefruit, peeled
12 cherries, halved and pipped
1-inch piece fresh ginger root, finely chopped
Maple syrup (optional)

Cut the melon into cubes and divide the grapefruit into segments. Place on individual serving bowls. Garnish with the cherries and the ginger (and add a splash of maple syrup to taste—if liked).

beans and tomatoes on toast

14 ounces cooked black-eyed peas (or navy beans or haricots)
2 tablespoons olive oil
1 red onion, sliced
1 garlic clove, sliced
½ teaspoon Florence fennel, finely chopped
1 teaspoon turmeric
1 teaspoon ground black cumin seed (or ground cumin)
½ teaspoon cayenne
2 teaspoons thyme, plus sprigs for garnish
Sea salt and freshly ground pepper
4 pieces of bread, toasted
8 thick tomato slices

Rinse, drain, and mash the beans. Stir-fry the onion, garlic, and fennel in the oil for 1 minute. Add the turmeric, cumin, cayenne, and thyme. Mix in the beans and heat through. Season to taste. Toast the bread and spread the bean mixture on top. Garnish with 2 tomato slices on each and a little thyme and black pepper. Serve hot.

fresh fruit salad

1 banana
1 kiwi or 2 passion-fruits
1 papaya
1 small bunch of grapes
2 peaches or nectarines
Seasonal berries to garnish
1 cup unsweetened fruit juice

Peel, deseed and slice the fruit. Place in a serving bowl. Add fruit juice and serve.

oatmeal with dried fruit and quinoa

2 cups rolled oats
4 tablespoons quinoa
5 ounces dried, unsulfured apricots
5 ounces raisins
5 ounces each of dried mango, pineapple, and apple
8 tablespoons plain soy yogurt

Soak the oats and the quinoa overnight in a saucepan with ¾ cup of water. Place the dried fruit in another small saucepan, cover with water and soak overnight too. In the morning, bring both to the boil (stirring the oats continuously), then cover and simmer each gently for 10–15 minutes. Serve the oatmeal in separate breakfast bowls, topped with the dried fruit (and liquid), and garnished with two spoonfuls of soy yogurt.

muesli

1¾ cups rolled oats
2 tablespoons each dried apricots, raisins, dates, chopped
1 tablespoon pecan nuts, chopped
1 tablespoon almonds, chopped
1 tablespoon sunflower seeds
1 tablespoon flax seed
2 tablespoons wheat germ
1 tablespoon wheat bran
Soy, rice, or almond milk
4 tablespoons plain soy yogurt
4 tablespoons fresh seasonal fruit

Combine all the muesli ingredients and serve with your choice of milk. Garnish each serving with a spoonful of yogurt and a spoonful of seasonal fruit. Serve.

fruity pancakes

1⅓ cups wheat flour
3 tablespoons gram flour
2 teaspoons baking powder
½ teaspoon salt (optional)
1¼ cups soy milk
1¼ cups water
3 tablespoons olive oil
Grapeseed oil for frying

For the filling:
5 ounces dried apricots, chopped
1 cup soy milk
10 strawberries, chopped
3½ ounces raspberries
1–2 guavas (or peaches), peeled and sliced
1 banana, chopped
Cinnamon
Maple syrup (optional)

Soak the apricots for the filling in the soy milk overnight. Next day, sift the flours with the baking powder and salt and mix well. Add the soy milk and the water a little at a time, stirring continuously with a whisk. Slowly add the oil, continuing to stir. Refrigerate for 15 minutes while you combine the filling ingredients. First place the creamed apricots in a bowl and then carefully fold in the other fruit. Cook the pancakes and place a couple of spoonfuls of the fruit filling in the center of each. Sprinkle with cinnamon and maple syrup. Serve immediately.

yogurt with fruit

2½ cups plain soy yogurt
1 apple, cored and finely chopped
1 mango, deseeded, peeled, and finely chopped
4 tablespoons blackberries (or other seasonal berries)
1 banana, peeled and finely chopped
Candied sweet violets (optional)

Divide the yogurt into individual serving bowls. Then divide the fruit between each and garnish with candied violets.

soups, appetizers, snacks, and sauces

SOUPS

basic vegetable soup

2 tablespoons olive oil
1 onion, chopped
3 garlic cloves, crushed
1 carrot, chopped
1 parsnip or parsley root, chopped
½ inch slice of celeriac, chopped
1 big handful of greens, curly kale or cabbage, chopped
1 leek, sliced
6½ cups water
14 ounces tomatoes, chopped
1 teaspoon thyme
1 tablespoon fresh lovage, chopped (optional)
1 bay leaf
1 tablespoon fresh parsley, chopped
Sea salt and black pepper to taste

Stir-fry the vegetables. Add the water and tomatoes. Bring to the boil and add herbs, and salt and pepper. Simmer for 30 minutes, or until the vegetables are soft. Serve this tasty vegetable soup with fresh bread, or use it to add flavour to stews and sauces.

cool tomato soup *(below)*

2 pounds fresh ripe tomatoes, quartered and stalks removed
2 scallions, finely chopped
4 tablespoons fresh (or 4 teaspoons dried) basil, finely chopped
Sea salt and black pepper to taste

Blend the tomatoes. Heat gently in a saucepan. Add scallions and basil. Season. Leave to cool and then chill well before serving.

healing soup

7½ cups water
1½ pounds potatoes, chopped
1 pound carrots, chopped
1 tablespoon fresh lovage or 1 teaspoon dried
1 tablespoon miso
1 teaspoon caraway seeds
1 teaspoon herbes de Provence
Sea salt and freshly ground black pepper to taste

Bring the water to boil and add the vegetables, lovage, miso, and caraway seeds. Simmer gently for 20 minutes. Add the herbes de Provence, blend, and heat through. Season to taste and serve with pan bread *(see page 274)*.

mint and melon soup

Flesh from 2 cantaloupe melons, chopped
1 cucumber, chopped and peeled
1 teaspoon maple syrup
1 tablespoon lemon rind, grated
1 cup water
3 tablespoons fresh mint, finely chopped
Sea salt and freshly ground black pepper to taste
Juice from 1 lemon
Lemon wedges (to garnish)

Heat the melon and the cucumber in a saucepan with the maple syrup, lemon rind, and water. Stir from time to time and simmer for 10 minutes. Add the mint. Blend, season and then add the lemon juice. Allow to cool, then refrigerate for 2 hours before serving. Serve with wedges of lemon.

black-eye pea and wild marjoram soup

2 tablespoons olive oil
2 shallots, chopped
1 garlic clove, crushed
1 teaspoon fennel seeds
2 teaspoons ground cilantro seeds
1 small fennel, chopped
1 small zucchini, chopped
14 ounces black-eyed peas, cooked
1 pound tomatoes, skinned and blended
5 cups diluted basic vegetable soup (see page 260)
2 tablespoons tomato paste
3 tablespoons fresh (or 3 teaspoons dried) marjoram, chopped

Gently stir-fry the shallots, garlic, fennel seeds, cilantro, fennel, and zucchini in the oil. Add the peas and the tomatoes, heat through, then add the soup and tomato paste. Bring to boil and add the salt, pepper and half the marjoram. Cover and simmer for 20 minutes. Add rest of the marjoram. Season and serve.

creamy cauliflower soup

1 cauliflower
2 tablespoons olive oil
2 shallots, chopped
1 small carrot, chopped
2 potatoes, chopped
5 cups diluted basic vegetable soup (see page 260)
1 cup soy milk
Sea salt and freshly ground black pepper to taste
1 bunch of parsley, finely chopped

Cut off the cauliflower flowerets and steam until tender. Chop up the rest of the cauliflower and stir-fry in the oil together with the other vegetables. Add the soup, bring to the boil and simmer for about 30 minutes. Blend, then add the soy milk together with the flowerets, seasoning and parsley. Heat through (but don't let it boil) and serve.

italian butterbean soup

14 ounces butterbeans, cooked
4 tablespoons olive oil
1 red onion, finely chopped
2 garlic cloves, finely chopped
4 stalks celery, chopped
1 pound 2 ounces tomatoes, peeled and chopped
5 cups diluted basic vegetable soup (see page 260)
1 tablespoon fresh thyme
1 teaspoon yeast extract
Sea salt and freshly ground black pepper to taste

Stir-fry the onion, garlic, and celery gently in the olive oil. Blend half the cooked beans with the tomatoes and half the soup, then add them together with the whole beans and the remaining soup. Stir well, then add the thyme, yeast extract, salt, and pepper. Bring to boil and simmer for 20 minutes. Adjust the seasoning and serve.

pumpkin soup

3 tablespoons olive oil
1 red onion, chopped
1 garlic clove, chopped
2 pounds pumpkin, peeled, deseeded, chopped
3 tablespoons fresh (or 3 teaspoons dried) marjoram
5 cups diluted basic vegetable soup (see page 260)
2 cups coconut milk
Sea salt and freshly ground black pepper to taste

Heat the oil gently in a big saucepan. Add the onion, garlic, and pumpkin. Stir-fry for 5 minutes, then add the marjoram, soup, and coconut milk. Bring to the boil, cover and simmer for 15 minutes or until the vegetables are soft. Add salt and pepper. Blend and serve, garnished with marjoram.

shiitake mushroom soup

3 ounces dried shiitake mushrooms (or 9 ounces fresh/bottled)
2 tablespoons olive oil
2 scallions, finely chopped
1 garlic clove, finely chopped
1 carrot, finely chopped
1-inch cube fresh ginger root, finely chopped
1 tablespoon soy sauce
1 teaspoon maple syrup
7½ cups water with 1 teaspoon miso
Sea salt and freshly ground black pepper

If using dried mushrooms, soak them in plenty of water for 20 minutes. Discard the stems. Heat the oil gently in a big skillet and stir-fry the scallions, garlic, carrot, and ginger root for 2 minutes. Add the mushrooms and sauté for another 5 minutes. Add the soy sauce, maple syrup, and water and miso one after the other. Bring to boil, cover and simmer gently for 30 minutes. Add the salt and pepper to taste.

spicy moroccan soup

2 ounces garbanzo beans
2 ounces pinto beans (or haricots)
3½ ounces green lentils, rinsed
3 tablespoons olive oil
1 garlic clove, finely chopped
1 onion, chopped
1 teaspoon ground black cumin (or ground cumin)
1 teaspoon ground cilantro
1 teaspoon caraway seeds
½ teaspoon cayenne
1 tablespoon turmeric
2 carrots, chopped
2 potatoes, chopped
3 celery stalks, finely chopped
1-inch piece fresh ginger root, finely chopped
1 pound tomatoes, blended
5 cups diluted basic vegetable soup *(see page 260)*
Sea salt and freshly ground black pepper to taste
2 tablespoons lemon juice

Rinse and soak the garbanzos and pinto beans overnight. Rinse again and place in a saucepan with the lentils. Add lots of water and cook for 30 minutes. Meanwhile heat the oil gently in a soup pan. Stir-fry the garlic and onion. Add the spices, then carrots, potatoes, celery, and ginger. Stir-fry for 5 minutes. Add tomatoes and simmer. Drain the cooking water off the legumes and rinse them. Add the legumes to the pan together with the soup. Bring to boil and simmer for 45 minutes, adding more water if necessary. Season, add lemon juice. Serve.

tibetan dumpling soup

10 ounces wholewheat flour
10 ounces white flour
½ teaspoon salt
2 tablespoons olive oil
½ teaspoon fenugreek seeds
1 garlic clove, crushed
1 red onion, sliced
3 tomatoes, chopped
1-inch piece of ginger root, finely chopped
½ teaspoon nutmeg, grated
½ teaspoon turmeric
3 tablespoons soy sauce
1 bunch of radishes, sliced
3½ ounces green peas
7½ cups diluted basic vegetable soup *(see page 260)*
3 salad onions, sliced
Sea salt and freshly ground black pepper to taste

Combine the flours and salt. Add enough water to make a stiff dough. Roll on a floured surface to form a long, finger-thick snake. Cut into ½-inch pieces and sprinkle with flour to prevent them sticking together. Heat the oil in a soup pan and add the fenugreek seeds. Stir-fry until dark brown, then add the garlic and onion. Stir for 3 minutes, then add the tomatoes, spices, and soy sauce.
Stir, cover, and simmer gently for 5 minutes, then add the radishes and peas. Cook for 2 more minutes. Add the soup, bring to boil and add the dumplings. Boil for 6–8 minutes until the dumplings are done. Add the salad onions. Season and serve.

welsh leek and potato soup

4 leeks, sliced
2 ounces vegetable margarine
4 medium potatoes, chopped into small cubes
7½ cups basic vegetable soup *(see page 260)*
Sea salt and freshly ground black pepper
1 bunch of chives

Gently sauté the leeks in the margarine, add the potatoes, cook for a few more minutes before adding the soup. Heat through and simmer for 30 minutes. Garnish with chives and serve hot. It is also delicious blended.

APPETIZERS

asparagus with ravigote

(below right)

2 bunches of asparagus, peeled
1 tablespoon lemon juice
Ravigote *(see page 267)*

Cut off the woody ends of the asparagus. Cook in lightly salted boiling water for about 10 minutes. (One method is to tie the asparagus in a bundle with cotton string and boil with tips sticking out of water.) Serve with ravigote dressing.

hummus with crudités and warm pitta bread

10 ounces garbanzo beans, cooked and drained
2 garlic cloves, crushed
4 tablespoons lemon juice
1 teaspoon sea salt
2 tablespoons tahini
1 tablespoon fresh parsley, finely chopped
1 teaspoon paprika
1 tablespoon olive oil

For the crudités:
2 carrots and 8 long radishes, sliced into slim sticks
2 celery stalks, sliced into sticks
¼ cucumber, sliced into sticks
8 cherry tomatoes (kept whole)
4 pitta breads, warmed and cut into wedges

Blend the garbanzos with the garlic, lemon juice, 4 tablespoons cold water, and sea salt. Add the tahini and blend again to a smooth paste. Adjust the seasoning and place in a serving bowl. Garnish with parsley and paprika and sprinkle with a little olive oil. Serve with crudités and warm pitta bread.

korean kimchi-style salad

1 small chinese cabbage, finely chopped
1 teaspoon unrefined sea salt
2 garlic cloves, finely chopped
1-inch piece of fresh ginger root, finely chopped
1 fresh chilli pepper, finely chopped
2 tomatoes, finely chopped
1 green bell pepper, finely chopped
1 carrot, finely chopped
½ cucumber, finely chopped

Place the chinese cabbage in a bowl. Add the salt and mix well. Add the rest
of the ingredients and serve with fresh bread.

broiled bell peppers

3 bell peppers, quartered longways and deseeded
Rich garlic dressing (see page 215)

Broil the peppers, with the skin facing the heat, until the skin is charred. Leave
to cool in a paper bag, then peel off the skin. Cut into long strips and place in
a shallow dish. Sprinkle with rich garlic dressing and serve with French bread.

vegetable kebabs

(pictured page 265)

16 button mushrooms, kept whole
12 cherry tomatoes, kept whole
1 red bell pepper, in chunks
1 green bell pepper, in chunks
2 zucchini, in chunks
1 big sweet potato or yam, parboiled, in chunks
1 eggplant, in chunks
4 shallots, halved
4 bay leaves, halved
4 barbecue skewers

For the marinade (makes 17fl ozt):
12 ounces tomato ketchup (see page 267)
Juice of 1 lemon
¾ cup red wine vinegar
6 garlic cloves, crushed
2 tablespoons raw cane sugar
2 tablespoons olive oil
2 tablespoons mustard

Mix all the marinade ingredients together in a bowl. Add the prepared kebab
ingredients. Mix gently, cover and leave to marinate for 2 hours. Thread the
vegetables on to the skewers and brush with marinade. Place the kebabs on
a hot barbecue and broil for 10 minutes, turning from time to time. Serve hot.

baba ganoush

1 big eggplant
2 garlic cloves, crushed
4 tablespoons tahini
4 tablespoons lemon juice
1 teaspoon ground black cumin, toasted
1 tablespoon fresh parsley, finely chopped
Sea salt to taste
1 teaspoon paprika

Prick the eggplant with a fork. Toast, turning from time to time, until the skin is black and charred. Cool under running water, then cut in half and scoop out the flesh. Chop the flesh finely, place in a bowl and mix in the rest of the ingredients, reserving a little parsley and the paprika to garnish. Adjust the seasoning, garnish, and serve with warm pitta bread, green salad leaves, tomato, and cucumber.

samosa parcels

4 scallions, finely chopped
1 tablespoon fresh ginger root, finely chopped
1 garlic clove, finely chopped
9 ounces marinated tofu, in small cubes
8½ ounces phyllo pastry
Sunflower oil
2 tablespoons soy sauce

Mix the scallions, ginger root, and garlic in a bowl. Gently stir-fry the tofu in a little oil. Turn off heat, add the soy sauce, stir, transfer to the bowl and mix well. Cut the phyllo pastry into long strips, about 3 inches wide. Brush each strip with oil. Take the first strip and put 1 teaspoon of filling on one end. Fold the end of the pastry over to form a triangle covering the filling. Keep folding the strip over itself in to form a triangular parcel. Repeat with the other strips. Brush the parcels with oil, bake at 425°F for 10 minutes until golden. Serve hot.

toasted tempeh with herb salad

8 tempeh slices
Sunflower oil
Sea salt
1 small red lettuce
1 bunch of watercress
1 bunch of nasturtium leaves and flowers (optional)
1 carrot, finely sliced
1 bunch chives, finely chopped
Lime dressing *(see page 267)*

Brush the tempeh slices with oil and toast them on a dry pan till golden. Sprinkle with sea salt and remove from heat. For each individual serving, arrange some salad and two slices of tempeh on a plate, sprinkle with dressing and serve.

tofumasalata

7 ounces smoked tofu
4 tablespoons lemon juice
1 teaspoon grated lemon rind
8 tablespoons water
1 shallot, chopped
1 garlic clove, chopped
3 tablespoons breadcrumbs
4 tablespoons olive oil
1 teaspoon paprika
Sea salt and freshly ground black pepper to taste

Crumble the tofu, and blend with the lemon juice, lemon rind, water, shallot, garlic, breadcrumbs, olive oil, and paprika. Adjust the seasoning and chill before serving with warm pitta, olives, and slices of cucumber.

SNACKS
marinated olives

10 ounces olives
4 tablespoons olive oil
2 fresh or dried chilli peppers, chopped
½ lemon (unpeeled), quartered and sliced
2 garlic cloves, sliced
1 teaspoon cilantro seeds, crushed
1 teaspoon dried thyme
1 teaspoon dried oregano

Gently press the olives with a rolling pin. Place in a bowl with the chilli peppers, lemon, garlic, cilantro, thyme, and oregano. Mix well, cover and allow to marinate overnight before serving.

toasted nuts and seeds

1 tablespoon cashew nuts
1 tablespoon melon seeds
1 tablespoon almonds
1 tablespoon walnuts
1 tablespoon hazelnuts
1 tablespoon sunflower seeds
1 tablespoon brazil nuts
Soy sauce
½ teaspoon sea salt
Few drops of tabasco (optional)

Mix together the cashew nuts, melon seeds, almonds, walnuts, hazelnuts, sunflower seeds, and brazil nuts and dry roast in a heavy skillet. Turn off the heat. Immediately add the soy sauce, sea salt, and tabasco. Stir well, remove from pan and serve.

tomato and cucumber canapés

1 cucumber, in thick slices
8 cherry tomatoes, halved
7 ounces walnuts, shelled
1 garlic clove
4 tablespoons water
5 tablespoons olive oil
Sea salt to taste
1 bunch of fresh parsley, finely chopped

Arrange the cucumber slices and the tomato halves on a large plate. Blend the walnuts, garlic, water, and olive oil to a smooth paté. Season to taste. Place a small spoonful of the paté on top of each slice of cucumber and tomato. Garnish with parsley and serve.

guacamole

4 small ripe avocados
2 teaspoons ground cilantro
2 teaspoons ground cumin
¼ teaspoon cayenne pepper
4 tablespoons lemon juice
2 garlic cloves, finely chopped
½-inch cube fresh ginger root, finely chopped
2 ripe tomatoes, finely chopped
Sea salt and freshly ground black pepper to taste
1 small bunch fresh cilantro leaves, chopped
2 carrots cut into sticks
1 packet tortilla chips

Blend the avocados with the ground cilantro, cumin, cayenne, lemon juice, garlic, and ginger until almost smooth. Transfer to a bowl, stir in the tomatoes, season, cover and chill before serving. Garnish with the fresh cilantro leaves and serve with tortilla chips and carrot sticks.

tofu balls

1 onion, grated
1 green chilli, deseeded and finely chopped
1 pound 2 ounces tofu, grated or crumbled
2 teaspoons ground cumin
1 garlic clove, crushed
1 organic lemon, juice and grated rind
Sea salt and freshly ground black pepper to taste
1 tablespoon olive oil
Grapeseed oil for shallow frying
Salad leaves (according to season)

Put the onion, chilli, tofu, cumin, garlic, lemon juice and rind, and olive oil in a bowl. Season to taste and mix well. Shape into small balls and shallow fry in the grapeseed oil till golden. Serve with a selection of salad leaves.

tzaziki

½ cucumber, finely diced
1¼ cups plain soy yogurt
1 teaspoon olive oil
2 garlic cloves, finely chopped
2 tablespoons fresh mint, finely chopped
Sea salt and freshly ground black pepper to taste

Place the cucumber in a bowl along with the yogurt, olive oil, garlic, and mint. Mix well. Cover and chill. Adjust seasoning. Serve with green salad leaves and warm pitta.

pan amb oli

4 slices of bread to toast
2 garlic cloves, halved
2 ripe tomatoes, halved
2 teaspoons olive oil
Sea salt and freshly ground black pepper

Toast the bread on both sides. Rub one side with the garlic, then squeeze on to a half tomato and rub in the tomato pulp (discard the skin). Sprinkle with ½ teaspoon of oil. Repeat for the remaining slices, season and serve immediately

SAUCES

lemon tahini dressing

(far left, bottom)

2 tablespoons lemon juice
1 tablespoon tahini
1 tablespoon maple syrup
1 tablespoon Dijon mustard
7 tablespoons olive oil
Sea salt and freshly ground black pepper

Mix together the lemon juice, tahini, maple syrup, Dijon mustard, and olive oil and blend or whisk to a thick, smooth consistency. Add seasoning to taste.

lime dressing

2 tablespoons lime juice
1 tablespoon Dijon mustard
1 teaspoon raw cane sugar
Sea salt and freshly ground black pepper
Olive oil

Combine all the ingredients, except the oil, in a small bowl and whisk together. Add the oil slowly, whisking continuously until you have a smooth dressing. (If you can't get the dressing to emulsify, try adding a little cold water.)

pesto sauce

(far left, top)

2 tablespoons pine nuts
1 bunch of fresh basil
2 garlic cloves, crushed
1 teaspoon coarse sea salt
4 tablespoons olive oil

Grind the nuts in a mortar or blender. Add the rest of the ingredients and mix to form a coarse paste. Add a little extra oil if necessary.

ravigote

1 garlic clove
1 teaspoon tarragon
2 tablespoons parsley, chopped
2 tablespoons chives, chopped
2 teaspoons capers
1 tablespoon Dijon mustard
1 tablespoon red wine vinegar
Pinch of freshly ground sea salt
¾ cup olive oil

Blend all the ingredients except the oil. Add the oil very carefully, a little at a time, until the mixture emulsifies, then slowly add the rest of the oil. Serve with cooked vegetables.

tomato ketchup

(far left, centre)

½ pound onion, finely chopped
1 pound red bell peppers, finely chopped
1 pound tomatoes, finely chopped
3 tablespoons olive oil
3½ ounces unrefined cane sugar
3 garlic cloves, finely chopped
1 fresh chilli pepper, deseeded, finely chopped
1 teaspoon mustard powder
2 teaspoons paprika
½ cup red wine vinegar
4 whole cloves, crushed
Sea salt and freshly ground black pepper to taste

Stir-fry the onion, red pepper, and tomatoes in the oil, then simmer for 45 minutes until they break down. Filter through a sieve. Add the sugar, cloves, chilli pepper, mustard powder, paprika, vinegar, and crushed cloves, and simmer very gently for 2 hours until you have a thick paste. Season. (This will keep in the refrigerator for 3–4 days. But if you want to keep it longer, pour the ketchup into clean bottles, put the tops on and place in boiling water for 20 minutes to sterilize the contents.)

main courses, side dishes, and salads

MAIN COURSES

amaranth and tofu puffs

1 ounce polyunsaturated vegetable margarine
8½ ounces marinated tofu, cubed small
8½ ounces amaranth leaves (or fresh spinach), chopped
Pinch of nutmeg
Sea salt and freshly ground black pepper to taste
1 packet of puff pastry

Melt the margarine, add the tofu and sauté for a few minutes. Add the amaranth (or spinach) and nutmeg and stir-fry until it goes soft and the water has evaporated. Season and set aside. Cut the pastry into squares. Dampen the edges. Place a portion of amaranth mixture on each square, fold one side over diagonally to form a triangle, seal well. Place on a greased baking tray and bake at 400°F for about 15 minutes or until golden.

casserole de puy

3½ ounces lentilles de Puy (brown lentils)
1 bay leaf
3 tablespoons olive oil
½ teaspoon cayenne
1 teaspoon turmeric
1 teaspoon each of cilantro, cumin, and mustard seeds
1 garlic clove, crushed
1 red onion, chopped
1 leek, sliced
8 ounces button mushrooms
1 potato
2 carrots
1 pound tomatoes, peeled and chopped
Sea salt and freshly ground black pepper to taste
Fresh cilantro

Put the lentils and the bay leaf on to boil in twice their volume of water. Cover and simmer while you prepare the other ingredients. Heat the oil in a large flameproof casserole. Crush the seeds in a mortar and add them with the other spices, then add the garlic, onion and leek. Stir-fry for 2 minutes, then add the mushrooms and stir-fry for a few more minutes. Add the potato, carrots, and tomatoes, heat through and add the partially cooked lentils (with the cooking water). Season with salt and pepper, add a little more water to make sure the dish doesn't dry out, then cover and cook in the oven at 350°F for 45 minutes. Garnish with fresh cilantro. Serve with mashed potato.

paella

3 tablespoons olive oil
8½ ounces long-grain rice
1 teaspoon turmeric
2 garlic cloves, finely chopped
1 onion, chopped
1 carrot, chopped
8½ ounces artichoke hearts
1 celery stalk, finely sliced
1 red bell pepper, deseeded and sliced
4 tomatoes, skinned and chopped
¼ cup basic vegetable soup *(see page 260)*
3½ ounces green peas
1 tablespoon fresh parsley, finely chopped
1 tablespoon fresh marjoram (or 1 teaspoon dried)
2 tablespoons cashew nuts
1 organic lemon, in thick slices
Sea salt and freshly ground black pepper to taste

Heat the oil in a large deep skillet and stir-fry the rice until golden. Add turmeric, garlic, onion, and carrot, and stir-fry for a few minutes. Add the artichoke hearts, celery stalk, and red bell pepper and stir-fry again for 2 minutes. Add the tomatoes and soup. Bring to boil and simmer for 5 minutes. Add the peas, then simmer until the rice is cooked. Add the herbs, cashews, and lemon slices. Season to taste. Serve hot.

artichoke hearts, fava beans, and shiitake

2 tablespoons olive oil
2 teaspoons ground cumin
1 bay leaf
1 teaspoon turmeric
8½ ounces shiitake mushrooms, halved
1 pound fava beans (shelled weight)
1 pound artichoke hearts, cooked
½ cup water
2 tablespoons lemon juice
1 small bunch of parsley, finely chopped
Sea salt and freshly ground black pepper to taste

Heat the oil gently in a large pan. Add the spices, then the mushrooms. Sauté for a few minutes, then add the broad beans with the artichokes and the water. Heat through, simmer until the beans are tender, then add the lemon juice and the parsley. Season and serve.

asparagus asian-style

1 bunch of asparagus, end cut off, peeled
2 tablespoons olive oil
1 teaspoon cumin powder
1 stalk lemongrass, finely sliced
1-inch piece fresh ginger root, finely chopped
3 medium carrots, julienned
1 bunch scallions, sliced
1 bell pepper, deseeded, finely sliced
2 tablespoons tamarind paste, dissolved in 1¼ cups hot water
1 handful beansprouts
2 tablespoons soy sauce
1 tablespoon maple syrup
1–2 tablespoons lemon juice
Sea salt and freshly ground black pepper to taste

Cut the asparagus into 2-inch pieces and set aside. Heat the oil in a wok, add the cumin, lemongrass, and ginger and stir-fry a few seconds. Add the asparagus, then the carrots, scallions, and bell pepper. Stir-fry for another 5 minutes. Add the dissolved tamarind paste. Simmer until the asparagus are cooked. Then add the beansprouts, soy sauce, maple syrup, and lemon juice. Heat through, season to taste and serve with rice or noodles.

butternut squash with bell pepper and tomato

(below)

1 butternut squash, deseeded and peeled
2 tablespoons olive oil
1 red onion, chopped
1 garlic clove, chopped
1 bell pepper, in strips
6 ripe tomatoes, skinned and sliced
2 tablespoons tomato paste
2 tablespoons fresh (or 2 teaspoons dried) basil, chopped
1 teaspoon paprika
2 tablespoons parsley, chopped
Sea salt and freshly ground black pepper to taste

Chop the squash into chunks. Heat the oil in a large pan, add the onion, garlic, and the squash, sauté for 2 minutes and then add the bell pepper. Heat through and then add the rest of the ingredients except the parsley. Cover and simmer for 20 minutes. Season, garnish with parsley and serve with rice or hasselbach potatoes *(see page 258)*.

sweet and sour vegetable parcels

4 thick slices of tempeh or tofu, chopped
2 scallions, finely sliced into strips
2 carrots, julienned
2 celery sticks, julienned
1-inch piece ginger root, cut into fine sticks
4-inch lemon grass stem
1 handful bean sprouts
8 sheets of phyllo pastry
Grapeseed oil
1 tablespoon soy sauce
2 tablespoons lemon juice
Vinegar
1 tablespoon maple syrup
1 tablespoon tomato paste
1 garlic clove, crushed
1 teaspoon paprika
1 broccoli, cut into flowerets
2½ ounces baby corns
1 red bell pepper, cut into strips

Stir-fry the tempeh. Add the vegetables one at a time in the order above, stir-frying in between. Add the lemongrass and beansprouts. Stir-fry again and season to taste. Brush the pastry with the oil. Divide the filling between the 8 sheets. Fold the corners of each sheet into the center and pinch the parcels together. Brush with oil and bake at 400°F for 20 minutes until golden. For the sweet and sour vegetables, mix together soy sauce, lemon juice, vinegar, syrup, tomato paste, garlic, and paprika. Sauté the broccoli, baby corns, and red bell peppers for 5 minutes. Add the sauce, heat through, and serve with parcels.

french onion tart *(left)*

For the short-crust pastry:
8½ ounces wheat or spelt flour
½ teaspoon salt
4½ ounces cold vegetable margarine
¾ cup cold water

For the filling:
1 pound 9 ounces onions, finely sliced
¾ teaspoon salt and a pinch of black pepper
8½ ounces tofu, crumbled
1 cup soy milk
1 tablespoon flour

Mix the flour and salt, then add the margarine by chopping it into the flour with a knife and a spoon until it forms small lumps. Crumble the dough with your hands until it looks like Parmesan (taking care not to let the dough get warm), then add cold water and knead the dough lightly to a smooth lump. Refrigerate until needed. Sauté the onions very gently in the oil. Stir from time to time, taking care not to let them brown. After 10 minutes, add the salt and pepper. Stir, then cover and cook very gently for 15 minutes. Remove the lid and let the liquid reduce for 5 minutes. Remove from heat. Blend the tofu, soy milk, and flour, and mix with the onions. Season to taste. Roll out the dough and place in a greased baking case. Add the filling and bake at 350°F for 25–30 minutes. Delicious hot or cold.

provençale-style kidney beans

2 tablespoons olive oil
1 red onion, sliced
2 garlic cloves, sliced
1 can red kidney beans
2 small zucchini, sliced
4 ripe tomatoes, skinned and chopped
½ cup basic vegetable soup *(see page 260)*
2 tablespoons fresh basil, chopped
3½ ounces small niçoise olives
Sea salt and freshly ground black pepper to taste

Heat the oil and sauté the onion and garlic gently for 2 minutes. Add the kidney beans, zucchini, and tomatoes and cook for 2 more minutes. Add the soup and the basil. Bring to boil and simmer for 10 minutes. Add the olives. Heat through, season, garnish with basil, and serve with wild rice.

greek casserole

4 tablespoons olive oil
8½ ounces tofu, cut into cubes
1 red onion, in thick slices
1 green bell pepper, in thick slices
2 garlic cloves, chopped
1 tablespoon wholewheat flour
1 pound 2 ounces ripe tomatoes, chopped
1 tablespoon tomato paste
2 teaspoons marjoram
Sea salt and freshly ground black pepper to taste

Stir-fry the tofu cubes in half the oil until they begin to brown. Remove from pan. Add the rest of the oil, then the onion. Sauté for a few minutes then add the green bell pepper and garlic. Sauté for a few minutes, turn down the heat and mix in the flour. Let it blend in for a minute, then add the tomatoes, turn up heat and stir well. Add the tomato paste, marjoram, and salt and pepper. Stir while you bring the mixture to boil. Add the tofu pieces and mix well. Place in an oven-proof dish and bake, covered, at 350°F for about 30 minutes.

spinach bouillabaisse

3 tablespoons olive oil
2 white onions, sliced
2 potatoes, sliced
1 pound 2 ounces fresh spinach, chopped
2 garlic cloves, crushed
1½ cups diluted basic vegetable soup *(see page 260)*
Pinch of cayenne
1 tablespoon fresh dill, chopped (optional)
1 tablespoon fresh parsley, chopped
Sea salt and freshly ground black pepper to taste

Sauté the onion and potato in the oil. Add the spinach and stir until it goes soft, then add the garlic, soup, and cayenne. Simmer for 10 minutes, add dill and parsley, and season to taste. Heat through and serve with fresh bread.

okra in sweet and sour tamarind sauce

4 tablespoons olive oil
1 teaspoon black mustard seeds
1 teaspoon ground cumin
1 teaspoon ground cilantro
Pinch of cayenne pepper
½ teaspoon turmeric
3 garlic cloves, finely chopped
1 pound fresh okra, trimmed
1¼ cups water
6½ ounces green beans, trimmed
2 tablespoons tamarind paste
2 tablespoons maple syrup
Sea salt and freshly ground black pepper to taste

Heat the oil gently in a skillet. Add mustard seeds, cumin, cilantro, cayenne, turmeric, and garlic. Stir-fry ½ minute, then add the okra. Stir-fry for 1 minute then add the water and the beans. Heat through and simmer for 10 minutes, stirring occasionally. Add the tamarind paste and the maple syrup. Simmer again for another 5 minutes. Season and serve with basmati rice.

shepherdess' pie

4 ounces lentilles de Puy (brown lentils)
3 tablespoons olive oil
1 bay leaf
1 teaspoon thyme
2 garlic cloves, finely chopped
2 shallots, chopped
2 carrots, finely chopped
10 ounces mushrooms, quartered
1 pound tomatoes, skinned and chopped
⅔ cup vegetable juice or soup(see page 260)
1 tablespoon soy sauce
2 tablespoons fresh basil, chopped
Sea salt and freshly ground black pepper to taste

For the topping:
3 large potatoes, chopped
2 sweet potatoes, chopped
2 ounces polyunsaturated vegetable margarine
Soy milk
Paprika

Put the lentils on to boil in three times their volume of water. Boil the potatoes and sweet potatoes in salted water until tender. Meanwhile heat the oil gently and add the bay leaf, thyme, garlic, shallots and carrots. Stir and add the mushrooms. Sauté for a few minutes (until the mushrooms give off their moisture) then add the tomatoes. Drain any remaining cooking water from the lentils and add them together with the soup and soy sauce. Simmer gently for 10 minutes. Add the basil and adjust seasoning. Remove from the heat and place in a large shallow ovenproof dish. Mash the potatoes with the margarine and soy milk. Add seasoning to taste and spread over the filling. Sprinkle with paprika and bake at 470°F for 10 minutes or until golden.

sweet potato curry

3 tablespoons olive oil
2 teaspoons black mustard seeds
1 teaspoon curry powder
1 red onion, sliced
2 green chillies, sliced
12 ounces sweet potatoes, peeled and cubed
8½ ounces corn kernels
1 spear broccoli, cut into flowerets
5 ounces fresh spinach, chopped
2 cups coconut milk
Sea salt and freshly ground black pepper to taste
2 tablespoons lime juice
1 bunch of fresh cilantro leaves, chopped

Heat the oil and add the black mustard seeds and the curry powder and stir-fry until the seeds start to pop. Add the onion and chillies, and stir-fry for another 2 minutes. Add the sweet potato, sweetcorn, and broccoli. Stir-fry for 5 minutes then add the spinach and mix well. Add the coconut milk and simmer gently for 10 minutes until the vegetables are soft. Season with salt, pepper, and lime juice. Garnish with fresh cilantro and serve with rice.

mushrooms with sage and thyme stuffing

12–16 large flat open mushrooms
2 tablespoons olive oil
3 garlic cloves, crushed
2 teaspoons thyme
3 tablespoons soy sauce
8 tablespoons breadcrumbs
4 tablespoons fresh parsley, finely chopped

Remove the stalks from the mushroom caps and scrape out the lamellae (gills) with a teaspoon. Place the caps upside down on a greased ovenproof dish or baking tray. Finely chop the mushroom stalks and stir-fry them in the oil with the garlic. Add the thyme and the soy sauce and stir-fry until the mushroom stalks give off their moisture. Add the breadcrumbs and stir until the liquid is soaked up. Remove from heat and add the chopped parsley. Fill the mushroom caps with the mixture and bake for about 10 minutes at 400°F.

winter hot pot

3 tablespoons olive oil
1 onion, sliced
2 carrots, sliced
1 parsnip, sliced
1 celery stick, sliced
7 ounces cooked garbanzo beans
10 ounces shiitake mushrooms, kept whole
¾ cup basic vegetable soup (see page 260)
Sea salt and freshly ground black pepper to taste
2 big potatoes, thinly sliced

Heat the oil in a deep, ovenproof casserole. Add the onion, carrots, and parsnip. Sauté for 5 minutes. Add the celery, garbanzos, and mushrooms. Stir-fry for another 5 minutes and then add the soup. Heat through, season, and cover with potato slices. Place in a preheated oven and cook at 350°F for 45 minutes.

spicy tofu burgers

1 tablespoon olive oil
1 onion, grated
1 carrot, grated
2 teaspoons ground cilantro
1 garlic clove, crushed
2 teaspoons tomato paste
8½ ounces tofu, crumbled
2 tablespoons breadcrumbs
2 tablespoons Brazil nuts, finely chopped
Sea salt and freshly ground black pepper to taste
Flour for coating
Grapeseed oil for frying

Heat the oil and gently stir-fry the onion and carrot until soft. Add the cilantro, garlic, and tomato paste and stir-fry for 2 more minutes. Place in a bowl and mix with the tofu, breadcrumbs, and nuts. Season and stir until the mixture sticks together well. Shape into burgers, dip in flour and fry till golden. Drain on paper and serve with steamed vegetables.

sweet chestnuts and kumquats

1 pound fresh (12 ounces dried) sweet chestnuts, shelled
3 tablespoons olive oil
1 garlic clove, sliced
1 bay leaf
2 celery sticks, sliced
2 leeks, sliced
3 tablespoons wholewheat flour
½ cup red wine
1¾ cups basic vegetable soup (see page 260))
Juice of 1 tangerine
3½ ounces kumquats
Sea salt and freshly ground black pepper to taste

If using dried chestnuts, you will need to soak them for 8 hours before cooking. If using fresh chestnuts, drop them in boiling water and peel them with a sharp knife. Heat the oil in a casserole, add the garlic and bay leaf, and stir for a few seconds. Add the chestnuts, celery, and leeks. Sprinkle with the flour, mix well, then slowly add the wine, the vegetable soup, and the tangerine juice. Heat through, then add the kumquats and salt and pepper. Cook covered in the oven at 350°F for about an hour. Serve with broccoli and wild rice.

SIDE DISHES

cucumber, tomato and pepper relish

½ cucumber, chopped
8½ ounces tomatoes, chopped
1 red onion, chopped
2 green chilli peppers, finely sliced
2 tablespoons lime juice
Pinch of unrefined sugar
Pinch of salt
2 tablespoons fresh cilantro leaves, chopped

Mix all the ingredients in a bowl and store in the refrigerator until needed.

red chilli relish

4 red chillies and 2 red peppers, stalk and seeds removed, chopped
4 ripe tomatoes, stalk removed, chopped
2 garlic cloves, peeled and chopped
3 tablespoons lime juice
Sea salt to taste

Blend all the ingredients, store in the refrigerator until needed.

khichuri—rice with lentils

7 ounces basmati rice, washed
3½ ounces red lentils, washed
1 bay leaf
2-inch cinnamon stick
1 teaspoon ground turmeric
5 cups water (approximately)
Sea salt to taste

Place the rice and the lentils in a saucepan with the spices. Add the water, bring to boil and simmer until rice is soft (about 30 minutes, depending on type).

lemon rice

10 ounces basmati rice, rinsed
2 lemon grass stalks, finely sliced
5 cups water (approximately)
Sea salt to taste
3 tablespoons lemon juice

Place the rice in a saucepan and add the water and the salt. Bring to the boil. Add the lemon grass and simmer for about 30 minutes until the rice is tender. Sprinkle with lemon juice and serve.

hasselbach potatoes

3 pounds potatoes, halved
Sunflower oil
Gomassio (sesame salt)
1 bunch of fresh dill, finely chopped

Place the halved potatoes on a chopping board, flat side down, and cut grooves in each (nearly all the way through to the bottom). Then parboil the potatoes in lightly salted water for 5 minutes, drain and cool under running water. Dry gently and place in a lightly greased large roasting pan. Brush well with oil. Bake in a preheated oven at 425°F for 25 minutes, or until crisp and golden. Sprinkle with gomassio and garnish with the fresh dill.

pan bread

8½ ounces wholewheat flour
2 teaspoons baking powder
½ teaspoon unrefined sea salt
1 teaspoon caraway seeds (optional)
1 cup water (approximately)

Sift the flour, baking powder, and salt together. Add the caraway seeds and then enough water to form a soft dough. Knead to a smooth consistency. Roll the dough into a sausage and divide it into 12 balls. Roll each ball on a floured surface into 5-inch rounds. Heat a dry heavy skillet and cook each bread (without oil) for 2 minutes on each side (or until brown spots appear).

spring greens and macadamia nuts

2 ounces macadamia nuts
2 tablespoons olive oil
2¼ pounds spring greens (or other greens), shredded
½ cup water or bouillon
1 tablespoon lemon juice
Sea salt and freshly ground black pepper

Toast the macadamia nuts in a dry skillet, then remove from heat. Heat the oil in a large pan or wok, add the spring greens and stir-fry for 5 minutes. Add the water, cover and simmer another 5 minutes. Add the lemon juice and macadamia nuts, season and serve.

tomato salsa

1 pound ripe tomatoes, finely chopped
2 scallions, finely chopped
1 red chilli pepper, finely chopped
4 tablespoons lime juice
1 bunch of fresh basil, finely chopped
Sea salt and freshly ground black pepper to taste

Mix all the ingredients well in a bowl. Season and serve.

swiss chard and juniper berries

2 tablespoons olive oil
6 juniper berries, crushed
1 pound Swiss chard (or other greens), shredded
Sea salt and freshly ground black pepper
½ cup water

Heat the oil gently in a large pan. Add the juniper and stir. Add the greens. Stir-fry for 2 minutes. Add water, cover and simmer for 10 minutes. Season and serve.

SALADS

carrot 'n' beet salad

10 ounces carrots, grated
10 ounces beet, grated
1 tablespoon fresh ginger root, finely chopped
2 tablespoons sunflower oil
4 tablespoons lemon juice
3½ ounces beansprouts
3 tablespoons sunflower seeds, roasted
3 tablespoons pumpkin seeds, roasted

Mix the grated carrots and beet with the ginger. Add the oil and the lemon juice, and mix well. Add the bean sprouts and mix gently. Garnish with the seeds.

salad niçoise

½ cup olive oil
2 tablespoons white wine vinegar
1 tablespoon lemon juice
1 tablespoon Dijon mustard
1 tablespoon maple syrup
7 ounces new potatoes in their skins, boiled in lightly salted water
Sea salt and freshly ground black pepper to taste
4 ounces marinated tofu, in small cubes
Soy sauce
8½ ounces tomatoes, in boats
½ cucumber, chopped into sticks
½ iceberg lettuce
4 tablespoons small niçoise olives
8½ ounces green beans, topped, tailed, and steamed
2 tablespoons fresh parsley, finely chopped
2 tablespoons fresh basil, finely chopped

Combine the oil, vinegar, lemon juice, mustard, and maple syrup in a bowl, whisk or hand-blend, then season to taste. Cut the cooled potatoes in half and add them to the dressing. Mix well and set aside. Sauté the tofu in a little oil, turn off heat and add a few drops of soy sauce. Add to the potatoes. Leave to cool a little, then add the rest of the ingredients and serve with French bread.

bulgur wheat salad

8½ ounces bulgur wheat, cooked and allowed to cool
1 bunch of scallions, sliced
2 tomatoes, chopped
1 green pepper, deseeded and cut into strips
½ cucumber, chopped
1 garlic clove
2 tablespoons fresh mint, chopped
2 tablespoons fresh parsley, chopped
2 tablespoons fresh cilantro leaves, chopped
4 tablespoons olive oil
3 tablespoons lemon juice
Sea salt and freshly ground black pepper to taste

Place the cooked bulgur in a salad bowl and mix with the rest of the ingredients. Serve cold.

artichoke salad

8 artichoke hearts
4 big ripe tomatoes, cut into boats
1 red onion, sliced
3½ ounces green olives

If using fresh artichokes, prepare them by breaking off the outer "petals." When you get to the softer inner ones, cut them off with a sharp knife as close to the heart as possible. Scrape out the "choke" with a teaspoon. (Leave the hearts in cold water while you prepare the others, to avoid discoloration.) Plunge the hearts into boiling water and cook for about 20 minutes (or until tender). Cool and place with the other ingredients in a salad bowl and serve with french bread and lemon tahini dressing (see page 251).

provençal mesclun salad

1 butterhead lettuce, shredded
A small handful of green leaves and herbs, as available (such as arugula, sorrel, radicchio, mustard cress, nasturtium leaves and flowers, parsley, mint, and/or basil)
Rich garlic dressing (see page 209)

Place the shredded lettuce in a large salad bowl, add the green leaves and herbs, mix lightly and add the dressing just before serving.

arugula salad

4 handfuls of arugula, shredded
1 small red onion, finely chopped
4 small ripe tomatoes, cut into boats
Lime dressing (see page 251)
4 tablespoons walnuts, roughly chopped

Place the arugula in a salad bowl, add the onion and tomato, and the dressing. Garnish with the walnuts and serve with fresh crusty bread.

catalan salad

2 pounds potatoes, boiled in their skins and allowed to cool
1 broccoli, cut into flowerets, steamed and allowed to cool
1 avocado, sliced
1 salad onion, chopped
1 red bell pepper, deseeded and sliced
1 yellow bell pepper, deseeded and sliced
3 tablespoons capers
4 tablespoons olives
3 tablespoons fresh parsley, finely chopped
1 tablespoon fresh thyme
Lime dressing *(see page 251)*

Cut the potatoes into thick slices. Place in a salad bowl and combine with the rest of the ingredients.

chinese salad *(pictured page 258)*

¼ Chinese cabbage, finely sliced
1 teaspoon fresh ginger root, finely chopped
1 teaspoon garlic, finely chopped
1 small red chilli pepper, deseeded and finely chopped
1 small bunch of watercress, chopped
3½ ounces mangetout peas, trimmed
2 scallions, finely sliced
8 ounces beansprouts
1 portion lime dressing *(see page 251)*

Place the Chinese cabbage in a salad bowl and add all the other ingredients. Mix well, add the dressing and serve.

florence fennel salad

1 bulb Florence fennel, thinly sliced
1 avocado, thinly sliced
3½ ounces pecan nuts
3½ ounces green olives
1 cucumber, thinly sliced
Rich garlic dressing *(see page 209)*

Mix all the ingredients with the dressing. Garnish with fennel tops and serve.

green lentil salad

2 ounces green lentils (dry weight), cooked and allowed to cool
1 small cauliflower, in flowerets
2 carrots, cut into peelings
7 ounces green peas, shelled
1 young zucchini, thinly sliced
1 bunch of watercress, chopped
7 ounces yellow beans, steamed and cooled
Lemon tahini dressing *(see page 251)*

Mix all the ingredients with the dressing and serve.

orange mango salad

1 orange, peeled and chopped
2 mangos, peeled and chopped
2 carrots, cut into peelings
1 handful of radicchio, finely shredded
1 red chilli, deseeded and finely sliced
1 teaspoon ginger root, finely chopped
3 tablespoons lemon juice

Mix all the ingredients in a salad bowl and serve.

pasta salad

12 ounces three-colored pasta twists, cooked
1 zucchini, grated
2 tomatoes, in boats
1 bunch of asparagus, trimmed and cooked, in pieces
1 bunch of fresh basil, finely chopped
Lime dressing *(see page 251)*

Cool the pasta and place in a salad bowl. Add all the other ingredients, add the dressing and serve.

potato salad

2¼ pounds new potatoes, boiled in their skins
1½ cups plain soy yogurt
1 shallot, finely chopped
1 small red bell pepper, finely chopped
2 tablespoons capers
1–2 tablespoons lemon juice
Sea salt and freshly ground black pepper to taste
1 small bunch of chives, finely chopped

Allow the potatoes to cool and cut them into thick slices. Combine the rest of the ingredients to make the dressing. Place the potatoes in a salad bowl and add the dressing, mix gently, garnish with chives and serve.

sweetcorn (maize) and sun-dried tomato salad

4 sweetcorns (maize), cut into chunks and boiled for 3 minutes
2 ounces sun-dried tomatoes, cut into strips
1 handful of arugula
1 small lettuce, shredded
2 tablespoons fresh basil, chopped
4 tablespoons walnut oil
2 tablespoons balsamic vinegar
Sea salt and freshly ground black pepper to taste

Put the corn in a bowl on a bed of tomatoes, arugula, lettuce, and basil. Whisk together the oil and vinegar and toss with the salad. Season and serve.

salad with sorrel and tempeh

2 tablespoons olive oil
8 tempeh rashers
1 handful of young sorrel leaves, shredded
1 little gem lettuce, shredded
Rich garlic dressing *(see page 209)*

Fry the tempeh in the olive oil until crisp and golden. Sprinkle with salt then cut into bite-size pieces. Place the sorrel and lettuce leaves in a bowl and add the tempeh. Pour the dressing over and mix gently.

tropical sunshine salad

3 carrots, cut into peelings
1 avocado, sliced
1 mango, peeled and sliced
1 handful of nasturtium leaves and flowers
1 pomegranate, peeled and pith removed
4 scallions, sliced
1 garlic clove, finely chopped
1-inch piece of ginger root, finely chopped
3 tablespoons safflower oil
3 tablespoons lime juice
Sea salt and freshly ground black pepper to taste

Combine all the ingredients in a salad bowl and mix well. Season and serve.

wild rice salad *(below)*

2 ounces wild rice (dry weight), cooked and cooled
1 Florence fennel, steamed, cooled and sliced
1 bell pepper, broiled and skinned *(see page 247)*
2 tomatoes, cut into boats
2 scallions, sliced
1 celery stalk, sliced
3½ ounces black olives, pitted
2 garlic cloves, crushed
Lemon tahini dressing *(see page 251)*
2 tablespoons fresh parsley, finely chopped, to garnish
2 tablespoons fresh basil, finely chopped, to garnish

Place the rice and fennel in a salad bowl, then add the rest of the ingredients. Add the lemon tahini dressing, garnish with the fresh herbs and serve.

desserts

raspberry gateau

8½ ounces wholewheat or spelt flour
1 tablespoon baking powder
2 ounces ground almonds
4 ounces raw cane sugar
½ cup sunflower oil
2 tablespoons malt extract
½ teaspoon vanilla (or almond) essence
1¼ cups warm water

For the topping:
1 cup plain soy yogurt
2 ounces blanched almonds, finely chopped and lightly toasted
12 ounces fresh raspberries
3 tablespoons maple syrup (optional)

Sift the flour and baking powder together. Add the ground almonds and sugar. Preheat the oven to 350°F. Grease a round cake tin with oil and sprinkle with flour. Combine the oil, malt, vanilla (or almond) essence, and warm water and quickly add the mixture to the flour. Mix as quickly as possible. Pour the mixture into the cake tin, smooth the top and bake for 20–30 minutes (until it doesn't stick to a skewer). Leave to cool a little, then remove from tin and place on a round serving plate and spread the yogurt evenly over it. Arrange the almonds and the raspberries over the yogurt and sprinkle with maple syrup.

baked apples

4 cooking apples, cored
10 dates, pitted and chopped
4 bananas, mashed
4 tablespoons macadamia nuts or walnuts, chopped
3 tablespoons tahini
3 tablespoons lemon juice
½ cup maple syrup

Preheat oven to 350°F. Cut a line horizontally around the middle in the skin of each apple. Mix half the mashed banana with the chopped dates and stuff the mixture into the apple. Sprinkle the nuts on top. Bake for 20 minutes. Mix the tahini with the rest of the banana, lemon juice, and syrup. Add a little water and stir to a rich sauce. Pour over the baked apples.

passion-fruit sorbet *(far right, back)*

1½ cups passion-fruit pulp, blended
4 ounces raw cane sugar
½ cup water

Heat the water and the sugar gently in a small heavy-based casserole until the sugar dissolves. Stir gently from time to time to loosen the sugar from the base of the pan. Bring to the boil and simmer for 1 minute. Cool, then mix with the passion fruit. Stir well then freeze the mixture in a shallow non-metal container until solid (4–6 hours). Just before serving, break up the frozen mixture into chunks and blend until smooth. Serve immediately.

blackberry crumble _(below left)_

2¼ pounds blackberries (or bilberries, raspberries or blueberries)
3 tablespoons raw cane sugar
2 tablespoons white flour

For the topping:
3½ ounces wholewheat or spelt flour
3½ ounces rolled oats
4 tablespoons chopped nuts
5 ounces vegetable margarine
4 tablespoons honey

Mix the blackberries with the sugar and flour in a pie dish. For the topping, mix the flour, oats, and nuts in a bowl, then rub in the margarine and honey. Cover the berries with crumble mixture and lightly smooth the surface. Bake at 400°F for 30 minutes until golden. Serve warm or cold.

nectarine surprise

4 nectarines, thinly sliced
4 tablespoons maple syrup
1 teaspoon fresh ginger root, grated
1 tablespoon fresh mint, finely chopped

Place the sliced nectarines in a bowl. Heat ½ cup of water and add the maple syrup and the ginger. Cool and pour over the nectarines. Leave to marinate in the refrigerator for a couple of hours before serving, garnished with mint.

raspberry sorbet _(right, front)_

1½ cups raspberries, juiced
6 ounces raw cane sugar
½ cup water

Heat the water and the sugar gently in a small heavy-based casserole until the sugar dissolves. Stir gently from time to time to loosen the sugar from the base. Bring to boil and boil for 1 minute. Cool before mixing with the raspberry juice. Stir well, then freeze in a shallow non-metal container until solid (4–6 hours). Just before serving, break into chunks and blend until smooth. Serve immediately.

tropical fruit salad

1-inch cube ginger root, finely chopped
4 tablespoons maple syrup (optional)
1 lemon, grated rind and juice
½ cup pineapple juice
8 lychees, peeled and pitted
1 mango, peeled and cut into cubes
1 pineapple, peeled, cored and sliced
4 kiwis, peeled and sliced
1 pawpaw, peeled, deseeded and sliced

Put the ginger, syrup, and juices in a pan. Heat gently and simmer for 1 minute. Pour into a bowl. Cool. Add the fruit and serve.

pear tart

4 big ripe pears, peeled, halved longways, cored and deseeded
Marzipan (optional)

For the short-crust pastry:
8½ ounces wholewheat or spelt flour
½ teaspoon salt
2 ounces raw cane sugar
4½ ounces cold vegetable margarine

Mix the flour, salt and sugar, and chop in the margarine with a knife and a spoon until it forms small lumps. Crumble the mixture with your hands until it looks like Parmesan (taking care not to let the dough get warm). Add 5 tablespoons cold water and knead the dough lightly into a smooth lump. Refrigerate until needed. Divide the pastry in two, roll out one half and place in a greased flan case. Press a lump of marzipan into the core of each pear half, then place the pears, face down, in the flan shell. Cover with the other half of the pastry. Press lightly down between the pears and firmly around the edge. Bake at 400°F for 20–30 minutes, until golden. Serve warm or cold.

juices
apricot and ginger

5 apricots, pitted
1 teaspoon fresh ginger root, chopped
½ cup apple juice
½ cup soy milk

Blend all the ingredients and serve with ice.

autumn fruit

2 apples, cored and quartered
2 pears, cored and quartered
½ grapefruit, peeled

Juice the ingredients and serve with ice.

beet and apple

8½ ounces fresh beet, quartered
3 apples, cored and quartered

Juice the beet and the apple and mix well. Pour into a tall glass and garnish with a slice of lime.

blackberry cream *(far right, front)*

3½ ounces blackberries
1 ripe banana
1 pear, cored and quartered
½ cup plain soy yogurt
1 tablespoon sunflower seeds

Blend all the ingredients and serve chilled.

caribbean smoothie

¼ pineapple, peeled, cored and chopped
½ mango, peeled and chopped
1 banana, peeled

Blend and serve chilled.

carrot and lemon with garlic

8½ ounces carrots
1 garlic clove, peeled
½ lemon, squeezed

Press the garlic through the juicer together with the carrot. Mix with the squeezed lemon and serve.

cool cucumber

1 cucumber
1 tomato
1 garlic clove, peeled
1 green bell pepper, quartered and deseeded
2 sprigs of fresh dill

Juice the ingredients, but keep a little dill as a garnish. Serve chilled.

cranberry spritzer

10 ounces cranberries (or ½ cup cranberry juice)
½ cup fizzy water
1 lemon slice

Juice the cranberries and mix with the fizzy water. Garnish with lemon.

creamy mango *(right, back)*

1 mango, pitted, peeled and cubed
1 banana, peeled
1 wedge of fresh coconut
1 orange, squeezed

Blend the mango, banana and coconut. Add the orange juice, mix well and serve.

green party

2 celery stalks with leaves
¼ Florence fennel
1 handful of arugula leaves (or other green leaves)
½ cucumber
1 tomato
Few sprigs of fresh basil
Slice of lime

Juice the celery, fennel, green leaves, cucumber, tomato, and basil. Garnish with lime and serve cool.

guava and apple

1 guava, peeled
¾ cup apple juice
1 slice of orange

Blend the guava with the apple juice. Serve in
a tall glass garnished with a slice of orange.

heart warmer

3½ ounces carrots
3½ ounces beet
2 celery sticks with leaves
2 garlic cloves, peeled
1-inch piece of ginger root, peeled
½ lemon, squeezed

Juice the carrot, beet, celery, garlic, and ginger.
Add the lemon juice, mix well, and serve.

height of passion

3 passion fruits, peeled
½ mango, peeled
¼ pineapple, peeled

Juice the fruits and serve with ice.

mango and lime

1 mango, peeled and pitted
½ cup almond milk
1 lime, squeezed
Pinch of cinnamon

Blend, garnish with a sprinkle of cinnamon, and serve chilled.

melon and orange

7 ounces cantaloupe melon, deeded and peeled
1 orange, squeezed

Blend the melon with the orange and serve with ice.

natural beauty *(far right)*

2 apples
½ cantaloupe melon

Juice and serve.

nirvana

1 ripe pear
6 strawberries
4 apricots
1 peach
1 slice of tangerine

Juice the fruits and serve garnished with a slice of tangerine.

papaya power

1 papaya, peeled, and pitted
1 lemon, squeezed

Blend the papaya with the lemon juice and serve with ice.

pina colada

½ pineapple, peeled, cored and chopped
4 tablespoons coconut milk
1 teaspoon lime juice
2 teaspoons maple syrup

Blend all the ingredients and serve with ice.

passion and lime

2 passion fruits
1 tablespoon maple syrup
1 orange, squeezed
½ lime, squeezed
2 tablespoons plain soy yogurt
Pinch of vanilla powder

Blend passion fruits, maple syrup, and orange and lime juice with yogurt and
vanilla. Pour into a glass and add fizzy water to taste. Serve with ice.

tomato cocktail

7 ounces tomatoes, quartered
1 carrot
1 small beet, quartered
3 lettuce leaves
3 spinach leaves
6 sprigs of watercress
4 sprigs of parsley
1 celery stalk with leaves
Few drops of tabasco (optional)
Pinch of celery salt

Juice the vegetables and greens. Pour into a glass and mix well, add a few
drops of tabasco and a pinch of celery salt, stir, and serve garnished with lemon.

pink pineapple *(far left)*

¼ pineapple, peeled, cored and chopped
1 orange, squeezed
5 ounces strawberries

Blend all the ingredients and serve.

grape and raisin smoothie

1 bunch of seedless grapes
1 carrot
2 tablespoons raisins, soaked in water overnight

Juice the ingredients and serve.

soft tutti fruity

6 strawberries
5 apricots
2 peaches
4 tablespoons apple juice
Maple syrup to taste (optional)

Blend the fruits with the apple juice and serve.

sunrise

1 apple, cored and quartered
2 carrots
1 tomato, quartered
1 orange, squeezed
1 slice of orange
Fresh mint

Juice the apple, carrots, and tomato and mix with the orange juice. Serve in a
tumbler garnished with a slice of orange and a sprig of fresh mint.

vegetable cocktail

1 small beet, quartered
1 handful of arugula (or other green leaves)
1 red bell pepper, deseeded and quartered
2 tomatoes, quartered
3 celery stalks, with tops
5 carrots
1 wedge of cabbage (or spring greens)
1 garlic clove, peeled

Juice the ingredients and serve.

herbal drinks and syrups

calming tea

1 part lavender flowers
1 part camomile
1 part lemon balm
1 part St. John's wort

Mix the herbs well. Use 1 teaspoon herb mixture per cup of boiling water. Place the herbs in a warmed teapot and pour boiling water over them. Cover and leave to infuse for 10 minutes.

camomile tonic

2 ounces camomile flowers
2 tablespoons lemon juice
3 tablespoons honey
3¾ cups organic white wine

Mix all the ingredients in a bowl. Cover and leave in a cool, dark place for 10 days. Strain through a cheesecloth and store in sterile bottles.

cold buster

½ teaspoon wild marjoram
½ teaspoon yarrow
½ teaspoon elderflowers
Small pinch of cayenne
1 cup boiling water
2 tablespoons lemon juice
Honey to taste

Place the herbs in a mug in a tea filter or strainer. Add boiling water. Cover and leave to infuse for 10 minutes. Remove the herbs, add the lemon juice and honey. Drink hot.

cough mixture

½ teaspoon licorice root
½ teaspoon thyme
½ teaspoon wild marjoram
½ teaspoon borage
1 teaspoon sweet violet
1 cup boiling water
1 teaspoon honey
Squeeze of lemon juice

Place the herbs in a warmed teapot. Add the boiling water, cover and leave to infuse for 10 minutes. Pour into a mug, add the honey and the lemon juice.

circulation booster

3 parts hawthorn flowers or berries
2 parts yarrow
1 part black mustard seeds

Mix the herbs. Use 1 teaspoon herb mixture per cup of boiling water. Place the herbs in a warmed teapot and pour boiling water over them. Cover and leave to infuse for 10 minutes.

cystitis relief

1 part yarrow
1 part echinacea
1 part cleavers
1 part celery seeds
1 part sweet violets

Mix the herbs well. Use 1 teaspoon herb mixture per cup of boiling water. Place the herbs in a warmed teapot and pour boiling water over them. Cover and leave to infuse for 10 minutes.

elderberry cordial

2¼ pounds ripe elderberries, rinsed with stalks removed
2½ cups spring water
2 tablespoons lemon juice
1 teaspoon citric acid (optional)
12 ounces unrefined cane sugar

Place the berries in a saucepan with the water, lemon juice, and citric acid. Bring to boil and simmer gently until the berries burst. Strain through a cheesecloth, add the sugar and bring back to the boil. Simmer again for 5 minutes. Skim and pour into sterilized warm glass bottles. Seal and store in a cool, dark place. Drink diluted with hot water.

elderflower spritzer

1 head of fresh elderflowers
1 slice of lemon
½ cup boiling water
1 teaspoon honey
Ice cubes
½ cup fizzy water

Place the elderflowers and the lemon slice in a small bowl. Add the boiling water and the honey. Cover and leave to cool. Strain and pour into a tall glass with ice, add the fizzy water, and serve immediately.

eucalyptus mix

3 parts eucalyptus leaves
2 parts camomile
2 parts thyme

Mix the herbs well. Use 1 teaspoon herb mixture per cup of boiling water. Place the herbs in a warmed teapot and pour boiling water over them. Cover and leave to infuse for 10 minutes.

garlic oxymel *(below)*

1 cup red wine vinegar
3 tablespoons fresh garlic, chopped
2 teaspoon black cumin seeds
9 ounces honey

Place the vinegar, garlic, and cumin in a small saucepan. Bring to boil, cover, and simmer for 5 minutes. Strain and add the honey. Bring to boil and simmer again, very gently, for another 5 minutes. Remove from heat and store in a clean jar. Take 1 tablespoon at a time.

green tea with mint

1 teaspoon green tea
1 tablespoon fresh mint, chopped
1 cup boiling water

Place the green tea and the mint in a warmed teapot. Add the boiling water, cover and leave to infuse for 5 minutes. Serve hot or chilled.

hay fever relief

1 teaspoon fresh horseradish, grated
1 teaspoon honey
1 glass of water

For the tisane:
2 parts elderflowers
1 part echinacea
1 part eyebright
1 part camomile
1 part licorice
1 part peppermint

Mix the grated horseradish with the honey and take with a glass of water. Make the tisane by mixing the herbs and adding 1 teaspoon of herbs per cup of boiling water to a warmed teapot. Add boiling water, cover, and leave to infuse for 10 minutes.

heart chai

1 teaspoon green tea
1 teaspoon black cumin seeds
½-inch of cinnamon stick
Small pinch of cayenne
1 teaspoon lemon balm
1½ cup soy (or rice) milk
1 teaspoon honey (optional)

Place all the ingredients, except the honey, in a small saucepan, bring to the boil and simmer gently for 2 minutes. Strain into a large cup, add honey (if liked), and serve.

immuni-tea

2 parts nettles
1 part licorice
1 part echinacea
1 part cleavers
1 part thyme
1 part borage

Mix the herbs well. Use 1 teaspoon of herb mixture per cup of boiling water. Place the herbs in a warmed teapot, add the water, cover, and leave to infuse for 10 minutes.

licorice mix

½-inch piece of licorice root, chopped
½-inch of cinnamon stick
½ teaspoon fennel seeds
½ teaspoon fresh ginger, chopped
1 cup water

Place all the ingredients in a small saucepan and bring to boil. Simmer gently for 5 minutes. Strain and serve.

lung-cleansing tea mix

1 part licorice root
1 part thyme
1 part eucalyptus leaves
1 part peppermint
1 part sweet violets
1 part elderflowers

Mix all the herbs well. Use 1 teaspoon per cup of boiling water. Place the herbs in a warmed teapot. Add the boiling water. Cover and leave to infuse for 10 minutes.

pick-me-up

1 part oats, whole grains, crushed
1 part lavender
1 part rosemary
1 part lemon balm
2 parts rosehips
1 part jasmine tea

Mix all the ingredients together. Use 1 teaspoon per cup of boiling water. Place the ingredients in a warmed teapot. Add the boiling water. Cover and leave to infuse for 10 minutes.

rosehip syrup

4 ounces rosehips
2½ cups water
4 ounces raw cane sugar

Place the rosehips and water in a saucepan. Bring to boil, remove from heat and leave to cool. Strain through several layers of cheesecloth to make sure seeds and fine hairs are discarded with the fruit. Bring the liquid back to boil, add the sugar and simmer gently until the volume is reduced by a third. Stir gently from time to time. Pour into sterile bottles and store in a cool dry place.

sage mix for sore throats

1 teaspoon sage
½ teaspoon cleavers
½ teaspoon fresh ginger, finely chopped
1½ cups boiling water

Place the sage, cleavers and ginger in a warmed teapot, add the water, and leave to infuse for 5 minutes.

si c

1 guava, peeled
3½ ounces blackcurrants
3½ ounces strawberries
½ papaya, peeled and deseeded
1 banana

Blend the ingredients and serve with ice.

sleepy time

2 parts passionflower leaves
1 part lavender
1 part camomile
1 part catnip

Mix all the herbs well. Use 1 teaspoon per cup of boiling water. Place the herbs in a warmed teapot. Add boiling water. Cover and leave to infuse for 10 minutes.

spicy chai

½-inch of cinnamon stick
½ teaspoon black mustard seeds
½ teaspoon fennel seeds
½ teaspoon licorice root
¼ teaspoon caraway seeds
1½ cup rice milk
1 teaspoon honey (optional)

Place all the ingredients in a small saucepan and bring to the boil. Simmer for a few minutes. Pour into a mug and serve with honey.

stress relief

1 part borage
1 part lavender
1 part lemon balm
1 part basil
1 part peppermint

Mix all the herbs well. Use 1 teaspoon per cup of boiling water. Place the herbs in a warmed teapot. Add boiling water. Cover and leave to infuse for 10 minutes.

tea for aches and pains

2 parts St. John's wort
2 parts meadowsweet
1 part rosemary

Mix all the herbs well. Use 1 teaspoon per cup of boiling water. Place the herbs in a warmed teapot. Add boiling water. Cover and leave to infuse for 10 minutes.

tea for ear infections

1 part St. John's wort
1 part echinacea
1 part rosehips
1 part elderflowers
1 part licorice root
1 part peppermint
1 part cleavers

Mix all the herbs well. Use 1 teaspoon per cup of boiling water. Place the herbs in a warmed teapot. Add boiling water. Cover and leave to infuse for 10 minutes.

tea for fever

½ teaspoon catnip
½ teaspoon borage
½ teaspoon camomile
Small pinch of cayenne
1 cup boiling water

Place the herbs in a warmed teapot. Add the boiling water. Cover and leave to infuse for 5 minutes.

tea for fungal infections

2 parts echinacea
1 part lemon balm
1 part calendula (marigold)
1 part cleavers

Mix the herbs well. Use 1 teaspoon herb mixture per cup of boiling water. Place the herbs in a warmed teapot and pour the boiling water over them. Cover and leave to infuse for 10 minutes.

thyme syrup

3 tablespoons dried thyme
2½ cups of water
12 ounces unrefined cane sugar

Bring the water to the boil in a small saucepan. Add the thyme and remove from heat. Cover and leave to infuse for 20 minutes. Strain and add the sugar. Heat gently until sugar dissolves. Pour into sterile bottles and store in the refrigerator.

tea for glands

1 part borage
1 part cleavers
1 part echinacea
1 part calendula (marigold)

Mix all the herbs well. Use 1 teaspoon per cup of boiling water. Place the herbs in a warmed teapot. Add boiling water. Cover and leave to infuse for 10 minutes.

tea for headache

1 part feverfew
1 part rosemary
1 part marjoram
1 part peppermint

Mix all the herbs well. Use 1 teaspoon per cup of boiling water. Place the herbs in a warmed teapot. Add boiling water. Cover and leave to infuse for 10 minutes.

tea for joints

1 part elderflowers
1 part St. John's wort
1 part celery seeds
1 part nettles
1 part black mustard seeds

Mix all the herbs well. Use 1 teaspoon per cup of boiling water. Place the herbs in a warmed teapot. Add boiling water. Cover and leave to infuse for 10 minutes.

tea for the skin

1 part nettles
1 part echinacea
1 part cleavers
½ part calendula (marigold)
1 part sweet violets

Mix all the herbs well. Use 1 teaspoon per cup of boiling water. Place the herbs in a warmed teapot. Add boiling water. Cover and leave to infuse for 10 minutes.

winter tonic

7 ounces ripe blackberries
2 tablespoons maple syrup
1 banana
½ cup almond milk

Blend and serve.

diet plans

detox and elimination diet

If you suspect you have a food allergy, but you are unsure what you are allergic to, one way to find out for sure is to keep a diet diary. Take seven pieces of paper and mark each one with a different day of the week. Carry the relevant piece of paper around with you everywhere each day for the following week, and record EVERYTHING you eat and drink and the time you had it. (It is easy to forget what you've eaten if you don't write it down immediately.)

At the end of each day, write down how (and where) you've been that day, whether you've had any allergy symptoms (such as migraine or stomach ache) and, if you are suffering from arthritis, whether your arthritis was better or worse (on a scale of 1 to 10) that day. Food allergy symptoms can start up to 24 hours after the allergen was consumed, so keeping a diet diary enables you to look back and identify possible offenders more easily.

If after a week it is clear that you have "good" days and "bad" days according to what you eat, you can start to create your own personal elimination diet by keeping your diet diary up to date and eliminating the foods you have found are not good for you.

Try the following diet plan to discover which foods or drinks to leave out (you can always reintroduce them after a while, to see if you still react to them). Choose a time when you haven't got too many commitments. If you suffer from any serious medical disorders, it is not advisable to undertake an elimination diet without medical supervision.

You may experience symptoms of withdrawal and detoxification (such as nausea, headache, the feeling that your teeth and tongue have a furry coat, and even diarrhea) but these symptoms should diminish after a couple of days, leaving you feeling fresher and more alert. Eat and drink (water or mild herb tea) every 2–3 hours and have plenty of the foods on the "allowed" list. Keep a record of everything you consume and note any reaction. Avoid using toothpaste during the diet—use salt or baking powder instead. This is a progressive plan in which you cut out more food groups each day, and reintroduce them according to the schedule given. Make sure you drink at least 4 cups of water each day.

DAY ONE

Cut out all stimulants (black tea, coffee, chocolate, cigarettes, alcohol) processed "convenience" foods, sugar (including sweets, honey and syrups), and foods containing additives.

DAY TWO

Cut out all dairy products, meat, fish, and shellfish.

DAY THREE

Cut out all wheat, buckwheat, corn, nuts and pulses, and foods containing these.

DAY FOUR

Cut out oxalic acid foods (spinach, rhubarb, strawberries) and foods belonging to the nightshade family (*solinaceae*): potatoes, eggplants, peppers, chillies, cayenne, paprika and tomatoes. Eat only steamed or raw vegetables, rice, and fruit.

DAY FIVE

Cut out rice and all citrus fruits (lemon, orange, grapefruit, lime, tangerine, kumquat, mandarin, clementine). Eat only steamed or raw vegetables and fruit.

DAY SIX

Eat only fruit.

DAY SEVEN

Drink only water.

DAY EIGHT

Eat only fruit.

DAY NINE

Eat only steamed or raw vegetables and fruit (except citrus, nightshade family and oxalic acid foods).

DAY TEN

Eat vegetables, fruits and rice. Reintroduce foods from the nightshade family. Observe any reaction.

DAY ELEVEN

Eat vegetables, fruits, and rice. Reintroduce citrus fruits. Observe any reaction.

DAY TWELVE

Eat vegetables, fruits, and rice. Reintroduce corn, nuts, and pulses. Observe any reaction.

DAY THIRTEEN

Eat vegetables, fruits, and rice. Reintroduce wheat, buckwheat, and fish. Observe any reaction.

DAY FOURTEEN

Eat vegetables, fruits, and rice. Reintroduce dairy products. Observe any reaction.

DAY FIFTEEN

Eat vegetables, fruits, and rice. Reintroduce shellfish. Observe any reaction.

DAY SIXTEEN

Start eating "normally" again, but note your reactions carefully when you reintroduce meat, sugar, oxalic-acid foods, stimulants, and food additives. Review your diet diary and take note of the food groups you reacted negatively to. Base your diet on what you discover.

traditional grape fast

A grape fast is cleansing and detoxifying. The best time to do it is at the end of the summer when grapes are cheap, and plentiful. Choose organic grapes, and eat as many as you like on the "grape" days. You should also drink plenty of water and have diluted unsweetened organic grape juice, little and often, throughout. Take plenty of time to rest, too. Avoid smoking during the fast.

DAYS ONE, TWO, AND THREE

Eat only grapes and drink only water and grape juice.

DAY FOUR

Eat nothing but drink plenty of water and grape juice.

DAYS FIVE, SIX, AND SEVEN

Eat only grapes and drink only water and grape juice.

gentle healing diet

If you are suffering from a chronic illness, or have been through a period of physical, mental, emotional, or spiritual stress, a gentle healing diet is a necessity to provide resources for healing. It is made up of foods that are highly nutritious, easily digested, and easily absorbed and used by the body. The diet contains the right amount of protein for growth and repair, and plenty of complex carbohydrates for sustained energy. It is low in fat but contains all the necessary essential fatty acids, and it is high in vitamins, minerals and other healing phytochemicals. Choose low-GI foods.

COMPLEX CARBOHYDRATES

Grains (such as quinoa, amaranth, rice, couscous, bulgur, whole wheat, barley, oats and rye), roots and tubers (such as parsnips, celeriac, carrots, potatoes, sweet potatoes, beet).

VEGETABLE PROTEIN

Beans, peas, and green leaves. (Meat is not suitable for this gentle healing diet because it is a very concentrated food containing no fiber, and it may contain residues of hormones, antibiotics, nitrates, and other additives or harmful substances.)

VITAMINS, MINERALS, AND PHYTOCHEMICALS

Organically grown vegetables, either raw or cooked, boiled, baked, or steamed depending on your taste, your state of health, and your digestion. Start with cooked vegetables if you find raw foods hard to digest and add some raw ones little by little.

Eat one or two pieces of fruit each day. But in this diet the aim is to build up resources by eating food that provides steady energy without too many short bursts upsetting blood-sugar levels. Most fruits contain simple sugars (disaccharides) that are digested and absorbed into the blood stream more quickly than the complex carbohydrates (polysaccharides) found in grains and many vegetables. Choose carbohydrate foods with a low GI value and eat fruits that are in season, and particularly fruits that improve digestion, such as papaya, pineapple, banana, and grapefruit. Lemons contain a lot of vitamin C and not too much sugar.

UNSATURATED FATS AND OMEGA OILS

Nuts, seeds and olive vegetable oils (apart from coconut and palm oil) all contain unsaturated and omega fats that are good for health.

DRINKS

The aim is to build up resources by eating nutritious foods and keeping the digestive load to a minimum. Drinks should follow the same guidelines and be limited to water, vegetable juices (without sugar), and herb teas (avoid the artificially flavored ones). Drink at least 4 cups of water a day.

SUGGESTED MENU
(CHOOSE ONE FROM EACH CATEGORY)

BREAKFAST
baked tomatoes on toast (page 258)
beans and tomatoes on toast (page 258)
muesli (page 259)
oatmeal with dried fruit and quinoa (page 258)
scrambled tofu (page 258)

SALAD AND SOUP LUNCH
curried quinoa and vegetable soup (page 205)
artichoke salad (page 275)
bulgur wheat salad (page 275)
carrot 'n' beet salad (page 275)

catalan salad (page 276)
florence fennel salad (page 276)
green lentil salad (page 276)
potato salad (page 276)
arugula salad (page 275)
salad niçoise (page 275)
sweetcorn and sun-dried tomato salad (page 276)
wild rice salad (page 277)
oriental salad with tempeh (page 209)
broiled endive and brazil nut salad (page 201)
black-eye pea and wild marjoram soup (page 261)
creamy cauliflower soup (page 261)
healing soup (page 260)
italian butterbean soup (page 261)
spicy moroccan soup (page 262)
tibetan dumpling soup (page 262)
welsh leek and potato soup (page 262)

DINNER
Starters
asparagus with ravigote (page 262)
baba ganoush (page 264)
hummus with crudités and warm pitta bread (page 262)
korean kimchi-style salad (page 263)
broiled bell peppers (page 263)
tofumasalata (page 264)
vegetable kebabs (page 263)

Main course
scandinavian beet burgers (page 179)
quinoa tabouleh (page 205)
amaranth and tofu puffs (page 268)
casserole de puy (page 268)
greek casserole (page 271)
mushrooms with sage and thyme stuffing (page 272)
paella (page 268)
provençale-style kidney beans (page 271)
shepherdess' pie (page 272)
spinach bouillabaisse (page 271)
sweet chestnuts and kumquats (page 273)
sweet potato curry (page 272)
winter hot pot (page 272)

SNACKS

spicy brazil nut paté (page 201)

marinated olives (page 264)

pan amb oli (page 267)

toasted nuts and seeds (page 264)

tomato and cucumber canapés (page 266)

guacamole (page 266)

tzaziki (page 267)

DRINKS

Pure water, herbal teas, freshly made vegetable juices and smoothies, dandelion or chicory coffee substitutes.

FOODS TO AVOID

- All sugars and foods containing added sugar
- All refined or processed foods and junk foods
- Fruit juices
- Stimulants (such as tea, coffee, alcohol, chocolate, fizzy drinks)
- Non-prescription drugs and supplements
- All foods containing saturated fats
- Additives
- Dairy products
- Meats
- Fish
- Foods with a high GI value

If you suffer from an arthritic condition, this healing diet may bring you relief from symptoms and pain. If it does not, you should consider modifying your diet to exclude the following: wheat, potatoes, tomatoes, peppers, eggplants, acidic fruits, spinach, rhubarb, strawberry, and vinegar.

glossary

Words in **bold** type also appear in this glossary.

ACETYLCHOLINE a chemical messenger needed for normal functioning of the central and autonomic nervous systems.

ANTHOCYANINS dark-blue flavonoid **antioxidants** that may reduce the "stickiness" of platelets and help prevent blood clots.

ANTI-CATARRHAL a substance capable of reducing secretions from mucous membranes.

ANTIBIOTIC a treatment for infectious disease that works by killing, or inhibiting the growth of, infecting organisms.

ANTICOAGULANT reduces the tendency of the blood to clot.

ANTIOXIDANT a substance that inhibits and controls the harmful action of **free radicals**. Vitamins C and E, zinc, and the trace element selenium are important antioxidants.

ANTISCORBUTIC prevents scurvy—a beneficial property of any food containing vitamin C (ascorbic acid).

ASTRINGENT any substance that causes binding and drying, for example to treat bleeding or diarrhea.

BENZOIC ACID an antiseptic primarily used to treat urinary-tract infections, and as a preservative in cordials and pickles.

BETA-SITOSTEROL a plant sterol that lowers blood cholesterol levels and is also believed to reduce tumor growth, particularly in the colon.

BIO-ACTIVE COMPOUNDS chemical substances, such as **antioxidants**, that are found in foods and known, or believed to have, beneficial effects on human health.

BIOFLAVONOIDS also known as flavonoids, a group of **bio-active compounds**, including **quercetin, kaempferol, rutin**, and hesperidin with **antioxidant, diuretic** and other wide-ranging properties. They reduce blood-cholesterol levels, and may protect against heart disease and some cancers.

BITTER PRINCIPLES a group of plant chemicals with a distinctive bitter taste. They stimulate secretion of digestive juices, activate the liver, and may act as natural **antibiotics**, antifungals, and anti-cancer agents.

BROMELAIN a protein-digesting enzyme found in pineapple. It mimics the action of pancreatic enzymes, and may reduce inflammation and swellings.

CAMPHOR a component of some volatile oils with warming, numbing, pain-relieving, and insecticidal properties.

CARMINATIVE relieves intestinal gas (flatulence).

CAROTENE a **carotenoid** in orange-colored plant foods.

CAROTENOIDS pigments with strong **antioxidant** properties found in brightly-colored plant foods. They are converted into vitamin A in the body.

CHLOROPHYLL a green pigment responsible for photosynthesis in plants that inhibits the growth of bacteria and soothes inflammation.

CITRIC ACID a plant acid that gives the distinctive sharp taste to lemons, limes, unripe oranges, currants, and raspberries. It has a cooling, thirst-quenching effect.

COUMARINS phytochemicals with natural anti-blood-clotting properties. May protect against stomach and breast cancer.

CRUCIFEROUS a member of the Cruciferae family of plants that includes cabbages, kale, mustard greens, turnips, and rutabaga. Cruciferous plants are rich in **glucosinolates**.

CURCUMINOIDS yellow pigments found in turmeric with anti-inflammatory properties. They enhance the action of adrenal hormones, and are beneficial to the liver.

CYANOGLYCOSIDES bio-active compounds found in some plants that may have medicinal properties.

DECOCTION a medicinal preparation made by boiling plant material (such as roots, wood, bark, nuts, or seeds) in water, usually for 10 to 15 minutes.

DEPURATIVE encourages the body to eliminate toxins.

DIAPHORETIC encourages sweating.

DIURETIC increases the flow of urine.

ESSENTIAL OILS also known as volatile oils, these are strong-smelling oils that give plants their characteristic odor, and have many pharmacological actions.

EXPECTORANT provokes expulsion of mucus from the lungs.

FEBRIFUGE a remedy that reduces fever.

FLAVONOID see **bioflavonoid**.

FOLATE, or folic acid, a type of B-vitamin so called because it is found in foliage.

FOLIC ACID see **folate**.

FORMIC ACID an irritant acid found in nettles.

FREE RADICALS by-products of metabolism that can cause damage to cell membranes by oxidation of fatty acids. Free radicals are neutralized by **antioxidants**.

GLUCOKININ a chemical found in various plants, including blueberry and garlic, that lowers blood-sugar levels.

GLUCOQUINONE a chemical found in nettle that may help lower blood-sugar levels.

GLUCOSINOLATES a group of more than 20 chemicals (including indoles and isothyocyanates) found in edible plants such as cabbage, cauliflower, and broccoli. They increase the activity of enzymes that help the body eliminate potential carcinogens, and thus help to protect against cancer. However, glucosinolates may inhibit iodine uptake by the thyroid gland if eaten in large quantities.

GLUTATHIONE a **free-radical** "scavenger" dependent on selenium for its **antioxidant** activity.

GLUTEN a protein contained in cereals such as wheat, barley, rye, and oats. Components of gluten called gliandins can provoke the immune reaction that causes celiac disease.

GLYCOSIDES compounds made up of a combination of sugars and non-sugars, found widely in nature, many of which have powerful medicinal actions (such as digitalis in foxglove).

HISTAMINE derived from the amino acid histidine and found in the tissues of animals and plants, it has various powerful effects on the body (including dilating small blood vessels, constricting the bronchial tubes, and stimulating the production of gastric juice), and is responsible for urticaria ("hives").

HYDROGENATED FATS found in many processed foods, these are made by adding hydrogen to polyunsaturated fats in a process known as hydrogenation. Hydrogenated and partially hydrogenated fats are more solid at room temperature than **polyunsaturated fats** (or oils), but the chemical and physical techniques used to produce them cause unwelcome changes, such as the production of unhealthy "trans" fats.

IMMUNO-STIMULANT boosts the body's natural defenses.

INFUSION a remedy made by steeping plant material (usually flowers and leaves) in hot water.

ISOFLAVONES a group of **bio-active compounds** found in cereals and legumes (including soy) that are structurally similar to human estrogen. Isoflavones may protect against breast cancer, but there is continuing debate about the effect of phytestrogens on infants fed on soy-based formula foods.

KAEMPFEROL a **bioflavonoid** found in many plant foods.

LACTOBACILLI a bacterial species that forms part of the body's healthy microbial ecology. Also found in live yogurt.

LECITHIN a complex phospholipid fat found in many body tissues, particularly the brain and nerves. It is also found in various foods. Plant lecithin may help the body to deal with excess cholesterol, and prevent abnormal blood clotting.

LENTINAN a polysaccharide found in shiitake mushrooms that enhances the immune response by stimulating cell activity. It has been investigated as a possible treatment for A.I.D.S. (in conjunction with other drugs) and cancer.

LEUKOTRIENE one of the eicosanoid family of chemicals, derived from arachidonic acid. It causes contraction of smooth muscle and is involved in the inflammatory response to injury.

LINOLEIC ACID one of the "essential" fatty acids (so called because they cannot be made in the body and thus have to be consumed in the diet). It is found in vegetables, nuts, grains, fruits, plant oils, eggs, and fowl, and is one of the omega-6 family of polyunsaturated fatty acids. It can be converted in the body to gamma-linolenic acid (GLA) and arachadonic acid, both of which have powerful effects on immune function, the inflammatory response, and cell metabolism.

LINOLENIC ACID an essential fatty acid necessary for normal health. One of the omega-3 family of polyunsaturated fatty acids, it is found in abundance in flax, mustard, and pumpkin seeds, soy and walnut oils, green leafy vegetables, meat, and meat products. It is converted in the body to eicosapentaeonic acid (E.P.A.—also found in fish oil) and docosahexaernoic acid (D.H.A.—also found in fish oil and some algae), both of which have beneficial effects on blood-fat levels and inhibit blood clotting.

LUTEIN an **antioxidant carotenoid** in many plant foods.

LYCOPENE an **antioxidant carotenoid** found in tomatoes. It is released from tomatoes when they are cooked, and its absorption into the body is improved by the presence of small amounts of oil or fat in the meal.

MONOUNSATURATED FAT a fatty acid that contains one chemical double-bond in its carbon chain. Olive oil is particularly rich in monounsaturated fatty acids, which are found also in many animal, fish, and vegetable fats.

MUCILAGE a complex carbohydrate found in many plants. It has a slimy texture when dissolved in water. Herbal remedies containing mucilage soothe inflamed mucous membranes.

OLEIC ACID one of the omega-9 family of unsaturated fats.

OMEGA-3 a group of unsaturated fatty acids containing **linolenic acid**, E.P.A. and D.H.A.

OMEGA-6 a group of unsaturated fatty acids containing **linoleic acid**, **linolenic acid** and arachidonic acid.

OXALATE also known as oxalic acid, a chemical found in various foodstuffs, including tea, rhubarb, and spinach, which, when present in the body in large amounts, encourages the formation of urinary stones. People suffering from urinary stones (or any form of gastro-intestinal malabsorption) should avoid foods containing oxalates.

PAPAIN a substance obtained from the juice of the papaya that mimics the action of digestive juices, thus aiding digestion.

PECTIN a soluble non-starch polysaccharide (N.S.P.) found in fruits and plants and used as a gelling agent in jams and preserves. Soluble N.S.P. in the diet helps protect against diseases associated with high blood cholesterol, such as coronary heart disease and gallstones.

PHENOLIC ACIDS substances found in freshly picked vegetables and fruits, wines, and teas that encourage detoxification and inhibit the formation of cancer cells.

PHYTOCHEMICALS bio-active compounds found in foods of plant origin with health-enhancing effects. They include allium compounds, carotenoids, coumarins, and bioflavonoids.

PHYTOHORMONES plant-derived chemicals, such as phytoestrogens, that mimic the action of human hormones.

POLYSACCHARIDES large carbohydrate molecules made up of chains of simple sugar molecules linked together. Starch is a type of polysaccharide.

POLYUNSATURATED FAT a type of fatty acid containing two or more double bonds in its carbon chain. It is found mainly in plant oils, and is an essential part of a healthy diet.

PORPHYRINS pigments found in the blood and tissues of animals, and also in plants and micro-organisms.

POULTICE a hot pack applied to the skin, prepared by mixing herbs (such as oats, flaxseed, or comfrey) with hot water and wrapping the mixture in a piece of linen or muslin.

PROTEASE INHIBITORS proteins found in plants, such as cereals and legumes, that may help protect against cancer.

QUERCETIN a **bioflavonoid** in foods such as onions, apples, tomatoes, berries, and tea. An **antioxidant**, it is thought to act as an antihistamine, and may help to treat allergies, as well as be valuable in the prevention of heart disease and cancer. There is, at present, little evidence to support this therapeutic claim.

QUINIC ACID a sugar compound found in fruits, such as apples, peaches, pears, plums, and some vegetables, that has antiviral and neuroprotective properties.

RUTIN a **bioflavonoid** with a reputation for toning and healing peripheral blood vessels.

SACCHARIDE another name for carbohydrate. Complex carbohydrates, fruit sugar, and glucose are also known as polysaccharides, disaccharides, and monosaccharides respectively.

SALICYLATE also known as salicylic acid, a chemical of plant origin that forms the basis for the drug aspirin. Plants containing salicylate have antiseptic, painkilling and anti-inflammatory effects. Thought best avoided in A.D.H.D. diet regimes.

SAPONINS bio-active compounds, traditionally used for their **expectorant**, **diuretic** and anti-inflammatory effects. They are found in many foods and herbs, including soy beans, licorice, violet, yarrow, oats, asparagus, and many other vegetables.

SATURATED FAT a type of fatty acid containing the maximum possible number of hydrogen atoms. It is usually solid at room temperature. Animal fats (including butter, lard, and suet) contain a high proportion of saturated fat, as do solid vegetable fats like coconut oil. Saturated fat can be made in the body and so is not needed in the diet.

SULFUR a mineral found in some plant foods and medicinal plants that has a cleansing, anti-rheumatic effect.

TANNIN a plant constituent that causes tissues to contract by precipitating proteins. Traditionally used to make leather by tanning animal hides, and used therapeutically to reduce secretions and discharges. It has an astringent action.

TARTARIC ACID a fruit acid found in grapes.

THYMOL a volatile oil with strong antiseptic properties.

TRYPTOPHAN an amino acid that can be converted into vitamin B3 in the body.

VALERIANIC ACID a volatile oil with sedative properties.

VASODILATOR causes blood vessels to widen (dilate).

VOLATILE OIL see **essential oils**.

top ten foods

The following lists give the top ten sources of vitamins, minerals, and trace elements. In each case foods are listed according to amount per portion, beginning with the highest.

WATER SOLUBLE VITAMINS

VITAMIN B1 (thiamin): peas, brown rice, yeast extract, potato, muesli, sunflower seed, pinto bean, cabbage, tahini paste, leek

VITAMIN B2 (riboflavin): yeast extract, tempeh, muesli, avocado, seaweed, oyster mushroom, corn, mushroom, peas, mustard leaf

VITAMIN B3 (niacin): yeast extract, tempeh, muesli, fava bean, peas, peanut butter, brown rice, soy bean, potato, wheat bran

VITAMIN B5 (pantothenic acid): fava beans, avocado, mushroom, tempeh, Brussels sprout, purple broccoli, endive, corn, sweet potato, potato

VITAMIN B6 (pyridoxine): tempeh, muesli, potato, avocado, bell pepper, banana, Brussels sprout, leek, lentil, curly kale

VITAMIN B12 (cobalamin); (f) = fortified: yeast extract (f), vegetable stock (f), vegetable margarine (f), soy milk (f), breakfast cereals (f), tempeh, seaweed, sourdough bread, shiitake mushroom, soy sauce

FOLATE (folic acid) (amount per portion): black-eyed peas, Swiss chard, savoy cabbage, spinach, fava bean, pinto bean, endive, Brussels sprout, curly kale, okra

BIOTIN: tempeh, soy bean, hazelnut, peanut, almond, muesli, black-eyed peas, mushroom, avocado, mangetout

VITAMIN C: guava, blackcurrant, red bell pepper, curly kale, orange, Brussels sprout, broccoli, green bell pepper, papaya, strawberry

FAT-SOLUBLE VITAMINS

VITAMIN A (carotene): sweet potato, carrot, red bell pepper, butternut squash, Swiss chard, spinach, curly kale, spring greens, mango, cantaloupe melon

VITAMIN D: Although a number of foods are fortified with vitamin D, only a few foods contain vitamin D naturally. The best way to ensure adequate vitamin D is to spend some time each day in the open air, as we all produce vitamin D internally by the action of sunlight on our skin.

VITAMIN E: wheat germ oil, sun-dried tomato, sweet potato, sunflower oil, safflower oil, sunflower seed, avocado, hazelnut, almond, butternut squash

VITAMIN K: broccoli, spinach, parsley, cabbage, curly kale, spring greens, cauliflower, peas, soy-based margarine, vegetable oil

MINERALS

CALCIUM: tofu, okra, spring greens, spinach, curly kale, tempeh, sesame seed, purple broccoli, scallion, dried fig

MAGNESIUM: Brazil nut, okra, melon seed, Swiss chard, brown rice, tempeh, sunflower seed, sesame seed, beans, spinach

PHOSPHORUS: brown rice, tempeh, tahini, muesli, peas, beans and lentils, nuts and seeds, corn, tofu, sweet potato

POTASSIUM: avocado, potato, sweet potato, dried apricot, squash, beans, banana, spinach, zucchini, Brussels sprout

TRACE ELEMENTS

IRON tempeh, lentils, potato, muesli, spring greens, endive, peas, tahini paste, cumin seed, dried peach

ZINC aduki bean, tofu, tempeh, lentil, muesli, pasta, wheat bran, garbanzo, tahini paste, brown rice

MANGANESE oyster mushroom, brown rice, muesli, tempeh, pine nut, tofu, blackberry, macadamia nut, hazelnut, aduki bean

COPPER tempeh, brown rice, aduki bean, pigeon peas, mushroom, melon seed, sunflower seed, cashew nut, tahini, soy bean

IODINE the most reliable sources come from the sea—fish and seaweeds, sea salt and iodized salt. The amount in plants varies depending on iodine levels in the soil.

SELENIUM Brazil nut, lentils, whole wheat bread, pasta, sunflower seed, pinto bean, red kidney bean, cashew nut, mushroom, soy bean

index

bibliography

R. Ballentine, *Diet & Nutrition* (Himalayan International Institute, U.S.A., 1982)

P. Belaiche, *Traité de Phytothérapie et Aromathérapie* (Maloine S.A. Editeur, France, 1979)

H. G. Bieler, *Food is Your Best Medicine* (Spearman, U.K., 1968)

K. Bock and N. Sabin, *The Road to Immunity* (Pocket Books, U.S.A., 1997)

P. Bocuse, *La Cuisine du Marché* (Flammarion, France,1976)

A. Braine, *Des Plantes pour Tous les Jours* (Presse Pocket, France, 1993)

C. and C. Caldicott, *World Food Café* (Frances Lincoln, U.K., 1999)

T. Cechini, *Encyclopédie des Plantes Médicinales* (Editions De Vecchi, France, 1993)

W. Chan, J. Brown and D. H. Buss, *Miscellaneous Foods,* supplement to *McCance & Widdowson's The Composition of Foods* (R.S.C. & M.A.F.F., U.K., 1994)

R. Creasy, *The Edible French Garden* (Periplus, U.S.A., 1999)

A. Del Conte, *Secrets from an Italian Kitchen* (Corgi, U.K., 1989)

M. Delmas, *Les Mille Recettes aux Mille Vertus* (Magnard/Le François, France, 1990)

A. Dolamore, *Olive Oil Companion* (Macmillan, U.K., 1988)

Dorvault, *L'Officine* (23rd edition, France, 1995)

Duhamel, *Cahiers de Phytothérapie* (Masson, France, 1995)

R. Elliot, *The Bean Book* (Fontana, U.K., 1979)

J. Ewin, *The Plants We Need to Eat* (Thorsons, U.K.,1997)

K. Fern, *Plants for a Future* (Permanent Publications, U.K., 1997)

B. Fichaux, *La Nouvelle Cuisine Familiale* (Les Editions Gabriandre, France, 1996)

J. S. Garrow, W.P.T. James and A. Ralph, *Human Nutrition & Dietetics*, *10th edition* (Churchill Livingstone, U.K., 2000)

M. Grieve, *A Modern Herbal* (Tiger Books, U.K., 1992)
J. Grigson, *Jane Grigson's Fruit Book* (Penguin, U.K., 1983)

S. Harrod Buhner, *Herbal Antibiotics* (Newleaf, Ireland, 2000)

K. Hartvig and N. Rowley, *10 Days To Better Health* (Piatkus, U.K., 1998)

K. Hartvig and N. Rowley, *You Are What You Eat* (Piatkus, U.K., 1996)

R. K. Henderson, *The Neighborhood Forager* (Chelsea Green, U.S.A. and U.K., 2000)

A. Hirsch, *Drink to Your Health* (Marlow, U.S.A., 2000)

D. Hoffmann *The Complete Illustrated Holistic Herbal* (Element, U.K., 1996)

B. Holland, I. D. Unwin and D. H. Buss, *Cereals & Cereal Products,* supplement to *McCance & Widdowson's The Composition of Foods* (R.S.C. & M.A.F.F., U.K., 1992, U.K., 1988)

B. Holland, I. D. Unwin and D. H. Buss, *Fruits & Nuts,* supplement to *McCance & Widdowson's The Composition of Foods* (R.S.C. & M.A.F.F., U.K., 1992)

B. Holland, I. D. Unwin and D. H. Buss, *Vegetables, Herbs & Spices,* supplement to *McCance & Widdowson's The Composition of Foods* (R.S.C. & M.A.F.F., U.K., 1991)

M. Jaffrey, *Eastern Vegetarian Cooking* (Arrow, U.K., 1990)

C. Kousmine, *La Méthode Kousmine* (Editions Jouvence, France, 1989)

H. Leclerc, *Précis de Phytothérapie* (Masson, France, 1994)

S. Mills, *The Dictionary of Modern Herbalism* (Thorsons, U.K., and U.S.A., 1985)

M.-A. Mulot, *Votre Santé par l es Elixirs* (Editions du Dauphin, France, 1986)

M. T. Murray and J. E. Pizzorno, *An Encyclopaedia of Natural Medicine* (Macdonald Optima, U.K., 1990)

C. R. Paterson, *Essentials of Human Biochemistry* (Pitman, U.K., 1983)

A. A. Paul and D. A. T. Southgate. *McCance & Widdowson's The Composition of Foods* (Her Majesty's Stationery Office, U.K., 1978)

A. A. Paul, D. A. T. Southgate and J. Russel, *Amino Acids and Fatty Acids,* supplement to *McCance & Widdowson's The Composition of Foods* (R.S.C. & M.A.F.F., U.K., 1992)

B. Pizzigoni, *La Cuisine Végétarienne pour Tous* (Editions De Vecchi poche, Italy, 1993)

M. Polunin, *Healing Foods* (Dorling Kindersley, U.K., 1997)

M. L. Rapaggi, *Erborare e Cucinare* (Edagricole Edizioni G. Agricole, Italy, 1995)

Reeves and E. Todd, *Immunology* (Blackwell Science, UK, 2000)

M. Romeyn, *Nutrition & H.I.V.* (Jossey-Bass, U.S.A., 1998)

E. Rothera, *Perhaps It's An Allergy* (Foulsham, U.K., 1988)

N. Rowley, *Basic Clinical Science* (Hodder & Stoughton, U.K., 1994)

N. Rowley and K. Hartvig *Energy Foods* (D.B.P., U.K., 2000)

N. Rowley and K. Hartvig. *Energy Juices* (D.B.P., U.K., 2000)

J. Santa Maria, *Chinese Vegetarian Cookery* (C.R.C.S., U.S.A., 1983)

K. Thesen, *Country Remedies* (Pierrot, U.K., 1979)

J. Valnet, *Aromathérapie* (Maloine S. A. Editeur, France, 1984)
J. Valnet, *Phytothérapie* (Maloine S. A. Editeur, France, 1983)

J. Valnet, *Fruits et Legumes* (Maloine S.A. Editeur, France, 1985)

Various authors, *A Taste of History* (English Heritage, U.K., 1993)

J. G. Vaughan and C. A. Geissler, *The New Oxford Book of Food Plants* (Oxford University Press, U.K., 1997)

J. Veissid, *Traité de Médecine Populaire* (Société Parisienne d'Edition, France, 1973)
R. F. Weiss, *Herbal Medicine* (A.B. Arcanum, UK, 1988)
World Cancer Research Fund in association with American Institute for Cancer Research, *Food, Nutrition & the Prevention of Cancer: a Global Perspective* (American Institute for Cancer Research, U.S.A., 1997)

R. C. Wren, *Potter's New Cyclopaedia of Botanical Drugs & Preparations* (Daniel, U.K., 1988)

acknowledgments

Kirsten Hartvig would like to thank:
Judy Barratt, Pamela Blake-Wilson, Geoffrey Cannon, Grace Cheetham, Richard Emerson, Peter Firebrace, Tara Firebrace, Allan Hartvig, Anders Hartvig, Simon Hickmott, Pip Martin, Jennifer Maughan, Ian Melrose, Anna Mews, Kathy Mitchison, Sue Mitchison, Françoise Nassivet, Manisha Patel, Liz Pearson, Dr Peter Pearson, Dr Nic Rowley, François Salies, Dr Joyce Thomas and Jaqueline Young for their help and inspiration in writing this book.

Duncan Baird Publishers would like to thank:
Dr Damien Downing (medical consultant, Food is Medicine)
Caroline Yates (recipe consultant, Food is Medicine)
Emma Bentham-Wood (photographer's assistant)
Juss Herd (assistant food stylist)
Ingrid Lock (indexer)
Vicky Carlisle (proofreader)

With special thanks to: Laurent and Marie Boileau, chefs, for testing and advising on the recipes in Food is Medicine.